THE POLITICS OF DEVELOPMENT

This book is destined to become essential reading in any university courses that consider the politics of development. It expertly unpicks the essentially political and painful nature of development, the core role of 'contestation', and the ideas, interests and institutions involved in both driving and blocking the expansion of the freedoms to be and to do that Amartya Sen identified as the true heart of human development. A wonderful addition to the literature. **Duncan Green, Professor in International Development, London School of Economics**

Development is political. That is the powerful and indisputable message of the authors of this book. Scholars and practitioners take note and start with this terrific and authoritative book. **James A. Robinson, Professor of Global Conflict Studies, University of Chicago**

Development is messy, contested, and deeply political. It impacts all aspects of our lives, especially if we are in particularly deprived communities and countries. It shapes age old problems like corruption, and more recent challenges like the climate crisis. The beauty of this book is that it covers the vast span of development, and its power-laden nature, in an engaging, accessible, and knowledgeable manner. It will be an excellent addition to reading lists. **Nikita Sud, Professor of the Politics of Development, University of Oxford**

The Politics of Development is an invaluable resource, bringing together in one place a lively and accessible overview of the politics of power, contestation and change. Not to be missed on any reading list in development studies. **John Gaventa, Professor, Institute of Development Studies**

The Politics of Development is clear and persuasive. It is centred on how institutions are shaped by people's interests, and the importance of ideas to understand when development does, or doesn't, happen. An important and lucid contribution in understanding how politics shape development. **Jakkie Cilliers, Chairperson of the Board, Head of African Futures & Innovation, Institute for Security Studies**

The Politics of Development is an insightful and thought-provoking book that illuminates the inherent link between politics and development. It offers a comprehensive framework to better understand global power dynamics and empowers readers to actively transform the world. A must-read for students of development everywhere. **Ivica Petrikova, Senior Lecturer in Politics and International Relations, Royal Holloway University of London**

THE POLITICS OF DEVELOPMENT

EDITED BY
CLAIRE MCLOUGHLIN
SAMEEN ALI
KAILING XIE
NIC CHEESEMAN
AND DAVID HUDSON

§ Sage

S Sage

1 Oliver's Yard
55 City Road
London EC1Y 1SP

2455 Teller Road
Thousand Oaks,
California 91320

Unit No 323-333, Third Floor, F-Block
International Trade Tower Nehru Place
New Delhi – 110 019

8 Marina View Suite 43-053
Asia Square Tower 1
Singapore 018960

Editor: Andrew Malvern
Assistant Editor: Daniel Price
Production Editor: Gourav Kumar
Copyeditor: Diana Chambers
Proofreader: Sarah Cooke
Indexer: Cathryn Pritchard
Marketing Manager: Fauzia Eastwood
Cover Design: Jennifer Crisp
Typeset by Knowledge Works Global Ltd
Printed in the UK

Library of Congress Control Number: 2023946196

British Library Cataloguing in Publication data

A catalogue record for this book is available from the British Library

ISBN 978-1-5296-6770-7
ISBN 978-1-5296-6769-1 (pbk)

Contents

Extended contents

About the editors and contributors

Editors

Sameen A. Mohsin Ali is an Assistant Professor of International Development at the University of Birmingham and researches governance and reform through the lens of bureaucratic and party politics, institutional design, and the politics of aid.

Nic Cheeseman is Professor of Democracy and the Director of the Centre for Elections, Democracy, Accountability and Representation (CEDAR) at the University of Birmingham.

David Hudson is Professor of Politics and Development and Head of the International Development Department, University of Birmingham, examining leadership, public opinion and migration.

Claire Mcloughlin is an Associate Professor of Politics and Development at the International Development Department, University of Birmingham, researching the politics of vital public service delivery and its effects on state-society relations.

Kailing Xie is an Assistant Professor at the International Development Department, University of Birmingham, researching discourse and identity, Feminist theorization of affect, and authoritarianism.

Contributors

Jasmine Burnley is a Doctoral researcher at the International Development Department, University of Birmingham, and development professional of over twenty years, focusing on the political economy of conflict and humanitarianism.

Eleanor Chowns is an Assistant Professor at the International Development Department, University of Birmingham, and practitioner interested in collective action, power and participation, and evaluation.

Harriet Croome is a Doctoral researcher and political ecologist at the International Development Department, University of Birmingham, examining how conservation and development reshape complex social-ecological interactions.

Niheer Dasandi is an Associate Professor in Politics and Development in the International Development Department, University of Birmingham.

Jonathan Fisher is Professor of Global Security at the International Development Department, University of Birmingham, exploring authoritarianism and insecurity in Africa and beyond.

Zenobia Ismail is an Applied social scientist specialising in knowledge syntheses for international development in sub-Saharan Africa. She has worked for the Knowledge for Development (K4D) programme.

Paul Jackson is Professor of African Politics at the International Development Department, University of Birmingham, researching rebel groups, security reform, conflict and post-conflict reconstruction.

Chris Lyon is a Teaching Fellow and researcher at the International Development Department, University of Birmingham, with a particular interest in normative political quandaries in development.

Fiona Nunan is Professor of Environment and Development at the International Development Department, University of Birmingham, conducting research into collaborative natural resource governance.

Emeka Njoku is an Assistant Professor at the International Development Department, University of Birmingham, and Associate Editor of the *Journal of Intervention and Statebuilding*.

Soomin Oh is a political scientist and Senior Research Fellow at Development Engagement Lab studying the distribution of public goods and services in developing contexts.

Chukwumerije Okereke is Professor of Global Environmental and Climate Governance and Director of Center for Climate and Development at Alex Ekwueme Federal University, Nigeria.

Kate Pruce is a Research Fellow at the Institute of Development Studies, Sussex, researching social protection.

Emily Scott an Assistant Professor at the International Development Department, University of Birmingham, researching humanitarianism, health, and forced migration in conflict and crisis, particularly in the Middle East.

Merisa Thompson is an Assistant Professor in Gender and Development, exploring gender and the intersectional dimensions of food and agriculture in the Caribbean and globally.

Bizuneh Yimenu is a Teaching Fellow at the International Development Department, University of Birmingham, specialising in comparative politics, political economy, public policy, and development.

Preface

Welcome to *The Politics of Development*. This book is for anyone who wants to understand how power, interests, rules and ideas have shaped and continue to shape who gets what, when, and how. It is an academic book, written in a non-academic style. It contains theories, but not for the sake of them; rather, to better understand the diversity of global challenges facing the world, from the perspective of everyday lived realities. It sees politics as both the obstacle and the way to solving these challenges.

Our aim is to equip readers with the curiosity, knowledge, and analytical tools needed to make sense of some of the critical questions facing our planet today – from rising inequality, to exclusion from vital goods and services, to the climate crisis, to violent conflict.

Why do we need a book about the politics of development? There are many great books about development in print, and many great books on the politics of development – many of which we cite in our chapters. None, however, brings together both in the way we do here – by defining the politics of development as a process of contestation and the movement towards people's desired futures – and providing readers with a framework not only for thinking about politics as a barrier to development, but analysing it as the way development happens.

The book comes out of our experience of teaching and working together at the International Development Department (IDD), in the School of Government, University of Birmingham. We are a collaborative department, with a diversity of methodological, regional and country expertise but, most of all, a commitment to making research speak to real-world issues. Since the department was formed in 1964, we have been learning from our students, past and present, about how to teach development, and how to encourage critical thinking. In turn, students continue to share and enrich our own critical thinking about the political dynamics behind some of the world's most pressing problems. In this sense, you could say that *The Politics of Development* has been 60 years in the making.

Most of us in the department work on some aspect of the politics of development, whether in our research or teaching, but also as practitioners, engaged with communities, organisations, governments, NGOs, or donors working in development. We are often all individually and collectively trying to convey that so many of the outcomes, decisions, failures, and successes are down to politics. In order to understand development, we have to understand politics. Politics isn't everything, but everything is political.

We purposefully ground the book in individual lived realities of inequality and injustice to encourage readers to connect with the topic on a human level and reflect on their own positionality and starting assumptions. By foregrounding the 'everyday' challenges people around the world face in accessing the vital resources they need to survive and thrive, we aim to show that politics is not detached from reality or something that happens only in formal arenas. Rather, politics happens everywhere, from Birmingham to Bandung. It is happening as much in hidden spaces as on national stages and global arenas.

Many readers will want more than to learn about the realities of the challenges that affect billions of lives, though: they want to get into the practicalities of 'doing development' or how to address them. We hope to facilitate this, in this book, by applying a problem-driven approach. In each chapter, we introduce a puzzle, or question that ordinary people living in any country around the world might ask. Sometimes these questions are provocative, but they are also everyday – for example, 'Why doesn't everyone get the same?' or 'How can I jump this queue?' and 'Can the planet cope with development?' These questions are deceptively simple, but intellectually, and in the real world, challenging to answer.

Understanding is not going to give you the answers, nor a guide on how to do development, but it is the basis of action. And in this book, we aim to show readers how to unpack these questions politically. From a political perspective, any development issue can be explained by understanding how institutions, interests, and ideas interact and intersect. The benefit of this approach to analysis is that it is simple, memorable, and accessible, yet intellectually robust. It allows us to bring the best disciplinary insights from the fields of economics, sociology, and politics to bear on the questions we pose, appealing to students trained within these disciplines, while also challenging them to think beyond disciplinary siloes.

A lot is at stake in this learning journey. Development challenges are everywhere, and increasingly pressing – including in supposedly 'developed' countries. But whether you are learning in a classroom, a lecture theatre, as a professional, a journalist, or in your bedroom, wherever you are, we hope this textbook will push you to question and contest something. We do not pretend there are any easy answers to the politics of development – instead, we aim to give you the analytical tools to understand why getting development right can be so hard, and how you can positively respond to some of the critical challenges facing governments, societies, and citizens around the world.

Acknowledgements

This book has been the result of the collective effort of a team of scholars in and around the International Development Department (IDD). The process of imagining, planning, and writing it has been as rewarding as the content. Our five-member editorial team, led by lead editor Claire Mcloughlin, have been so proud of and grateful to our co-authors in and around the IDD – all sixteen of them! The process of developing the book involved lively meetings, writing retreats, editorial feedback, reviewers' comments, revisions, and numerous requests for further edits. The fact that we hit our deadlines, with so many moving parts, was a miracle. And we thank all the authors for their respect, collegiality and brilliance.

We have had the great fortune of working with a stellar team at Sage publishers. Andrew Malvern, our commissioning editor, has been the human embodiment of enthusiasm. His interest and encouragement from the very start, through to his careful shepherding of the project through all stages, from concept, to structure, to advice on covers, has always been positive, joyful, and constructive. Daniel Price's calm and clear guidance and positive feedback on earlier drafts helped make the process of refining the text run smoothly. We are grateful to Jen Crisp, Sage's design director, for her striking cover. We would also like to thank the Board of Directors for their support for all our requests to make the book as inclusive as possible.

Finally, but also most importantly, we would like to thank our students, who, through their curiosity and thirst for knowledge, provided both the inspiration for the book, and in many practical ways made it better – not least through focus groups and trial read-throughs, during which, in the spirit of contestation, they told us exactly what they liked, did/didn't understand, and thought was right or wrong about what we had written. We hope that this book will inspire many more lively classroom interactions.

Sincerely,
The Editors

Part 1 Understanding the politics of development

1 Why is development political?

Claire Mcloughlin, David Hudson, Nic Cheeseman, Sameen Ali, and Kailing Xie

Image 1.1 Australian students protest in Sydney, 2019, to demand urgent action on climate change. Image by Holli via Shutterstock.

Learning outcomes

- Define the politics of development as a process of contestation.
- Critically assess how diversity, scarcity and colonial legacies drive the politics of development.
- Begin to understand how institutions, interests and ideas shape lived realities.

Connecting politics to lived realities

We have reached a defining moment in human history.

The people of the world have asked us to shine a light on a future of promise and opportunity.

Ban Ki-moon, New York, 25 September 2015

When United Nations Secretary General Ban Ki-moon spoke these words at the adoption of the 2030 Agenda for Sustainable Development, it marked the culmination of four years of intergovernmental deliberation and contestation. A new set of 17 Sustainable Development Goals (SDGs), with 169 associated targets, was adopted as the world's 'to do list' for ending poverty and hunger, tackling inequalities, empowering women, and protecting the planet (see Figure 1.1). Achieving them, the Secretary General remarked, was a promise made by all leaders, to all people, everywhere.

Figure 1.1 Sustainable Development Goals (SDGs)
Source: un.org

Decisions made in high-profile global arenas may seem a distant concern for many ordinary people. Yet in theory at least, these goals were forged from lived realities. In the process of setting them, the UN had led an extensive consultation with a million people around the world in order to understand their everyday challenges and priorities. The resulting report, 'A Million Voices: The World We Want' (2013), revealed a common sense of injustice, insecurity, and poverty. People expressed deeply felt inequalities – between men and women, rich and poor, class and caste, ethnicity, and across urban and rural divides – in access to vital resources such as land, health, water or housing. Younger generations were losing livelihoods, facing precarious employment, and missing out on access to quality educational opportunities. Many women and girls felt acutely vulnerable to violence, both inside and outside of their homes, and blocked from accessing the necessary justice to redress discriminations against them. All of this was compounded by pressures from unplanned migration, fragile ecosystems, and the rising frequency of extreme weather events.

The great promise of the SDGs lay in closing the gap between 'the world we want' and the actions of some of the most powerful people and organisations capable of enabling or blocking its attainment. In practice, though, as witnessed in the intervening decade, the connection between what people need, value or are entitled to, and what they get, is always, everywhere, mediated by politics. In the broadest sense, politics is a universal and pervasive feature of all collective human activity. Its function, as one of the leading political thinkers, Adrian Leftwich, put it, is to 'organise and express the interaction of people, resources and power' (2004: 101). As such, politics has profoundly shaped lived experiences around the world. The deprivations, insecurities, and injustices reported in the UN consultation were not inevitable, nor did they occur by chance. They are the result of choices, made by people, holding unequal power and control over resources. The rules that shape decision-making often benefit and protect those in power and embed these inequalities, meaning that some are simply better positioned to protect their interests, and their share of wealth and opportunity, than others. And in contexts of scarcity and diversity, where there is never enough to go around, opposing views on how resources *should* be allocated inevitably have to be negotiated or contested. This is the stuff of politics. This is the stuff of development.

Everything about development is political. The Sustainable Development Goals themselves could not have been adopted without politics – the process of contestation between interests, rules, choices, decisions, and non-decisions. The outcomes of politics left its mark on which indicators were chosen, and how they are phrased. Take Goal 10, for example. It aims to 'reduce inequality within and among countries' but avoids committing countries to any action to address arguably the more insidious problem of 'extreme inequality'. The targets set, and measured, in relation to this goal relate to 'economic inclusion', rather than the distribution of wealth between the top and bottom of the economic ladder. Although argued on a technicality (precision of measurement), the real reason behind this is political. As a target, 'economic inclusion' avoids challenging the powerful vested interests of the very elites who have accumulated extreme wealth, many of whom were present or represented at the negotiations (Fukuda-Parr, 2019).

Explicitly recognising that everything about development is political encourages us to *analyse* it politically. Imagine, for example, the range of processes, reforms, choices, actions, and investments that could be undertaken to tackle SDG 1: No poverty. You might think of improving the opportunities for decent employment or eradicating precarious jobs, but trade unions are not always as powerful as private sector interests who use money, lobbying, unfair contracts, and new laws to tame the power of workers. Think of the design and building of roads to enable people to trade goods and travel between urban centres – an engineering task? Yes, but also deeply political. Where does the investment come from (World Bank or China)? Who wins the contracts (the best bidder or the one with political connections)? Where does the road go and who does it serve (near the local MP's house)? Think of the risks of being affected by climate-related disasters; while this is partly geographically determined, it is also fundamentally caused by some of the world's largest economies and energy companies not taking responsibility for climate change, or properly funding the 'loss and damage' suffered by the world's most vulnerable countries and peoples. Hence, when we apply political thinking to such developments, we get closer to the reasons why they do or do not happen, and in whose interests.

This book is about why all development is political. It is about the effects of politics on the distribution of resources, rights, and freedoms that people need and value. It is about the political dynamics behind the everyday lived realities that prevent people from realising their version of 'the world we want'.

In this chapter, we set out the fundamental what, why, where and how of the politics of development. By defining our key terms and concepts (itself a product of contestation), we lay the foundations of what is to come. We begin to explore some of the fundamental reasons why politics is unavoidable, how it is shaped by past and present power dynamics, and the expansive nature of the spaces where it happens. We introduce our approach to analysing the politics of development – what we call our three 'I's: institutions, interests, and ideas – that form the book's intellectual framework. Contrary to the universalising tendencies of the SDGs, there is, of course, not one development 'to do list' for the world, but many. But this book, and this chapter, aim to show that politics is both the obstacle and the way to address it.

Defining the politics of development

Everyone has a view on how decisions *should* be made, how people *should* behave or think, and ultimately, as coined in the classic political science work of Harold Lasswell (1936), 'who should get what, when, how'. But studying the politics of development is not about normatively judging the relative merits of different perspectives on what is right, wrong, good, bad or unfair for society. Instead, it is about critically analysing the *processes behind these outcomes*. That is, what goes on inside the pervasive and ubiquitous struggles that hold the potential to alter the human condition: whether it's legislating to combat discrimination and exclusion, building and maintaining vital social or physical infrastructure, enforcing land rights and property ownership, recognising identity, or indeed, agreeing indicators and targets for measuring progress towards the SDGs.

In this book, we define the politics of development as a process of *contesting alternative desired futures* (see Box 1.1). By alternative desired futures, we simply mean different versions of the way things are and should be – what people believe is right or wrong for themselves or for society, what they need or value, how they believe certain goods should be distributed, and how they contest that allocation. In practice, as we come to explain later in this chapter, the 'things' that are contested under the banner of 'development' could be physical or social, material or non-material, but they are always desired by someone, because they satisfy or further their basic needs and wants.

> ## Box 1.1   Defining the politics of development
>
> The politics of development is the *unavoidable process of contestation over alternative desired futures*.
>
> - **What is contested?** The desired distribution of material or non-material resources such as authority, rights, and freedoms in a society.
> - **Why is it unavoidable?** Contestation is unavoidable due to the universal facts of diversity of interests, goals and identities, scarcity and inequality, and colonial legacies.
> - **Where does it happen?** Contestation happens everywhere and anywhere that decisions are made over the allocation of resources that are valued or needed.
> - **How does it happen?** Formal and informal rules for resource allocation are contested by more (or less) rational actors with competing interests, holding a range of ideas about what is right and fair.

What does it mean to contest such things? When we think about *how* individuals or collectives 'contest' anything, it implies resistance or rejection, agitation, or dissent. We might imagine, for example, villagers mobilising against environmentally harmful deforestation by sabotaging the equipment of logging companies, or disenfranchised groups tapping into the oil pipes laid by multinational corporations to claim what they perceive as their fair share of wealth. These are contestations, but they are acute manifestations of it. More routinely, contestation is not necessarily antagonistic. And it is much broader in its scope. In this book, we understand contestation as the exercise of human agency – or the capacity to act – in ways that we want to achieve what we want. Nobel Laureate Amartya Sen called this 'well-being freedom', or 'what a person is free to do and achieve in pursuit of whatever goals or values he or she regards as important' (Sen, 1985, 2000).

Wherever resources are claimed or allocated, some form of contestation is unavoidable. Rarely is the exercise of power and decision-making unrivalled. There will always be diversity of interests, goals and preferences between groups, societies or indeed nations about who should get what, when, how. Some will want to maintain the status quo, others to modify or overturn it. This competitive struggle for power and influence is exacerbated by scarcity of vital resources, whether fresh water, arable land, clean air, or quality education. Scarcity is not only naturally occurring, but human-made. Inequalities in distributions of the things people need to survive and prosper were baked into lived realities through colonial injustices and their continuing legacies. These histories also explain why contestation over resources continues to be dominated by powerful individuals, groups and corporations that hold more power and influence to secure their interests.

Contestation happens everywhere and anywhere – wealthy as much as poorer countries, homes as much as parliaments. As we shall see in this book, its prevalence and form does not fit with outdated categories of 'developing' versus 'developed' countries. But what is common is that wherever it occurs, it is shaped by three social forces – what we call in this book our 'three I's of the politics of development: institutions, interests and ideas'. What we mean by this is that anywhere there is contestation over alternative desired futures, there are:

- formal structures and informal rules or institutions in place;
- being contested by more (or less) rational actors with competing power and interests;
- driven by underpinning ideas about what is right and fair.

This definition of the politics of development is distinct, in two senses. First, we do not approach politics as an add-on or a discrete academic angle on development, but rather, as *the way development happens*. In effect, there can be *no development without politics*. In contrast to the development 'canon' – a collection of key theories, concepts, and works that have historically shaped the field of development studies – our approach places politics more squarely *within* the definition of development (see Table 1.1). Early development theories critically analysed politics as an *outcome* of development or a *cause* of underdevelopment and inequality. Post-development theory was critical in foregrounding the political *effects* of development interventions and encouraging more inclusive, contextually sensitive, and socially just approaches to addressing development challenges (Ferguson, 1994; Kothari, 2001). It directly challenged the discourse of 'development' as *depoliticising* the conflicts and divisions in society (Ziai, 2017). While these theories were foundational, they did not analyse politics, or contestation, as the active *means of* development, in the way we do in this book.

Reflective question

What factors shaped the evolution of ideas about the place of politics in development?

Table 1.1   The place of politics in the development 'canon'

'Canon' theory	Place of politics	Classic text
• Modernisation theory	• 'Modernisation' – a linear and technologically driven progression from traditional society to a modern industrialised economy – would inevitably *lead to political change* as countries democratised and political participation deepened.	• Walt Whitman Rostow's *The Stages of Growth: A Non-Communist Manifesto (1960)*
• Dependency theory	• European colonial powers *hindered Africa's economic and social progress through politics* – specifically, exploitation, extraction of resources, and unequal trade relationships.	• Walter Rodney's *How Europe Underdeveloped Africa (1972)*
• Post-development theory	• The *very idea of development is political* – it perpetuates unequal power dynamics and cultural imperialism. Development interventions reinforce existing power structures.	• Arturo Escobar's *Encountering Development: The Making and Unmaking of the Third World (2011)*

Second, while we cannot and should not deny or sanitise the damage that politics has inflicted on desired futures, our point of departure in this book is to analyse politics as an empirical phenomenon, rather than lament or deplore it. In many ways, politics has something of a bad reputation. People assume that it is to do with self-interested and self-serving power, corruption, venality, or opportunism that is anti-social and corrosive of the common good and social justice. And much of this, as we will see in the book, is true. But this is also a partial view. Politics, as Otto van Bismarck famously said, is also 'the art of the possible'. It is also about working to bring about change through pragmatism, leadership and compromise. Politics is not just an obstacle to progress; it is also the way change happens. Indeed, we hope to show that the point of understanding how politics can block development, is to also understand how progress can be unlocked *through* it.

The above summary of the what, why, where and how of the politics of development provides the impetus and intellectual scaffolding for this book. In the rest of this chapter, we unpack, justify, and illustrate it.

What 'development' is contested?

You will not be surprised to read that there is contestation over the very meaning of the term 'development'. Is it a process or an outcome? Ends or means? And what *is* the end goal? To some extent, to use the well-known idiom, 'where you stand depends on where you sit'. Different perspectives on development depend on disciplinary biases and subjectivities that shape vantage points. Economists may see the *end goal* of development as growth and wealth, and the *means* as commodities, labour, extractive industries, trade relations. Political scientists may see the *end goal* as the maturity and stability of political systems, and the *resources* as participatory institutions or democratic values. Sociologists may see *the end goal* as human well-being, and the *resources* as rights, freedoms, or social capital. Development can mean any or all these things, but crucially, bracketing it as one or the other is reductive in the sense that it may not coincide with what people themselves need or want in any given setting. In effect, the more important question is *who* should define development?

Our answer is those who seek it. Not all people, societies or countries aspire towards a common end-point – or 'Getting to Denmark', as the famous metaphor for an ostensibly 'well-functioning' society goes (Fukuyama, 2014). Rather than focus on universalised and instrumentalised benchmarks of growth or advancement, we apply a people-centred lens on development in this book. We align with the more holistic view of well-being advanced by the human development approach, pioneered in the works of Amartya Sen, Mahbub ul Haq and Martha Nussbaum. For Sen (1999), the Nobel Laureate economist, development means an expansion of capabilities, freedoms and choice; for ul Haq (1995), the fulfilment of human potential; for Nussbaum (2011), the process of creating conditions that enable humans to lead lives they value. We use the term 'alternative desired futures' to capture these intrinsic, people-centred meanings (see Box 1.2).

Box 1.2   Development as alternative desired futures

From a people-centred perspective, development is the *process* of pursuing goals that people define as *desirable* and beneficial to their life prospects, wellbeing, or dignity. People interpret what is desirable differently because they are rooted in different lived realities, hence, there is not one desired future, but *alternative* versions of it.

Achieving alternative desired futures requires resources, of course. By resources, we mean the production, supply and distribution of something tangible or intangible, material or ideational, that enables individuals or collectives to achieve their goals and aspirations. But, as Abraham Maslow (1943) famously noted with his hierarchy of needs, there are many layers to this. There may be immediate material needs, such as access to food, shelter, or medicines. There are also the less tangible resources that may need to be in place for people to provide for their needs. These non-material resources, such as power, autonomy, rights, authority, representation, and freedoms, are gateways to achieving material resources, but they may also be valued as intrinsic end-goals, in and of themselves (see Table 1.2).

Table 1.2   Resources to achieve desired futures

Material	Non-material
• Health, education, housing, access to clean water, money, minerals, natural resources, land, weapons, guns and ammunition, books, technology, oil, wind, sea, fisheries, agriculture, food.	• Power, knowledge, skills, agency, authority, representation, rights, social capital, participation, voice, inclusion, recognition, freedom, decision-making power, trust, legitimacy.

Reflective question

How do non-material resources enable access to material resources?

Notice we jettison the normative framings of 'progress' or 'good change' (Rostow, 1960; Chambers, 1997) as synonyms for development. Development is not synonymous with these terms because it is rarely an unqualified and universally good thing. This was powerfully, and famously, captured by James Ferguson, a leading post-development scholar, in his 1990 book *The Anti-Politics Machine: Development, Depoliticization, and Bureaucratic Power in Lesotho*. It demonstrated how seemingly 'technical' investments in infrastructure and resources benefit those in power who can control and manipulate them, while marginalising and harming others. In effect, there are always winners and losers: one version of a desired future is often achieved at the cost of another. At worst, this results in deliberate exclusions, at best unintended trade-offs and consequences. For instance, in Pakistan, citizens' receptiveness to essential childhood vaccinations – for polio, measles, diphtheria, tuberculosis – provided free at their doorstep is shaped by their prior experience of the state meeting their needs – or not (Ali and Altaf, 2021). China's prioritisation of GDP growth through privatisation of state-owned enterprise in the 1990s has led to the drastic degradation of the living standard of the socialist workforce who were forced into redundancy and urban poverty.

Image 1.2 A Sotho shepherd in Lesotho, the research site of James Ferguson's 'The Anti-Politics Machine'. Image by Matthias Kestel, via Shutterstock.

The crucial point is that the very process of development *produces* trade-offs: the uneven distribution of resources unavoidably affects the ability of different individuals or groups to meet their needs. This potential for trade-offs in development is part of the reason why contestation is unavoidable, which we elaborate on next.

Why is contestation unavoidable?

Wherever there is a felt deprivation or experience that does not conform to individual or societal expectations, needs or wants, there is potential for contestation. Unmet needs, undesirable distributions, and felt injustices – as expressed in 'the world we want' – are part of lived realities. What we need to ask now, is why do these gaps exist in the first place? Are they natural or human made? Our answer is that they are socially, politically, and historically constructed. More specifically, *scarcity and inequality* mean the supply of resources and opportunities results in contestation. The *diversity of interests, goals, and identities* means that the demand for alternative distributions amplifies this. All of this is undeniably rooted in colonialism, which is not only a legacy, but a continued lived reality.

Diversity of interests, goals, and identities

Even if the planet had infinite resources, there would still be contestation. Why? Because, of course, people, societies and nations have varied goals, needs, identities and values. In other words, there is not one 'desired future', but many.

Diversity of interests and preferences is a product of identity and lived experience (which includes, among other things, a person's age, gender, caste, ethnicity, tribal affiliations, mental and physical health, capability, education, and income). Identity, as we shall see in Chapter 10, is not fixed, but transient; not singular but intersectional (people hold multiple identities at the same time). Values and preferences are socially constructed through exposure to different belief systems, media, cultures and customs, ideologies, norms, and ideas.

Diversity is a key driver of contestation because it means that when faced with the same options, people may make different choices. Indeed, they may even *conceive* of their choices differently. Not everyone needs, wants, prioritises, or is willing to pay for the same resources. The process of pursuing development requires understanding and navigating this divergence. In a small municipality in Eastern Nepal, for example, a household survey was conducted to determine whether and how much people would be willing to pay for municipal solid waste-collection services (Rai et al., 2019). Waste collection is a major challenge in crowded urban environments all over the world, but is often unfunded and deprioritised by councils, relying instead on citizen contributions. In this municipality, though, older respondents were more eager to pay to change the status quo compared to younger people who migrate for work, larger families (who produce more waste) more so than smaller ones, families with more space to store waste, more so than those who did not. The fate of this reform effort – the degree to which it is resisted or accepted – rests on the council arbitrating between these diverse needs and preferences.

Heterogeneity of preferences may seem like something confined to people's heads, but even at the micro level, it can have much wider social ramifications for the *collective* achievement of alternative desired futures. To illustrate, briefly, a simple choice experiment was conducted among sheep smallholder keepers in Burkina Faso. Their collective goal is to selectively breed sheep to maintain disease resistance. Each farmer is presented with cards that depict a ram-purchasing scenario, where the attributes of the ram are displayed alongside the purchasing price. The results reveal that some groups are more willing to take risks than others: purchasing larger but less disease-resistant sheep (Tindano et al., 2017). These farmers can only achieve their collective goal by adhering to a common framework, but this hinges on their ability to contest, coordinate and resolve their divergent choices. In turn, this ability is influenced by scarcity of resources, and inequality in access to them.

Scarcity and inequality

Contestation is *inevitable* wherever there are competing claims to a finite or fixed set of resources. Humankind faces the stark reality that the resources upon which we depend for our survival – whether housing, energy, food, water, fuel – are unevenly distributed between nations and peoples, and in some cases are dwindling in supply. Geographies of uneven distribution can be natural – such as Bolivia's coastline – or manmade – such as access to life-saving vaccines. This scarcity and inequality fuels competing interests in accumulating and controlling access to them.

Scarcity permeates spaces of contestation from the global to the local level. Viewed through a political economy lens (how the economic marketplace affects politics (Ravenhill, 2017)), we see the influence of scarcity in the clamouring of major powers for influence in resource-rich regions – for example, why China's enthusiasm to deepen its diplomatic and security ties with the Pacific – a region rich with fisheries, timber, maritime resources, trade, and shipping routes – has provoked alarm and counter-posturing by the US, Australia, and the UK. Within countries, discourses of scarcity have been manipulated to legitimise water, land and green 'grabs', in which large swathes of agricultural land and productive resources are traded in deals between private investors and governments. Ostensibly, this is to provide for future needs more equitably, but in practice, it has pernicious effects on local livelihoods (Mehta, 2019). And between groups, competing claims to sought-after resources drive protracted contestations. For example, in the oil politics of the Niger Delta, competing claims over ownership and the distribution of revenues has escalated into protracted, violent conflict between the people of the Niger Delta, the Federal Government, and multinational corporations (Onah, 2022).

These examples keenly illustrate that scarcity is not just a natural phenomenon, but a politically constructed reality. Resources are scarce because people, groups and nations hoard and compete over them. As Amartya Sen (1982: 1) famously remarked, 'starvation is the characteristic of some people not having enough food to eat. It is not the characteristic of there being not enough food to eat'. Scarcity is both a product of politics, and a cause of it. Consider, for example, the urgent crisis of the world's food systems being unsustainable. Food production (e.g., rearing cattle) produces carbon emissions, environmental degradation, and has devastating effects on biodiversity. Yet the political economy of food is resistant to change: powerful transnational corporations (seed producers, agrichemical and agri-food corporations and retailers) are resisting policy reform, and individuals are unwilling to adapt consumption (e.g., for red meat) in the collective interest (Béné, 2022). In these ways, scarcity is created and (re-)produced through interests, choices, and power relations.

The acute conundrum of scarcity prompts us to reflect on whether it is even possible, or desirable, to achieve development – that is, whether the planet has infinite capacity to realise all of humanity's wants and needs. In the current ecological crisis, the unfettered pursuit of capitalist production may ultimately be self-defeating because it will destroy our habitat in the process. This is the central premise of 'sustainable development' – a framing of development that urges meeting the needs of people in the present without jeopardising the needs of future generations. In recognition of the earth's environmental ceiling, development is recast as 'meeting the needs of all people within the means of the living planet' (Raworth, 2017).

Politically constructed scarcity and inequality ensures that the distribution and supply of resources will always be contested. The diversity of interests, goals, and identities ensures alternative demands for distribution of resources and opportunities. When the two come together, contestation becomes inevitable. But politics is also the exercise of power, in its various forms (see Box 1.3). Inequalities of power and locked-in legacies of colonialism mean that most of the world's population does not even get to fully contest, on fair terms, what they need or are entitled to. Inequality in the capacity of different nations or peoples to exercise power over the processes that determine their needs and wants is entrenched, and rising. The gap between rich and poor is widening: The average disposable income of the richest 10 per cent in OECD countries is around 10 times higher than that of the poorest 10 per cent, compared to 7 times higher a quarter of a century ago. The inevitability of contestation reflects this uneven power. And unequal power, in turn, begets unequal outcomes.

Box 1.3 Politics as the exercise of power

Power as control and influence: to Robert A. Dahl, a prominent political theorist, power is the ability of an individual or a group to influence the choices and behaviours of others. 'A has power over B to the extent that he can get B to do something that B would not otherwise do' (Dahl, 1957: 202–3). In this reading, power is a social relationship – a behavioural outcome of human interaction.

Power as the ability to act in concert: the German–American historian and philosopher, Hannah Arendt, argued that power is the capacity of people to influence and shape the course of events through shared action (Arendt, 1970). In this reading, power is not an individual attribute, but arises from people acting together via cooperation, persuasion, and collective deliberation.

Power as diffuse: in contrast to Dahl, the French philosopher Michel Foucault was concerned with how power is exercised through various social institutions, practices, and discourses (Foucault, 1982). In this reading, power doesn't just restrict or control – it creates knowledge, shapes subjectivities, and establishes norms.

Colonial legacies

There has never been a level playing field in the process of contesting power or resources due to the history and enduring legacies of colonisation. From more than five hundred years – between the early fifteenth-century conquests, to the 'scramble for Africa' in the nineteenth and early twentieth centuries – a vast number of countries, spanning almost every region of the world, experienced some form of direct or indirect rule, economic exploitation, influence, or intervention, by European colonisers. The lived experience of being colonised was violent and dehumanising in numerous ways, depending on whether the colonisers' primary interest was in the dispossession of land, the extraction of resources, or the exploitation of labour (see Kothari and Klein, 2023). The harms inflicted ranged from suppression of languages and traditions, to loss of livelihoods and cultural heritage, to discrimination, segregation, forced displacement, murder and ethnic cleansing.

Colonisation underlies contemporary global, structural inequality. In crude terms, some countries are rich and others are poor because rich countries use their power and wealth to create the conditions under which it is harder for poor countries to transform their situation. The conditions that enabled growth in some of the world's largest economies no longer exist because those countries 'kicked away the ladder' (Chang, 2002). Britain, for example, exploited colonies by plundering their natural resources while preventing those countries from growing their own export industries. For instance, Patnaik (2019) concluded that in colonising India, Britain drained approximately US $45 trillion from the region between 1765 and 1938. More broadly, Britain and the US benefitted from free trade, then turned to protectionism (introducing customs tariffs, banning exports of raw materials) to grow their manufacturing industries, and then moved back to free trade to open up markets to sell their goods to, as discussed in Chapter 7.

As we will show throughout this book, legacies of the trauma and injustices of colonial rule continue to shape contemporary contestations. A major reason for this is that colonisation embedded egregious and discriminatory systems for allocating 'who gets what, when, how', to facilitate extraction and domination. Pillage and social engineering left deep scars in communities, carried across time through intergenerational trauma, continued marginalisation, the denial of rights and identities, and embedded structural inequalities. This is evident in the impact of colonisation on Australia's first peoples who, like many indigenous communities, suffered collective marginalisation and suppression. In Australia, this included the brutal removal of Aboriginal and Torres Strait Islander children from their families and later policies of assimilation. Collective traumas continue to have adverse effects on educational outcomes, employment, livelihoods, and well-being, including the higher prevalence of ill health in indigenous communities (Menzies, 2019). In these and many other ways, colonialism is not history, but lived reality (see Box 1.4).

Box 1.4 Why colonialism is not history

In the early 1900s, European countries including Belgium, France, the UK and Portugal presided over empires in which a small number of colonial officials governed the lives of millions of African, Asian and Caribbean people. Following the Second World War, an upsurge in nationalism and a desire for self-determination saw successive waves of countries gaining independence – from Belgian, British, and French rule in the 1950–1960s, and from Portuguese rule in the 1970s – but this did not mark the end of colonialism as a set of institutions, ideas and interests (Kothari and Klien, 2023).

As we will examine in chapters of this book, colonialism lives on through various enduring effects, including how it interacted with 'traditional' governance structures and created a duality of ideas and rules; stratified access to education in ways that reproduced inequalities; created lop-sided economies dependent on the export of raw materials, and laid the foundations for authoritarian and often violent political systems and social orders.

Postcolonial scholars continue to critically analyse these legacies of colonial rule, including in the contemporary works of Argentine professor Walter Mignolo in his 2021 book, *The Politics of Decolonial Investigations*, and in *On the Postcolony*, a book written by Cameroonian philosopher and political theorist, Achille Mbembe, published in 2001. In these and similar works, authors explore the complexities of postcolonial societies, examining the social, political, economic, and cultural dynamics that shape them after the end of formal colonial rule. In doing so, they stress both the exploitative and authoritarian legacy of empire – which typically constructed highly repressive systems of government – but also the agency of colonised people to subvert and resist colonial expectations. Mignolo, for example, argues that 'the combination of the self-fashioned narratives of Western civilisation and the hegemony of Eurocentric thought served to eradicate all knowledges in non-European languages and praxes of living and being', but also that 'coloniality has provoked the emergence of decolonial politics', which creates the potential for 'overcoming of the long-lasting hegemony of the West and its distorted legacies'.

Mbembe, meanwhile, coined the term 'necropolitics' to refer to 'the power and the capacity to dictate who may live and who must die'. In other words, who governments consider of greater or lesser value shapes our experiences every day, both domestically and internationally. A good contemporary example of the latter is access to vaccinations during the COVID-19 pandemic. Vaccines for COVID-19 were developed in the West and were then hoarded by countries like the US and Canada, while the rest of the world waited months before the vaccines reached their populations (Khetpal, 2021), as discussed in Chapter 7.

Colonial power relations also continue to structure the international system, shaping the flow of ideas, money, trade, and even migration. For instance, the leadership of international organisations such as the World Bank and International Monetary Fund are drawn from Western states – most notably, the US – and so their policies are shaped by the understanding of politics and economics that is dominant in Western capitals. As we show in Chapters 7 and 10, these policies impact the lives and livelihoods of billions of citizens living in the rest the world.

The present-day impacts of colonialism reach into every aspect of our lives, including the social and personal. Nathan Nunn and Leonard Wantchekon (2011), for example, have found that the transatlantic and Indian Ocean slave trade – which forcibly transported 12–13 million Africans across the Atlantic in the most terrible conditions over a span of 400 years – continues to shape how societies operate today. Remarkably, writing over a hundred years later, they use 'individual-level survey data with historical data on slave shipments by ethnic group' to show that individuals whose ancestors were heavily raided during the slave trade are less trusting today'.

For her part, Durba Mitra (2020) argues that British colonisers and their Indian collaborators used their ideas of what was socially acceptable and what was not to shape and control women's sexuality in the subcontinent, with continuing impacts on contemporary notions of sexuality in South Asian countries. Mitra's work is particularly valuable because it demonstrates the insidious and often subconscious way that colonial ideas and institutions continue to shape how we think today.

Although it was experienced in diverse ways, colonialism often engineered fault lines of contestation between spaces, castes, and ethnic groups *within* countries by privileging certain groups over others. It also denied inclusive and accountable political systems to most colonised peoples until close to independence, laying foundations for the authoritarian governments that would later emerge in countries such as the Democratic Republic of Congo, Kenya, Nigeria, and Pakistan (Opalo, 2019; Cheeseman and Fisher, 2019). Contestation emerges from tensions within the so-called 'hybrid' forms of governance left behind: systems that blend traditional and customary authority, such as, chiefly, systems with formal government institutions. Traditional leaders, for example, retain considerable legitimacy in settling local disputes sub-Saharan Africa, but do not always make decisions in ways that recognise women's formal rights to inherit land. In tribal regions in Afghanistan and Pakistan, decisions on disputes are often controversial due to disagreements on values and norms between informal conflict resolution forums that operate parallel to the formal structures of justice of the state.

Reflective question

In what ways did colonisation make contemporary contestation inevitable?

Where does contestation happen?

By virtue of their visibility (to social scientists, at least), the most obvious spaces to examine contemporary, political contestation are *formal* decision-making forums and arenas. Such formal arenas exist at all levels, from the transnational to local: global summits, national legislatures, high-level political dialogues, town councils, village gatherings. However, in this book we adopt a perspective that invites readers to observe politics in arenas not conventionally described as 'political'. Agency is also alive, habitual even, in the micropolitics of everyday life – whether it be in schools, churches, hospitals, police stations, in homes or on street corners. As Hay (2002: 3) puts it, 'all events, processes and practices which occur within the social sphere have the potential to be political'.

Spaces of contestation are vast because the social sphere is vast and, indeed, expanding. Especially in this digital age, we observe contemporary contestations in familiar and new spaces: in Kenya, where a fictional superhero became a hashtag phenomenon – #Makmende – providing a viral platform to contest the quality of governance and leadership in the lead up to the 2017 election (Mukhongo, 2020). In Nigeria, where the prolific use of WhatsApp by influencers, political parties and ordinary people is simultaneously strengthening and undermining democratic consolidation (Cheeseman et al., 2020). On street corners of shantytowns in Argentina, where goods and services are traded for political favours (Auyero, 2001).

What these examples illustrate is that politics is not confined to the sphere of government, or to the processes of representation or accountability that occur within them. Formalised spaces where policies are made, elections are held, or interest groups formally compete for influence – the focus of the traditional 'arena view' of politics (Dahl, 1957) – are valid sites of enquiry, but they are merely the tip of the iceberg. Indeed, by the time politics is rendered visible in formal arenas, there was likely a more hidden history of contestation leading up to it. If we focus only on how politics reveals itself in formal spaces, we will overlook the underlying dynamics operating beneath the surface: such as the back-room deals, and agenda setting and lobbying from private companies, or, within the household, the informal politics of the care provided by women that allows men to be overrepresented in formal spaces.

Contestation is multilayered, from transnational, to national, to local. A quick appraisal of the contestation around SDG 6 – clean sanitation and water – illustrates the point. At the transnational level, this goal is the outcome of negotiated frameworks and agenda-setting, reflected and revived through campaigns such as the UN General Assembly's Water Action Decade (2018–2028), which Antonio Gutteres described as 'a roadmap to enhance the water agenda'. At the national level, as in Chile, the distribution of access to water is influenced by contestations between the state and powerful agribusinesses who fund political parties and have control over the media narratives around water scarcity (Madariaga, 2021). And at the local level, people experiencing scarcity and unequal distributions mobilise their agency to contest access. For example, after 21 days without drinking water, more than 10,000 people gathered in Kafr el Borollos, rural Egypt, to block access to the coastal highway, sparking a series of popular protests known as the 'thirst revolution' (El Nour, 2021).

These layers of contestation may appear dispersed, even fragmented, but they can also be viewed as interconnected parts of an overall political ecosystem. In theory, at least, there may be feedback loops operating between transnational, national, and local action: if political actors are responsive to public pressure, if high-level bureaucrats faithfully implement global normative frameworks, and if civil society use on-the-ground investigations and research to inform policy advocacy.

Does 'development' occur only in 'developing' countries?

It should be evident from this pluralist, multilayered definition that development is not a phenomenon that occurs only or even largely in so-called 'developing' countries. Artificial and normatively constructed binaries between 'North' and 'South' or 'Developed' and 'Developing' perpetuate stereotypes and stigmatise countries. The terms 'global south' and 'developing country' reflect colonial notions of 'advanced' and 'primitive' societies (Dados and Connell, 2012). Post-colonial scholars, including Achille Mbembe (2001), and Walter Mignolo (2021), have extensively critiqued the construction of these Western and Eurocentric categorisations for reproducing these power dynamics.

Aside from the intrinsic reasons to jettison archaic labels, the categories simply no longer hold empirically. Several middle-income countries, notably Indonesia and India, have significant numbers of people living in poverty, due to income inequality, regional disparities, and rapid urbanisation. In India, for example, just over 10 per cent of the population fall below the International Poverty Line of US $2.15 per day – a measure set by the World Bank and used by the UN to monitor extreme poverty around the world (see ourworldindata.org).

This is an extreme illustration, certainly, but it shows how national classification systems mask wide income inequalities *within* countries, including in terms of vulnerability to climate change, and exclusions from vital public services such as health and education, which, as we will see throughout this book, intersects with identity.

No level of development can buffer countries from the effects of the climate crisis on ecosystems, or infectious diseases that travel across borders, or managing access to vital energy or water supply. Think about the global challenge of contaminated water sources – an issue that, according to the World Health Organization, affects around one in four people on the planet, exposing them to risk of preventable diseases such as diarrhoea, cholera, dysentery, typhoid and polio (WHO and UNICEF, 2021). This is a problem not only in resource-poor cities, such as Dhaka in Bangladesh, or Nairobi in Kenya, but was also the lived reality for residents of the US city of Flint, the poorest city in the US, whose water was contaminated with dangerous levels of lead between 2014 and 2019, exposing up to 12,000 children to poisoning. Here, as in the cities in Africa, the underlying drivers include insufficient political commitment or investment in the vital infrastructure that could make water safe.

The blurring of boundaries between North/South or Developed/Developing has prompted a lively debate about whether we can now say that development is truly 'global', in the sense that challenges are increasingly shared and therefore demand shared solutions (Horner and Hulme, 2019; Horner, 2020). Critics of the idea of 'global' or universal development argue that it flattens lived realities and obscures the injustices of some countries, groups and individuals being more adversely affected by global challenges than others as a result of colonial legacies and inequality (Kothari and Klein, 2023). In this book, we navigate this line between universality and specificity by offering an approach to analysing the politics of development that can be applied universally to *reveal* the diversity and injustices of lived experience. Our starting point is that contestation is universally possible, because deprivation is universally possible. This does not mean, of course, that the scale or nature of deprivation looks the same everywhere. However, by analysing contestation, we may get closer to understanding, empirically, the gap between people's lived realities and desired futures and the historical legacies and power relations that have (re-)produced this. To this end, we now turn to the approach we advocate, and which we apply throughout this book, for analysing *how* contestation happens.

Reflective question

To what extent do you agree it is problematic to approach development as a 'global' challenge?

How does contestation happen?

Anywhere that resources, rights or power are contested, whether in the backstreet markets of Doha or the corridors of the G7 summit, institutions, interests, and ideas are involved. This means that there are formal structures and informal *rules* in place, being contested by more (or less) rational actors with competing *interests*, holding a range of *ideas* about what is right and fair. In this section, we introduce these three I's of the politics of development.

These are not conceptual abstractions, but a framework for thinking and analysis. To illustrate this, we show below how the three 'I's help us to understand the politics behind one of the most pressing contemporary global challenges: the learning crisis (Box 1.5). Here, as throughout this book, we do not discuss theory for theory's sake, but show how theories can be applied in the real world.

Box 1.5   The learning crisis

The World Development Report, 2018, 'Learning to Realize Education's Promise', was highly significant in raising awareness of a critical challenge: in spite of increased access to education, a large number of children around the world are still not acquiring foundational skills and knowledge. In many low- and middle-income countries, students are going to school, but not actually learning. The Global Education Monitoring Report 2021/2 revealed, for example, that at least 80 per cent of students in Cambodia, Myanmar and the Philippines leave school without minimum proficiency in literacy and numeracy. This crisis is a stark illustration of inequality of opportunity, exacerbated by prolonged school closures during the COVID-19 pandemic. Remedying it is the focus of SDG 4: 'Ensure inclusive and quality education for all by promoting lifelong learning'.

Institutions

Institutions are the rules that shape people's behaviour (see Chapter 3). Nobel prize-winning economist Douglass North (1990) defined them as 'the rules of the game in society'. Just as the rules of the game influence how players play a game of chess or a sports match, so do they influence behaviour and outcomes in society. If one were to change the rules of the game – for example, having two Queens in chess or the goalkeeper in a football match being able to use their hands in all the pitch – it would fundamentally change how people would play.

The same goes for society: if the institutions are changed, then people behave differently. For example, think of the institutions of property rights or criminal justice – these rules produce more or less stable and predictable patterns of behaviour when people make investment or business decisions, or when they decide to follow or break the law. The institutions, or rules of the game in society, produce incentives for individuals to do or not to do certain things; pay taxes, cooperate with the police, or open a shop. If there were no or very weak institutions protecting property rights or criminal justice, we might expect a lot less investment and entrepreneurship, and a lot more crime and disorder.

Another important distinction is between formal and informal institutions. The rules that shape society are not just formal (e.g., constitutions, laws, regulations), but can also be informal (unwritten) social norms around gender roles, queuing, or deferring to traditional authority such as elders (Helmke and Levitsky, 2004). Even though they are not formalised or written down, these rules are often just as powerful in shaping who gets what, when, how. For example, in Sri Lanka after the tsunami, international aid agencies widely distributed fishing boats to revive local livelihoods. They neglected to appreciate, though, that social institutions based on ethnicity or caste determine who can legitimately fish. In some cases, as a result, boats were left unused because their distribution did not conform to these norms (Blaikie, 2010).

What this shows is that informal rules and institutions are just as essential as formal rules in understanding how things really work. Informal institutions can be just as powerful as formal institutions, because although they are not codified, they can still be enforced. Think of how a close-knit community can punish an individual who breaks their rules – for example, by marrying an outsider, they are ostracised. The effect of punishments like this may be just as great as the effect of the punishment the government levies or breaking formal rules, such as financial or material sanctions, or even incarceration.

Finally, and crucially, institutions are not fixed. While institutions are often 'sticky' and tend to be stable over time – which academics refer to as path dependency – they are ultimately humanly designed and maintained, meaning that change can and does happen (Thelen, 2003; Pierson, 2004). And when people contest development, this is what they are seeking to do: create, maintain, shape, add to, avoid, undermine, or demolish the existing rules. Indeed, contestation might be necessitated by a clash of formal and informal rules.

From an institutional perspective, then, can we analyse the learning crisis as a problem of insufficiently strong *rules*? For example, we might ask why there are no monitoring systems around teacher attendance or performance, or accountability for results. Why don't governments, line ministries, teacher–parent groups, ordinary citizens, effectively exercise oversight of the quality of what is delivered in the classroom (see Box 1.6)?

Box 1.6 Institutions and the learning crisis

The rules that (re)produce the learning crisis include everything from state-society relations, to school-level management, to household choices:

- **At the societal level,** the historical dynamics of state-society relations, or 'social contract' (see Chapter 14), can determine whether the right to education is embedded in laws or constitutions, and whether people are, in practice, free to claim it.
- **At the management level,** school management systems are supposed to ensure effective monitoring, training, and professional development.
- **At the household level,** household hierarchies and systems of authority may influence homework routines, or norms around deference to teachers, which in turn influence the likelihood that parents will seek to hold teachers to account for underperformance.

Many key thinkers over the past few decades, such as Francis Fukuyama (2014), Elinor Ostrom (1990), Dani Rodrik (2000), and others, see the primary challenge of development as building strong, stable, peaceful, prosperous, inclusive, and accountable institutions. While compelling, there are limits to this approach. An important one is that while institutions are good at explaining continuity, they are notoriously bad at accounting for change. This is why we also need to consider interests.

Interests

Rules do not make rules, people do (see Chapter 4). To return to the metaphor of the rules of the game, Adrian Leftwich coined the idea of people 'playing games within the rules' – i.e., that the rules of chess or football do not determine outcomes but shape them. To understand this, we need to understand agency and where interests come from.

From an interests perspective, another way we might approach the problem of the learning crisis is to ask: Why haven't people taken more direct action to address it? Why haven't politicians invested more effort into solving the problem? Why don't people protest about it? In other words, why aren't people acting in what seems like everyone's interests?

When we think about contestation, we can always ask what differing interests people have in certain outcomes. Some people have vested interests in maintaining the status quo because it provides them with benefits. Those who have power will seek to defend their advantage, and those who are disadvantaged will be marginalised. So how does this play out in relation to the learning crisis (see Box 1.7)?

Box 1.7   Interests and the learning crisis

Who are the key players, what are their interests, and what influence or power do they have?

- **Unions** Achieving quality education requires governments to adopt and implement reforms that go against the vested interests of powerful teachers' unions (Hossain and Hickey, 2019).
- **Politicians** The popularity of 'free education' was a vote winner after the reintroduction of multiparty politics in sub-Saharan Africa in the 1990s, helping political parties win elections in Tanzania, Kenya and Mozambique. But politicians usually show greater interest in expanding access than improving quality: politicians love a ribbon-cutting ceremony, but less so challenging unions (Batley and Mcloughlin, 2015). The results of quality improvements are likely to extend beyond a single electoral term, making it a much murkier investment from the perspective of winning electoral support.
- **Bureaucrats** Facing different metrics of their own performance, they might also find it easier to increase *attendance* in schools than battle unions over teachers' performance.
- **Teachers** Improving quality means making teachers subject to greater scrutiny and performance measurement, which may not be in their short-term interests.

As we can see from the box, even those with interests in challenging the status quo may fail to act on these interests. If people were always, everywhere, collectively rational, humanity would have achieved much more in terms of the common good (Weale, 2004). But many global challenges – from climate change denial to political apathy over policy reforms – are often the result of *collective action dilemmas*, where people do not act in the common interest (Olson, 1965). For communities to achieve a common interest or purpose, people have to work together, but the benefits of co-operation depend on the co-operation of others. There is always a risk that individuals will 'free-ride' on the benefits, without contributing to them (Olson, 1965). So, for example, if a school has many teachers, some teachers may choose to 'free-ride', or coast on, the hard work of others to achieve results (Bruns et al., 2011). Or if a group of parents decide to mobilise to demand improvements in the quality of teaching, classrooms, or provision of textbooks, other parents observing this may themselves fail to mobilise, thereby undermining the collective movement – the common fate of so many parent-led initiatives.

But simply understanding interests is not enough. People do not act freely without the opportunities and constraints that institutions, as the rules of the game, provide. Where institutions and interests come together is the concept of incentives. Incentives are created by institutions: the rewards and punishments associated with different actions (Ostrom et al., 2002). Good institutions incentivise coordination, and missing or bad institutions incentivise the kind of self-seeking and negative outcomes such as teacher absenteeism detailed above. The limits with just looking at institutions, interests and incentives is that self-interest is assumed to be obvious – self-interested and utility maximising actors will respond consistently and predictably to incentive structures. However, they do not (Hudson and Leftwich, 2014).

Instead, people typically face many overlapping sets of rules, and sometimes must interpret which ones to follow and why. This is not always an open choice, and they can – as the previous section suggested – play games within the rules. This is what the political scientist Mark Blyth (2003) means when he says that institutions do not come with an instruction sheet. Instead, people must interpret the opportunities and risks facing them, often in a situation of uncertainty. This means that people need to engage in 'an internal conversation' to understand what their interests are, and why and how to act (Archer, 2003). Therefore, people's ideas, beliefs, and values – both in their heads and in society – are also vitally important for understanding the politics of development.

Ideas

While it is essential to ask *what* different interests people have in certain outcomes, this leaves open the question of *why*. Why do people have preferences in the first instance? Why do they make certain choices about which rules to follow or not?

Human behaviours are influenced by more than material interests. They are also shaped by ideas (see Chapter 5). Ideas are the values, philosophies, ideologies, norms, and beliefs that people hold. For at least 20 years, scholars have been proving that 'ideas matter' for development, because they shape how political problems are understood, define solutions, and inform what people think is right and fair (Hudson and Leftwich, 2014). Much of this discussion falls under the umbrella of 'discursive institutionalism', first coined by Vivien A. Schmidt (2008). She argued that understanding how change happens requires ideational analysis: investigating the people who carry ideas, the content of ideas, and the discourses through which they are conveyed.

Everything contains ideas. Discursive institutionalists argue all institutions are sustained by normative ideas and beliefs, because the actors involved think they are the right ones or the natural way of the world. Tax systems, for example, contain ideas about reciprocity, entitlements, and what it means to be a productive citizen. The National Health Service in the UK is etched into national identity because of the idea that healthcare should be free at the point of delivery, regardless of ability to pay (see Chapter 5).

Ideas are not just embedded into the rules (institutions), they are the active ingredient in making them. It is no coincidence that whenever there is a need to persuade, legitimise, or mobilise collective action, people in power tell stories that convey ideas. Through plots with 'drama, heroes and villains', stories provide a dramatic imperative behind a certain course of action, and cast people as actors within it (Mayer, 2014, 3). Stories and narratives can motivate co-operation or incite violence.

Ideas also influence contestation because they shape behaviours, and choices at the individual, collective and national level. Individually, people obey the law not only because of threat or fear of punishment, but because the rules are considered 'legitimate', meaning normatively fair and right (Tyler, 2011). They decide whether to take up potentially life-saving vaccinations because of ideas, myths and stories surrounding them. They can also mobilise agency. When people were protesting in Egypt's thirst revolution mentioned earlier, this was not only a distributional conflict, but a symbolic struggle for the value of human dignity (El Nour, 2021). At the national level, ideas can change the course of nations. Sarah Phillips (2020) convincingly shows that Somaliland's post-conflict peace is less sustained by the power of its institutions than a discourse about the country's proximity and propensity to war that motivated the maintenance of order.

Another way of examining the learning crisis, then, would be to examine how ideas at individual, collective and national levels are shaping whether quality education is available, valued, or prioritised. Critically, what ideas or discourses are driving demand for change or perpetuating the status quo (see Box 1.8)?

Box 1.8 Ideas and the learning crisis

In the case of the learning crisis, it might be less immediately obvious what role ideas play, but once you focus on them, they are everywhere you look.

- **Education contains ideas** Education can become associated with normative ideas about the rights of the people or social justice at critical junctures of crisis and change

(Mcloughlin, 2024). Such ideas can become tied to the social contract because they are intimately bound up with national identity (Paglayan, 2021).

- **Elite attitudes shape policy choices** Whether elites see investment in quality education as beneficial may depend on the ideas they hold about the value of education and people's entitlement to it. In some cases, political commitment to education is bolstered when it is framed as essential to nation-building or the realisation of national identity (Hossain, 2005).
- **International norms and frameworks, including the SDGs** These are normative ideas around which local civil society can mobilise collective action and pressure politicians.
- **Education is a symbol of social prestige** This is deeply rooted in many cultures around the world, where people make tremendous sacrifices to send their children to school.

Despite their pervasiveness, it can be challenging for social scientists to isolate and prove that ideas have explanatory power because they are very hard to quantify and measure. For this reason, ideas, much like other intangible variables, such as leadership, have often been neglected. This problem has been compounded by colonial legacies and the flawed assumption that politics in some parts of the world, such as Africa, are not 'ideological' and hence are not shaped by the power of ideas. All development processes, wherever they take place, are shaped by how people understand politics and what they think about the appropriate distribution of resources. Berman (2001) argues that to understand ideational transformations, we must consider the context in which ideas lose their traction, who advocates for new ideas to replace them, and what factors explain why some ideas resonate where others do not.

Summary and conclusion

The politics of development is the process of contestation that happens wherever there are competing visions of, or motivation for, changes in the allocation of resources as well as inequalities of power. Contestation is intrinsic to the pursuit of alternative desired futures. In this process, different institutions, interests and ideas compete with one another and through compromise or domination, differences are resolved or not, and the outcomes are accepted as more or less legitimate. Everyone participates in the politics of development; the question is how. There is no universal set of expectations, or indeed opportunities, to contest change.

We can better understand how contestation happens if we examine its core ingredients: the formal and informal rules set by institutions, the interests and incentives of people, leaders, and elites and who stand to win or lose, and the underpinning beliefs and ideas that drive people's thoughts and behaviour. Sometimes, as we shall see in the book, these three 'I's are obstacles to progress. But they are also levers to work *through* politics. An institutional perspective on the learning crisis, for example, might suggest changing the rules by tweaking incentives, sanctioning or rewarding good performance at individual or school level. A focus on interests might call for negotiating with powerful unions to dampen opposition. An ideational lens might suggest informational campaigns to promote the right to education.

The borders between these levers are porous, of course. The point is, there is not one blueprint. While diagnosing the political causes of underdevelopment is a vital element of the book, we also want to show that progress can be made, often against the odds. The book will not provide 'implications for policy', which are often trite and unrealistic, but rather focus on stories of change. It is not a prescription. It is not a 'how to'. It aims, instead, to facilitate critical reflection and understanding, as a basis for action. And we do this by starting not from lofty theories, but from lived realities. Because in the same vein as the Million Voices campaign, understanding how the politics of development is already connected with our lives is the basis for understanding how we can work through it to achieve a fairer future for everyone.

How to use this book

Readers will have their own starting points, life histories, identities, and ideas that will in turn, influence their positionality and perspectives on the very serious issues we address in this book. This diversity is precisely why in the real world, the politics of development is contested. It is why it is complex, unpredictable, and non-linear.

We aim to carve a path through this complexity by providing the raw elements of a social scientific approach to the politics of development. We apply insights from a range of disciplinary perspectives and methodological dispositions, from the fields of anthropology, economics, sociology, political economy, and geography, to examine the lived realities of politics. In doing so, we aim to challenge readers to think beyond disciplinary siloes that, in the real world, do not exist anyway.

In the spirit of contestation, we invite readers to engage with, reflect on, accept, or object to the propositions made in this book. Our aim is not to impart a true version of reality, itself a fiction, but to stimulate critical thinking and enquiry-based learning about its contestability. That is why you will encounter *Reflective Questions* throughout the text, prompting you to critically consider our arguments and examples, and how far they apply to your existence and experiences, and confirm or refute your prior assumptions about how the world works.

The book is written so that it makes sense whether read as a whole or in parts, in a linear or non-linear way. Nevertheless, there is a logic behind the structure. To help orient readers and educators towards specific ideas, concepts, theories and puzzles they may be looking to explore, in whichever order, we have included an tour of the book (see page 28). This sets out the learning outcomes of each chapter, key concepts and theories it explains, and the reflective questions raised. In sum, though, the book is split into three parts:

In *Part I: Foundations: Interests, Institutions, Ideas*, we explore the three 'I's' of the politics of development in greater depth, analysing and illustrating the strengths and limitations of their explanatory power and why we need all three to appreciate how contestation works.

In *Part II: Change-makers: Government, Market, People Donors*, we scrutinise the interests and ideas held by some of the primary political actors engaged in contesting development and ask whether they have the motivations, power, and opportunities to enable or constrain it.

In *Part III: Challenges: The Politics of Development from the Ground Up*, we apply our three I's to analyse the processes of contestation around the everyday challenges facing people all over the world, as they seek to get by and get ahead, ending with what happens when contestation fails and turns violent.

Before we begin this endeavour, though, we must first situate the book in a critical assessment of how scholars can even claim to know these things, who holds power in this claim-making, and why. In other words, whose knowledge counts. It would be inexcusable not to ground a book about politics in an appreciation of the politics of knowledge, because historical legacies and global inequalities generated knowledge asymmetries that have profoundly shaped whose everyday lived realities are represented, and on whose terms. If any part of this book is compulsory reading, it is this (next) one.

Discussion questions

- What does a political approach reveal about who gets what, when, how that a purely technical approach cannot?
- *Why* is development political? Which of the three underlying drivers – diversity, scarcity and colonial legacies – do you think are most significant, and why?
- Think of another global development challenge, like the learning crisis. What are the underlying institutions, interests or ideas that (re)produce it?

Tour of the book

Chapter	Learning outcomes	Theories and concepts	Reflective questions
Understanding the politics of development			
1 Why is all development political?	• Define the politics of development as a process of contestation. • Critically assess how diversity, scarcity and colonial legacies drive the politics of development. • Begin to understand how institutions, interests and ideas shape lived realities.	• Development as 'alternative desired futures' • The place of politics in the "canon" of development studies • Power	• What factors shaped the evolution of ideas about the place of politics in development? • How do non-material resources enable access to material resources? • In what ways did colonisation make contemporary contestation inevitable? • To what extent do you agree it is problematic to approach development as a 'global' challenge?
2 Whose knowledge counts?	• Critically evaluate the social construction of knowledge about development. • Analyse how knowledge production is contested via ideas, interests, and institutions. • Understand some of the key barriers to, and levers for, decolonising knowledge about development.	• The Western "canon" of development studies (modernisation and dependency) • Decolonisation • Postcolonialism • Orientalism	• How does power shape the construction of 'facts' about development? • Do you agree that colonial influence allowed for theories to be privileged above lived realities in 'doing development'? • Is having a control group fair in the context of development interventions? • To what extent has colonial influence on knowledge production shaped the reading lists of your courses, especially but not exclusively those that aim to study development?
Foundations: institutions, interests, and ideas			
3 Do institutions rule?	• Define institutions, and distinguish between different types of institutions (formal, informal, inclusive, extractive) and their functions in society. • Assess the mechanisms via which institutions shape contestations over desired futures. • Critically evaluate the debates about the role of institutions in development. • Assess key enablers and constraints to institutional reform.	• The state as an institution • Rational choice institutionalism • Historical institutionalism • Sociological institutionalism • Formal institutions • Informal institutions • Social norms • Path dependence • Critical junctures	• Think of an institution. How and why does it have consequences for who gets what, when, how? • Do you agree that inequalities can be explained by studying patterns of institutional development during colonial rule? • Think of an important institution that affects freedoms or capabilities in your world. Has it been contested or changed? Why/why not? • What comes first, the 'right' rules or inclusive development?

	Chapter	Learning outcomes	Theories and concepts	Reflective questions
4	Development in whose interest?	• Define interests and the critical role they play in shaping institutions in development. • Understand how interests are formed, beyond purely rational choice explanations, through ideas and power. • Describe mechanisms for aligning interests towards desired futures.	• The structure-agency problem • Elite capture versus elite control • Political settlements • Collective action • Rational fools • Power to pursue interests	• Do rules control people or do people control rules? • How do agreements between ruling political elites shape everyday lived realities? • To what extent could desired futures be achieved if everyone always acted exclusively in their own self-interest? • What mechanisms can align individual and collective interests?
5	What's the big idea?	• Describe how ideas matter in our everyday lives and become developmentally consequential. • Analyse the emergence and dominance of ideas as a function of institutions, interests, and power. • Understand how ideas are manufactured and deployed within processes of contestation over who gets what, when and how.	• Normative ideas • Ideologies • Beliefs • Discursive institutionalism • Nationalism	• How does an ideational perspective encourage us to think differently about the world around us? • What ideas are most consequential in your life? Why? • What new ideas have emerged and gained traction in your lifetime? What explains this change? • To what extent can nationalism be the driving force behind economic development? • Do you agree that institutions (rules) can only legitimately change when ideas change?

Change-makers: state, people, market, aid

	Chapter	Learning outcomes	Theories and concepts	Reflective questions
6	Are some governments better than others?	• Understand the difference between democracy and authoritarianism, and what it means for a country to become more and less democratic. • Critically evaluate whether these terms are useful when explaining development outcomes. • Assess the extent to which states are able to shape development outcomes in the modern world.	• Authoritarianism • Democracy • The developmental state	• Are states less powerful today than they were in the past? • What aspect of democracy is most important to you? Free speech? Multiparty elections? The right to join any organization you choose to? • Do you agree that at times it can be legitimate to prioritise building state capacity over democratic processes? • Do you agree that the effectiveness of the East Asian model could not be replicated in a democracy? • Has your country moved towards or away from democracy in the last five years?

(Continued)

	Chapter	Learning outcomes	Theories and concepts	Reflective questions
7	Should markets rule?	• Trace the historical development of the concept of free trade and the contestation between free trade and interventionist policies. • Examine the influential ideas, interests, and institutions behind the promotion of the market by global institutions. • Evaluate the rationale behind the implementation of interventionist policies for economic development.	• Comparative advantage • Opportunity cost • Absolute advantage • Mercantilism • Free trade • Washington Consensus	• How do imbalances in the global economy produced by colonial power dynamics shape lived realities? • Do you think that you are based in a country that was disadvantaged or advantaged by the Washington Consensus? • Do you think promoting global trade relationships through trade liberalization is worth compromising on to support for local industries through protectionist policies? • In what ways can state intervention promote more equitable market outcomes?
8	Power to the people?	• Critically evaluate the extent to which people power can shape the pursuit of desired futures. • Understand the political dynamics of social movements, participation, and deepening democracy. • Analyse how power is claimed and contested by people through ideas, interests and institutions.	• Social movements • Contentious politics • Popular participation • Deepening democracy	• Is participation intrinsically valuable or only instrumentally valuable for development? • What would motivate you to join a social movement? why? • Is grassroots participation always helpful in achieving desired futures? Why/why not? • What conditions are needed for participation and deeper democracy to work?
9	Follow the money?	• Understand the diversity of development donors and how their interests can shape who gets what, when how. • Understand how donors' ideas, values, and beliefs influence development policy and practice. • Discuss how the global aid architecture is being contested, including through localization and reparations.	• Development donors • Institutional donors • Philanthrocapitalism • Remittances • Political conditionality • Localisation • Reparations	• Are the wealthy qualified to decide people's futures simply because they have accumulated wealth? • Why is the influence of 'emerging donors', many of which were previously classed as 'developing countries', growing? • What does the nature of conditionalities reveal about donor interests in giving aid? • Can we shift the power in the global aid architecture?

	Chapter	Learning outcomes	Theories and concepts	Reflective questions
Challenges: The politics of development from the ground up				
10	How does my identity matter?	• Understand what identity is, how it is socially constructed, and how this is shaped by colonial legacies. • Critically evaluate what positionality and intersectionality add to the analysis of identity. • Analyse how the contestation of identities becomes developmentally consequential.	• Identity as practice • Identity as a category of analysis • Intersectionality • Positionality	• Do you agree that identity is not static? Why or why not? • Can you think of a real-life example where individuals have little control over how they are categorised into certain identity groups that significantly affects their life chances? • Should all identities be protected by the state? Why? • Do you agree that identity motivates political participation? • Can political participation transform people's identity?
11	Why doesn't everyone get the same?	• Critically evaluate the politics of inequality and inclusion • Define vertical and horizontal inequalities and the constitutive and instrumental case for social inclusion • Understand the role of interests, institutions, and ideas in driving exclusions, particularly the uneven distribution of public goods.	• Social inclusion and exclusion • Sen's Capability approach • Distributive politics • Spatial exclusion	• Do you agree that the SDGs and the LNOB agenda are an inadequate means of addressing inequality? • In what ways does social exclusion prevent people from pursuing their desired futures? • Can you think of exclusions in your context that have both constitutive and instrumental elements? • How do the characteristics of public goods influence political elites' interests to allocate them and *to whom*? • How does identity influence people's power to *address* exclusions? • Thinking about an exclusion you are familiar with, what policies do you think could work to address this?
12	How can I jump this queue?	• Identify a range of 'games within the rules' and evaluate their developmental impacts. • Critically analyse the interests, institutions, and ideas behind two such games - bribery and clientelism. • Analyse what motivates politicians, bureaucrats and citizens to engage in games within the rules.	• Petty corruption • Street level bureaucracy • Clientelism • The Weberian state ideal • Principal-agent theory	• Why is there a difference between official rules and how they get implemented in practice? • Do you think corporate lobbying of governments is a form of rent-seeking? • How does power influence which groups are more or less susceptible to bribery? • Do you agree that clientelist systems can supplement democratic processes? • Should bribery be analysed as a principal agent problem or a collective action problem?

(*Continued*)

	Chapter	Learning outcomes	Theories and concepts	Reflective questions
13	Can the planet cope with development?	• Analyse who pays the price of environmental degradation from a political perspective. • Understand the interests, institutions, and ideas behind the commodification of nature. • Evaluate how environmental protection and justice are contested.	• Sustainability and sustainable development • Political ecology • Environmental justice • Commodification of nature • Mitigation and adaptation • Doughnut Economics	• Is environmental protection a constraint on development for the world's poorest countries? • Why are politicians attracted to neoliberal solutions to environmental challenges? • Could an environmental justice lens inform fairer and more effective political decisions on environment and development dilemmas? • Could the ideas of post-growth, planetary boundaries and doughnut economics challenge entrenched interests, institutions and ideas for a fairer, greener future?
14	When do people accept authority?	• Define authority and explain why compliance with authority matters for development. • Analyse how interests, institutions, and ideas affect whether people accept authority, or not. • Critically evaluate what drives contestation over authority beyond the state.	• Legitimate authority • Social contract theory • The virtuous circle of governance • Procedural justice	• Is 'good' authority always 'legitimate' – and is 'bad' authority always illegitimate? • Why is coercive authority experienced unevenly within countries? • Do the services on your doorstep influence whether you think the state is legitimate or not? • Does the idea of the social contract apply beyond the Western context?
15	When does contestation turn violent?	• Critically evaluate the politics of defining and analysing conflict. • Understand major reasons why contestation turns violent, including the impact of ideas, institutions, and interests of domestic and international actors in shaping conflict dynamics. • Evaluate the roles that identity and inequalities play in sustaining conflict and undermining the chances of peace. • Assess the evolving politics of peacebuilding and evaluate how power and interests underlie prospects for resolving conflict and addressing its underlying causes.	• Greed versus grievance • Rational choice theory, interests and conflict • Communalising colonial policies • Identity-inequality nexus • Peacebuilding and the 'local turn' • Hybridity in peacebuilding	• What are the differences between a "terrorist", a "criminal", and a "revolutionary"? • Is every contemporary conflict "international" to some extent? • What leads civilians to take up arms and participate in violent conflict? • Whose interests operate for or against peacebuilding, and how? • Is what ways is the language and practice of 'peacebuilding' political?

2 Whose knowledge counts?

Global inequalities, knowledge production and the need for decolonisation

Zenobia Ismail

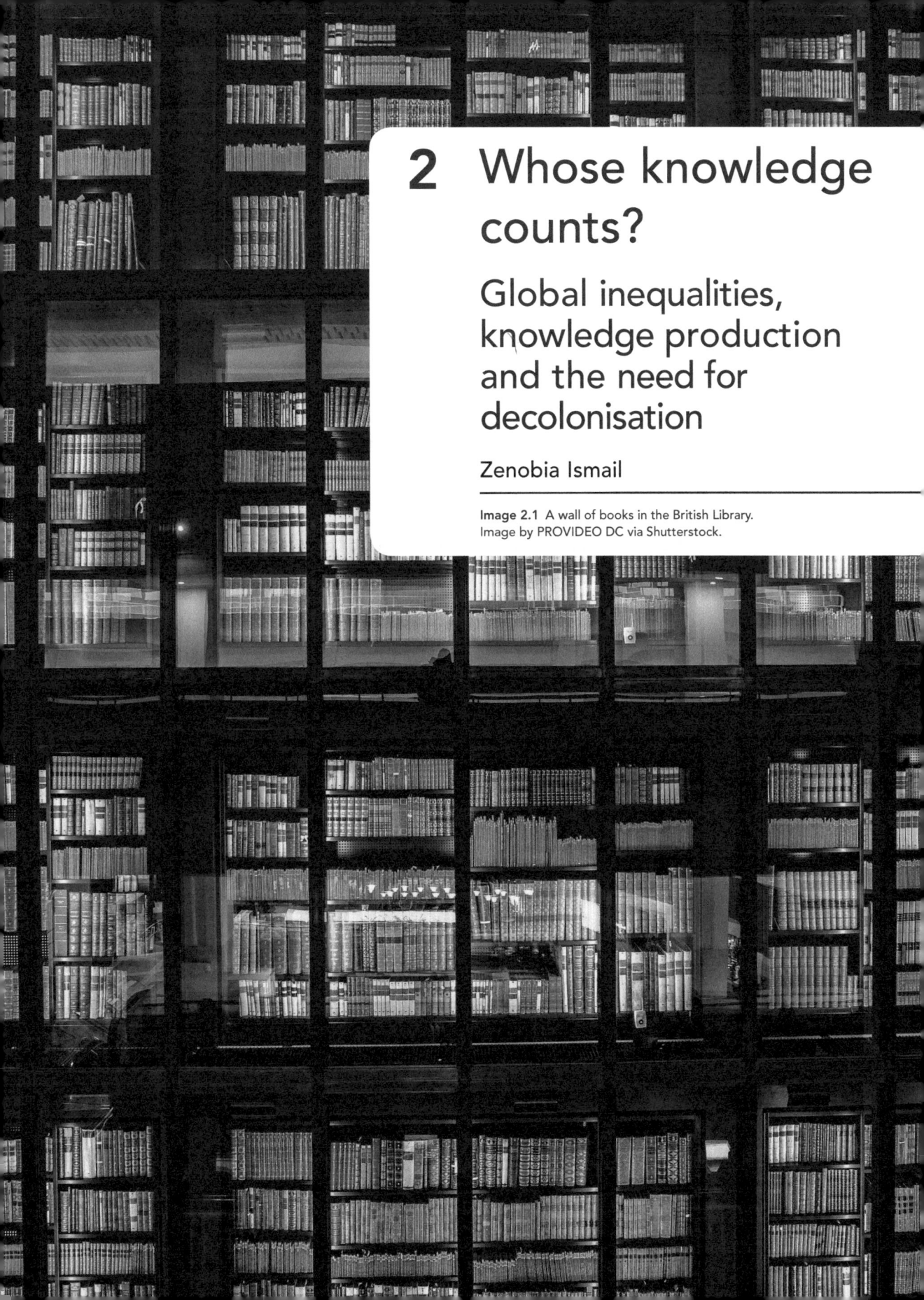

Image 2.1 A wall of books in the British Library. Image by PROVIDEO DC via Shutterstock.

> ## Learning outcomes
>
> - Critically evaluate the social construction of knowledge about development.
> - Analyse how knowledge production is contested via ideas, interests, and institutions.
> - Understand some of the key barriers to, and levers for, decolonising knowledge about development.

The politics of knowledge

In 1981, Takeshi Hirayama, chief epidemiologist at the National Cancer Research Institute in Tokyo, released results from a long-term study on 540 women whose husbands smoked. It found that the more their husbands smoked, the more likely women were to die from cancer. In response, the tobacco industry commissioned their own study, led by a scientist who claimed that Hirayama made serious statistical errors (Oreskes and Conway, 2011). The media was pressured to present both sides of the story, thereby nullifying the damaging evidence that smoking caused cancer. More broadly, the tobacco industry successfully paid a handful of scientists and economists to discredit research that highlighted the health risks of smoking well into the 1990s, delaying the eventual consensus around its carcinogenic effects, and causing hundreds of thousands of unnecessary deaths.

This example, in which those with power, money, and influence harnessed knowledge production to promote their own interests, may seem particularly stark and shocking. Yet it plays out in much more subtle but no less significant ways, across the social and political world. This book endeavours to capture and convey the everyday politics of development and encourage critical engagement with the forces that reproduce it. But we cannot embark on this pursuit without first acknowledging that everything we, as writers, and you, as readers, think we know about development is filtered through the politics of knowledge production. From what research is published, where, to whose voices are represented, how they are promoted, and gain influence, to where and by whom they are taught, knowledge creation is itself an arena of contestation. Power has shaped the production of this book – for example, both in terms of the authors' privilege to write it, and the fact that you are reading it, as opposed to something written by someone from another part of the world.

Think about where the knowledge and ideas you have about countries that you have never visited comes from. It could be Afghanistan, Kenya, India, or Venezuela. Who are the main tellers of these stories? And what are their interests in telling them? Do you question their accounts if they themselves are outsiders without lived experience, or do not speak the local language? Reflecting on these questions is necessary because it reminds us that knowledge does not just 'exist' – it is generated and created. All of us are producers and consumers of it. And this matters because it frames not only how we understand and experience the world, but also how we approach and engage with it. Maybe you won't visit a country if you've heard it is unsafe, for example. In other words, the politics of knowledge has real consequences every single day.

Colonial rule left a profound legacy on whose knowledge counts by (re-)producing unfair hierarchies of knowledge creation and dissemination. Empire spread the idea that European civilisation (including philosophy, science and art) were somehow superior to the relatively unsophisticated rest of the world. Colonising countries enriched themselves at the expense of the colonised, using this wealth to invest greater resources in education and research, thereby reproducing their privilege as suppliers of knowledge. The legacy of this period is still felt today: Western academic institutions typically have more resources, time, power, opportunity and connections at their disposal to conduct research and publish it in elite journals. Academics at Western institutions serve on the editorial boards of many journals where they exert influence over whose ideas and knowledge are published. Many studies have mined databases to show that most of the work published about the Global South is written by researchers from the Global North. This inequity is driven in part by the continued premium on Western evidence and methodologies over local, endogenous forms of knowledge production. As a result, these lived realities are often obscured from view.

Over the last decade, this stark inequality in global knowledge production has mobilised movements such as #RhodesMustFall and #BlackInTheIvory to challenge academic practices and promote diversification and decolonisation. While there is growing consensus that the current situation is untenable, however, there is less agreement on exactly what needs to be done to put things right. Do we just need to see more non-Western scholars and topics in curricula and reading lists? Or does development studies need to go much further to fundamentally rethink the methods, concepts and ideas on which it is based?

This chapter positions the entire book in this critical contemporary debate. It asks what knowledge is, and how it is contested. It explains how colonial legacies led to academics and researchers based in wealthier countries dominating the production of knowledge. It shows why identifying and confronting the political drivers of global knowledge inequalities is not only intrinsically important for social justice, but also essential for appreciating the everyday experiences of the politics of development among historically marginalised communities.

What is knowledge?

The simplest definition of knowledge is what we believe or know (Zagzebski, 2017). Contrary to how this sounds, though, knowledge isn't just a description of what goes on in inside our head. Rather, it is socially constructed. We consume knowledge because we are socially exposed to it, whether through our relationships, kinship ties, or families, our habits of reading print and online media, listening, debating or telling stories. In today's multi-verse, an overwhelming amount of knowledge is out 'there', in the collective world, but we must decide, subjectively, what knowledge to place in our own minds. That involves a process of cognitive deduction, of filtering what seems true or untrue, what fits with or challenges our worldviews, and who to believe when, and why. Thus, from a sociological perspective, knowledge is not just its content, or the ideas we accept as real, but the social processes through which they come to be so (Chandra, 2010).

What we choose to believe matters, ultimately, because it can make us act in a particular way. As Chapter 5 on the power of ideas demonstrates, what we think shapes whether we decide to buy something, follow the rules, or understand the likely benefits, risks and consequences of our actions and adjust or proceed accordingly. Because knowledge is so foundational to human behaviour, there is power to be gained in producing it. This basic fact drives the proliferation of spaces, online or otherwise, where people, businesses, political parties, and organisations seek to influence and persuade us to believe something. In these spaces, knowledge is claimed, substantiated and, because there is always a diversity of perspectives, contested. Disinformation and conspiracy theories compete with scientific evidence or 'facts', making it difficult for the everyday consumer to 'know' what – or who – to believe.

Why does this matter for knowledge about development, in particular? It matters because popular awareness and consciousness about the issues that affect people's lives, and their willingness to act towards desired futures, depends on who wins these contestations.

Take, for example, the climate crisis. Even though extensive research and data proves that climate change is the greatest threat to our long-term existence, conflicting information distributed by climate change deniers has made this a contestable fact (Treen et al., 2020). This process was not organic, but actively encouraged by corporations in the fossil fuel industries, who seek to manipulate the narrative to protect their interests. Similarly, despite much evidence on the efficacy of coronavirus vaccines, disinformation spread on social media by 'antivaxxers' and politicians ideologically opposed to state intervention contributed to vaccine hesitancy during the COVID-19 pandemic. In sum, knowledge is a sociopolitical process in which the most accurate analysis, or that which would benefit the achievement of desired futures, is not always the most widely shared or influential. The reason for that is power.

Reflective question

How does power shape the construction of 'facts' about development?

The power of knowledge production

Development can be undermined by not having the right knowledge. This extends to the exclusion of *people* with relevant, lived experience and understanding of local conditions from decision-making institutions – a particular theme of colonial subjugation. For example, in 1947, the British government decided to invest in large-scale groundnut production in Tanganyika (present-day Tanzania). They planned to clear 5,000 square miles of forest and produce 56,920 tons of groundnuts. Frank Samuel, Managing Director of the United Africa Company – part of Unilever, the largest margarine producer in the UK, which wanted a cheap supply of groundnut oil – was excited by the prospects of the scheme and lobbied the British government to support it. The Overseas Food Corporation, which managed the project, conducted a survey of the area in only seven weeks but overlooked key features that were well known to local inhabitants (Hogendorn and Scott, 1981). In Kongwa, where the project got underway, the terrain proved difficult to clear, the heavy clay soil was unsuitable, and the rainfall inadequate. The project, doomed to fail from the outset, was abandoned in 1954 after a devastating review of its failures. In the subsequent years, local farmers utilised the cleared land for successful cattle farming, demonstrating what could be achieved with the right knowledge of conditions on the ground.

The groundnut scheme has become a well-known cautionary tale about the risk of assuming that outside experts and scientific knowledge always know best. It illustrates how an institution (the United Food Corporation) used its influence with the British government to secure access to cheap groundnut oil and thus further its own interests. Had colonial governments and officials listened to the communities that lived and farmed these areas, they would have found out that the scheme would not work and saved a vast amount of time and resources. Yet despite the notoriety of the groundnut project, the practice of privileging knowledge from the Global North continues to this day.

How do colonial legacies influence knowledge production?

As is demonstrated by the groundnut example, knowledge and power are intertwined. The roots of this ultimately lie in colonialism. The discourse of 'international development' only began when former colonies attained independence (Cooper and Packard, 1997; Mignolo, 2007), propelled by the notion that colonial rule had 'underdeveloped' them (Rodney, 1972). Contemporary development studies is therefore unpalatably yet inescapably rooted in colonialism, and has often been criticised as a means for former colonial powers to continue to exercise power and influence over former colonies (Mignolo, 2009; Ndlovu-Gatsheni, 2012).

Some of the core assumptions that were built into development studies as a discipline reflected the idea of empire. Most notably, through its 'white-gaze', development studies characterised other 'races' of the South as regressive in comparison to the progressive 'North' (Pailey, 2020). There is a great hubris and irony in early, Euro-centric development scholarship that frowned upon, and considered malformed, certain manifestations of politics – corruption, patronage – given that very similar dynamics characterised the European and North American states at a certain stage of their own developments. Early politics in the UK, for example, was notoriously corrupt, with landlords buying their votes in 'rotten boroughs'. Meanwhile, many of the best-known terms we have for electoral manipulation, such as gerrymandering – the art of redrawing constituency boundaries so that the same level of political support delivers a party more seats – come from the United States (Cheeseman and Klaas, 2019).

Some respected intellectuals who played an important role in shaping academic and policy understandings of development, at the same time held racist views or were proponents of colonialism. For example, Bronislaw Malinowski, an influential anthropologist who studied the traditions of Trobriand islanders, referred to them as 'savages' (Malinowski, 1921). Ida Pruitt wrote an incisive life history of Ning Lao T'ai-t'ai, a working-class Chinese woman, that contains valuable social history, but also notes that she could only find time to interview Ning while eating her breakfast (Ning, 1945). The philosopher, John Stuart Mill, argued powerfully for individual liberty and self-mastery, but was a colonial officer in British-ruled India and opposed self-rule because he believed the 'natives' were still in their 'infancy' (Gani and Marshall, 2022). Rudyard Kipling wrote the much-loved children's story *The Jungle Book*, but also the now infamous poem, 'The White Man's Burden', which reflected his support for the American annexation of the Philippines in 1898. These examples highlight the complexity of the intellectual output of this era, which provided insights into the lives of colonised peoples, but from a problematic – often orientalist – perspective that was frequently misleading (see Box 2.1).

Box 2.1 Orientalism

Orientalism emerged when postcolonial literary critics such as Edward Said, Giyatri Spivak and Homni Bhabha examined the relationship between knowledge and power, a theme that is central in this chapter. Said (1978), for example, argued that Western media, film and academia use distorted lenses to describe Arab culture and history, which he described as orientalism. An orientalist view of colonised regions sees them as distinct and opposite to the Western colonisers. In other words, colonised regions were misrepresented in Western art or media as being exotic, childlike and backward. Such negative depictions supported the perceived superiority of Western civilisation, including its ideas or knowledge and educational institutions.

Orientalism has been criticised for presenting a simplified or essentialist view of the contrast between East and West that is overly static, as opposed to postcolonial approaches that seek to challenge and overcome such dichotomies. Despite these criticisms, however, orientalism laid the foundation for current debates on who produces knowledge, and why some ideas and institutions have more power than others. In other words, it played an important role in highlighting how the rules and standards for evaluating science in the West can be used to dismiss local or indigenous knowledge for lacking rigour.

This process was not only driven from the outside. Religious conversion and the aspiration to follow the example of wealthier countries encouraged some of those in poorer states to adopt similar assumptions. This set the scene for a process of 'development by emulation', in which former colonies sought to advance their economies by adopting similar policies to those it was assumed had promoted the advancement of powerful states in the North, such as industrialisation, export-led growth and urbanisation (Mignolo, 2009). These policies were based on ideas such as the efficiency of free markets and comparative advantage of nations championed by economists such as Adam Smith and David Ricardo (see Chapter 8). In this way, colonial legacies continued to shape the core ideas and theories that came to dominate thinking about development and how to achieve it – or, the Western 'canon' (see Box 2.2). As we shall see, it also influenced the methodologies that determined how knowledge was produced and the pedagogy that affected how knowledge was taught or learned at academic institutions (Langdon, 2013; Mitova, 2020).

Box 2.2 The Western 'canon' of development studies

The Western 'canon' of development studies is commonly traced back to the middle of the twentieth century and has tended to be defined and dominated by economists. The prevailing orthodoxy this gave rise to was that the binding constraint to development was a lack of capital given that there was high underemployment and therefore abundant human capacity (Harrod, 1939; Domar, 1946).

This universalist, linear view was further embedded by the emergence of Modernisation Theory, epitomised by W.W. Rostow's (1960) *The Stages of Growth: A Non-Communist Manifesto*. Modernisation Theory posited that all economies had to go through a series of stages. They start in a traditional society, characterised as agricultural, religious, with localised trade, and a hierarchical rigid social structure, and proceed to a high mass-consumption modern economy, characterised as mainly urban, scientific, with expanding trade, politically inclusive, with high levels of investment and production. This, according to Rostow and other modernisation theorists, was 'development'.

These economic growth-focused approaches were challenged (initially unsuccessfully) by the basic needs approach which tried to put the emphasis on poverty, not just economic growth (Chenery, 1960). Yet it was not until later, in the 1970s, that the first Southern view of development really punctured the canon. Building on the ideas of Argentine economist Raúl Prebisch, figures such as the Guyanese historian and activist Walter Rodney (1972) began to articulate a critique of global inequality that emphasised the role of colonial and neo-colonial exploitation. More specifically, Dependency Theory or structuralism argued that one of the reasons 'peripheral' parts of the world were poor was that they had been actively underdeveloped by wealthy states, and that the stages of development as set out by Modernisation Theory were, in fact, impossible to realise because of the structure of the world economy. This included the unequal terms of trade between rich and poor countries, the international division of labour that was exploited by multinational companies, and the tendency for former colonies to become highly indebted, all of which made developing countries dependent on wealthier countries.

This breakthrough was partial and short-lived, however. Rather than building on this critique of the global economic system, the 1980s saw the rise of neoliberalism and the 'Washington Consensus' associated with the return of neoclassical economics (discussed in Chapter 8) and a shift to the political right in the US. The failures of development were again put down to a sclerotic state, monopolies, and tradition in general. The solution, from a neoliberal perspective, was to sweep these away and enact widespread liberalisation of the economy (Williamson, 1990), a move that only served to empower economic experts in institutions such as the World Bank and the International Monetary Fund. Partly as a result, the late 1980s and early 1990s saw the emergence of another wave of critique, sometimes described as *Post-Development scholarship*. The key themes of this literature were that development was essentially a form of neo-colonialism and its power was manifested in part through discourse – i.e., that there are countries and peoples whose goal should be to become more like the West, reinforcing some of the very problems it purports to solve. Post-development scholars include the likes of James Ferguson (1994), James Scott (1998) and, probably most famously, Arturo Escobar's *Encountering Development* (2011).

> As the 1990s rolled in, a new paradigm of human development was in the ascendency, which drew inspiration from the basic needs approaches in the 1960s, demonstrating the cyclical nature of trends in development literature. Some examples of human development approaches are:
>
> 1. Feminism, which emphasises equal rights among sexes (Biewener and Bacque, 2015), beginning with a women in development approach and evolving to gender and development.
> 2. 'Participation lit', which focuses on bottom-up approaches for tackling development challenges and empowering people living in poverty (Chambers, 1994). This includes critiquing the focus on urbanisation as a means of development and the exclusion of rural voices in development planning and programming.
> 3. A focus on Institutions (see Chapter 3) and the role of politics on international development, especially from the 2000s onwards.

Some of the overarching theories described in Box 2.1, such as the modernisation approach, were overly abstract, anachronistic, and unfit for analysing the real politics of development. As with other grand theories, they were vulnerable to criticism for their weak predictive power, generalisability, and relevance to people's everyday lives. One reason for this is that they were not, in fact, particularly concerned with the politics of development, but rather with foregrounding various social, relational, industrial, and technological factors as more or less powerful explanations of development trajectories. Normatively, they were often influenced by exclusively Western ideas and experiences, or worse, 'othering' the ideas of colonised peoples (Kothari, 2006). In this sense, past orthodoxy tells us how *not* to think about/do development, just as it provides us interesting models to think with. By marginalising scholars and forms of knowledge from the Global South, they made development less accessible and relatable, and privileged ambitious theories over everyday realities.

Reflective question

Do you agree that colonial influence allowed for theories to be privileged above lived realities in 'doing development'?

Over the last sixty years, postcolonial thinking has emerged as an interdisciplinary approach grounded in the use of postmodern critique (which in this context often refers to the critique of unfair power structures) to study how 'colonized peoples transformed in relation to colonizers, opening processes of hybridity and creating creative resistances, sometimes digested by dominant/imperial/hegemonic discourses' (Botella-Ordinas, 2013). Contemporary postcolonialism builds on this reservoir of ideas and reflects on how the colonial legacies continue to influence global power asymmetries and current debates on national security, nuclear proliferation, migration, international aid and land rights. In addition, it calls for a stronger focus on the power dynamics relating to race/ethnicity, gender and class across social science and humanities (see Box 2.3).

Box 2.3   Postcolonialism

Postcolonialism refers to ideas and perspectives that developed after former colonies attained independence. Seminal postcolonial scholars, like Franz Fanon and Albert Memmi, discussed how people in colonised places internalised imperialist worldviews and racial hierarchies through the adoption of the coloniser's language, culture, religion and education system and consequently came to believe that they were inferior (Nair, 2017).

The term 'postcolonial' can be used to refer both to the period that followed independence, and the project of reclaiming the history and agency of those people subordinated by colonialism. The Kenyan author Ngũgĩ wa Thiong'o, for example, has written of the need to decolonise the mind (1986), encouraging others to write in their original language rather than the one imposed by colonial powers.

Such challenges to colonial ideas and ideologies did not only emerge after the end of colonial rule. In opposition to imperial attitudes and prejudices, which often regarded colonialised people as lacking a sophisticated culture or history, Senegalese political leader and philosopher Leopold Senghor and the Martinican politician and poet Aimé Césaire developed the idea of *négritude* in the 1930s. *Négritude* celebrated the unique identity and culture of African peoples, not only to position them as equal to other races, but also arguing that Black societies had distinctive features that meant that in some respects they were superior. Partly as a result, *négritude* rejected the French colonial aspiration of assimilation which anticipated that indigenous people in Francophone Africa would eventually become French through education and acculturation (Kohn and McBride, 2011).

While postcolonial thinking has been influential, it is yet to transform the practices and understandings of development, in part because these are sustained by differential access to research funding, information, and a global audience, as discussed in greater detail below.

Who funds knowledge production?

Funding for producing knowledge about development is concentrated in wealthier countries with government research schemes, such as the United Kingdom Innovation Research (UKRI) fund. Academic institutions in these countries have better access to funding for creating knowledge through research. In addition, academic institutions in these countries also benefit, disproportionately, from well-developed industrial sectors (e.g., pharmaceuticals or Silicon Valley) that collaborate with universities, particularly in science and engineering

(Gani and Marshall, 2022). Although the private sector is a valuable source of funding for research, there are cases where powerful pharmaceutical companies can influence the type of research that is conducted, and sometimes even the presentation of research results so that they appear more favourable and beneficial to the positioning of the company at the apex of the global production chain (Jefferson, 2020; Reutlinger, 2020).

Access to funding is, by contrast, often much more challenging in less wealthy countries, although this does not mean that they do not invest in education. A study by the Organisation for Economic Development and Co-operation (OECD) found that government spending on education (including research and development) as a percentage of total government expenditure is highest in Chile, South Africa, India, Brazil and Mexico. These countries spend far more on education than OECD countries on average – as indicated in Table 2.1. It is no coincidence that these countries have some of the best known universities outside of Western countries. However, it is also important to note that a lot of this money goes on primary and secondary school education, rather than university education and research. Moreover, funding for universities is often targeted at teaching students rather than creating the necessary environment for academics to conduct research and publish papers.

Table 2.1 Total government expenditure spent on education (including research and development)

	Primary (%)	Secondary/post secondary (%)	Tertiary (%)
Chile	5.9	6.1	5.4
South Africa	7.3	6.3	3.3
India	3.9	5.7	4.9
Brazil	4.1	6.3	3.6
Mexico	5.4	5.3	3.2
OECD average	3.4	4.3	2.8

Source: OECD, 2022

It is also important to keep in mind that universities in the Global South typically receive far less money in terms of grants and philanthropy, which constrains their ability to set their own research agendas. Moreover, many have yet to recover from the negative impact that the structural adjustment policies implemented in the early 1990s had on their education sectors (see Chapter 6; Gani and Marshall, 2022). Researchers in regions such as sub-Saharan Africa have to contend with low levels of funding for research, low salaries, heavy teaching loads and inadequate libraries (Crawford et al., 2021). They are often ineligible for research grants that are available in well-resourced countries because of restrictions on nationality. Furthermore, lack of funds (Gani and Marshall, 2022) and visa regulations make it difficult for academics in the Global South even to travel to academic conferences in the Global North.

Who can act as gatekeepers, and who gets read?

An additional challenge to overcoming global knowledge inequalities is that the editorial boards of many peer-reviewed journals are usually dominated by academics from wealthier countries who may act as gatekeepers by requiring articles to utilise specific methodologies, or to engage with the work of specific authors in the 'canon' in order to be published. This is important because the 'gold standard' in research is a peer reviewed article – i.e., a piece of work that is published after two or three peers have submitted it to a rigorous, anonymous review process. Given this, it is particularly significant that limited access to archival material, a lack of funding for original research, English language requirements, lack of access to mentors who have the time to provide guidance and more latent issues relating to unconscious bias – ingrained prejudices that the holder may not realise they have – and overt racism all serve to discriminate against the research work of scholars based in the Global South (Crawford et al., 2021; Gani and Marshall, 2022). As a result, they are less likely to be published in the most highly cited journals, and hence to shape the academic debate.

A study by Briggs and Weathers (2016) finds that researchers based in Africa produce only a small proportion of the articles in the two main peer-reviewed journals on Africa. Although the number of women published in *African Affairs* and the *Journal of Modern African Studies* increased over time, the number of African-based authors declined to just 15 per cent in 2013 (Briggs and Weathers, 2016), despite efforts by the journals to encourage submissions. Similarly, just 3 per cent of articles published in leading European and North American journals between 2008 and 2017 were written by scholars based in the Global South. Even in the *International Feminist Journal of Politics,* less than 5 per cent of articles were written by Southern authors (Crawford et al., 2021).

The situation is somewhat different when it comes to the reports of international organisations, think tanks and NGOs, which is often referred to as 'grey literature'. Organisations like the World Bank, United Nations Development Programme (UNDP), United States Agency for International development (USAID), conduct research that often approximates academic methods, but is usually not peer reviewed. Likewise, philanthropic foundations such as the Gates Foundation, Aga Khan Foundation, Mo Ibrahim Foundation, and civil society organisations like the Foundation for Democratic Process in Zambia, Lead Pakistan and the Self-Employed Women's Association (SEWA) in India, also produce analytical reports. These represent an important source of knowledge, and are often produced using consultants from the relevant country, especially when they are produced by local civil society organisations. Many of these reports, such as the evaluations of donor programmes, are not released to the public, however, and so do not shape the broader debate. Even if such material is published, it may not find a large audience if organisations do not have effective communications infrastructure, not least because such reports are less likely to be prioritised by search engines such as Google Scholar (Krauss, 2018).

How is knowledge produced in practice?

Knowledge is produced by individuals and organisations through structured processes like conducting interviews for a research project or teaching a course, and through the lived experiences of people and organisations, such as participating in environmental justice campaigns, doing smallholder farming or running a business.

In the social sciences there are three broad methodologies for conducting scientific research (Table 2.2). These methodologies are influenced by Western thought on science and the ethnographic work scholars like Malikowski, Mary Douglas and others. These methodologies became dominant, and so scholars based in institutions where they can obtain the relevant training and access to funds have an advantage in terms of producing 'scientific' knowledge that conforms to these Western standards.

Table 2.2 Research methods used in social science for primary data collection

	Qualitative research	Quantitative research	Experimental research
• Description	• Obtains rich information with unstructured interviews, focus groups and participant observation	• Obtains large amounts of data with a structured questionnaire and data capture	• Aim is to compare a treatment group with a placebo or control group to determine if the treatment was effective
• Number of respondents	• Tends to be small	• Tends to be large	• Tends to be large
• Statistical significance	• Not applicable	• Can be estimated	• Differences can be estimated
• Data types	• Text or visual • Thick descriptions	• Numerical and statistical	• Numerical and statistical
• Data collection methods	• In-depth interviews • Focus groups • Ethnography	• Surveys • Large observational studies	• Surveys • Measurements (e.g., weight gain) • Tests (e.g., mathematics ability, cholesterol levels)

Qualitative research and ethnography (participant observation) can be useful for gathering local knowledge and representing local voices in scholarship. This data is collected through interviews with relevant individuals, and focus groups with small numbers of participants (usually 5–10), and is often very detailed, which is sometimes called 'thick' analysis. Quantitative methods may also be used to collect data – for example, conducting large surveys that elicit thousands of responses and then using statistical programmes such as Stata or SPSS to analyse them. Meanwhile, experimental research methods seek to replicate scientific approaches, using strategies such as randomised control trials where respondents are randomly allocated to a treatment group and a control group so that the effect of the treatment can be isolated and estimated. For example, imagine a research project to determine whether a youth employment programme that offered training and access to micro-finance is effective in terms of generating employment and experiment can be performed. The treatment groups would get the training and micro-finance, and the control groups would get nothing. A few months later, a survey can be done to measure employment levels across both groups. If the number of employed people is the same or very similar in the treatment and control groups, then it appears that the programme was not successful.

In general, quantitative research and experiments are often regarded as 'more scientific' than qualitative research because the use of large samples and statistical analysis generates a greater sense of certainty. This has significant consequences, because this kind of analysis requires access to expensive computer software and specific technical skills that assume a degree of mathematical capacity, which are less likely to be easy to access outside of wealthy states. As a result, an emphasis on such methodologies may be inherently exclusionary to researchers based in some countries. Which countries are most impacted by these forms of exclusion vary, and it is important to recognise that the Global North/ Global South divide is often an unhelpful oversimplification. Where mathematical skills are concerned, for example, the TIMSS international study on maths and science education finds that East Asian countries lead the way, while the Middle East, Morocco, South Africa and Pakistan lag behind (Mullis et al., 2019). This is also true in other areas. Wealthier and larger countries in the South that have English as an official language tend to be better represented in terms of academic publications and citations, such as India, Nigeria and South Africa, meaning that there is inequality within the North and the South, as well as between them.

The idea that quantitative approaches are inherently more scientific is also misleading, and can lead to important issues related to ethics and data quality being overlooked. For example, cross-national surveys are lauded for their great explanatory power but are sometimes based on data that is not strictly comparable, leading to estimation problems and flawed statistical modelling (Keeves et al., 2006). Similarly, randomised control trials for new drugs can occur in countries with lower safety standards and involve people who cannot afford access to the treatment that is being developed, giving rise to thorny ethical dilemmas (Bittker, 2021). Thus, although the methods used in international development are constantly evolving, there remains a serious concern that the way that data is collected – especially from those who are living in poverty – can be extractive (USAID, 2022). This is especially the case when organisations or companies in wealthy countries publish the data gathered from local communities and claim intellectual property rights over it. When this happens, the individuals and communities that gave up their time to make the study possible may lose control and ownership over their knowledge – indeed, they may not even be able to access it due to costs or paywalls.

Image 2.2 Black Lives Matter demonstration signs in a window of All Souls College at Oxford University, UK, 2020. Image by Chris Dorney via Shutterstock.

It is important to note that there are many other ways that knowledge is shared, such as blogs, opinion pieces and articles in the news media (Lucas, 2022). These can provide important insights into contemporary events, although they may lack the rigour and scrutiny of peer reviewed research. One potential advantage of such mediums, however, is that they can create vehicles for local communities and concerned citizens to tell their own stories. This is particularly important because although local knowledge can be incorporated into peer-reviewed publications and grey literature, some kinds of knowledge – such as oral history, with stories that are passed down the generations in communities that do not have a history of literacy – are much less likely to be fore-grounded in such formats, and may be more amenable to other kinds of approaches such as the use of videos, animation and creative media to communicate communal knowledge.

How can knowledge be decolonised?

Scholars have been writing about knowledge disparities between wealthy countries and their poorer counterparts since the 1970s (Decker and McMahon, 2020). Recent political debates sparked by movements like #RhodesMustFall and #BlackLivesMatter were helpful in galvanising conversations about the colonial legacies of many academic institutions and the dominance of Western ideas and theories in their syllabi. Yet, although debates on decolonising knowledge production generally start by acknowledging that development knowledge is heavily influenced by the Western 'canon', they often stall when it comes to forging agreement on what needs to be done (Krauss, 2018; see Box 2.4).

> ## Box 2.4 What does it mean to decolonise knowledge?
>
> Decolonisation theory builds on postcolonialism's reflection on the physical, psychological and social impact of the colonial legacy and how this continues to foster inequality. It posits that many of the inequalities we can observe in the world today can be traced back to the colonial era, when imperialist countries benefitted from slavery and the exploitation of natural resources at the expense of colonised countries. There remains considerable debate, however, over exactly what it means to be truly 'decolonised'.
>
> Mitova (2020) observes that epistemic decolonisation can either be moderate, entailing the diversification of knowledge and inclusion of marginalised voices, or so radical that it calls for the rejection of theories and knowledge emanating from the Global North.
>
> Some influential decolonisers, such as Walter Mignolo (2007, 2009) propose moving away from Western categories of thought (which are heavily influenced by classical Greek philosophy) and developing new perspectives and theories. More radical scholars like Mignolo and Sabelo Ndlovu-Gatsheni (2018), discuss the need for epistemic disobedience (Mignolo, 2009), or epistemic recentring (Mitova, 2020) in order to bring the periphery to the centre. In particular, they object to concepts such as modernity and progress which are deeply influenced by European philosophies relating to the Enlightenment and liberalism (Ndlovu-Gatsheni, 2012). One challenge for these broader attempts is to develop an alternative worldview that is both comprehensive and does not rely on colonial ideas.

While these criticisms are all founded on reasonable concerns, there is a good argument that knowledge should be challenged and probed rather than simply discarded, not least because there is considerable disagreement about exactly what should replace the 'canon' (Crawford et al., 2021). Indeed, in some ways our focus should be less on specific arguments and theories, and more about changing the process of researching development to ensure that it is inclusive, ethical and consistently critiques existing assumptions, power structures, and inequalities. This means paying attention not only to what research is published, but also the conditions under which it is produced, and how we can develop alternatives to market-driven models that include the voices and perspectives of marginalised groups (Krauss, 2018). Understood in this way, decolonising knowledge production is an ongoing process (Mitova, 2020) that includes reassessing established knowledge, developing alternative or new knowledge, and transforming the process of knowledge production. In other words, capturing alternative desired futures authentically.

Some of the challenges that will be involved in this become clear as soon as you start to consider practical solutions to these deep-rooted issues. Diversifying Western educational institutions by recruiting scholars from outside of the West might initially seem like a clear win for decolonisation, for example. But what if this contributes to a further process of brain drain, taking some of the most effective researchers and teachers out of their home countries so that they do not train and inspire the next generation? A better solution might therefore be to set up academic exchanges to enable the circulation of individuals and ideas, while instigating new programmes to empower academics and practitioners based in the Global South to have a stronger voice in global academic and policy debates. This is easier said than done, however. Journals and conferences in the North, such as the African Studies Association of the UK, the British Academy, and the Development Studies Association, are increasingly seeking to level the playing field by offering writing workshops, discounted membership and travel grants (Crawford et al., 2021). Yet this will only have a modest impact in the absence of efforts to address structural constraints, such as the large classes, limited time for teaching, and lack of institutional incentives to publish that are common in many universities.

Another institutional issue that must be tackled is the way that research funding is distributed by academic and development organisations. At present, it is all too common for funders to tie grants to a very specific agenda that is set by those in the North, rather than the communities and individuals the research is designed to assist. Short deadlines and demanding application processes also mean that researchers have little time to develop meaningful collaborations. As a result, what often happens is that researchers in Western institutions scramble at the last minute to find collaborators in the South, effectively asking them to join projects whose scope and methods have already been identified. When this happens, there is a considerable risk that rather than a genuine collaboration, those based in the country to be studied effectively act as data collectors, and enjoy little control over the intellectual foundation or direction of the project.

Changing this situation requires funders to empower researchers and communities facing development challenges to set their own agendas, allowing researchers more time to establish meaningful collaborations, and resourcing pre-bid workshops to enable all participants to play a full role in project design. It is also important that researchers commit to inclusive independent advisory boards that feature representatives of the communities to be researched, establishing joint ownership of intellectual property, and presenting research back to participants in an accessible way (Dodsworth and Cheeseman 2018). Researchers should also make sure that they comply with the ethical standards of the country and communities concerned, not just the institution and country issuing the funding. This will mean taking time to share the design of studies with local communities so they can play a more interactive role, and giving them the power to veto elements of the research that they find inappropriate or disrespectful.

In many cases, those pioneering these new approaches are based in countries like Bangladesh, where the International Centre for Climate Change and Development (ICCCD) – a collaboration between a UK think tank, the Bangladesh Centre for Advanced Studies, and Independent University, Bangladesh – places great emphasis on locally led adaptation (LLA) programming. The ICCCD finds that this approach, in which 'local communities, community-based organisations, small businesses, community members, citizen groups, local governments, and local private sector entities at the lowest administrative level are consulted and included as decision-makers in the climate adaptation interventions that affect them', leads to a more equitable distribution of power and resources (ICCCD, n.d.). Furthermore, local innovation and knowledge are elevated which contributes to more effective resilience-building, while developing a Community of Practitioners in Bangladesh who can play a central role in the co-production of knowledge and policy implementation in the future.

Listening to local communities and incorporating local or indigenous knowledge into development programme decisions is critical for building trust and relationships with communities that can themselves contribute to better development outcomes (USAID, 2022). The Biovision Africa Trust, for example, starts new programmes in communities by learning about the current practices and challenges. Only after listening to local experiences and common frustrations does the Trust propose its plans for intervention, which the community is invited to respond to and modify, building respect and a genuine sense of collaboration (USAID, 2022).

Issues around gender and racial bias also need to be addressed – for example, by ensuring that all journal editors and individuals who sit on hiring committees have unconscious bias training. Journals also need to be further incentivised to revise existing working practices, and one way to do this would be to track the submission and publication rate of journals by location, with publishing houses and editors encouraged to espouse an editorial vision that promotes inclusion (Crawford et al., 2021). We must also recognise that the barriers described in this chapter do not only exist on one dimension and instead are intersectional, with women and individuals from the LGBT+ community most likely to suffer discrimination. In the light of this, there will also be a need to ensure that more specific and targeted support is provided to marginalised groups. There are already positive steps in this direction – such as the Merian Institute of Advanced Studies in Africa at the University of Ghana, a collaboration between African and European researchers that holds dedicated workshops for female academics with sessions on publishing and applying for research grants, but much more is needed.

Reflective question

To what extent has colonial influence on knowledge production shaped the reading lists of your courses, especially but not exclusively those that aim to study development?

Many of these issues are only likely to be fully rectified in the long-term, but there are also things that can be done now. Knowledge can be decolonised by broadening the reading lists for courses on international development to include books and articles produced outside of the 'usual suspects'. Where feasible, the publications of researchers and local civil society organisations based in the Global South should be incorporated into the syllabi. Lead Pakistan, for example, produces several publications on climate change across countries in the Global South that can be incorporated into courses on governing environmental resources. Similarly, the Self-Employed Women's Association (SEWA) in India produced a report on the impact of COVID-19 on self-employed women using survey data. The inclusion of these reports is critical for decolonising knowledge production, because they contain knowledge that may challenge dominant narratives and policy responses for climate change, pandemics and other issues.

Summary and conclusion

This book aims to anchor the politics of development in the day-to-day experiences of citizens. But legacies of power and knowledge asymmetries necessarily limit this pursuit, in practice, particularly the degree to which the voices of the most marginalised are represented on their own terms.

Progress towards decolonising knowledge and decentring the Global North is underway. International non-government organisations, such as ActionAid and Oxfam, have moved their headquarters to locations in the Global South. International organisations or agencies, such as the World Bank, Ministry of Foreign Affairs of the Netherlands and the (Canadian) International Development Research Centre, support civil society organisations and knowledge networks like SEWA and Lead Pakistan to produce high quality research publications and shape the global debate. Philanthropic organisations that are based in Africa and Asia, like the Mo Ibrahim Foundation and the Aga Khan Foundation, are also playing an important role in providing different perspectives on international development. The Aga Khan Foundation, for example, continues to support development initiatives for people in Afghanistan after the Taliban takeover, in contrast to development agencies in the UK and US that quickly withdrew aid.

More needs to be done, though, and fast. Local knowledge relating to ecological and agricultural practices that has been passed down from one generation to another will have insights that experts, whether based in the West or the capital city of the country concerned, are likely to miss. It is therefore only by working in collaboration with local communities that we can develop truly effective responses to pressing global challenges such as climate change. The decolonisation process is therefore not only ethically important, it is essential to get development right. This does not mean, however, that we should always idealise the 'local', or assume that a given community will have a settled position on a given issue, or an inclusive one. Indeed, each community has its own internal inequalities. The voices of women and other historically marginalised groups are often drowned out by more wealthy men, for example. Empowering local communities without entrenching these injustices may therefore require creating safe spaces for different groups and individuals to express their views without fear of retribution, while encouraging those who hold power to take on board the views of everyone.

Working in this way will take more time, and will cost more money, than the top-down development models of old. But the advantages will far outweigh the costs. Genuine partnerships will provide new skills and experience to development practitioners, enriching their understanding and capabilities. The risk of major and costly development failures such as the Groundnut Scheme will be reduced, and these savings may well exceed the additional resources needed to work in a more bottom-up way. And a genuine sense of partnership will generate a stronger foundation from which to tackle future challenges. Building this future will require not just new institutions, but also new ideas, changing the way we think. This book, and its emphasis on the lived experience of those struggling for development around the world, represents our contribution to this effort.

Discussion questions

- Think about who is seen to be an 'expert' in your country – what do these people have in common, and how does this vary depending on the issue?
- If you were doing a research project yourself, what could you do to include local knowledge?
- Who should be involved in developing a level playing field for knowledge production?
- What are the responsibilities of academic institutions, governments and philanthropic foundations?

Suggested further reading

Aloudat, T. and Khan, T. (2022) 'Decolonising humanitarianism or humanitarian aid?', *PLOS Global Public Health*, 2 (4).

Kessi, S., Marks, Z. and E. Ramugondo (2020) 'Decolonizing African Studies', *Critical African Studies*, 12 (3): 271–82.

Part 2
Foundations: institutions, interests, and ideas

3 Do institutions rule?

Order, incentives, and norms

Jasmine Burnley, Niheer Dasandi, and David Hudson

Image 3.1 Ribbons tied on a fence at Imjingak unification park in the Republic of Korea, 2019. Image by trabantos via Shutterstock.

> ## Learning outcomes
>
> - Define institutions, and distinguish between different types of institutions (formal, informal, inclusive, extractive) and their functions in society.
> - Assess the mechanisms via which institutions shape contestations over desired futures.
> - Critically evaluate the debates about the role of institutions in development.
> - Assess key enablers and constraints to institutional reform.

The power of rules

'Do institutions rule?' is a bit of a pun (and not ours). Institutions *are* the rules, in that they provide the framework for how things get done – as, for example, in the rules of a chess game. But also, as some social scientists argue, rules really do 'rule', in the sense that they are the most important determinant of prospects of achieving desired futures (Rodrik et al., 2004). But do rules really rule? What are the limits of this viewpoint? To kick off our exploration of the three 'I's of this book's intellectual framework, this chapter takes a closer look at how and why institutions 'rule', and when they have the power to shape the distribution of resources, rights, and freedoms in society.

Consider the example of piracy off the coast of Somalia. With the assistance of international aid agencies, the government of Somalia made a set of international agreements to allow foreign vessels to fish its territorial waters. But when the Somali state collapsed in 1991, so did these rules. In this metaphorical sea of lawlessness, in which the foreign-funded Somali Navy no longer had authority or capacity to police its waters, large international fishing vessels began plundering its rich fish stocks. Local fisherfolk, who experienced the impacts of this disorder on their livelihoods, responded by using small boats to police the waters themselves. Yet their efforts to prevent what they perceived as foreign invaders from stealing their resources were often unsuccessful.

Seeking a stronger deterrent, and backed by more aggressively enterprising *abbaanduule* ('warlords'), this activity quickly transformed into piracy. If you have seen Hollywood depictions of this, as per the movie *Captain Phillips*, you might imagine an onset of chaos, violence, and anarchy. In a more subtle version of reality, though, what transpired was the evolution of a complex set of agreements and arrangements (rules!) for dividing up ransom money between the businessmen funding the pirate ships, and subcontractors providing food, access to port and sex workers (Pham, 2010). The disintegration of the formal rules, and the order and stability that they provided, was not replaced by anarchy, but by other rules that solved problems, created alternative sources of livelihoods, and restored a new form of order, albeit one that served different interests.

In time, as the informal rules of piracy disrupted a critical international trade route, the international community countered by establishing a multi-national anti-piracy coalition – the United States coordinated Combined Task Force 151 (CTF-151), NATO's

'Operation Ocean Shield' (originally 'Operation Allied Protector'), and the European Union Naval Force (EU NAVFOR) 'Operation Atalanta'. A couple of dozen warships began patrolling the waters, eventually succeeding in curbing piracy incidents, and ultimately re-establishing the preferred international, rules-based order.

What does this example tell us about rules? First, that rules have the power to determine the distribution of resources – who gets what, when, how. Second, that rules can be formal or informal, from international agreements, to the mutually serving pacts between pirates and warlords. Third, that people have an interest in creating, maintaining, or contesting rules, in order to protect or serve their interests. This is why there will always be attempts to make and enforce rules. Even the most seemingly anarchical spaces have rules: Somali pirates splitting the profits of ransom 50/50 with their warlord benefactors, for example. But the Somali piracy case also suggests that the relationship between rules, order and developmental gains is not so clear-cut, and actually depends on who has the power to make them, and in whose interests they ultimately work.

In this chapter, we explore some of the critical debates about how institutions affect contestations over desired futures. In turn, we ask what institutions are, how they work, how they shape development, and how they change.

Why are institutions important? Because they arrrrrr

To understand why rules matter, even in apparently lawless scenarios, we can look more closely at pirates, this time, in historical perspective. Pirates operating around the Caribbean in the early eighteenth century were, like their contemporary Somali counterparts, roaming around in an apparent void of rules. They functioned outside of the law, attacking merchant ships, stealing their cargo and valuable goods, and engaging in extortion (see Leeson, 2014). Pirate ships usually had around 80 crew members. To successfully plunder the merchant ships, the crew needed to carefully coordinate their attack, so captains needed absolute authority over how they engaged in battle. During the onslaught, crew members had to follow the captain's orders. During normal operations, another pirate officer, the quartermaster, otherwise led the crew, facilitating day-to-day coordination, distributing resources (including loot), disciplining crew members, and arbitrating disputes among them.

While these officers – the captain and the quartermaster – were essential for coordinating pirate activities and maintaining order on the ships, there was also the risk that they would abuse their authority by using their special powers to serve their own private interests rather than those of the whole crew. To safeguard against this, the crews needed agreements with them – rules that placed limits on how the officers could use their privileged position. They also needed to be able to enforce these rules, particularly because expeditions could last for many months, meaning that it could be a long wait to jump ship, literally!

Surprisingly, given the apparently lawless nature of their activities, the specific rules that pirates established to enforce relations between officers and crew members was *constitutional democracy* (Leeson, 2014). The crews of pirate ships democratically elected captains and quartermasters. A popular vote on officers' behaviour or performance could be held at any time the crew members wanted. If the crew believed the captain or quartermaster was using their powers in ways that weren't in keeping with the agreements, they could dispose of the officer and elect a new person in their place. Hence, pirates established democratic checks and balances as a way of privately enforcing the rules. However, that wasn't enough. For these democratic checks to be effective, crew members needed to be able to agree on what constituted an abuse of power. Without this, they would not be able to coordinate their voting to successfully depose officers that abused their power. To do this, they needed constitutions.

Pirates' constitutions clearly stated the powers of the captain and quartermaster, when they could use them, and when and how the crew could use collective action mechanisms (such as voting). These constitutions also clearly established important rules such as how looted booty should be distributed on board. Pirates wrote all of this down in constitutional documents referred to as *articles*. Prior to joining a pirate crew, new members would be asked to read the crew's articles, and sign the constitution to show they knew them. This process ensured that all crew members had shared knowledge and understanding about what was considered legitimate and illegitimate behaviour by officers.

These rules, and their mechanisms of enforcement, are examples of *institutions*. They directly shaped the way that pirate ships operated and how both officers and crew members behaved on expeditions. Why? Because they provided clear incentives for the captain and quartermasters to use their powers in the collective interests, or else risk being voted out. They also helped ensure that crew members followed the captain's orders during battles, because they had confidence that the captain's orders were given in the collective interest.

Why are we still talking about pirates? Because these eighteenth-century pirates tell us a lot about where institutions come from, how they work, and how they can impact people's behaviour. The same motives for rule-making in this case – to agree mechanisms for accountability, to protect the (perceived) collective interest, to generate trust and order – also exist across everyday spaces of contestation, whether in the family, or in political forums. This is why institutions are a fundamental feature of all social organisation, and why they emerge organically, even in the least likely scenarios.

What are institutions and how do they work?

As the pirates demonstrated, a key challenge for human societies is establishing order so that people can interact in ways that avoid violence and chaos. Douglass North (1990: 3), a Nobel Prize winning economist, set out a case for understanding institutions as 'the rules of the game in a society or, more formally . . . the humanly devised constraints that shape human interaction.' These rules provide a structure to everyday life, and so reduce uncertainty about how people act, allowing societies to function more smoothly.

Take the example of a traffic-light system: rather than people guessing whether cars on the road will stop, the colour of the traffic lights establishes when drivers must stop and when they can go, reducing uncertainty and the potential for conflict. Traffic lights can be seen as an example of a formal institution, in that if a car was to keep driving – even though the traffic light was red indicating that the driver should stop – then the driver would be breaking the country's laws, and the government would punish them with a fine or worse. Hence, formal institutions can be understood as explicit rules, procedures, and regulations that govern a system.

Institutions can be *formal* or *informal* (see Box 3.1). Helmke and Levitsky (2004: 727) define informal institutions as 'socially shared rules, usually unwritten, that are created, communicated and enforced outside officially sanctioned channels'. To give a concrete example: people queue in line to buy concert tickets, or to collect water from a standpipe, not because it's official law but because there may be a social expectation, or a social norm, that everyone will wait in line until their turn. Alternatively, there could be an informal rule that the elderly, or the infirm, or men (in patriarchal societies), should get priority. If someone was to cut the line and go straight to the front, they may not be breaking any written rules, but they may provoke the anger of all the other people waiting for breaching socially acceptable behaviour. Perhaps as a result, others would socially sanction them somehow, or try to themselves push to the front of the line, leading to the overall breakdown of the queuing system. As a result, it might take everyone much longer to get to the front.

> ## Box 3.1 Formal and informal institutions
>
> *Formal institutions* refer to established and codified structures, rules, and regulations that are officially recognised and often written down. These institutions are often visible and easily identifiable because they are explicitly defined and have a formal structure (e.g., laws, constitutions, government agencies, and courts).
>
> *Informal institutions* are unwritten, unofficial, and often implicit rules, norms, and practices that guide behaviour within a society or organisation. Unlike formal institutions, they are not codified in official documents, but they can be just as influential in shaping behaviour and outcomes. They are often shaped by social customs, cultural traditions, and shared understandings (e.g., social norms, taboos, and traditions).

In thinking about the rules that affect contestations over desired futures – or who gets what, when, how – we can disaggregate between political, economic and social institutions (see Table 3.1). Economic rules focus on issues such as who owns what in society, and how government revenue can be earned and redistributed – for example, via taxation. Social and family institutions, such as expectations around marriage, parenthood, and caregiving, shape the household division of labour and opportunities for individuals to pursue livelihoods and freedoms outside of it. Political institutions shape how disputes should be resolved, who has decision-making power and over what.

Table 3.1 Rules that affect who gets what, when, how

Economic	Social	Political
• Markets, financial rules, property rights, work–life balance, tax laws, labour regulations, intellectual property laws.	• Marriage, parenthood, caregiving, gender norms and roles, identity, patriarchy.	• Electoral systems, accountability systems, political participation, citizenship, constitutions, justice systems, human rights.

Reflective question

Think of an institution. How and why does it have consequences for who gets what, when, how?

These institutions do not exist in siloes, of course. They intersect to provide a framework for cooperation, coordination, and conflict resolution. Some institutions straddle all three domains – political, economic, social. For example, as we will see throughout this book, particularly in Chapter 6, the state is a multilayered set of institutions shaping who gets what, when, how. It contains both formal rules about how power should be exercised, and informal meanings, ideas and norms that are interpreted through and take shape in everyday lived realities (see Box 3.2).

Box 3.2   The 'state' as formal and informal rules

The state refers to the institutions, or rules, that structure political, economic and social life in a given country. More than a physical apparatus exerting control over a territory, the state also contains a set of ideas and agreements about how power *should* be exercised, and indeed, what limits should be placed on actors seeking to use it.

In this way, the state transcends any individual, government or institution. The leader or party that runs a country at any given time are part of the state, but they are not the entirety of it. Driving a car is a good analogy: a government may operate or 'drive' the state, but the state also includes the vehicle, and the rules of the road. It also means that the specific combinations of formal and informal institutions, which can be more or less inclusive, mean that the question of whether a government is more or less democratic or authoritarian is a nuanced one (for more on this, see Chapter 6).

Viewed in this way, the concept of the state seems to encompass a lot: all the people, rules, apparatus and machinery via which governing institutions exercise power. Ambiguous, isn't it? What does it mean, in practice? To locate the state in a more grounded, everyday perspective, ethnographers have studied how people themselves conceive of and encounter the state. Their work contests the Western notion of the 'state' as a set of universal functions or features, revealing citizen-state relationships to be much more variegated and shaped by colonial legacies of control over territory, knowledge or resources (Hansen and Stepputat, 2001).

How do institutions work?

Institutions are all around us, and it is not possible to step outside of them. But *how* do they shape our behaviours? In other words, how do they work? In Table 3.1, we outline three of the main approaches to understanding institutions. In sum, rational choice institutionalism argues institutions 'rule' because they are how people pursue their interests (think back to the Somali piracy example); historical institutionalism says institutions 'rule' because past decisions (rules) constrain the choices we have in the present; and sociological institutionalism makes the case that institutions 'rule' because if we don't follow them, we face social sanctions.

Despite important differences, these approaches all emphasise several key factors in how institutions influence behaviour. As in the queueing example, they do so through a combination of incentives, sanctions, and norms. Our friend, Douglass North, as well as famously defining institutions as the rules of the game, also later described them as 'incentive systems, that's all they are. It is important to understand that because being incentive systems, they provide a guide to human behavior' (North, 2003: 1). How do incentives provide a guide to human behaviour? What are incentives?

You probably have a sense of what incentives are – we use the language of incentives all the time; children are incentivised by parents to do well on a test with a reward,

Image 3.2 Rules in action - Traffic in Ho Chi Minh City, Vietnam, 2023. Image by CravenA via Shutterstock.

employees are incentivised to perform better at work by bonuses. But people are also disincentivised to do certain things. A classic example is the punishments you might receive for breaking the law, such as fines or being locked up. So, we can define incentives as the external stimuli of rewards and punishments that are related to certain types of actions (Ostrom 2000). Incentives, such as rewards or recognition, therefore, encourage individuals to follow the rules, while sanctions, such as punishments or exclusion, disincentivise individuals from breaking them.

As well as incentives, rules are also enforced through powerful social expectations often known as social norms (see Box 3.3; Bicchieri, 2012). Social norms are followed not because people calculate the costs and benefits of incentives, but because people think that other people will follow them and that they should be followed. This then creates a powerful reason to follow the norm, because failure to do so could lead to social stigma and even being ostracised by the community. Ideas – one of the other three 'I's of the politics of development – also work together with norms and incentives to shape how rules are developed and enforced. As Chapter 5 tells us, ideas are the ingredients that people draw upon to inform which rules are deemed the right ones to follow, which means that people's understandings of what is best for them – or for society at large – evolves against the backdrop of sets of ideas. Norms and ideas are particularly important concepts for the sociological institutionalist approach (see Table 3.2).

> ## Box 3.3 What are social norms?
>
> Social norms refer to the shared expectations, beliefs, behaviours or standards of appropriateness or inappropriateness within a particular social context. Social norms shape how people relate and co-operate. They are enforced through social mechanisms, such as approval, disapproval, and reputation or social sanction.

Table 3.2 Approaches to understanding how institutions work

Rational choice institutionalism	Historical institutionalism	Sociological institutionalism
• Focuses on the behaviour of individual actors within institutions. • Individuals make rational decisions based on their self-interest and institutions are created to serve specific purposes that benefit them. • Institutions are tools or frameworks that individuals use to maximise their benefits and achieve their goals. • *Therefore, according to this approach, individuals weigh the costs and benefits of their actions and make decisions that align with their personal interests; institutions provide rules, norms, and structures that guide these decisions.*	• Emphasises the significance of historical context and path dependency in shaping institutions and their outcomes. • Past decisions and events influence the development and functioning of institutions over time. • Institutions are often shaped by historical circumstances and, once established, can be difficult to change due to the inertia and constraints within existing structures. • *Therefore, this approach recognises that institutions are not formed in a vacuum; they evolve from earlier decisions, which can set trajectories that persist, even when circumstances change.*	• Focuses on the role of societal norms, values, and cultural beliefs in shaping institutions. • Institutions are not just rational creations but are also influenced by broader social factors. • Social pressures and collective behaviour influence the development, maintenance, and stability of institutions. • *Therefore, this approach highlights that institutions are not solely based on individual calculations but are also deeply embedded in the social fabric.*

Source: Hall and Taylor (1996).

In addition to ensuring that people follow the rules, the incentives, sanctions and norms provided by institutions also shape people's behaviour more broadly. Norms, for example, may also be followed because they shape our assumptions about what is normal, such that we don't even question why the current rules we live under exist. And it is because of this that political institutions, in particular, are also widely viewed as fundamental to the distribution of material and immaterial resources, and central to explaining why we see such differences in levels of development, or people's ability to achieve their version of it, around the world.

How do institutions shape development?

Institutions provide the necessary social infrastructure to harness the behaviour of self-interested actors, whether they be politicians, citizens going about their everyday lives, or pirates. They are the coordination mechanism to provide order and ultimately peace, justice, economic growth and allow society to function smoothly. They are the glue that holds society together. Without institutions providing and upholding laws, contracts, property rights, and trust, life would be 'nasty, brutish, and short' – in other words, too unpredictable for people to thrive or even survive (Hobbes, 2017: 113).

Why are North and South Korea so different?

If institutions can be said to 'rule' in the everyday sense, how does this scale up to influence development at the macro level? Consider the opposing pathways of North and South Korea. After the Second World War, Korea was partitioned along the 38th parallel, with the Soviet Union occupying the North and the United States the South. Ongoing tensions resulted in the Korean War that ended in stalemate in 1953, making the divide permanent. Up until that point, Korea had been a single country for over a thousand years, meaning that the North and the South shared the same history, geography, and culture and living standards. However, after partition, the fortunes of the North and the South diverged sharply. Now, the average North Korean can expect to live ten years less than the average South Korean (Kim et al., 2001). Given their shared history, culture, and geography, this divergence can surely only be explained through human-made political and economic institutions that came after partition. But how?

The two countries adopted very different rules for political organisation. In North Korea, authoritarianism, coupled with a centrally planned economy and no property rights (all property is owned by the state), failed to incentivise innovation and productivity. People's basic rights were consistently violated. The country stagnated. South Korea, on the other hand, developed more inclusive political and economic institutions that extended rights to all people, placed limits on what the government could do, and fostered growth. Their constitution states that 'the right of property of all citizens shall be guaranteed'. The country rapidly industrialised, becoming one of world's largest trading countries – a so-called economic miracle (see Amsden, 1989). It is now one of the largest producers of cars, mobile phones, and semiconductors as well as being a cultural powerhouse, from K-pop to gaming and movies.

What are inclusive and extractive institutions?

The fate of these two halves of a (former) country speaks to a distinction between *inclusive* and *extractive* institutions (see Table 3.3). Daron Acemoglu and James Robinson (2012) in

Table 3.3 Characteristics of extractive and inclusive institutions

Extractive institutions	Inclusive institutions
• Power concentrated in the hands of a narrow elite. • Few constraints on the elite's power. • Elite able to seize people's property. • Extractive economic institutions structured by a narrow elite. • Economic institutions used to extract resources from the rest of society and enrich a narrow elite.	• Power broadly distributed across society. • Constraints on the arbitrary use of power. • Property rights of wide sections of society protected. • Inclusive economic institutions structured by society. • Inclusive economic institutions provide equitable resource distribution across society.

Source: Acemoglu and Robinson (2012).

their well-known book, *Why Nations Fail*, explain that extractive institutions concentrate power in the hands of a small political elite, place few constraints on how this elite exercises its power, and enables this elite to extract resources from the rest of society. In contrast, inclusive institutions distribute power widely across society, constrain the power of politicians, and provide public services ensuring that there is broadly a level playing field across society in terms of people's opportunities.

Inclusive institutions, so the argument goes, are good because they protect people's rights, harness the talents and energy of their whole society, and provide people with incentives to invest resources. Extractive ones are bad because they restrict rights to a privileged few, extract resources from the rest, and inhibit and disincentivise innovation and productivity. Inclusive political institutions place limits on the power of politicians over citizens' lives, incentivising politicians to work *for* their citizens – no matter how imperfectly – as voters can hold them to account. Where such political institutions do not exist, politicians are able to 'amass their own fortunes and to pursue their own agendas, ones detrimental to those of the citizens' (p. 42). Inclusive institutions may, in turn, also create incentives for citizens to 'become educated, to save and invest, to innovate and adopt new technologies, and so on' (Acemoglu and Robinson, 2012: 42), making a country more likely to harness the potential energy, creativity and entrepreneurship held across society.

The importance of these different types of institutions can be seen when we consider one of the worst development outcomes – *famine*. In 1973, Ethiopia experienced a major famine, in which tens of thousands of people died of starvation having had their land and livelihoods taken away from them by wealthy landowners and the government who ran roughshod over private property rights. The country was ruled by the authoritarian Emperor Haile Selassie. Ethiopia's extractive institutions placed virtually no constraints on his power, and so he ruled with absolute authority with little accountability. The absence of public accountability meant that he did little to try to prevent the famine or help Ethiopians who couldn't access food. Instead, he simply tried to cover it up. The absence of a free press meant that many people in the country were unaware that the famine was even happening until the international media began to report on it.

Another Nobel Prize-winning economist, Amartya Sen (1999), has found that famines, like the one in Ethiopia, only take place in such authoritarian contexts with extractive institutions.

In more democratic settings with inclusive institutions, leaders have strong incentives to avoid such crises, because otherwise the public will vote them out of office in elections. Furthermore, inclusive institutional contexts include a free press, which can ensure that people in the country receive information about what's going on in the country to ensure that such crises can be prevented. This means that famines do not take place in settings with inclusive institutions and helps to explain why authoritarian states are more likely to deliver particularly disastrous developmental outcomes, as discussed at greater length in Chapter 6.

Beyond specific examples such as North and South Korea, and Ethiopia, many argue that institutions are the principal reason why we see such large differences in wealth, health, education, and general living standards around the world. Turning again to the work of Acemoglu and Robinson (2012), they have argued that to understand these global inequalities, we need to consider the impact of European colonial rule, and specifically how the different European colonial powers set up different types of institutions around the world. They argue that in some colonies, such as in North America, European settlers established inclusive institutions. The climate and geography in such places suited Europeans and they were able to settle in these places with relative ease. It was, therefore, worthwhile for them to set up inclusive institutions that distributed power among the settlers (though not among indigenous populations who, unlike the Europeans, were for the large part excluded from being given access to rights, resources and freedoms).

Reflective question

Do you agree that inequalities can be explained by studying patterns of institutional development during colonial rule?

In other places, however, such as the Democratic Republic of Congo, Europeans faced a climate and geography that was harsher, which led to European settlers experiencing high mortality rates. In these places, where they could not settle in large numbers, they installed extractive institutions with the primary purpose of allowing the Europeans to extract natural resources to be transferred back to Europe. Therefore, these extractive colonial institutions served to enrich Europe and impoverish European colonies in Africa, Asia, and the Americas. According to Acemoglu and Robinson, these differences in colonial institutions explain the differences in living standards we see around the world, particularly as many former colonies still have these extractive institutions in place.

Many argue that for development to happen, what is needed is for countries to develop not extractive but inclusive institutions. Inclusive institutions – formal and informal – are the ones that create the 'right' incentives for everyone – not just the elite – to benefit from development. Of course, it is not just institutions that have legacies that carry into the future. As some scholars have indicated, it is also policies and practices established by richer countries – often former colonial powers – that can have enduring impacts on how development occurs today. Some of these are explored further in Chapters 7 and 8. But if inclusive institutions have a key role to play, what is stopping countries everywhere from changing their extractive institutions or setting up new inclusive ones? The answer to this puzzle lies in the degree to which institutions – or rules – can change.

Can institutions change?

If institutions play such a crucial role in the distribution of resources that people need to pursue desired futures, and inclusive institutions can promote higher standards of living than exclusive institutions – then why can't people simply change the institutions of a country? A big idea around institutions is that they provide long-term stability. This is something that political scientists – particularly those associated with the historical institutionalist approach – call 'path dependence', which is the idea that once institutions are in place, it is difficult to sway them from the course they are on. How so?

Why do institutions tend to resist change?

There are two main reasons for this path dependence (see Box 3.4). First, political institutions distribute power unequally to different actors. This means that specific institutional arrangements have the effect of empowering some actors, while marginalising others. This inequality enables those with power to consolidate their positions, increasing power asymmetries over time, which makes it harder, and hence less likely, that rules can be changed (Mahoney and Thelen, 2009). Second, as we have already discussed, actors within a given institutional arrangement – set of rules – adapt their behaviour and beliefs in line with the incentives and constraints provided by them. As Pierson (2004: 10) argues, once the rules of the game are established, 'even citizens' basic ways of thinking about the political world will often generate self-reinforcing dynamics', with the result that political alternatives that might once have been a possibility are lost. In effect, there is a kind of inertia in the rules we follow, and the more we follow them, the harder it is to change them.

Box 3.4 Are rules path dependent?

The concept of path dependence was originally coined by economic historian Paul David. In reference to the persistence of the QWERTY keyboard layout, he argued that historical events and decisions can lead to the persistence of certain trajectories even if there are more efficient alternatives. Scholars of institutional development, such as Kathleen Thelen (2004) and Paul Pierson (2004), have applied this idea to examine how historical choices influence and constrain future developments. In other words, the historical sequence of events creates a trajectory that is difficult to deviate from due to the lock-in effects it generates.

Understanding the origins and consequences of path dependence can help us understand the 'stickiness' or resistance to change often encountered in development processes. It can also help us to understand why inequalities – of access to resources and rights – are so often reproduced by configurations of power, i.e., because they are supported by institutions and rules whose futures have been at least partially written by the weight of their past direction of travel.

This can be seen with the example of unequal access to resources in US public schools. In the nineteenth century, when public education systems were being established in the US, funding was often tied to local property taxes. This created disparities, as communities with higher property values had more resources to allocate to their schools. Over time, communities that started with more resources were able to provide better educational facilities, materials, and opportunities, which in turn led to higher academic performance and graduation rates in wealthier areas. As these disparities persisted, the local property tax-based funding mechanism became entrenched. Efforts to equalise funding across districts faced resistance from wealthier communities that were unwilling to give up their advantages. Over the decades, the disparities in resources and educational quality became deeply embedded in the education system. Schools in lower-income areas struggled to attract and retain qualified teachers, update curriculum, and provide adequate facilities. Despite recognising the issue, changing how the schools were funded proved deeply challenging – politically and logistically – despite parents in poorer neighbourhoods taking the issue to court. Part of the problem is that there is no language guaranteeing children the right to education in state constitutions (Turner et al., 2016).

More broadly, in countries with extractive institutions, where power is restricted to a small political elite, this elite will have greater power and access to resources, which it can use to block any change to institutions. Similarly, in a country with more inclusive institutions, where power is distributed more widely, there will be other actors such as an independent media and civil society organisations who have sufficient power and incentives to prevent attempts to undermine these institutions.

When they do change how does that happen?

While path dependency is important, it is also clearly true that change does happen and institutions are created, overturned, or transformed (see Canen and Wantchekon, 2022). For example, Chinese foot binding (*chánzú*) was a custom, or informal institution, that existed for nearly a thousand years. It was a practice passed on from mothers to daughters whereby they bound their feet as children to stop growth. The 'four smaller toes were curled underneath towards the centre of the foot's sole until the bones were broken' (Wilson, 2013). It was seen as a sign of beauty and marriageability. Yet despite lasting for a thousand years, it disappeared in a generation. Similarly, opposition to same-sex marriage in many countries across the globe has been challenged or overcome very recently after centuries of anti-homosexual sentiment and laws (Paternotte, 2015). How was this possible?

Within the argument for path dependence, there is recognition that there are 'moments' of uncertainty, where some kind of event or shift creates space for the self-reinforcing dynamics of particular rules, set on a particular path, to be broken open – creating a 'critical juncture' (see Box 3.5; Capoccia, 2015: 147). Critical junctures show that institutions are not just sticky and resistant to change – they can be broken open by sudden and unexpected events. The abolition of slavery undermined the power of local white plantation owners and expanded the legal rights of emancipated Afro-descendants in forced colonies (Owolabi, 2023). Coloni-sation, as a critical juncture, embedded systems of 'decentralized despotism' that exacerbated ethnic and regional divides, favoured some groups over others, and laid the foundations of post-colonial intergroup contestation and political repression (Mamdani, 1996). While in some countries, extractive colonial institutions persisted with new authoritarian leaders replacing the colonial powers; in other contexts, independence movements gave rise to new inclusive political institutions that enabled groups of people, who had been excluded from decision-making under colonial rule, to shape their countries' politics and development.

Box 3.5   Why critical junctures can change the rules

Critical junctures refer to pivotal moments or periods in the development of an institution where important decisions or events have the potential to significantly shape the trajectory of future developments. These junctures may be due to shocks or disruptions that lead to the breakdown of institutions and processes of path dependence.

Some have criticised the notion of institutional change only occurring during such critical junctures. This is because critical junctures are associated with sudden *exogenous* change. In other words, change is only seen to take place when some external factor leads to a disruption. In recent years, there has been growing recognition that change can also take place incre-mentally through *endogenous* or internally driven change. This criticism is linked to a wider critique of the economic and incentives-focused view of institutions – often labelled rational choice institutionalism (see Table 3.2). This economistic approach to institutions as incen-tive systems can be an overly materialistic, calculating, and bloodless way of understanding the social world (Hudson and Leftwich, 2014). People are not just cost–benefit calculating machines, they are also driven by values, passions, and ideas and have to interpret the world; incentives are not just mechanical. What motivates individuals is taken up in Chapter 4, on interests and where they come from.

How does this fit within our definition of development as contestation over alternative desired futures? Politics of development, then, involves contestations over the interpretation and implementation of the rules. Thelen and Mahoney argue that within institutions there are actually 'struggles over the meaning, application, and enforcement' of the rules – and not only this, those struggles are intertwined with how the resources allocated by the rules are distributed (2004: 11). Likewise, Mark Blyth (2003: 698) has the lovely line that 'structures do not come with an instruction sheet'; people have to interpret the costs and benefits and in doing so they draw on their beliefs, values and cognitive shortcuts – in other words, ideas – to understand how they should act (Hay and Wincott, 1998). In sum, contesting the rules is a central ingredient in how the politics of development happens.

Many thinkers argue that even though institutions are responsible for much of how our societies, economies and policies work, they may be slowly contested, sometimes so slowly that change is not noticeable. Thelen and Mahoney argue that 'piecemeal change' can be just as important for shaping human behaviour as big bang critical juncture change (2004: 1). They highlight the British House of Lords, which began its life as a deeply undemocratic institution, but which over time has become part of the constellation of institutions that form the UK's democratic governance system and one that is frequently looked to as an example of how democracies should work. As the British House of Lords has existed for hundreds of years – a long time before development came to the UK, it also raises an important question about what comes first – development, or institutions? Did the pirates make rules because they had valued goods (loot) to protect, or did the rules mean they gained more of them?

> ### Reflective question
>
> Think of an important institution that affects freedoms or capabilities in your world. Has it been contested or changed? Why/why not?

Development and institutions: what comes first and why does it matter?

For a long time, the accepted view was that growth needs to happen before development can be kickstarted (Ang, 2016). But in the last few decades, the new orthodoxy is that institutions are seen as *the essential prerequisite* for development. The argument runs that without institutions, there can be no real development that will allow countries to move from places of poverty, inequality and conflict, towards life as lived by people in the rich world (Ha Joon Chang, 2011). Francis Fukuyama (2011) calls this the 'getting to Denmark' problem. Denmark is a metaphor; an idealised example of a state that works really well. But this leads to a mistaken assumption that if other countries adopt the institutions that Denmark has, then they will work like Denmark.

But do institutions really rule? A critique

Is it really so simple, and, if so, how do countries with the 'wrong' institutions operate at all? Let us return to the example of North Korea: in North Korea, people do not vote for their leaders, rather the state is controlled by an elite who seized power and then kept hold of it by handing it down to selected individuals over generations. People have some freedoms, but their options about what they own or purchase, where they live and what kind of jobs they do, are strictly limited; they cannot access independent press or travel overseas, or even speak freely to people outside of their country. But North Korea is not a state in anarchy, it still has institutions that provide the people that live there with rules about how to interact, what the rewards and punishments of following or disobeying those rules will be, offers them some protections against insecurity and gives them some rights.

People's access to opportunities in North Korea are structured by the 'songbun' – a system of classifying each person's status in the country (Kim, 2022). Whether you have high or low status in the songbun system will determine your life chances – what school you attend, whether you can go to university and if you can get a job that doesn't consist of factory work or hard labour. The advocacy organisation Human Rights Watch tells the story of Choi Seung Chol who was born in North Korea. He recounts that 'The dream for me and all my friends was to get a job with power, and become a corrupt government official' – for Choi, it was clear that being one of the lucky few with privileged access to resources and decision making was the only way to make a good life for himself (Robertson, 2016).

As discussed earlier, the type kind of institution that distributes access to resources in this way can be described as 'extractive'. Remember that extractive political institutions concentrate power in the hands of a narrow elite and the economic institutions that go along with them are often structured by those in power to extract resources from society and funnel them to that elite. This uneven access to economic resources enriches these elites, consolidating their power further. Yet some of these kinds of authoritarian political systems have achieved much higher levels of economic growth – think Singapore, China, and indeed South Korea for so many years! Why have they managed to achieve this while apparently being governed by the wrong institutions? One answer is that it might come down to specific actions of an individual leader, such as the growth-promoting Lee Kuan Lee who ruled Singapore from 1965 until 1990. Another, as Chapter 6 explains, might be that some states have better institutional barriers that somehow limit the abuse of power, despite not being fully inclusive.

Reflective question

What comes first, the 'right' rules or inclusive development?

But even when they do deliver on growth, the development that occurs with these types of extractive institutions doesn't tend to benefit everyone equally, especially when extractive institutions go hand-in-hand with a lack of internal checks and balances. This can help to explain why Choi and his friends saw joining the elite as the only real way to get to the resources that would provide him with the means to a good life: many North Korean institutions have been designed to extract resources and condense them into sources of wealth and power for those at the top. Using examples of the development of countries from Asia, Africa, the Americas and Europe over hundreds of years, Acemoglu and Robinson show that even when extractive institutions do work, the growth they generate routes profits back to those elites, keeping resources and power in the hands of the few, not the many.

So, we can think of it this way: inclusive institutions spread power, allow all people access to rights, resources and freedoms, and hold those in power to account. Extractive institutions can promote rapid economic transformation under the right conditions, but also help those in power to extract resources for their own benefit and hang onto that power to keep others from spreading wealth and rights.

But is this really what history tells us? Ha Joon Chang, a world-renowned economist from South Korea, writes: 'today's rich countries acquired most of the institutions that today's dominant view considers to be prerequisites of economic development after, not before, their economic development – democracy, modern bureaucracy, IPRs, limited liability, bankruptcy law, banking, the central bank, securities regulation, and so on' (Chang, 2011). So not only do the 'right' institutions *not* always come first, but in fact history demonstrates that the developed world got to be the way it is, without the very institutions that poorer countries are now requested to have in place in order to develop themselves.

Ha Joon Chang teaches us not to think of the relationship between institutions and development as a one-way street. In fact, economic development can change institutions as much as the other way around. The growth that took place in South Korea for example happened even though they didn't have fully inclusive institutions that provided citizens completely free choice over what they did and how. When it was separated from North Korea following the Korean War, the authoritarian government of South Korea was put in place by powerful foreign powers which wanted to ensure that it was sufficiently strong, successful and protected from being seized by the communist regime in the North. For decades, South Korea prioritised growth and economic development, and only then, when economic development was beginning to flourish, did the authorities in South Korea begin to introduce the kind of inclusive political institutions that allowed free elections and an independent press. A more general point is that it is often convenient for international actors to downplay the role of international rules, power and inequalities and frame poverty as a 'domestic' issue, whether this is weak institutions or bad policies (Hudson and Dasandi, 2014). See Chapter 7 for more on the role of international organisations in the global political economy.

Yuen Yuen Ang (2016) gives us an even more compelling example of why development does not simply follow institutions. Charting the progress of China out of its poverty trap, she argues that economic development was built on weak institutions. Development is a 'co-evolutionary' process – where states and markets interact – one doesn't simply follow another (2016: 3). She describes China's weaker, and less effective institutions as the 'raw materials' for building markets. As China liberalised, local governments did not have the rule of law or professional bureaucracies regarded as institutional prerequisites for growth. So local leaders leveraged what they had: 'Every county and town mobilised the entire civil service to use personal networks to find investors, and those who succeeded were rewarded with bonuses. In this way, local leaders harnessed a key strength of communism (the ability to mobilise) and of rural conditions (strong personal ties).' Mobilising all civil servants to recruit investors using personal relations is not 'good governance', but it worked. Ang argues that 'normatively weak institutions can be functionally strong' and that inclusive institutions could actually be part of the problem of being poor, not the solution.

So what should we do?

Why is this important? For decades, the international community has built its policies in developing countries around getting the 'right' institutions in place, so that development can take off. What if this was the wrong approach, or worse, has distracted poor country governments with inappropriate, or ill-fitting reforms while their potential to develop with the raw materials they have just got away? What happens when you get this wrong – you try to build institutions before development or do development without institutions?

Scholars have increasingly demonstrated the flaws in expecting low- or middle-income countries to make reforms that are only possible in high-income countries – something that Andrews et al. (2017: 57) call *premature loadbearing*, when 'an organization is overwhelmed with the complexity of the tasks being demanded of it'. In other words, doing too much too soon! Consider the numbers. Afghanistan – a country in which the international community tried and failed to state-build – has about US$10 per year to spend on each of its citizens. Compare this to the US$17,554 the US has available for each of its citizens per year. Expecting the Afghan government to implement the same reforms the US government has only recently introduced is not sensible.

The problem this creates – again using a term coined by Andrews et al. (2017) – is that this leads to something called *isomorphic mimicry* – that is, many governments try to *look* like successful states in order to get the investment, legitimacy, and aid – for example, procurement reform: many development organisations require partners to adopt laws requiring competitive bidding in order to receive financial support. Isomorphic mimicry conflates form and function: 'looks like' substitutes for 'does' – instances or levels of training count even if practice doesn't improve; numbers of children in schools count even if learning doesn't improve (recall the learning crisis, unpacked in Chapter 1), well-presented budget documents count even if they don't regulate and inform spending outcomes. In this way, crucially, having rules in place does not guarantee that they will produce the intended outcomes. In other words, as we explore in greater depth in Chapter 12 of this book, rules only have their desired effect if they are implemented as intended.

Summary and conclusion

In this chapter, we have seen that a key explanation for the glaring inequalities we see around the world is institutions, what they look like, how they work, and for whom they work.

We have discussed how institutions can be both formal and informal. They can be written down (as in a constitution) or they can be unwritten norms of behaviour, with both influencing people's behaviour. We have reviewed the arguments for why we want institutions in the first place, suggesting that the answer can be found in the powerful ways that institutions – the rules of the game – provide structure to everyday life, and so reduce uncertainty about how people act, allowing societies to function more smoothly.

Do they rule? Often, and in important ways, and not always, and never absolutely. People can interpret them differently and choose to navigate differently. We have seen that institutions do not all operate in the same ways. Some are inclusive and are built around extending rights to resources and power broadly across society, while others are extractive, and uphold rules that extend rights to a few, privileged and powerful actors only. These different types of institutions have important implications for countries' development outcomes.

We have looked at the arguments about what comes first – development or institutions. It's a classic chicken-or-egg question (the chicken came first), but it's important not to assume that making changes to institutions will mean everyone 'gets to Denmark'. For one thing, institutions can be very hard to change in the short term. Institutions are quite literally the manifestations of historical legacies, so they 'institutionalise' an existing practice and maintain its reproduction, and it is through this process that such practices really become 'rules' of the game, which can be very difficult to alter. In addition, the focus on institutional fixes may result in inappropriate reforms for the context and risks overloading developing country governments. There are no short cuts when it comes to institutions – the process of contesting them, and legitimising them, is as important as getting there.

Discussion questions

- What are some of the reasons that people follow the 'rules of the game'?
- How do different types of institutions distribute resources, rights and freedoms differently?
- How are institutions affected by historical legacies, path dependencies and sudden changes?
- Should we consider getting the 'right' kind of institutions in place as an essential prerequisite for development?

Suggested further reading

Acemoglu, D., Johnson, S. and Robinson, J. (2006) 'Understanding prosperity and poverty: geography, institutions and the reversal of fortune', *Understanding Poverty*, pp. 19–36.

Ang, Y.Y. (2018) 'Autocracy with Chinese characteristics: Beijing's behind-the-scenes reforms'. *Foreign Affairs*, 97 (39).

Chang, H.J. (2011) 'Institutions and economic development: theory, policy and history', *Journal of Institutional Economics*, 7 (4): 473–98.

Woolcock, M., Szreter, S. and Rao, V. (2011) 'How and why does history matter for development policy?', *The Journal of Development Studies*, 47(1): 70–96.

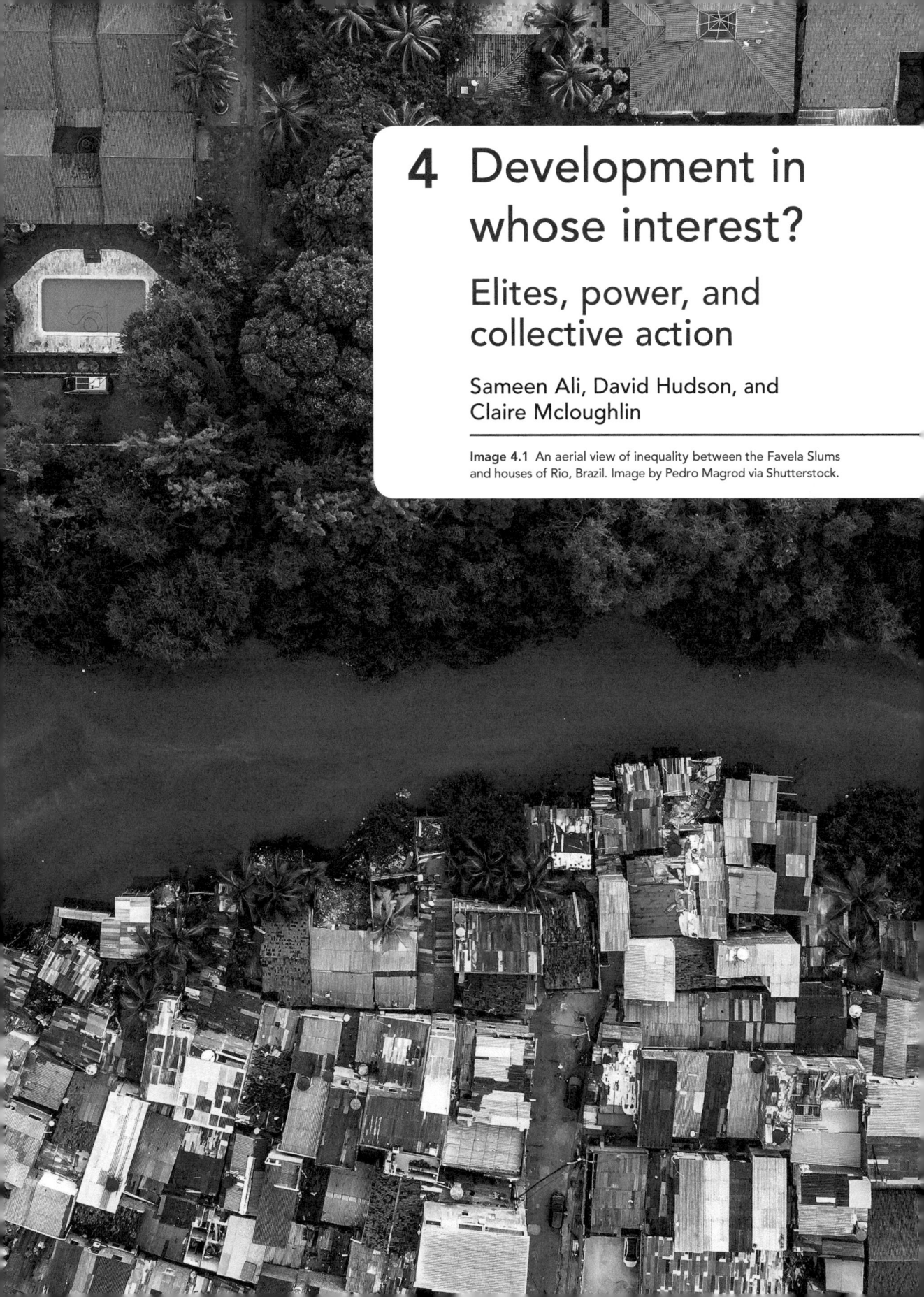

4 Development in whose interest?

Elites, power, and collective action

Sameen Ali, David Hudson, and Claire Mcloughlin

Image 4.1 An aerial view of inequality between the Favela Slums and houses of Rio, Brazil. Image by Pedro Magrod via Shutterstock.

> ## Learning outcomes
>
> - Define interests and the critical role they play in shaping institutions in development.
> - Understand how interests are formed, beyond purely rational choice explanations, through ideas and power.
> - Describe mechanisms for aligning interests towards desired futures.

'Just because you do not take an interest in politics doesn't mean politics won't take an interest in you.'

Pericles

Winners and losers in development

In rural China, the policy of 'one homestead for one household' allows villagers to obtain a single plot of agricultural land from the local government at the discretion of village cadres and officials. But faced with choices over the sale of land rights, local political elites have strong incentives to misuse their decision-making power for personal gain. Why? Because the cost of compensating villagers unable to secure their due allocation is minor, compared to the profit that could be gained from selling the land off to rich business owners and developers instead. The potential payoffs are not only financial, but in support for re-election in the village.

Elites pursue these payoffs at the cost of ordinary people's rights and entitlements. Lower-class villagers do not have the means to bribe village cadres with luxury banquets and gifts, so many of them lose their lands and, subsequently, their livelihoods. In turn, they cannot afford to purchase the lavish apartments built on the misappropriated land. Their protests are suppressed, in part, because middle-class villagers, themselves beneficiaries of the jobs generated by commercial developments, are not willing to risk their own livelihoods to join the lower-class villagers in contesting the glaringly unfair distribution (Ruan and Wang, 2023).

This 'winner and losers' scenario, too often characteristic of how development plays out in practice, is ultimately driven by the power of interests. For good or for ill, interests are the engine of who gets what, when, how. But in the same way that there are alternative desired futures, interests may be diametrically opposed. And as in villages across rural China, elite interests often matter – in an empirical (not normative) sense – much more than others. The interests of ruling elites underlie whether development happens in the wider interests of society and is inclusive of deprived groups or is distorted to serve the narrower priorities of the most powerful (Amsden et al., 2012). If powerful ruling elites exclusively pursue their self-interests, the collective interest can get lost by the wayside. This matters because, as we saw in Chapter 3, whether institutions are inclusive or extractive is a key nexus of development prospects.

For these reasons, we cannot analyse whose version of a desired future is being pursued without understanding interests – the second of our three 'I's' of the politics of development. But where do interests come from, and how are they formed? Are they always a malevolent force that undermines inclusive development? Can they be harnessed towards inclusive development?

This chapter considers different perspectives on these puzzles. As per the book's approach, we argue that interests are not inherently good or bad for development, but they are an active ingredient in the process of contesting it. Whose interests prevail, ultimately, is dictated by power relations. This is why, as Pericles' quotation underlines, no matter how we feel about interests, icky or otherwise, we ignore them at our peril.

Rules don't just exist, they are made

In Chapter 3, we were introduced to the importance of institutions, or rules of the game, and how they shape the pursuit of desired futures. But if we think more deeply about rules, and where they come from, we must necessarily also engage with what drives individual human beings to make and enforce them. Here, we need to examine something social scientists call 'agency', or, more simply, how and why humans behave in ways intended to achieve a desired result. As Adrian Leftwich (2010) argued, the real politics of development lies in agency. This fundamental people-oriented starting point was eloquently captured by Margaret Levi (2006: 10) in her American Political Science Association Presidential Address, when she said that 'institutions are empty boxes without leaders and staff who have the capacity to produce the public goods the public demands'. In other words, rules do not just exist, they are made.

If this wasn't the case, then all rules, everywhere, would look the same. On that note, Levi highlighted the contrast between Pakistan's and India's approaches to rule-making – in this case, state-building – after partition in 1947. Despite their similar colonial experience, the two founding leaders of these new countries, Muhammad Ali Jinnah and Jawaharlal Nehru, had very different visions for the rules. As Maya Tudor argued in her book *The Promise of Power* (2013), Nehru wanted to establish a secular state that could accommodate diverse religious and linguistic groups, while Jinnah prioritised a state that would protect the rights of Muslims. India eventually took the path of pluralist democracy, while Pakistan descended into an unstable autocracy. But it was not just the vision of their founding fathers that shaped these countries' divergent paths. Political parties, and the interests they represent, also mattered. In India, the Indian National Congress was closely connected to the emerging middle class, who shared aspirations for political freedom, economic development, and social progress. The Muslim League, in Pakistan, held its power base among the Northern landed aristocracy, with much less appetite for reform, as both Jalal (1995) and Adeney (2007) have argued.

Reflective question

Do rules control people or do people control rules?

Agency, then – meaning the power to act and choices we make – fundamentally shapes institutions. Real people make real choices that determine how institutions turn out. But this does not mean that all people, even the most powerful political elites, can make such choices in a limitless plane of open possibilities. They are always constrained by their context. Think about the example above – political elites pursued their visions, but they also created systems of rule designed to cater to their primary support base. In this way, their choices were also shaped by the rules, or structures, already in place. So, choices are never entirely free. But the rules are not destiny, either. This puzzle, of understanding the interaction between people and rules, is one that preoccupies much academic thought. Often associated with the work of Anthony Giddens (1984), it is known as the classic 'structure–agency problem' (Box 4.1).

Box 4.1 The structure–agency problem

The structure–agency problem examines how individuals' actions and choices *(agency)* are influenced by larger social forces and rules *(structure)*. It provides a way of thinking about whether and when people can use agency to pursue their needs, goals and interests versus when they cannot because of the already-existing rules.

Why does the structure–agency problem matter for the politics of development in particular, though? In sum, because if the process of development entails contesting, defining, and shaping rules, as we saw in Chapter 3, then this necessarily must involve *people* interpreting and shaping them through their capacity to act. A fascinating case of what this entails, in practice, is described in Rebecca Abers and Margaret Keck's (2013) study of Brazilian water politics. Governing Brazil's freshwater resources is a complex undertaking, involving an entanglement of competing interests, from mining extraction, hydroelectric power generation, irrigation, tourism, cattle-raising, to, of course, providing safe drinking water. The state (an institution in itself) generated a new legal framework (new rules) in the form of *river basin committees* to make decision-making more coherent across the sector, and to try to resolve some of these competing interests. But the new law was ambiguous and short on detail: it did not tell leaders how to establish or operate these committees in practice. Getting them up and running therefore relied on the ability of local leaders to accumulate the 'practical authority' to get things done, by reworking and testing ideas, debating, transforming organisational resources, problem-solving and connecting people. Some committees (institutions) succeeded, some failed. None of them followed the expected trajectory. Same rules, different agents, different outcomes. It is this ability of agents to shape institutions that makes them developmentally consequential. But is the decisive role of interests a good or a bad thing for development?

Are interests good or bad for development?

Interests have a bad reputation. As exemplified in the case of Chinese village cadres profiteering on their control over land distributions, we often think of interests as a malevolent force: a heuristic for the myriad ways in which people pursue their own goals at the cost of how things ideally *should* be, resulting in unfair outcomes. Politicians are assumed to be driven by their interest in getting elected and staying in power. And those in business are assumed to be driven by their interest in making a profit. As Adam Smith famously put it in *The Wealth of Nations* (1776), 'it is not from the benevolence of the butcher, the brewer, or the baker, that we expect our dinner, but from their regard to their own self-interest'.

To some extent, this scepticism is justified. Globally, there is evidence that around 7.5 per cent of aid is stolen by national elites, measured by sharp increases in bank deposits in offshore financial 'havens' (attractive places to hide and launder funds) after aid is disbursed to aid-dependent countries (Andersen et al., 2022). This, and the China example, reflect a wider concern over 'elite capture' in development, wherein elites use their disproportionate influence, power, wealth, or status to manipulate resources in ways that serve their own interests. It is important to stress, though, that elites are not a homogeneous category; they may gain power, status and influence economically (through wealth, land, business interests), politically (via election, inherited roles, traditional authority), or socially (due to their caste, profession, kinship ties, voluntary work, religious activities). Plus, as Musgrave and Wong (2016) argue, there is a difference between 'elite capture' and 'elite control' of development projects and programmes (see Table 4.1). In other words, we should not automatically equate elite involvement in decision-making with extractive institutions.

These subtleties remind us not to take the importance of interests to mean that society is populated with self-interested sociopaths. While elite capture generally connotes detrimental outcomes, elite control can be benevolent *or* malevolent, depending on how it influences

Table 4.1 Elite capture versus elite control of development

	Elite capture	Elite control
• What is it?	• Elite misappropriation of public resources or funds to their own end.	• Elite control of access to resources.
• How does it happen?	• Monopolising project benefits, siphoning resources, neglecting the interests and needs of the marginalised.	• Occupying key leadership positions on development initiatives and projects, dominating decision-making.
• Is it good or bad for development?	• Considered to always induce inequitable outcomes, and therefore undermine development.	• May not negatively impact the distribution of outcomes. May facilitate project leadership and management.

the distribution of resources. This was revealed to be the case in one widely cited study of community-driven poverty alleviation projects in Indonesia (Dasgupta and Beard, 2007). Here, local community organisations received funding they could disburse either in the form of providing micro-credit to local entrepreneurs, constructing physical infrastructure, or improving human resources through training. In the neighbourhoods they studied, researchers found varying degrees of elite control, elite capture and democratic self-governance. But at the same time, even in the cases of elite capture, benefits continued to be delivered to deserving members of the community. One of the reasons for this, as has been found in other studies (Lund and Saito-Jensen 2013; Ali 2020), is that communities are not passive observers; they mobilise to protect projects from elite capture by demanding a voice, participating in meetings, and so on.

So maybe self-interest isn't always a bad thing? Indeed, sometimes self-interested elite competition may generate the conditions for economic prosperity. Economists Whitfield and Buur (2014) have studied the logic behind this: the goal of political elites is to remain in power, but doing so requires money, so they choose policies that align with the interests of powerful groups – whether the financiers of political parties, or firms or families who dominate key sectors – in return for political funds. Since political elites benefit in this way from the prosperity and patronage of the industries in which their major financiers operate, they develop a mutual interest in addressing any key productivity-constraining problems faced in these industries. This generates a political interest in running the industry as effectively as possible. The result of this combination of political and economic interests is the creation of what the researchers termed 'pockets of efficiency' within the state bureaucracy. These are agencies and organisations, staffed only by trusted bureaucrats, with the highest levels of technical expertise necessary to implement vital policies that support powerful industries. This is the story behind the relative efficiency of the cocoa sector in Ghana, led by the Ghana Cocoa Board (COCOBOD). Here, various coalitions of ruling elites have consistently supported cocoa bean exports over time, not only because it is a key source of financing for the state, but because the ruling party's electoral strongholds are in key cocoa producing regions. Many smallholder farmers are involved in cocoa cultivation, and their livelihoods are directly dependent on the sector's success. Ghana is now one of the world's largest cocoa producers and exporters, and cocoa plays a significant role in both employment and export earnings. The point is that the pursuit of self-interest is not necessarily detrimental to other people's interests. Sometimes, rather than winners and losers, there can be win–wins.

Image 4.2 A farmer holds a cocoa bean in Östliche Region, Ghana. Image by Nhorv via Shutterstock.

Political settlements

The Ghana case highlights that the alignment of interests between political and economic elites can stabilise institutions, or rules-based orders. This is why to understand interests, we need to move beyond the individual level, to explore the balance of power and alignment of interests *between* elites, and the formation of 'intra-elite' agreements or pacts. How elites organise power and distribute resources between them, and the degree to which they share this across wider society, is the central concern of political settlements theory (see Box 4.2).

Box 4.2   Political Settlements Theory

Political settlements are agreements among powerful elites, whether political or military, bureaucratic or business, about how to share power and distribute benefits, or rents (economic rewards). The aim of this 'settlement' is to end war or, at least, to minimise the threat that certain powerful elites will instead resort to violence to control access to resources and power.

The work of the economist Mushtaq Khan has been hugely influential in showing how political settlements shape development prospects. In an important paper, 'Political settlements and the governance of growth-enhancing institutions' (2010), he argued that the nature of a political settlement significantly affects the governance of institutions, which in turn impacts economic growth and development outcomes. 'Developmental settlements' often involve a capable state that can enforce regulations and provide public goods. In contrast, 'predatory or neo-patrimonial settlements' might suffer from weak state capacity and poor policy implementation.

The political settlements approach provides insights into how states overcome violence and disorder, and what puts them on a path towards inclusive (or otherwise) growth. For example, the idea that elite bargains can propel economic development was popularised in Stefan Dercon's (2022) book, *Gambling on Development*. In it, he argued that to advance growth, a country's elites have to shift from protecting their own interests and wealth in the short term, and take a gamble that supporting a shared 'development bargain' will benefit them. The work of the Effective States and Inclusive Development (ESID) Research Program made an extensive contribution to this field by developing a typology of political settlements and systemising their measurement (Kelsall et al., 2022). They identified two key factors that differentiate the nature of political settlements in practice. One, the *social foundation*, or support base, of the settlement. A broad support base generates incentives to cater to the general population. Second, the *concentration of power*. The more concentrated power is within a ruling coalition, the greater the prospect of achieving consensus on policy objectives. Inclusive settlements may ensure a broader distribution of benefits, whereas extractive ones concentrate benefits in the hands of a few.

Political settlements may sound like a lofty and distant configuration of power at the national level, so how do their effects cascade down to the everyday politics of who gets what, when and how? Diana Mitlin's (2022) work on the politics of shelter provision in three East African cities – Hawassa, Mogadishu, Nairobi – illustrates how. In these cities, each characterised by land insecurity, national and urban elites use clientelism, corruption and violence in the shelter sector to advance their legitimacy and popularity – i.e., serve their interests. They generate rents from the corrupt sale and control of lands, their gangs – what some local residents call 'cartels' – supervise construction and use coercive tactics to extract rewards, all the time cloaking these actions in modernist visions of the future. These city-level contestations are reflective of national political settlements that hinge on territorially managing key electorates and legitimising the state by promoting the idea of transformation. In this sense, the local mode of elite extraction reflects the national political settlement. The nature of the rules at the top filter down to the local level.

Reflective question

How do agreements between ruling political elites shape everyday lived realities?

While the political settlements approach has contributed valuable insights to the study of politics and development, it is not without its critics. As a version of elite theory, historically dominated by male scholars, political settlements can be 'gender blind', where they overlook how gender norms are reflected in and reproduced in them (Nazneen and Mahmud, 2015). Focusing on elites and their interests also obscures the everyday interests of non-elite, ordinary citizens, whose interests are also collectively contested – a topic we turn to next.

Collective Action Dilemmas

However desired futures are imagined, achieving them requires a range of actors, not only elites, to resolve their interests in ways that can deliver it. One of the knottiest problems with interests, though, is that what is in people's private interests and what is in the wider, public interest are often not perfectly aligned. Imagine, for example, the problem of delivering a vital public good such as clean streets. To pay for this good which can, in theory, benefit everyone, governments need to mobilise domestic resources in the form of taxes. Having a well-resourced government budget so that the streets are clean is in everyone's interest. Paying taxes, though, is not in many people's private interests. Problems occur when people pursue their own self-interest at the expense of the collective interest. For example, they avoid paying taxes, which, in the long-term, means the streets stay unsanitary.

Even if you agree that having a particular good is, well, good, sharing a common interest with others is not the same as *acting* on it. You may ask, what do I gain versus others? What are the costs, to me, of paying my share, or doing my part? Can I pursue alternatives that benefit me more? How you answer these questions has consequences, beyond your own actions.

It may be in your interests to tackle climate change over the long term, but you also drive a car to work on a route you could otherwise walk to save yourself valuable time. It may be in your interests that corruption is reduced, but you may also pay a bribe to ensure that your child secures a place at the best local school.

These tussles between what is good for you, versus what is good for everyone, create the basis for what is known as the *collective action problem* (Olson, 1965). This problem is exacerbated by the fact that in practice, individuals can benefit from the collective efforts of others, while themselves avoid paying any personal cost, whether in terms of money, materials, time, energy or labour. In effect, they know that their streets will be cleaned even if they themselves do not pay tax for this service, because most other people *will* choose to pay their taxes. This is called the 'free-rider' problem (Olson, 1965).

Under what real-world conditions do collective action problems occur, though? Imagine a scenario in which patients queue at a remote, rural health facility, seeking access to vital medical care. Knowing that the facility is chronically understaffed and unlikely to abide by scheduled appointments, people show up hours earlier than their allotted time to ensure they are one of the lucky ones who gets seen that day. This exacerbates the chaos, in which people jostle and compete to be seen. Everyone is unhappy, but no one wants to complain because the personal costs of making a fuss are too high; they may be branded a troublemaker and forego their chance of getting much-needed medical assistance. Although everyone has a shared interest in the facility operating more fairly and efficiently, the personal nature of their problems means they have a diversity of preferences of what this should look like. Should elderly people, children, or cancer patients get priority? Identifying shared goals is also difficult because community trust is low – there are multiple ethnic groups and religions using the facility, and it is hard for people to imagine room for solidarity. Those who can afford to pay a bribe to facilitate their place in the queue will do so. Those who can avoid the clinic entirely, opt out and pay privately, will take this option. These actions undermine the collective power of these individuals to demand accountability and to pressure the clinic to operate more fairly.

The example of the health clinic may be stylised, but it is not a fiction. It is a scenario that plays out regularly in some of the most resource-constrained environments, where services are poor, dilapidated, or even absent, and people find it hard to aggregate their individual experiences into collective demands for accountability. If we take the collective action problem seriously, we can assume that just like in this scenario, achieving desired futures therefore requires getting people to forego their individual interests in the pursuit of collective ones. The question of *how* to do this is the key concern of collective action theory (see Box 4.3).

Box 4.3 Collective Action Theory

Collective action theory is a framework for understanding how and why individuals come together to pursue common goals. It explores the conditions under which people are more likely to cooperate and act collectively, whether in the form of protests, strikes, lobbying, or forming interest groups, coalitions or social movements, despite disincentives and free-rider problems (where people can benefit without contributing).

In his foundational work *The Logic of Collective Action: Public Goods and the Theory of Groups* (1965) Mancur Olson was pessimistic about the ability of self-interested individuals to work in the interests of a group. He did, though, argue that small, homogeneous groups are more likely to overcome collective action problems because the members share similar interests and have a stronger sense of group identity and solidarity.

One of the implications of Olson's theory was that selfish humans would inevitably overuse and deplete any shared resources that require collective action to manage sustainably, such as rivers or forests. This was known as the 'tragedy of the commons'. But the groundbreaking work of Elinor Ostrom, for which she won the Nobel Prize in Economics in 2009, challenged this pessimistic view. In her book *Governing the Commons: The Evolution of Institutions for Collective Action* (1990), she showed that communities *can* achieve sustainable co-operation by developing effective rules, building trust to overcome uncertainty, and through active participation in decision-making.

While the lived realities of collective action problems gives us cause for pessimism regarding the pursuit of shared interests, it also *assumes* that interests are formed and calculations are made in a particularly narrow and self-serving way – essentially, that everyone can only think of what is right for them, and that their version of a desired future gives no regard for others. Of course, this is not always the case. To understand the potential for overcoming the collective action problem, we need to look more closely at where interests come from. Crucially, we must examine whether interests are always rational.

How are interests formed?

How do people *know* what is in their interest in the first place? The starting assumption for many scholars, including Mancur Olson, is Rational Choice Theory. Individuals are assumed to evaluate carefully the costs and benefits that arise from different courses of action and then choose the one that maximises their perceived net benefits (utility). It is assumed that the primary form of rationality is an egoistic, self-interested or self-seeking one. From a rational choice perspective, everyone acts in a goal-oriented manner all the time, with the expectation of maximising rewards.

Rational choice theory is premised on mathematical modelling and game theory. The most famous presentation of the theory is the prisoner's dilemma, a game where two sets of actors must make a decision: they can cooperate to the benefit of both parties, or one or both can pursue their individual interest, betraying the other. This 'economic approach to politics' has been summarised and critiqued well by Merilee Grindle (2001: 349) as:

in seeking to explain the behaviour of politicians, rational choice theorists generally assert that politicians naturally prefer more power to less; survival in office to defeat; re-election to loss; influence to irrelevance. Voters naturally prefer politicians who provide benefits that improve their individual welfare to those who do not. Bureaucrats naturally prefer higher budgets to lower ones, more discretion to less, more opportunities to promote their own welfare to fewer, career promotion to demotion. These individuals are distinct from economic actors only in that they are conceptualized to be interacting in a political market in which competition is about power to provide or receive benefits from public policy, public investments, and resources controlled by the government.

The limits of rationality

So what's wrong, or incomplete, with this view of the world? Consider the 'rational voter paradox' (Downs, 1957). Given the fact that we all know the probability of a single vote making a difference to the election outcome is close to zero, a truly rational citizen would never bother voting. But of course, that's not true, and citizens often take on costs to vote, from minor inconvenience to risking life and limb. If people always acted rationally, why does a firefighter go into a burning building to save someone they don't know? The reality is that individuals are guided by a wider repertoire of motivations than only self-interest. In fact, the assumption that people are *exclusively* driven by maximising their own gain is exposed as a rather a silly one by Amartya Sen (see Box 4.4).

Box 4.4 Rational Fools

The economic approach to explaining behaviour is based on the assumption that people only give a truthful answer as long as there are economic incentives for doing so.

But this, in practice, would make social life quite unworkable. As Amartya Sen (1977: 332) put it: 'when asked a question, the individual gives that answer which will maximize his personal gain. How good is this assumption? I doubt that in general it is very good. ("Where is the railway station?" he asks me. "There," I say, pointing at the post office, "and would you please post this letter for me on the way?" "Yes," he says, determined to open the envelope and check whether it contains something valuable.)'

So, if people are sometimes but not always rational in the narrow self-interested sense, how can we make sense of their behaviour the rest of the time – is it just irrational? James March and Johan Olsen (1984) provide a useful language for navigating this. They argue that when people are trying to maximise their benefits and minimise costs (getting elected, maximising the budget) they are following a 'logic of consequences'. Alternatively, there is also a 'logic of appropriateness'. This is where people ask themselves what kind of situation they face, what is expected of them, and what they should do given their role in a political community. Similarly, one of the key contributions from the pioneering work of Elinor Ostrom (2000), which critiqued rational choice theory, was that the world contains multiple types of individuals, some more willing to cooperate than others. Willingness to cooperate is not just a utility calculation – it is shaped by the social norms, ideas, and power relations in which people are situated.

> ## Reflective question
>
> To what extent could desired futures be achieved if everyone always acted exclusively in their own self-interest?

Hence, the incentives provided by the rules, as discussed in Chapter 3, do not determine what people consider to be in their interests in a mechanistic sense – there is slippage as they *make sense of* their interests. And, contrary to the assumptions of rational choice, people rarely enjoy perfect information about what is in their interests. Instead, they struggle with uncertainty. However, people are 'skilful' in the sense that we practise and get better at this navigation (Fligstein, 1997). And people are 'strategic' in the sense that they reflect on different courses of action available to them (Hay, 2002). The sociologist Margaret Archer (2003) has a wonderful expression to capture how this interplay between people and their context – 'an internal conversation' – works. What she means by this is that people reflexively deliberate about what their 'ultimate concerns' are – what matters to us, who we are. We have internal conversations about our physical well-being, our competence, and our self-worth, to define our version of a desired future.

The metaphor is to consider the difference between someone trying to negotiate a maze compared to someone trying to navigate between two points on a map with a contoured topography. In the former, the pathway to the centre of the maze is fixed. In the latter, people can choose any number of different routes from A to B, but some routes are more likely to be selected, and some are likely to be neglected if they are unknown or difficult. In short, institutions do not come with an instruction sheet (Blyth, 2003).

However, just because we get to construct our own interests does not mean that we can pursue them. And this is where power comes in.

Power to pursue interests

In all societies, particular communities hold greater decision-making power than others, and are more likely to be able to pursue their interests. Such dominance may be socially constructed out of the value or superiority placed on certain ethnic, linguistic, or religious identities, a subject we explore further in Chapter 10. In India and other parts of South Asia, for example, caste is a form of inherited social hierarchy that serves as a crucial determinant of who is able to dominate ideational or decision-making space and pursue their interests. Alongside other intersectional identities (gender, class, and so on), caste operates to produce 'both "categorical exclusion" and "opportunity hoarding"' (Mosse, 2018). Exclusion on the basis of caste experienced by Dalits (the 'lowest' caste) is by no means an anachronism, nor is it limited to the subcontinent. Indeed, caste-based discrimination and harassment plagues applicants to and employees in technology companies in Silicon Valley (Rai, 2021). Ultimately, any basis of exclusion (gender, religion, class, race, ethnicity, and so on) is a matter of the assertion of power. Power is what determines our agency and our ability to pursue our interests.

Power can be exercised to *secure interests* in various ways (see Table 4.2). As we saw in Chapter 1, the most straightforward way of conceiving of the exercise of power is as influence over others. 'A has power over B to the extent that he can get B to do something that B would not otherwise do' (Dahl, 1957: 202–3). This definition sees power as relational and focused on the making of decisions arising out of a conflict of interests or preferences. Building on Dahl's definition, others expanded our understanding of the exercise of power: Bachrach and Baratz (1970) added agenda setting as shaping decision-making or non-decision-making as the second face of power, limiting the options available to individuals. Lukes (1974) goes a step further and adds manipulation, covert control over the agendas and decision-making to limit behaviour, as the third dimension of power.

Table 4.2 How power affects the pursuit of interests

Type of power	Form	Example
• Decision-making power	• Power that is openly expressed and observable; the open 'face' of power.	• Access to decision-making roles and influence; powerful individuals who get to decide at key decision-making points (Dahl, 1957).
• Agenda-setting	• Power that operates behind the scenes by determining what topics are up for discussion in the first place.	• Agenda setting through differential access to decision-makers, typically using lobbying, or private deals (Bachrach and Baratz, 1962).
• Manipulative	• Power that can influence people without them even realising it (Gaventa, 1980), involving persuasion and manipulation to shape how people think, act and what they believe.	• Charismatic speeches, media coverage and narrative building, framing.

Decision-making power is crucial for enabling elites to serve any interests they have in accessing state resources or bypassing state processes. Access to politicians, bureaucrats, businesspersons, lobbyists, enhanced through connections and networks enables decision-making (or non-decision-making) to advance a narrow set of interests. For instance, COVID-related procurement in the UK was heavily influenced by elite relationships and interests. Baroness Mone, a Conservative member of the House of Lords, came under investigation for referring a company to the UK government's 'VIP lane' to secure COVID contracts. The profits from this company were secretly paid to Mone and her family (Conn, 2022).

Through their access to networks and resources, elites are able to exercise *agenda-setting power* – in other words, what gets discussed, in what forums, and when – such that 'demands for change in the existing allocation of benefits and privileges in the community can be suffocated before they are even voiced; or kept covert; or killed before they gain access to the relevant decision-making arena; or, failing all these things, maimed or destroyed in the decision-implementing stage of the policy process' (Bachrach and Baratz 1970: 44). For instance, the Sackler family, owners of the pharmaceutical companies that produced the drugs causing an opioid epidemic in the United States, were able to use their wealth and connections to influence key decision-making bodies such as the WHO (Clark and Rogers, 2019) and the National Academies of Sciences, Engineering and Medicine (Jewett, 2023). As a result, these bodies produced reports and guidance that encouraged opioid prescription and use as a best practice.

The third face of power, *manipulation*, involves the covert or latent exercise of influence or control. It is the ability to influence behaviour 'by influencing, shaping or determining his very wants' (Lukes, 1974: 27). The exercise of power in this manner can be observed through our everyday lives – in the ways we are socialised into society, the influence of the media over our lives, our beliefs and identity, and how they shape our behaviour, and the ability of some to shape the preferences of others – in other words, to prevent a conflict of interest from ever arising in the first place that might lead to the exercise of the first or second faces of power.

As we will discuss in greater depth, in Chapter 9, one of the ways that interests shape development is via the power of international aid actors to pursue their own agendas above and beyond what is in the interests of the countries they purport to assist. Asymmetrical power dynamics between aid actors and the governments of post-colonial countries can lead to prescriptive policy solutions that are barely contested. This is revealed in the analysis of how cash transfer programmes were adopted and implemented across Africa (Ouma and Adesina, 2019; see Box 4.5).

Box 4.5   The agenda-setting power of international aid

Cash transfer programmes have now been widely adopted as an means of social protection across Africa. Ouma and Adesina (2019) use a Foucauldian view of power similar to Lukes's notion – that power is in operation everywhere in our lives and is exercised relationally – in unpacking the power of international institutions such as DFID and UNICEF to shape this policy agenda. In Kenya, this power was exercised in several ways, including:

- By excluding certain political actors from the policy-making and implementation process for fear of elite capture.
- By exercising hegemony over the funding, staffing, and knowledge production aimed at promoting a particular policy approach.

Can interests be tamed?

Whether we consider the interests of local elites, ordinary people or international actors, interests matter because, in the words of Elinor Ostrom (2009), they determine the 'distribution of benefits and harms' to those in and outside a group. The question, then, is how, and when, can interests be shifted towards the achievement of more benefit and less harm to societies?

One answer is incentives. Olson's (1965) theory proposed that collective action problems can be overcome by giving 'selective' incentives, meaning only to group members and not to free riders. These could be in the form of sanctions, tangible rewards such as resources or money, or intangible benefits such as social recognition or a sense of belonging. What this does, in effect, is to encourage people to alter their *perception* of what is in their interests.

Experience in Lagos State, Nigeria, illustrates this in practice. The irregular flow of revenues available to the State government has been a perennial problem (Utomi et al., 2007). But amazingly, between 1999 and 2005/6, revenues increased more than a staggering hundred-fold. How? The State governor had an interest in radical reforms to secure a more stable budget. So he incentivised better revenue collection by allowing the State revenue board – whose job it was to collect taxes – to retain 5 per cent of all revenues collected. The revenue board was allowed to spend this 5 per cent on its own operating costs, salaries and bonuses. Change happened, then, by aligning the private interests of the revenue service (in increasing its own resources) with the public interest in maximising tax revenues. As Lagos State became increasingly reliant on local, as opposed to federal, revenues, it became increasingly sensitive to local demands for improved performance, and more accountable to its tax-paying citizens, establishing a 'fiscal social contract' (Moore, 2004). While this is just one example, it is indicative of the suite of reforms set out in the World Bank's 2017 Word Development Report, *Governance and the Law*. The task of governing effectively, ultimately, is to shift the incentives of those who are in or possess power, and therefore reshape their preferences towards the common good.

How, though, do non-elites – the other side of the interests' equation – secure their interests? The vast majority of people lack the power, wealth, connections, access or the recognition to easily command their will. But maybe, instead, they can restrain the power of elites to selfishly pursue them. One way is to augment the power of representation in institutions such as legislatures. In Kenya, for example, Opalo (2019) finds that legislative strength and independence constrains the unchecked powers of the Kenyan President. During periods when the legislature has been strongest, presidents have issued fewer 'Legal Notices' or rules issued by the executive have the force of law. These findings question the conventional wisdom that presidential power is untrammelled on the continent. In other words, that decision-making always follows the interests of the executive.

Of course, legislative measures to curb executive interests are only open to those living in democratic polities where there is a meaningful understanding of citizenship that includes participation. How do citizens get the state to respond to their interests where such mechanisms are weak or cut off? For example, in rentier states, the social contract makes it difficult for citizens to exercise influence in a manner that serves their interests over those of the state. Because these states draw their income from rents (through oil or mineral wealth), they do not rely significantly on taxation for their revenue. This shapes the evolution of institutions and power structures in these countries, and the ability and indeed will of citizens to make demands of the state (Barkey and Parikh, 1991). In many other contexts, patronage relationships are the key avenue through which citizens – politicians, bureaucrats, voters – pursue their interests.

'Power to the people' (the subject of Chapter 8) – in the form of participation, collective action and social mobilisation – is sometimes the only way to (forcefully) align interests. This takes many forms, but may strategically require some attempt at rebalancing power differentials via acts of non-compliance, active resistance, or even self-sabotage. In an example of the latter, communities in northern Nigeria have boycotted polio vaccination – something they recognise hurts both their own interests and those of the state – as a way of gaining leverage over the state to force it to improve services in their area. By increasing their bargaining power, they were successful in extracting concessions on holding an otherwise unresponsive and/or unaccountable state accountable (Grossman et al., 2018).

Reflective question

What mechanisms can align individual and collective interests?

Addressing power imbalances, then, requires groups to organise to build their collective voice and power. But how can subaltern groups do this when they begin from a place of disempowerment and structural disadvantage? One answer is trust-building. Goopta (2000) identifies how sex workers in Calcutta went from being in commercial competition and distrustful of one another, to an organised group with high levels of solidarity. Group formation and maintenance was a function of actively crafting shared values, norms, and identity. Although many sex workers joined the group for personal reasons (self-esteem, education), their commitment was transformed through taking on the roles of peer educators and activists. Further mobilisation, protest, and the creation of cooperative services such as savings and credit helped further maintain the collective identity and extend the group's agency. In other words, collective action problems can be overcome by developing shared interests.

Summary and conclusion

In this book, we argue that interests, and securing them, becomes essential when people's lived realities don't match their expectations. When people have an aspiration for more and for a better life, interests and their pursuit can dominate choices and behaviours. Take scarcity, for example, introduced as one of the drivers of contestation in the book's Introduction. Scarcity is not inevitable – it is manufactured, and there are interests behind it. Our entire social world, and the rules that govern it, do not just exist, they are *made* via interests.

The challenge is that there are many reasons why the pursuit of interests can undermine the achievement of desired futures: the diversity of interests, the ways individual interests can undermine collective action, or the interests of the few (with power) overriding the interests of the many (without it), exclusive and extractive political settlements, or elite capture. Too much focus on the 'rules' distracts us from their real drivers, operating beneath the surface.

Institutions work in ways that people want them to; they can subvert, use them, or co-opt them. As such, we need to see interests for what they are: the engine of development.

The question is how to resolve and reconcile these tensions in interests: because they exist, and they generate real incentives to block or facilitate development. In the same way that power is the core reason why certain interests are pursued, and whose interests win and lose, then power is also the answer to rebalancing and aligning interests. Whether that power is institutionally designed or reclaimed by the people, the only way to offset the selfish pursuit of powerful interests is to shift the power to those whose interests are not (yet) served.

Discussion questions

- To what extent do you think the selfish pursuit of individual interests is the cause of the world's development challenges?
- Find a recent newspaper article on a collective action problem that interests you. Who are the actors involved and how were their interests formed?
- In your specific country context, who are the key agents exercising agenda-setting power? What are their interests and preferences? Who gets left out when these interests are prioritised?

Suggested further reading

Escoffier, S. (2018) 'Mobilisational citizenship: sustainable collective action in underprivileged urban Chile', *Citizenship Studies*, 22 (7): 769–90.

Kruks-Wisner, G. (2018) 'The pursuit of social welfare: citizen claim-making in rural India', *World Politics*, 70 (1): 122–63.

Ostrom, E. (2009) *A Polycentric Approach for Coping with Climate Change* (1 October). World Bank Policy Research Working Paper No. 5095.

Singh, P. (2015) 'Subnationalism and social development: a comparative analysis of Indian states', *World Politics*, 67 (3): 506–62.

5 What's the big idea?

Ideology, beliefs, and discourse

Nic Cheeseman, Claire Mcloughlin, and Kate Pruce

Image 5.1 Refugees arrive in Lesbos, Greece, on a boat from Turkey in 2015. Image by punghi via Shutterstock.

Learning outcomes

- Describe how ideas matter in our everyday lives and become developmentally consequential.
- Analyse the emergence and traction of ideas as a function of institutions, interests, and power.
- Understand how ideas are manufactured and deployed within processes of contestation over who gets what, when and how.

The power of ideas

As we have seen in Chapters 3 and 4, dominant explanations for social change focus on institutions and interests, and how these drive people's everyday opportunities to pursue the material or symbolic resources they desire to live a fulfilling life. This is important, but it is not the whole story of how people survive and thrive. Humans aren't driven purely by rational calculations – the choices we make are often also guided by our beliefs about what is right and appropriate. To fully understand the politics of development, we must therefore go beyond these explanations, and ask 'what's the big idea?'

Ideas shape the politics of development in the most fundamental ways imaginable. They influence not only how we try to address development challenges, but also what we think constitutes a problem in the first instance. What is poverty, for example? All sorts of normative ideas and stereotypes are attached to being 'poor', which could denote a certain income, lifestyle, social class or caste. In one country, you might be considered poor if you can't afford to eat. In another, if you don't have a smart phone. Deeply held views about the causes of poverty, particularly the idea of deservingness – i.e. who deserves assistance – matter because in turn, they influence whether and how we respond to it. If we believe poverty is caused by a lack of income, then the logical solution is to enhance income via growth. By contrast, if we think poverty results from the unequal distribution of resources, this implies redistributing the benefits of growth so that they reach citizens more equally. Our inclinations do not emerge from a vacuum but are shaped by the ideas and beliefs we hold, including our ideological beliefs. Those who subscribe to neoliberal ideology (described in detail in Chapter 7), for example, are likely to believe that the poor need to work their way out of poverty, and that providing too much assistance can lock people in a 'dependency trap'. Critics of neoliberalism, on the other hand, argue that this view is unfair and exists in part to justify the inequities of capitalist wealth distribution (Fischer, 2018). Because our beliefs influence our behaviours, people living in poverty may face 'povertyism' – a term coined by the United Nations to capture discrimination based on stigmatised notions of the poor as lazy, socially inferior, or responsible for their situation. Such discriminations include being excluded from vital public services or employment on the grounds of socioeconomic disadvantage. In these ways, it is impossible to disassociate the lived reality of poverty from individually or collectively held ideas about its origins, manifestations, and meanings.

This chapter takes us squarely into this 'ideational realm' and explores the power of the third of our three 'I's – ideas – in shaping the politics of who gets what, when, and how. We set the scene by outlining what we mean by the 'ideational', before considering how ideas influence the pursuit of desired futures. We explore the emergence and dominance of certain ideas to show they are always, everywhere, structured by and refracted through power relations. Finally, we examine how ideas are strategically evoked and projected onto the processes of contestation at the heart of the politics of development. Crucially, we explain how and why ideas are a dynamic ingredient in the creation, maintenance, and evolution of institutions, shaping interests and framing versions of reality that, when broadcast into the public sphere, can determine the course of individual and collective futures.

Ideas, and why they matter

What do we mean when we talk about ideas? In simple terms, ideas are the perceptions we have about the world around us. When you decide which leader to vote for in an election, you are – at least in part – considering whose ideas about how to run the country are closest to your own. If you instead struggle with the question of whether to vote at all, you may find yourself weighing up the demands of civic duty against a desire not to spend time and money getting to the polling station – two very different ideas about how citizens of a country should behave. More broadly, everything you do, from what time you wake up in the morning to what you think is appropriate for breakfast (from cooked meats to raw fish, rice and beans, and chocolate spread on toast), through to what you expect the government to provide to its people, is driven by ideas about how human life should be organised.

One key reason ideas matter is that *everything contains an idea*. Take the state, for example. We might naturally assume that it has infrastructural and bureaucratic power, whether in the form of the police, military, parliaments or palaces, or border patrols. Michael Mann (1984) famously depicted the state in this way, as an autonomous, territorially defined entity with the capacity to physically penetrate society and implement its rules. But the state isn't just a physical entity; it is also a set of ideas and norms – a 'structure of intelligibility' that helps people make sense of the rules that govern authority (Steinberger, 2004). It reflects judgements and beliefs about the purpose of authority, the appropriate way to exercise power, and the restraints that should be placed upon it. Indeed, for many remote communities, dislocated from the state through geography or exclusion, the state is nothing *more* than an idea, because it often has little tangible presence in their everyday lives. In this way, an ideational perspective can encourage us to critically evaluate the assumptions we make about the 'material' world.

Ideas also matter for how societies function because they are never merely 'in our heads' – they are unavoidably social and shared or 'inter-subjective' (Geertz, 1994). This means that ideas are constructed by sharing experiences, knowledge, and understandings via social interaction. Research in social psychology has demonstrated that human beings tend to be very susceptible to what they believe others like them think and do. As we discussed in Chapter 4, one of the best-known conceptualisations of how we are shaped by the societies within which we live was provided by James March and Johan Olsen (1996). They suggest that individuals don't always make decisions by calculating which course of action would benefit them most as an individual, as suggested by rational-choice approaches to human behaviour. Instead, they argue that individuals naturally think about what would be socially appropriate in each situation, which they famously called 'the logic of appropriateness'.

Reflective question

How does an ideational perspective encourage us to think differently about the world around us?

Indeed, we are often unaware of the hold that norms, prejudices, and ideologies have over our understanding. When a belief is widely shared, it may appear to be natural, inevitable, or ordained, such that we may not question it – even when it is against our own interests. Think about how often you have critiqued some of the fundamental building blocks of our political lives. When was the last time that you asked why our political systems assume that where you were born should dictate where you are allowed to live? Or why international law assumes that governments have a right to rule as they please within their own territory, and to use any natural resources that exist for the exclusive benefit of their own citizens, rather than all of humanity? These questions are pertinent because the modern political world is premised on the idea that national borders are sacrosanct and must be protected. On this basis, scared families who risk their lives to cross dangerous seas on flimsy boats are sent back by countries that could afford to support them. This idea is so pervasive it seems 'natural', but in reality, it is a human and political construct.

Engaging with and contesting ideas, then, is how people communicate and interact with others, and agree what actions are appropriate. Ideas form a 'web of related elements of meaning' (Carstensen, 2011: 600), that provide cognitive shortcuts and interpretive filters to enable people to make sense of the world they inhabit. Whether we read them in books like this one, are taught them in classrooms, or imbue them from conversations with friends, ideas play a profound role in shaping both individual and collective consciousness. But what ideas are relevant to development, in particular?

An ideational lens on development

Many of the ideas associated with development and change – from philosophies and ideologies, to everyday attitudes and prejudices, to social norms – are contestable and contested (see Table 5.1). As we saw in Chapter 2, many of these ideas also profoundly shaped the production of knowledge *about* development; they helped determine whose ideas speak loudest, and get heard, when people try to make sense of lived realities.

Crucially, as we can see from the table, many ideas about development are fundamentally *normative*, in the sense that they contain moral judgements about what is good or bad for society (see Box 5.1). They infer priorities in terms of who should get what, when, how, based on who *deserves* what, or what is *fair* or (in)tolerable. They often contain an interpretation

Table 5.1 Contested ideas about development

Type of idea	Philosophies	Ideologies	Attitudes and beliefs	Prejudices	Social norms
Definition:	A theory or attitude that acts as a guiding principle for behaviour.	A system of beliefs about how economic, social, or political life should be organised.	A set of emotions, beliefs, and behaviours towards a particular object, person, thing, or event.	Preconceived, biased opinions not based on reason.	Ideas that generate expectations of how we should act.
Examples:	Equality, social justice, distributive justice, human rights.	Patriarchy, feminism, neoliberalism, capitalism, communism, socialism, Marxism.	Deservingness, moral appropriateness (legitimacy), fairness, tolerance, respect, deference, religious beliefs.	Racism, sexism, povertyism, ageism, religious, or gender identity-based.	Gender roles, customs, traditions.

Box 5.1   What's in a 'normative idea?

Many scholars, including John Campbell (2020) and Vivienne Schmidt (2008), analytically separate 'normative' ideas from cognitive, or 'causal' ideas. While causal ideas explain how things happen, or why they occur, normative ideas contain values, standards, or judgments about what is right, just, ethically or morally acceptable – for example:

- Cognitive idea: 'Widespread poverty can lead to civil unrest.'
- Normative idea: 'We all have a moral obligation to help those in need.'

---

of the end-goal of development, too, whether ending injustice, overturning patriarchy, or achieving gender equality. It is this normative character of ideas about development that makes them fundamentally contestable.

Take the idea of equality, for example – in any given context, it could mean equality of opportunity *or* of outcomes, greater representation, safeguarding minority rights, or affirmative action. The strength of feeling, or valence, of this idea, is likely to be influenced by cultural norms, historical experiences, and societal values. Ideas are contingent, in that they are influenced by, and can reinforce or replace the other ideas around them at a given point in time. Gender equality has a very different meaning in Sweden than it does in Saudi Arabia, for example. In Sweden, it means that men and women have equal opportunities to pursue education, careers, and leadership positions, and that gender-based discrimination is actively discouraged. In Saudi Arabia, it means ensuring that women have access to education and employment opportunities within the boundaries set by cultural and religious norms. The point is, if we want to understand the meaning of ideas about development, we have to understand not only its content, but its context.

When social scientists study the influence of ideas, attitudes, beliefs or any other mind-generated thoughts over our choices and actions, they are applying an 'ideational' lens. The study of political ideas and their hold on the human imagination has a long history, but one of the most extensive treatments has come from the discursive institutionalism school (see Box 5.2). Importantly, applying an ideational lens doesn't preclude examining the tangible, material, or geographical drivers of (or constraints to) development, whether it is the construction of cities, the extent of natural resources, or manufacturing via global value chains. Rather, it encourages us to examine *how* these processes are also powered by, and interact with, ideas.

Box 5.2   Discursive institutionalism – the home of the ideational

Discursive institutionalism was first coined by Vivien Schmidt (2008, 2010) to refer to a 'fourth' new institutionalism – one that emphasises ideas and the mobilisation of ideas as key to explaining institutional change. This approach was deliberately conceived as an antidote to instrumental or interest-based accounts of human choice and agency, and became an umbrella term for a wide range of approaches that take ideas seriously.

Discursive institutionalism is an interdisciplinary approach that spans sociology, political sociology, international relations and organisational studies, for example. Scholars in this tradition study the power of language, discourse, and communication in shaping political behaviour, governance systems, or policy outcomes.

An ideational lens also draws attention to the *variety of discursive spaces* where such meanings (shared or otherwise) are generated, deliberated, and contested: from the micro-level discussions over family meals, to church sermons, to village and community forums, to media opinion columns, and to, of course, the proliferation of online forums and social media in our digital era. Jürgen Habermas (1989) called the discursive spaces where people articulate their mutual interests and form judgements about what is right and wrong for society the 'public sphere'. While this remains an influential term, it presupposes a Western model of democratic deliberation that is at odds with the lived realities of how ideas are shared through traditional, private means in other societies. Pacific communities, for example, transmit moral teachings and share lived experiences across generations, through indigenous oralities such as 'tok stori', 'a Melanesian term for telling stories, and making sense of life' (Sanga et al., 2018). Indigenous knowledge systems can impart vital, localised knowledge about climate change adaptation, such as in the rural Mutoko district of Zimbabwe, where communities have been adapting to rainfall scarcity by reviving indigenous practices (Mugambiwa, 2018). In these ways, the ideational is as much alive in the everyday as it is in more 'formal' kinds of public contestation.

How ideas connect to lived realities

Analysing the spaces where ideas circulate or make meaning is one thing, but how do ideas connect to our material world? How do they influence lived realities? Although ideas are everywhere, they can be difficult to pin down. Schmidt (2008) argued that in practice, studying ideas requires attention to the people promoting them, the 'carriers' of ideas; their meaning and value, or 'content'; and the interactive process via which ideas are conveyed, or 'discourse'. Nevertheless, the challenge of isolating the effects of ideas from other, social or economic factors, looms large. So can we really say that ideas matter for development? How?

In practice, scholars have addressed this challenge using a variety of methods, from opinion surveys, to interviews with policy-makers and decision-makers, or textual analysis of policy documents, and discourse analysis of political speeches, all the way through to data-mining social media to explore how ideas are articulated in the public sphere. Using these methods, they have provided evidence that ideas are developmentally consequential (see Box 5.3).

Box 5.3   How do we know that ideas have developmental effects?

- In her book, *Ideas and Institutions: Developmentalism in Brazil and Argentina* (1991), Kathryn Sikkink uses a comparative case study methodology to show how the idea of 'developmentalism' was adopted by governments in Brazil and Argentina, and why this was done more successfully in the former than the latter.
- In *The White Man's Burden: Historical Origins of Racism in the United States* (1974), Winthrop D. Jordan shows how the attitudes and beliefs about race held by Europeans and early American settlers were used to justify colonialism, slavery, and social hierarchies.
- Jimi Adesina's edited book on *Social Policy in the African Context* (2021) demonstrates how ideas such as neoliberalism have shaped specific social policy trajectories in Africa and the direction of development itself, leading to 'sticking-plaster' responses rather than a transformative approach to addressing social problems.

If ideas are developmentally consequential, how does this happen? Below, we discuss four key mechanisms that take ideas out of our heads to shape the future in concrete ways.

First, normative ideas (and our perceptions of other people's ideas) *motivate us to act*. They are an invisible social glue that binds communities around a collective moral code. They give us reasons to care (or not) about who gets what, when and how. Religious ideas, for example, are often particularly powerful in this regard. Religious networks and gatherings can generate social trust, provide valued social contact that can improve mental health, and enable communities to achieve common objectives (Qayyum et al., 2020). Indeed, in many countries, faith is embedded into people's everyday survival strategies: systematic reviews of documented evidence have found that in some African countries, Faith-Based Organisations (FBOs) provide 44 per cent of health services (Kagawa et al., 2012).

Second, beliefs can generate social expectations about how we *should* appropriately behave in social situations – in other words, they become social norms. In her book, *Norms in the Wild*, Christina Bicchieri (2017) defines social norms as behavioural rules that satisfy two criteria: people believe that others follow them, and people believe that others think they *should* be followed. These rules may or may not align with people's own preferences, but that is precisely the point – people follow them not necessarily because they correspond with preferences, but because of the weight of social expectations, and sometimes the threat of social sanction for not doing so. This will not be the case in every human interaction, of course – people may decide to rebel against convention or to reject the beliefs of their community – but our basic desire to fit in and be accepted means that it often applies.

Because ideas generate social norms, or expectations of behaviour, they also determine people's *freedoms and choices*. The religious ideas discussed above enable social capital in some scenarios, but in other circumstances, constrain opportunities. Religious ideas may determine what women can do, wear, when they can get married, to whom, whether they can get pregnant or not, or leave their house unaccompanied, or drive a car. In many cases around the world, ideas affect the rules we live by in ways that can be deeply detrimental or harmful to those involved. Gender norms, underpinned by patriarchal belief systems, restrict opportunities for women to influence decisions that directly affect their lives. In village ward councils in Tanzania (Eaton et al., 2021), where there are firmly held ideas that women should show respect and subservience, it can be challenging for a woman to speak out in public, as it is taken to mean that their husbands have 'lost control' over them. Ideas, then, can actively block women's voices and representation.

Finally, perhaps the most discussed mechanism through which ideas become consequential is through the *policy-making decisions of elites*. All policies, such as legislation that bans child marriage or criminalises domestic violence, are shaped by elites, who not only have interests, but ideas. Have you ever thought about why governments address some problems but not others? This is partly due to limited time and resources; it is not possible to prioritise all existing problems at the same time. But what determines which ideas rise up the agenda? One answer is that which policies gain attention is determined by the political ideologies, worldviews, assumptions, and biases held by leaders and bureaucrats. As Bilal Baloch shows in his book *When Ideas Matter: Corruption and Democracy in India* (2021), when faced with acute credibility crises, ruling elites will choose policies, narratives and justifications that align with their philosophical beliefs about the nation and/or their ideas of social or economic development.

Reflective question

What ideas are most consequential in your life? Why?

These examples demonstrate how ideas have consequences for development. But this does not explain *why* certain ideas become influential in the first instance. Why do some ideas take hold in societies, and others do not? The answer is that ideas are also shaped by who holds power in a given context – a subject we turn to next.

How ideas (re)produce power

Given the developmental importance of ideas, the question of under what conditions they emerge and spread is key. The extent to which an idea is influential is shaped by the content of the idea, the credibility of the messenger, and the degree to which they fit with existing ideas. But the decision of individuals to promote certain ideas over others is rarely neutral or random, and instead tends to reflect their own interests or the interests of others that they are connected to. Who benefits, for example, from the current system of international law, and the emphasis it places on respecting existing borders and national sovereignty? This system essentially protects the existing distribution of global wealth. Is that just an accident or is it by design? If it is not an accident, which groups and institutions work to sustain it, and how?

The central point to keep in mind here is that political ideas are always, everywhere, produced through and reflect the distribution of power. The process through which ideas become policy is not a purely meritocratic competition in which the best policies always win out, but is rather shaped by the existing set of political institutions and distribution of power. Indeed, the power of ideas explains why 'those engaged in politics are trying to create, influence, frame and communicate ideas all the time' (Schmidt, 2008). Ideas interact with power in three main ways (Carstensen and Schmidt, 2016; see Box 5.4).

Box 5.4   Ideas and power

- Power over ideas: imposing ideas and resisting the inclusion of alternatives.
- Power through ideas: persuading others to accept and adopt certain views.
- Power in ideas: establishing hegemony or institutions that constrain what ideas are considered.

First, power asymmetries provide some groups with disproportionate control *over* ideas. Just as some social media platforms use algorithms that accelerate the spread of certain kinds of messages and restrict the flow of others, political institutions can constrain some ideologies and promote others. A classic example would be an authoritarian country in which the government controls all the TV and radio stations, such as Rwanda. In such a context, ideas and ideologies that are in line with the ruling orthodoxy face few barriers, but those that question the government's achievements – or challenge the key principles on which it is based – can be forced underground. The great lengths that authoritarian leaders go to suppress rival ideas and ideologies demonstrates just how powerful they are. In the Rwandan local government elections of 2021, for example, 'the government's repression of legitimate opposition parties and strict control of the media helped to ensure an overwhelming victory for the RPF [ruling party]' (Freedom House, 2023).

Second, power operates *through* ideas – meaning that some groups may use ideas to influence people in ways that are not in their best interests. Examples include the caste system in India, or identity-based discrimination more broadly (see Chapter 10). In many social settings, the dominant ideas passed on by parents, preached by religious leaders, and in some cases even taught in school, suggest that it is natural – perhaps even God given – that some people would be born into power and privilege, and others would not. This is most striking when it appears to harm the individual concerned. Consider why, for example, significant numbers of women in some countries hold attitudes and beliefs that both legitimate gender inequalities and help to sustain them. A recent study by the Pew Research Centre found that in Nigeria and Tunisia, less than half of the population felt that gender equality was 'very important', including a large proportion of women (46 per cent in Nigeria). Moreover, while most Americans say that gender equality is important, women are less likely to hold this view than men (89 per cent as compared to 93 per cent). The point is that because ideas are created and maintained through existing power structures, they can legitimate unfair and unequal distributions of resources – even to some of those who may be discriminated against.

Finally, power *in* ideas means that ideas can lock-in certain institutional arrangements that favour the powerful. As set out in Box 5.5, the famous German economist and philosopher Karl Marx argued that that what we might call 'ruling ideas' are neither accidental or neutral, but serve to legitimise political and economic systems that are deeply unjust. In other words, he claimed that ideology distorted reality, masking how capitalist societies exploited one group for the benefit of another, and hiding the fact that the system was based on the consistent use of violence. Marx was writing about European societies such as France, Germany, and the United Kingdom, and the exploited groups he was thinking about were peasants in feudal societies who were effectively owned by their landlord, or the working class in capitalist societies who were paid a pittance for their labour. Over the last 170 years, however, Marx's insights have inspired a broader literature on how the persistence of certain ideological beliefs can mask the injustice of inequality and oppression within a much wider range of societies and groups.

Box 5.5 The power of ideology

The term 'ideology' describes a system of ideas, ideals, and assumptions that people hold about how the world (should) work. Today, most theorists view ideology as neither inherently good nor bad. American anthropologist Clifford Geertz (1994), for example, defined ideology as systems of thought that enable us to understand and make decisions by simplifying reality.

Historically, though, ideologies have been considered deeply problematic because they contain claims to truth that may not be fact-based, but are nevertheless politically powerful. Karl Marx and Friedrich Engels (1965), for example, argued that ideology enables ruling elites to legitimate and consolidate their dominance over the masses. Key to this is the emergence of 'false consciousness', whereby people support ideas that in fact exploit them.

Philosopher Antonio Gramsci, who was imprisoned by the Italian dictator Benito Mussolini and so had particularly sharp view of the power of authoritarian ideas, later developed the Marxist notion of ideology into the concept of 'hegemony', meaning the control of subordinate groups by dominant ones. One of Gramsci's most influential ideas was the 'manufacture of consent', meaning the manipulation of the media, universities and religion to legitimate an economic and political order that did not operate in the interests of most citizens.

Later Marxist theorisation extended the idea of 'dominant' and 'subordinate' groups beyond class, to include other axes of oppression such as gender, race, and ethnicity. The postcolonial theorist Gayatri Chakravorty Spivak (2005), for example, critiqued Marxian ideas for neglecting the 'subaltern' – groups systemically marginalised through colonialism.

How ideas emerge and spread

It should be clear by now that contesting development necessarily entails interpreting ideas, deploying them, and seeking to change them. But how do ideas change? One explanation is our innate desire to fit in. Recent literature on social psychology tells us that what we believe and do evolves in line with what we perceive other people to believe and do (Tankard and Paluck, 2016), and so once a set of ideas starts to take hold, it can create a self-reinforcing cycle in which more and more people start to conform to the norm. This is a useful starting point, but it doesn't explain what drives the evolution of ideas at a more general level – what changes lead to the emergence of new thoughts and make others seem old-fashioned. It is tempting to think that as we learn more, we become frustrated with flawed ideas and discard them in favour of something better.

The physicist and philosopher Thomas Kuhn (1962), for example, argues that scientific thinking evolves through a series of paradigm shifts that are triggered by a growing recognition that our existing ideas are flawed. Kuhn suggests that we begin with a period of normality in which people believe the current orthodoxy. This view becomes increasingly untenable, however, due to the growing weight of evidence exposing serious flaws. At some point, the weight of evidence becomes so strong that the discipline is thrown into crisis, and this encourages more critical thinkers to conduct 'extraordinary' research that is more exploratory, leading to new breakthroughs. Eventually, a new paradigm emerges that holds sway and becomes the 'new normal' – though with some resistance from those who remain attached to the previous ideas, until once again, new problems emerge, and the cycle begins all over again. The kind of process that Kuhn describes is thus characterised by long periods of stability and then sudden 'revolutions' that are followed by further periods of stability. These shifts do not necessarily always bring us closer to 'truth', but they can lead to progress.

New political ideas are more likely to be adopted if they are aligned with existing arrangements, but paradigm shifts can occur in the policy arena also. The introduction of tobacco control policies, such as smoking bans, took many years, with powerful tobacco companies framing the freedom to smoke as promoting both the economy and civil liberties. Although the first studies began to provide scientific evidence about the harmful health effects of tobacco in the 1950s, tobacco control policies were not introduced in Europe until the mid-2000s and in many other countries they still do not exist. Norms that are taken for granted can therefore place limits on policy debates. Reframing smoking as a public health issue beyond the individual, based on increasing knowledge about the dangers of passive smoking, contributed to a new worldview on tobacco which enabled the enforcement of more stringent controls than had previously been possible (Cairney, 2009), which in turn led to a decline in the number of smokers and hence the emergence of new norms. Evidence can thus play a role in policy paradigm shifts, but not always in the way we would expect; what matters is not just the idea, but how acceptable it is to different groups.

Reflective question

What new ideas have emerged and gained traction in your lifetime? What explains this change?

Ideas do not simply spread because of their quality or timeliness, but also because they are promoted by powerful networks, institutions, and interests. The spread of neoliberalism is a case in point. From the early 1970s, an idea began to captivate the policy-makers in some of the most powerful countries in the world. Within the neoliberal school of thought, government-controlled industries and services came to be viewed as inherently inefficient monopolies with no incentive to provide a better service. Competition between companies, on the other hand, was lauded on the basis that it gave business leaders incentives to innovate and reduce costs to outmanoeuvre rivals, leading to better and cheaper products. Neoliberalism was not a new ideology but proved to be a highly effective reformulation of the belief that small governments and free markets are the best way to run a country. A key element of this approach was that individuals were expected to do more for themselves, with states providing fewer services, and so imposing fewer taxes.

Within a decade, neoliberal ideas had permeated numerous governments and many of the most powerful development institutions. In the process, they contributed to the International Monetary Fund and the World Bank adopting Structural Adjustment Policies (SAPs) that imposed spending cuts on many countries in Latin America, Africa, and Asia. In turn, SAPs led to governments reducing expenditure on health and education, and removing government subsidies on food and fuel, sparking criticism that they increased poverty and inequality while undermining the infrastructural development and human capital required for economic transformation. So how did such controversial and unpopular policies spread so far, so quickly?

The answer to this question lies in the capacity of powerful individuals, networks, and institutions to spread – and to an extent impose – their ideas on others. One reason neoliberal ideas caught on was the socioeconomic context. In countries such as the US and UK chronic stagflation – the combination of inflation and stagnation – generated a strong sense that a new economic approach was desperately needed. There was also a facilitative context at the international level because the sustained economic difficulties faced by some economies in Asia, Africa and Latin America raised serious concerns about whether governments would be able to pay back the loans they had contracted, challenging the sustainability of the system.

As we have already seen, however, political ideas rarely spread organically, and the reason those neoliberal ideas came to be seen to be the solutions to the world's economic problems was rooted in the distribution of power within *knowledge networks, political institutions, and likely winners and losers.*

- *Knowledge networks.* Well-known academics such as the Nobel Prize winner Milton Friedman promoted neoliberal economics at influential universities and institutions. In turn, a group of economists from Latin America who trained under Friedman, known as the Chicago Boys, subsequently introduced these ideas to their own countries, most notably in Chile. In this way, educational networks played a key role in passing on ideas from one generation to another, and from one country to another.
- *Political institutions.* In many cases, such policies were not adopted willingly. Some governments in sub-Saharan Africa, Latin America and Asia sought to resist neoliberal

ideas, but had little choice because the institutions that controlled access to international finance made the adoption of these rules a condition of accessing vital loans and support. The role of power here was twofold. First, the ability of the US government to determine the leadership of the World Bank – at a time when the voices of Africa, Asian and Latin American countries were marginalised – was critical to the Bank's adoption of a neoliberal approach. Second, the Bank's power to enforce restrictive conditions on governments in economic crisis empowered it to demand that these policy goals were adopted across a remarkably broad range of countries.

- *Winners and losers.* Like any economic policy, neoliberal approaches created winners and losers, and so supporting their adoption was in the *interests* of certain social groups. At the domestic level, wealthier citizens – including political leaders, senior bureaucrats, and economic advisers – benefitted from lower taxes. They also had the means to access private healthcare and education when state provision was low quality. Meanwhile, poorer citizens often suffered because they lost public services that they could not replace with their limited incomes, and rarely actually benefitted from the promised 'trickle-down' of wealth from the rich to the poor. At the international level, free trade policies also advanced the interests of their authors. On one hand, the removal of import restrictions and duties opened an increasing number of foreign markets to Western multinational companies. On the other hand, rules that prevented governments from protecting their infant industries – for example, through subsidies – meant that these firms were forced to compete with stronger rivals in other countries, making it less likely that they would grow to a point at which they would become sustainable. While free trade has several advantages when it comes to boosting global wealth and productivity, in practice SAPs and free trade agreements contributed to an increase in the gap between rich and poor countries.

In this way, the spread of neoliberal ideas reshaped development policy in much of the world, but not all of it. In some countries, leaders deliberately implemented as few neoliberal reforms as they could get away with. In others, such as the Soviet Union, governments continued to be driven by a very different ideology, rooted in communism or socialism, for much of the 1970s and 1980s. Under these visions it was the state rather than the free market that was seen to be the driving force of progress (see Chapter 7). The approach of communist governments was therefore to assert state control over industry and business in order to direct economic activity in the belief that this would be more efficient and lead to a more equal and fair society. Although the high level of government control necessitated by the kind of communism practised in countries such as the Soviet Union and North Korea meant that these systems were prone to corruption and abuse (Chapter 6), the ideological commitment of successive leaders – as well as a desire to protect their own interests – prevented effective reform. The contrasting approach of the United States and the Soviet Union during this period is thus testament to the power of ideas to shape government policies, and through them, development outcomes, in ways that are not always in the interests of most citizens.

How ideas shape who gets what, when and how

So far, we have shown that ideas are not merely organic by-products of our everyday social interactions; instead, they reflect conscious efforts by people operating at multiple levels to gain and wield power by shaping how we think. But how do people, organisations, political leaders, and policy-makers *use* ideas to influence who gets what, when and how? How do ideas work in the political process of contesting resources that people need or value to achieve the life they want? Below, we discuss three ways this can happen.

Underpinning Institutions

First, ideas shape who gets what, when, how, because they underpin institutions. Institutions are essentially *rules designed to achieve desired ideas* (see Chapter 3; Campbell, 1998). Ideas propel institutions into being, giving them meaning and legitimacy. Even political regimes, as a set of institutions, can rise or fall on the strength of their ideas. In many post-colonial African states, for example, aspiring elites who did not have the capacity and resources to rule exclusively through coercion alone shrouded brute force in ideas about the importance of 'strong man' rule to ensure unity and stability, to legitimise what might otherwise be seen to be an unjustifiable abuse of power (Cheeseman and Fisher, 2019).

Big ideas, such as what justifies the state's authority (see Chapter 14), or what it means to be a citizen, help to embed institutions into the national psyche. Consider the role of the UK's National Health Service (NHS) in forming British identity. On one level, the NHS is simply a government-run institution that provides basic health. But on another, it is inseparable from the post-war ideas it came to symbolise – about the right to health, access, affordability and equity – which gave the NHS a distinctive and important place in the national imagination (Webster, 2002). Standing on the steps of Number 10 Downing Street on the day of his party's electoral victory in 2019, Boris Johnson hailed the National Health Service as 'that simple and beautiful idea that represents the best of our country'.

We may shudder at the politicisation of ideas that bind nations, but nationalism – a strong sense of identity, loyalty, and attachment to the idea of a specific nation or ethnic group (see Box 5.6) – has played a significant role in driving economic development. As Liah Greenfeld (2003) argued in her book *The Spirit of Capitalism: Nationalism and Economic Growth*, nationalism was the key motivation, or 'spirit' behind the development of growth-oriented strategies in a number of advanced economies (e.g., the US, Germany, Japan). In these cases, it fostered a sense of collective identity and common purpose, which increased social cohesion, cooperation, and trust, and in turn, created a conducive environment for economic activities and innovation.

Reflective question

To what extent can nationalism be the driving force behind economic development?

Box 5.6 How ideas shape nations

Nationalism is a belief in protecting and promoting the interests, culture, identity, and sovereignty of one's nation. Benedict Andersen (1983) argued that the idea of the nation is not primordial – i.e., natural and inevitable – but rather constructed by political leaders and societies on the basis of a combination of factors, including shared customs and beliefs. Andersen's work was important in demonstrating that the nation-state is itself the product of ideas. These ideas are brought to life in Wale Adebanwi's 2016 book, *Nation as Grand Narrative: The Nigerian Press and the Politics of Meaning*, which shows how media practices, language use and discursive practices shaped the national identity.

Mahmood Mamdani (1996) pushed some of these ideas further, arguing that far from emerging organically, the creation of nation-states was an inherently violent endeavour, in which a supposed common identity only emerged after processes of ethnic cleansing and is sustained by the marginalisation of minorities.

Institutionalised ideas about national norms and values do not always persist, however. We see this dynamic in the case of social cash transfers in Zambia. When the scheme was first introduced by donors in 2003, the Ministry of Finance was extremely resistant on the basis that it would be financially unsustainable, generate welfare dependency and was out of line with past practice (Hanlon et al., 2012). Against this, a coalition of donors and government bureaucrats made a convincing argument that cash transfers were an effective poverty reduction policy, using evidence from positive impact evaluations from Zambia's pilot cash transfer schemes. The election of a new government in Zambia in 2011 facilitated the acceptance of the new policy, and the expansion of social cash transfers, because it more closely aligned with the 'pro-poor' manifesto of the new ruling party. At the same time, perceptions in communities that the most 'deserving' households were those unfit or unable to work due to circumstances beyond their control led to changes to the targeting criteria. In these ways, the alignment of institutions and ideas, as well as interests, was central to the adoption and design of the policy (Pruce and Hickey, 2019; Pruce, 2022).

Crucially, because all institutions *contain* ideas, they cannot be legitimately changed without challenging the ideas that underpin them (Hudson et al., 2018). The power of the NHS and its role in forming post-war national identity, fundamentally shapes how political

Image 5.2 An image that appears on the 5 Kwacha note in Zambia, which features the Kariba Dam, the largest man-made reservoir in the world. Image by Anton Ivanov on Shutterstock.

leaders approach the topic of reforming it, for example. Politicians who would prefer to disband the NHS and introduce a private system of healthcare have often been forced to pursue more modest reforms because to go further would be unpopular with many voters. This means that to make fundamental changes to the NHS, its opponents will likely need to build a coalition of thought leaders – newspaper editors, civil society leaders, social media influences – to change the way that British people think about the NHS and what it represents.

> ### Reflective question
>
> Do you agree that institutions (rules) can only legitimately change when ideas change?

Making sense of interests

Second, ideas help people to make sense of what is in their interests. We may imagine that our interests are purely rational and our ideas are subjective. But, as we have said, this is not true. Indeed, some scholars argue that there is no such thing as material interests, only *perceived* interests, based on how we interpret our material reality (Hay, 2011). In sum, ideas shape what we think we need.

In Timor-Leste, the veterans who fought in the independence struggle against Indonesia have elevated status in society and receive many benefits from the government, including cash transfers and scholarships for their children's education. There is a powerful narrative valorising the veterans which works in the interests of the veterans themselves, and many politicians who also participated in the independence war. Other citizens, including pregnant women, mothers and people with disabilities also receive cash transfers from the government, but the amounts are much lower than the veterans' payments, leading to equity concerns. This uneven distribution of funds is difficult to contest as the veterans' right to receive high levels of government assistance is deeply embedded in Timorese society, and, as a result, some of those who are in effect discriminated against do not perceive the situation to be unjust or against their own interests (Pruce et al., 2023).

This is a two-way street, of course, because our existing understanding of our interests shapes what ideas we think of as being most acceptable. To return to Zambia, those who are most opposed to cash transfers are often wealthier and hence do not stand to gain from them. The strongest resistance to cash transfers came from former Minister of Finance, Ng'andu Magande, who had worked his way up from a poor background in a Zambian village and believed that others should be able to do the same. This is not to say that all poorer citizens believe cash transfers are a good idea, but interests, based on personal experience, shape support for distinct policy positions.

Framing realities

Finally, ideas shape contestation by 'framing' situations in ways that persuade people to think or behave differently. To be successful, ideas have to be performed and framed in ways that appeal to and elicit sympathy and support from their intended audiences. Framing can make the difference between the success or failure of efforts to change institutions. In Jordan, for example, a coalition managed to introduce new legislation protecting women from domestic violence in a highly conservative society by avoiding a 'women's rights' frame and instead using a 'family frame' that appealed to the principles of Sharia, focusing in particular on the suffering of children and the elderly (Tadros, 2011).

Framing can be decisive in persuading ordinary citizens to see certain behaviour as right and appropriate, but this is not always easy to get right. Research by Cheeseman and Peiffer (2022) has found that anti-corruption messages are often ineffective and, in the worst cases, can backfire and increase people's willingness to pay a bribe. The reason is that many of the messages employed by international donors and government anti-corruption agencies raise awareness about how bad a given situation is. A classic example would be 'we need to stop corruption because it is so rampant that it is undermining public finances'. The intuition behind this message is clear: if we can only persuade people that a situation is important, we can persuade them to behave 'better'.

Yet this intuition is often wrong, because it fails to factor in how human psychology works. Such anti-corruption messages implicitly tell people that many of their fellow citizens are not following the rules. This creates a risk that those receiving the message will deduce, consciously or unconsciously, that it is socially appropriate to do the same. Such messages may also trigger individuals to think that the problem is so big that it is intractable. The appropriate thing to do, therefore, may not be to join the fight against corruption, but rather to 'go with the flow'. This is why the narrative frames used to change ideas have to be carefully considered – otherwise they may backfire and fail to achieve their goals.

Summary and conclusion

This chapter has analysed the power of ideas in the politics of development. It is impossible to provide a complete account of the politics of development – the process of contesting alternative desired futures – without factoring in the ideas of citizens, leaders, and bureaucrats. We have seen that interests and institutions matter, but also that people must have *ideas* in order to form their interests and the institutions they operate within. Indeed, ideas shape not only our interests and institutions, but also what we think the rules *should* look like. In the same way that different kinds of maps highlight certain features of the landscape and obscure others, the ideational lens provides a particular way of viewing the world. For example, it underlines the deeper meanings and value that people wish to attain in their lives, beyond instrumental or material rewards.

We may think that ideas are all in the mind, but they have real causal effects on individual and collective choice and agency. They shape how problems are identified and understood, define acceptable solutions to them, and determine the choices that people can make, as well as when those choices are taken away.

Ideas do not become powerful by osmosis, but because they are actively embedded and reproduced by people in the pursuit of power. Ideas are functions of power relations in three key ways: by imposing ideas on others (power *over*), persuading others to adopt ideas (power *through*) and constraining the options of what is feasible (power *in* ideas).

The power of ideas means that they are often used strategically in contestations over who gets what, when, how. Changing institutions, or the rules of the game, implies also changing the underlying ideas that create and sustain them. It implies using ideas to shape how people interpret their interests. And it implies framing desired futures, and their particular value to society, in ways that will appeal to these interests.

Discussion questions

- Think of a global development challenge – for example, the learning crisis discussed in Chapter 1. What are the ideational causes and dimensions of this challenge?
- How do ideas become developmentally consequential?
- Which of the three ways that ideas matter for contesting development do you find most compelling, and why?
- Now that you have reached the end of our three 'I's chapters, what is the relationship between interests, institutions, and ideas? Why do we need all three?

Suggested further reading

Mehta, J. (2010) 'The Varied Roles of Ideas in Politics: From "Whether" to "How"', in Daniel Béland and Robert Henry Cox (eds), *Ideas and Politics in Social Science Research*. Oxford: Oxford University Press. Ideas and Politics in Social Science Research | Oxford Academic (oup.com)

Schmidt, V.A. (2010) 'Taking ideas and discourse seriously: explaining change through discursive institutionalism as the new "fourth" institutionalism', *European Political Science Review*, 2 (1): 1–25.

Part 3
Change-makers: government, market, people, donors

6 Are some governments better than others?

Democracy, authoritarianism, and developmental states

Nic Cheeseman

Image 6.1 Marina Bay, the heart of the financial district of the 'East Asian Tiger' of Singapore. Image by marcobrivio.photography via Shutterstock.

Learning outcomes

- Understand the difference between democracy and authoritarianism, and what it means for a country to become more and less democratic.
- Critically evaluate whether these terms are useful when explaining development outcomes.
- Assess the extent to which states are able to shape development outcomes in the modern world.

Is democracy necessary for alternative desired futures?

Democracy is a political system in which, at least in its ideal form, power is held by the people, who can select the government and vote it out if they think another leader or party can do a better job. In the 1990s, democratic ideas and institutions appeared to be in the ascendency, following the collapse of one of the world's most prominent authoritarian states, the Soviet Union. But that was deceptive, and the last twenty years have seen a pronounced period of democratic erosion – the transfer of power from citizens to governments who rule through the use of force rather than the consent of the people. So how does this influence the pursuit of development?

The short answer is that there is no short answer. A loss of political rights clearly has worrying implications for human rights and the ability of citizens to live free of repression and censorship – or, as we described in Chapter 1, development as 'freedom'. Yet if we focus on the ability of citizens to achieve improvements in their economic conditions, things are less clear. Researchers and political leaders have spent many years disagreeing about whether democracy is needed to fuel innovation and growth, or whether the best way to enable development is to shift power to the state, removing checks and balances so that the government can get things done. Authoritarian regimes free leaders up to make decisions without having to compromise, but this can enable them to abuse their authority. Democracies disperse power more broadly, preventing any one group from dominating, but this can lead to continual compromises that stymie radical change. This chapter investigates what these trade-offs mean for developmental outcomes and how sustainable they are. Are poorer countries best served by authoritarian governments that can pursue rapid change, or democratic ones that prevent the abuse of power?

One reason for this controversy is that what looks like the most suitable political system may be different depending on where you live. It is easy to argue that democracy should be prioritised whatever the consequence when you are writing from a comfortable office in Birmingham. This trade-off might seem much more questionable to someone living in poverty in a country that has never provided sufficient jobs for its people. For citizens struggling to makes ends meet, the idea of a strong leader who can use their power to get things done can be very attractive, especially if the process of democratisation might exacerbate ethnic and social tensions.

This appeared to be the case in Mali in August 2020, when a military coup that removed President Ibrahim Boubacar Keïta – known as IBK – from power was celebrated in the streets by thousands of people. The sight of citizens welcoming the military overthrow of an elected president after his government lost popularity for failing to deliver either economic growth, or security from jihadi insurgencies, from jihadi insurgencies was taken by some commentators to imply that Malians had chosen authoritarian order over democratic uncertainty. Read in this way, events in Mali supported the argument of authoritarian leaders such as Rwandan President Paul Kagame that certain countries face so many challenges that they cannot 'afford' democracy. On this interpretation, the military had simply carried out the will of the people. For example, Ousmane Diallo, a protestor and former soldier, told the BBC (2020), IBK's fall meant that 'The people are victorious'.

Yet if we look a little deeper, it is less clear that this is what the people of Mali were signalling. One of the reasons that public anger had grown was that Keïta himself was accused of authoritarian practices, undermining his own democratic legitimacy. Many of those who went to the streets celebrated the coup not because they wanted an efficient authoritarian future, but because they hoped that it would lead to a transition to a more genuine and effective democratic political system. In his interview with the BBC, Diallo went on to state that 'the military should not be thinking now that they can stay in power'.

This chapter explains the options facing citizens like Diallo. It asks whether governments and the states they control still have the potential to shape development in the era of globalisation (a government is the particular system and leaders who hold political power in a given state, while a state is the broader set of political and economic institutions that shape the distribution of power - see Chapter 3: 54). It shows why we need to go beyond the binary of democracy vs. authoritarianism. It explores which kinds of government are best placed to effect rapid economic transformation, which generate inclusive and sustainable economic gains, and how we can prevent the abuse of state power.

The evidence suggests that on average democracies tend to do better than authoritarian political systems on social indicators such as education and healthcare. But the chapter also demonstrates that some of the greatest economic transformations of the last fifty years have occurred under authoritarian governments. This complex reality means that regime type does not tell us that much about how effectively a government can realise the hopes, dreams and desired futures of its people. What really matters is finding political institutions and ideas that empower the state to play an effective role in promoting development, while ensuring that leaders are incentivised to limit the extent to which power is abused. This 'sweet spot' is not the preserve of either democratic or authoritarian systems.

Can states drive development as they could in the past?

Over the last thirty years, media, policy-makers and academics have become increasingly preoccupied with the question of whether government control of the state has become less important in the face of powerful international actors and global forces. This focus is rooted in the idea that globalisation has reduced the significance of state borders and structures by undermining the capacity of leaders to protect their citizens from wider economic trends (Stiglitz, 2017). A good example is the difficulty many governments have had in managing inflation after the Russian invasion of Ukraine in 2022 disrupted global food supplies and so increased food prices.

In the economic sense, globalisation refers to the growing interdependence of the world's economies and is marked by lower barriers to the movement of goods and people, higher levels of international trade, and greater integration among customers and businesses in different countries due to new technology. The rise of populist leaders promising to take back control of the economy – from the European Union, global markets, or international financial institutions – has often been explained as a response to popular frustration with the way global trends can shift jobs from one country to another, and change the make-up of societies through immigration (Bajo-Rubio and Yan, 2019).

Yet while it is clearly true that the choices governments face are bound by forces beyond their control, this does not mean that the state is irrelevant. As Linda Weiss (1998) has argued, not only can governments make important decisions about how far the free market is allowed to determine the direction of the economy (see Chapter 7), but the influence of external pressure is itself shaped by the strength of domestic economic and political institutions. This point is well illustrated by the variation in tax policies that exist across different states today. Facing the same global economy, countries such as Sweden have far higher levels of taxation than countries such as the United States (Figure 6.1).

This policy difference has a tremendous impact on citizen's lives. In the US, citizens pay lower taxes and so may think of themselves as having greater control over their finances than their Swedish counterparts. They also, however, receive fewer services from the state, and have weaker safety nets to catch them if they hit hard times. Moreover, the US government has less scope to redistribute wealth from the rich to the poor in order to give a greater

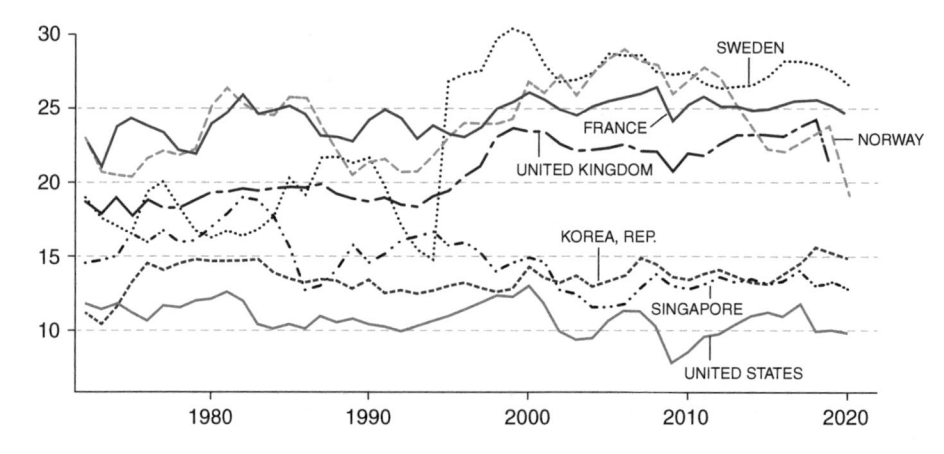

Figure 6.1 Tax revenue as a percentage of GDP in selected countries, 1975–2020
Source: Created by the author from data collected by the World Bank (2023).

proportion of society financial security, which can leave them extremely exposed to economic chocks (Albiston and Fisk, 2021).

These differences matter not only to how citizens live their everyday lives, but also to how able governments are to protect less wealthy citizens from the changes generated by globalisation. Thus, far from globalisation rendering the state obsolete or impotent, the capacity and willingness of governments to intervene in the economy productively will continue to play an important a role in shaping who gets what, when and how in the future. In turn, this raises the question of how different kinds of political system encourage different kinds of development.

Reflective question

Are states less powerful today than they were in the past?

Beyond Democracy vs. Authoritarianism

In general, the headline conclusion of cross-national studies that investigate the effect of the political system on economic performance is that democratic governments have the edge when it comes to economic growth (Calagrossi et al., 2020). While some authoritarian governments perform better than their democratic counterparts, the dire performance of many military regimes and one-party states drags down the average. Democracies often struggle to outperform the best authoritarian states, but are less likely to experience economic and political disasters (Przeworski et al., 2000). In this sense, the type of government does matter.

Simplistic comparisons between democratic and authoritarian states may obscure as much as they reveal, however. Averages can be misleading. Imagine three centre-forwards in a football team, one who always scores five goals a game, one who always scores one goal a game and one who scores none. The average goals per game for the three forwards is two, but if we went to a game and bet money on any one of the forwards scoring two goals, we would lose our stake. The performance of authoritarian states on development is a little like this: some perform extremely well, and some perform very badly, and the average – which sits in the middle of the two – does a poor job of capturing either dynamic. Indeed, there is as much variation between the most and least effective authoritarian governments as there is between democracies and autocracies overall.

We therefore need a more nuanced approach. Even if democracies perform best on average, for example, it could still be the case that more hierarchical political systems have advantages in delivering rapid economic transformation. This is clear from the fate of the Sustainable Development Goals, and in particular Goal 1, which is to end poverty everywhere. Modest progress has been made towards this goal, but what is remarkable is that 75 per cent of the reduction in global poverty over the last 40 was achieved by just one country – China. By maintaining a strong focus on a broad-based economic transformation, and adopting targeted policies designed to improve living standards in areas of endemic poverty, the Chinese Communist Party government lifted an incredible 800 million people out of poverty (Liu et al., 2020). For all of this period, China was a not only a highly authoritarian state, but actually experienced a decline in the quality of political liberties (VDEM, 2023).

Another reason that we need to move beyond simplistic comparisons between democratic and authoritarian states is that the distinction between the two is often much harder to draw in practice than it is in theory, as set out in Box 6.1.

Box 6.1 Democracy and authoritarianism: theory and practice

- *Theory*. Theoretically, the distinction between democracy and authoritarianism is clear. Democracy requires governments that are 'of the people, by the people, for the people', and in its modern incarnation this involves citizens voting for the party and leader they prefer through a variety of different electoral systems. Direct democracy, in which citizens meet *en masse* to make decisions, has mostly died out, as it requires too much time for modern life. Most countries therefore practise representative democracy, in which citizens elect individuals to represent them in the legislature. Another key principle of contemporary democratic rule is that power should be balanced – for example, between an executive, legislature, and judiciary. Many democracies also have a specific bill of rights or constitutional provisions designed to protect the rights of minorities. By contrast, authoritarian governments hold power through force. Although they may be popular and pursue policies designed to boost their legitimacy, their ability to retain control is founded on the repression and control of dissent. This usually involves censoring the media, making opposition parties illegal, and deploying the security forces to harass and detain critics. A legislature and a judiciary may exist, but they lack independence from the government and so power is not dispersed but rather centralised under the ruling party and executive.
- *Practice*. In practice, relatively few countries are either full democracies or complete autocracies. Instead, they exist on a broad spectrum between the two, and often include elements of both democratic and authoritarian practices (Levitsky and Way, 2002). We know this because over the last fifty years, many indices have been created to try to measure how democratic (or otherwise) countries are, including the 'Freedom in the World' ratings from Freedom House, the Democracy Index of the Economist Intelligence Unit, and the Varieties of Democracy (VDEM) dataset. These indices usually generate their overall rating, such as VDEM's 'Electoral Democracy Index', by giving countries a score for how they perform in a range of different aspects of democracy: Are multiparty elections held? How free and fair are they? Do citizens enjoy a full set of political rights and civil liberties? Take a look at Table 6.1, which shows some (but not all) of the indicators that VDEM takes into account. The scores

for these variables are then combined into an index, which in the case of VDEM runs from 0 (least democratic) to 1 (most democratic). When countries are evaluated in this way, it turns out that more countries are in the middle of the spectrum (i.e., around 0.5) rather than at the extremes (0 and 1).

Table 6.1 Some of the indicators included in VDEM's Electoral Democracy Index

Theme	Indicator
Freedom of expression	• Level of government censorship
	• Harassment of journalists
	• Level of media bias
	• Freedom of discussion for men
	• Freedom of discussion for women
Freedom of association	• Are any parties banned?
	• Barriers to parties operating freely
	• Degree of opposition parties' autonomy
	• Are multiparty elections held?
	• Civil society repression
Voters	• Percentage of population with suffrage
Clean elections	• Electoral management body autonomy
	• Level of election vote buying
	• Level of election government intimidation
	• How free and fair are elections?
Elected officials	• Is the lower chamber of the legislature elected?
	• Is the upper chamber of the legislature elected?

What this means in practice is that in regions such as post-communist Europe, South Asia and sub-Saharan Africa, almost all states hold elections, but they often do not lead to political change because leaders have worked out how to manipulate them. As Cheeseman and Klaas (2019) have argued, many contemporary leaders hold elections in order to gain legitimacy and access to international financial assistance, but manipulate them to such an extent that they are unlikely to lose power. These 'counterfeit democracies' typically deny citizens political rights and civil liberties, and prevent the emergence of an independent media and judiciary that might hold the government to account. To reflect this, they are given names such as 'electoral-authoritarian' or 'competitive-authoritarian' (Levitsky and Way, 2002) to indicate that they combine elements of democracy and authoritarianism. In turn, the fact that so many states are neither fully democratic nor fully authoritarian means that these labels are of limited help to understand the relationship between political institutions and development.

Indeed, a better question is what kinds of authoritarian political system, and what kinds of democratic systems, are best suited to promoting rapid economic transformation and inclusive and sustainable development?

> **Reflective question**
>
> What aspect of democracy is most important to you? Free speech? Multiparty elections? The right to join any organisation you choose to?

Which type of government is the best placed to deliver rapid economic transformation?

Responding quickly and decisively to major challenges is important for governments, especially those with a weak infrastructure, limited economic activity and large numbers of unemployed. For example, post-independence states that had to deal with colonial legacies of underdevelopment often felt that they could not afford to develop slowly because they would fall further behind other countries. Citizens are also unlikely to be patient if they lack the basic requirements for a healthy life. Think about how willing you would be to wait for a long-term process to slowly lift you out of poverty if your children were forced to drink dirty water, you had no electricity, and healthcare was unaffordable.

This sense of urgency was well captured by President Julius Nyerere after Tanganyika (later Tanzania) gained independence in 1961, when he told his people that 'we must run while others walk' (Akanle and Adésìnà, 2018). Nyerere argued that this meant that Tanzania could not afford the disagreements and disunity that he claimed democracy, and more specifically political competition between rival parties, would bring. This idea proved to have tremendous resonance, especially in Tanzania and other newly independent African states. It was one of the main justifications that Nyerere presented for introducing a one-party state, in which opposition parties. By preventing disagreements over who should be the government, a single-party system would be more efficient.

> **Reflective question**
>
> Do you agree that at times it can be legitimate to prioritise building state capacity over democratic processes?

A similar intuition lies behind research that suggests authoritarian regimes may have advantages at low levels of development. Perhaps one of the most influential versions of this argument is the large literature on the 'developmental state' (see Box 6.2). In the words of Thandika Mkandawire (2001: 2), developmental states were distinctive for their capacity to implement economic policy wisely, with this capacity rooted in a variety of: 'institutional, technical, administrative and political factors'. This strong focus on the capacity of development states to drive long-term change naturally encouraged an emphasis on state power rather than democratic constraints.

Box 6.2 The developmental state

A 'developmental state' refers to a specific type of government that promotes rapid economic growth and development. It is often associated with the economic success of countries such as South Korea, Singapore, Japan and Taiwan. These political systems were characterised by a strong central authority and the use of state intervention to direct economic activity into productive areas and protect infant industries until they become internationally competitive. In its most generic sense, developmental states emphasise the achievement of long-term development as a primary goal (Mkandawire, 2001).

Scholars such as Öniş (1991), however, have also highlighted specific features that are common to successful developmental states. These include a long-term economic plan designed and funded by the state, 'a developmental discourse dominated by the need to industrialize and the role of the state in fostering industrialization, the exclusion of the majority of the population, and a highly institutionalized public sector bureaucracy' (Schneider, 1999: 278). East Asian developmental states were also 'characterized not only by a high degree of bureaucratic autonomy and capacity, but also by the existence of a significant degree of institutionalized interaction and dialogue between the state elites and autonomous centers of power within civil society' (Öniş, 1999: 123). This enabled politically dominant governments to drive development without being distracted by elections, while ensuring that they faced some constraints to prevent the abuse of power.

This tendency was exacerbated by the belief that focusing on long-term goals meant giving the bureaucracy a degree of autonomy from short-termist political pressures, and hence insulating the government from social pressure such as trade union demands for higher wages. Responding to these demands would mean abandoning fiscal discipline and strategic goals in order to satisfy the short-term needs of influential constituencies such as urban workers. While democracy empowers such demands by making governments compete for popular support in regular elections, authoritarian political systems weaken them. As Jose Maria Maravall (1994) has put it, 'The proauthoritarian theses rest on the argument that dictatorships enjoy a greater political capacity and a higher level of insulation from particularistic demands than do democratic regimes'. Indeed, some researchers have identified its autonomy from social pressures and short-termist political calculations to be the most fundamental feature of the developmental state (Öniş, 1991).

Although some foundational thinkers did not argue that democracy was inherently inimical to the emergence of developmental states, others did (Maria Maravall 1994). A classic argument along these lines ran that voters and in particular poorer citizens were likely to oppose the reallocation of resources from consumption to investment needed for capital accumulation, forcing governments to compromise on their long-term goals. Another held that dictators were better placed to make and enforce decisions quickly, and thus overcome collective action problems both inside and outside of government, while rejecting populist pressures to prioritise short-term needs over long-term growth. A similar argument has been recently made by Dambisa Moyo (2018), who has written that 'democracy doesn't deliver' because 'endless elections, unqualified leaders, uninformed voters, and short-term thinking are impeding economic growth'.

Where political institutions are compromised and leaders are incentivised to engage in clientelism and patronage around elections by prevailing social norms, as discussed later in Chapter 12, political competition and the desperation to win an election can drive corruption, vote buying, and worse (Cheeseman and Klaas, 2019). In low-quality multiparty systems, the combination of low levels of political trust and winner-takes-all political dynamics – in which citizens worry that if their party loses power they will be denied access to state resources and services – means that electoral competition can intensify inequalities and tensions between different ethnic groups and classes. This is particularly significant, because Frances Stewart (2000) has shown that an important driver of political conflict is the growth of horizontal inequalities, when pronounced differences in wealth and opportunity emerge between rival ethnic, religious or regional groups (see Chapter 11). Not only does this mean that some citizens enjoy a much worse quality of life that others, but it has also contributed to election violence in countries such as Côte d'Ivoire, India, and Kenya.

Even when this does not happen, media bias, disinformation, and the simple short-term desires of citizens to have a better standard of living now, rather than in the future, can lead to problematic policy. Many of the world's most established democracies, for example, have routinely failed to take the measures required to tackle climate change due to the significant cost it would impose on voters (Willis, 2020). This is also true for other 'future' problems, such as ensuring that governments have sufficient resources to fund the pensions of today's workers. Taken together, these claims imply that centralised and authoritarian kinds of government may have advantages when it comes to both maintaining political stability and long-term economic planning.

Yet, as we shall see, the evidence actually demonstrates that most authoritarian states have not managed to achieve this, and – contra Moyo – are more corrupt than their democratic counterparts. In turn, this demonstrates that the type of political system that exists is not always a useful guide as to the prospects for development (see Box 6.3).

Box 6.3   Are voters the problem?

Moyo's complaint about 'uninformed voters' reveals a hidden assumption about developmental states – the idea that leaders and technocrats know best what is right for a country, and that allowing citizens to have a say can just get in the way. This is well demonstrated by the beliefs of Lee Kuan Yew, Prime Minister of Singapore between 1959 and 1990. Lee was both a founding father of his country and a key inspiration behind its economic approach, having led the campaign for independence. In power, Lee presided over the remarkable transformation of Singapore from a 'small port town' into a 'global financial hub' (Alam, 2015). During this period, GDP per capita increased from US$428 to US$11,860, as the country moved from being 'low income' to 'high income'.

One of the most striking things about Lee's tenure was his willingness to speak bluntly about how he achieved this. In an interview with *The New York Times* in 2010, he said he 'had to do some nasty things, locking fellows up without trial'. This was not something he was apologetic about, however. In 1998, looking back on his time in office, he reflected on whether democracy would have better suited his country. He concluded that the idea of asking the people what they think was 'childish rubbish. We are leaders. We know the consequences. You mean that ice-water man knows the consequences of his vote? They say people can think for themselves? Do you honestly believe that the chap who can't pass primary six knows the consequences of his choice when he answers a question viscerally on language, culture and religion?' (Han et al., 2015: 134).

Lee remains hugely popular in Singapore, where his party is still in power. Yet in many cases where leaders have not used their authority to promote long-term economic growth, it is precisely the democratic checks and balances that he derided – including competitive elections – that have constrained the abuse of power by the government and driven better developmental outcomes.

China is perhaps the most famous contemporary example of a country that appears to have benefitted from an authoritarian development model, but it is not alone. Some of the fastest growing economies of recent years include Djibouti, Ethiopia, Rwanda, and Saudi Arabia. Going back a little further, many of the biggest economic success stories of the 1970s and 1980s occurred under authoritarian systems in countries such as Singapore, South Korea, and Taiwan. Although they are very different countries in terms of their histories and size, these 'East Asian Tigers' employed a similar set of policies to drive rapid development. However, our understanding of why these countries enjoyed success has shifted over time. Initially, the dominant view was that their growth was based on an export-orientated growth model fuelled by empowering the private sector and opening up to the free market. In other words, the emphasis was placed on policies that were consistent with neoliberal orthodoxy, as the World Bank and IMF sought to use the success of these governments as a poster child for the Washington Consensus (see Chapter 7).

This changed rapidly in the mid-1980s when researchers such as Alice H. Amsden (2001) and Chalmers Johnson (1995) challenged the idea that economic success came from having a small state and an unregulated market. Instead, they told a very different story, emphasising the extent to which economic transformation depended on states playing a central role in managing the impact of domestic and international market forces. Effective developmental states invested heavily in education, infrastructure and specific areas of the economy to promote rapid industrialisation. As part of this approach, they also provided subsidies and protection to businesses operating in sectors the government wished to encourage, enabling them to grow in size, strength and productivity before exposing them to international competition.

The state-led nature of this development model was critical to its success, because it generated a new comparative advantage for these countries in important emerging markets such as electrical goods and information technology (Kohli, 2004). Without this, Singapore, South Korea, and Taiwan would have been stuck with the economies they had in the 1950s, which were predominantly based on agriculture. This is a weak foundation for transformative economic growth, because the economy is dependent on the price of exports on world markets, with most jobs being relatively low skilled, while 'value added' activities, such as manufacturing is done in other countries. An effective and interventionist state was therefore central to the development of the modern dynamic economies that have given rise to some of the world's best known brands, such as Acer, Hyundai, LG, and Samsung. In turn, industrialisation contributed to rapid economic growth, creating higher skilled and higher paid jobs.

Although there is some debate about how necessary authoritarianism was to this process, there are a number of ways in which it facilitated these developments. First, economic transformation required governments to pursue a long-term plan over many years. While successive democratically elected governments could have agreed to implement similar policies, it is also possible that elections would have brought to power parties and leaders with a very different vision, leading to an inconsistent approach. The repression of organised labour also meant that there were no powerful trade union groups representing workers who could use their influence – for example, by going on strike – to force the government to prioritise short-term concerns over long-term plans (Kohli, 2004). In this sense, the effectiveness of East Asian developmental states could be said to have depended 'on the destruction of the left and curtailment of the power of organized labor plus other popular groups' (Öniş, 1991). This would not have been possible in a democracy, where government policy is more likely to be responsive to demands for subsidies and protections for workers and non-strategic sectors of the economy, undermining global competitiveness.

Reflective question

Do you agree that the effectiveness of the East Asian model could not be replicated in a democracy?

Many of the authoritarian states that are currently promising to deliver long-term growth to their subjects have also been called 'developmental', including China, Ethiopia, Rwanda, and Tanzania. It is not always clear, however, that they merit this title. Some lack the 'institutional, technical, administrative and political' capacity or the autonomy from social pressures and short-termist political pressures this implies, while others have not pursued classic developmental state goals such as industrialisation. The increased use of the term 'developmental state' may therefore reflect the fact that it became a popular idea and reference point among policy-makers and the media, and should not be taken as evidence that there are actually more development states today than in the past. As Laura Routley (2014) has argued, 'the ephemeral, buzzword, nature of the concept of developmental states' highlights how the concept has become 'utilised in ways that are unexpected and come to mean different things in different contexts'.

With great power comes great responsibility

Efficiency, and the ability to implement long-term plans, is not only about making and implementing decisions quickly and consistently. It is also about avoiding waste. One of the challenges for all governments – and particularly authoritarian ones with weaker checks and balances – is minimizing corruption and the diversion of state resources. While corruption can thrive under any political system, there are good reasons to think that it may be particularly problematic under authoritarian rule. In the absence of a free media and independent judiciary, there is no one to expose and punish corruption, and public pressure is easier to ignore. It is therefore not surprising that, according to Transparency International's Corruption Perception Index, all of the ten most corrupt countries in the world are authoritarian. Meanwhile, all but one of the ten least corrupt countries in the world are democracies. The exception is Singapore, which is not fully democratic or authoritarian today, but sits between these two extremes (see Table 6.2), holding tightly controlled elections.

Table 6.2 Least and most corrupt countries according to the Corruption Perception Index, 2022

	Democracies	Semi-democratic countries	Autocracies
Top 10 least corrupt countries (listed in order, least corrupt first)	Denmark Finland New Zealand Norway Sweden Switzerland Netherlands Germany Ireland	Singapore	
	9	1	0
Top 10 most corrupt countries (listed in order, most corrupt first)			Somalia Syria South Sudan Venezuela Yemen Libya North Korea Haiti Equatorial Guinea Burundi
	0	0	10

This helps to explain why a critical factor in the evolution of an effective developmental authoritarian state is the presence of certain constraints that promote the balancing of power – and so limit the abuse of office – without undermining the autonomy of the bureaucracy. This kind of a system is essential, according to Öniş (1991: 124), to ensure that developmental states develop 'infrastructural power' in which a strong state implements 'policies through a process of negotiation and cooperation in society', and avoids 'despotic power' in which state elites abuse their positions and can easily start to implement flawed policies.

Such constraints typically fall under three headings: top-down discipline, limiting the size of the bureaucracy and the power of key government agencies, and maintaining a balance between military, bureaucratic, political, and economic elites. This set of factors is most likely to exist when institutions divide power between different actors, and this division is underpinned by a shared idea that stability and restraint is not only valuable but essential.

1   *Discipline*. Where discipline is concerned, the governments of East Asia were particularly committed to achieving their goals because they faced an external threat from nearby regimes, which encouraged them to perform well both in order to both legitimate their development strategy and protect their sovereignty. Put another way, the presence of an external threat encouraged a shared idea about the imperative of acting in the national interest, with rapid economic transformation understood as critical for national security. The government of Taiwan, for example, aspires to be an independent sovereign nation, but is still considered to be Chinese territory by the Chinese government. Becoming economically strong was therefore an imperative for the Taiwanese elite in order to be able to have the financial foundation to resist being reabsorbed into China.

2   *Limiting the size of the bureaucracy and key agencies*. The discipline described above helped to ensure that technocrats operated within constraints, despite being empowered to engage in long-term planning. One consequence of this was that the size and power of bureaucracies and government agencies did not become bloated and overstaffed in the way that they did in many one-party states elsewhere in Asia and in Africa. In turn, this made it possible to restrain the cost of the civil service and oversee its activities. When it came to key government agencies – such as the Economic Planning Board (EPB) in South Korea and the Ministry of International Trade and Industry (MITI) in Japan – they were empowered by giving them sufficient responsibility to enable them to drive industrialisation, but constrained by limiting the extent of their control over some aspects of economic and political decision-making.

3   *Maintaining a balance*. The constraints placed on key agencies helped to ensure that they did not become governments in themselves, and remained under the guidance of political leaders. This kind of balancing was complemented by another – namely, a willingness to share influence between military, political, bureaucratic and economic elites – as well as certain groups within civil society. Through a process of continual engagement and negotiation, all these groups came to support the focus on long-term

economic development, but also had a vested interest in preventing other groups from expanding their powers in a way that would enable them to dominate others. They therefore became that rare thing: self-restraining states. In turn, this helped to sustain discipline and maintain limits on the size and power of the bureaucracy and key agencies, which is why Singapore was able to emerge as one of the least corrupt countries in the world, despite Lee's distaste for democratic checks and balances (see Box 6.3). This is not to say that corruption did not occur in these developmental states – we know that it did – but it was relatively low and predictable, and so did not deter investors, or waste resources, to an extent that undermined economic transformation.

Another way of putting this is that what matters for economic success is not just whether a state is authoritarian and aims to be 'developmental', but whether it features internal institutional constraints and external drivers of discipline that limit the abuse of power. When these are not present, the absence of checks and balances in authoritarian systems can lead to 'despotic power', with negative consequences, including the repression of minorities, civil conflict, and political instability (Table 6.3). As Chipo Dendere (2021) has demonstrated, in countries such as Zimbabwe, corruption, economic exploitation and repression have gone hand in hand. On one hand, the ability of those in the ZANU-PF government to use their access the state to become wealthy gives them an even stronger motivation to retain power at any cost. On the other hand, the use of force to repress the opposition undermines political accountability, enabling poor quality and corrupt government to continue indefinitely. As a result, Zimbabwe has suffered hyperinflation, institutional decay, a cholera outbreak and the collapse of their currency, and is still ruled by the same party.

Table 6.3 Impacts of Constrained and Unconstrained Authoritarian Governments

	Classic examples	Common features	Consequences
Unconstrained authoritarian	• Democratic Republic of Congo • North Korea • Zimbabwe	• Lack of discipline and rule following at all levels • Bloated government and bureaucracy • Concentration of power in the hands of a small number of people	• High levels of corruption and graft underpinned by immunity for those in power • Higher risk of conflict and human rights abuses • Lower levels of economic growth
Constrained authoritarian	• Singapore • South Korea • Taiwan	• Disciplined government and bureaucracy • Limits on the size and cost of the government and bureaucracy • Balance between key agencies • Balance between military, bureaucratic, political elites and influential social forces	• Repression of organised labour • Limited corruption • Higher levels of economic growth

The case of Zimbabwe illustrates the dangers of 'authoritarian development': the conditions that came together in the East Asian cases rare, and so most authoritarian states lack strong internal constraints. It also suggests that authoritarianism may work better for development in some regions than others. In many sub-Saharan African states, for example, the tendency for power to be highly personalised in the president (Tapscott, 2021), along with the absence of an external threat to foster agreement on the idea that economic transformation is necessary for national survival, has given rise to a particularly inefficient and dysfunctional form of authoritarianism (Chang and Golden, 2010).

Although Rwanda has managed to maintain a high level of discipline comparable to the East Asian experience under the firm grip of President Paul Kagame – perhaps in part due to the fear of a repeat of the 1994 genocide in which over 800,000 people were killed – his country is the exception rather than the rule. In sub-Saharan Africa more broadly, a majority of the most authoritarian states experienced some form of armed conflict in 2022, compared to none of the continent's high quality democracies (Africa Centre for Strategic Studies, 2021). In line with this, Takaaki Masaki and Nicolas van de Walle (2015) find that there is a large gap in performance between democracies and authoritarian states in Africa, with democracies achieving significantly higher levels of economic growth.

Which types of government deliver the most inclusive and sustainable development?

How efficiently a government can act is only one way to think about how political factors can shape development. Another is how inclusive and sustainable the development process is. Sustainability is important to make sure that short-term gains are not lost through conflict or mismanagement. Inclusion is important to ensure that development gains are fairly shared across a population, and because human beings value being included in the decisions that impact their lives (for a detailed discussion of inclusion, see Chapter 11).

Considerable research now suggests that inclusion and sustainability are actually linked. Giving individuals and groups a stake in political and economic institutions provides them with an incentive to defend them, and so reduces the prospects for social conflict and political instability (Lijphart, 1999). The most influential version of this argument was made by Daron Acemoglu and James Robinson in their book, *Why Nations Fail* (2012), which we introduced in Chapter 3. In addition to having greater political durability, they argue that inclusive institutions have also been shown to have a positive effect on economic growth. More specifically, they suggest that long-term progress is more likely when economic institutions encourage broad investment in physical capacity, technology and human capacity. In turn, inclusive economic institutions are more likely to emerge when political institutions create effective constraints on power-holders, limit rent seeking by those in power, and allocate power to groups with an interest in broadly conferring and protecting property rights. When this happens, Acemoglu and Robinson argue, countries grow faster because inclusive economic institutions drive greater investment, education, and public goods provision.

Inclusive institutions are not exactly the same thing as democracy, because they refer to a broader range of economic institutions 'that allow and encourage participation by the great mass of people in economic activities that make best use of their talents and skills and that enable individuals to make the choices they wish' (Acemoglu and Robinson, 2012: 74). Nonetheless, Acemoglu and Robinson are clear that the inclusive institutions that they refer to are common features of democratic political systems. This explains why they find that 'Democratization increases GDP per capita by about 20% in the long-run'.

Growth is a crude measure of development, however, so it is important that a large body of research has also found that democracies have an advantage in the provision of public services (Chapter 11). To see how inclusive political institutions can provide political leaders with incentives to deliver the services citizens need, and contribute to a process of democratic strengthening – let us look at the case of Ghana. In the early 1990s, Ghana appeared to be a poor prospect for either democratisation or sustainable development. The country had experienced a series of coups since independence and was ruled by a populist autocrat in J.J. Rawlings, nicknamed 'Junior Jesus' due to his charismatic appeal. GDP was just US$ 5.96 billion in 1993, the year after multiparty elections were introduced, not that much higher than the US$ 2.20 billion in 1960. Yet, as pressure grew for democratisation (Cheeseman, 2015), Rawlings proved willing to introduce political institutions that were both robust and had a degree of independence from the executive. This meant that when he stepped down in 2000 having exhausted presidential term limits, it was possible for the opposition to win power. Despite a number of major election controversies, repeated transfers of power and improvements to the political system subsequently built trust between rival parties and meant that elections did not generate the negative side-effects described by Moyo. In 2023, Ghanaian GDP stood at over US$77 billion, a dramatic increase since 1993.

Better still, despite ongoing worries about clientelistic and corrupt politics both inside and outside of parliament, close elections drove a spirit of accountability, as voters demonstrated their willingness to 'kick the bums out', to use that famous phrase. Ahead of the 2016 Ghanaian elections, for example, voters in the Volta region put up signs that read 'no lights, no votes'. The signs were a message to the ruling National Democratic Congress (NDC) government that it should not assume that it could rely on their votes if it failed to deliver on promises of electrification. The warning turned out to be prescient. Despite being known as the 'World Bank' of the NDC due to the significance of its support to the party's prospects, voters in Volta played a critical role in facilitating a transfer of power to the opposition New Patriotic Party (NPP). While historic loyalty and ethno-regional voting patterns meant that few NDC voters could be persuaded to actually vote for the NPP, many stayed at home, making it easier for the opposition to win the presidential election.

Image 6.2 Voters gather at the tolling booths during the municipal elections in Cape Town, South Africa in 2011. Image by ImageArc, via Shutterstock.

The transfer of power did not necessarily mean that voters in Volta got their lights, of course. The new government's power base outside of the region generated an incentive to direct resources elsewhere. But there is evidence that even poor quality elections can drive better service delivery. Robin Harding and David Stasavage (2014) show that the reintroduction of multiparty elections in Africa in the early 1990s shifted the incentives facing political leaders, and encouraged them to pursue policies that were popular with voters such as introducing free education. In this way, the change in political institutions was quickly followed by the introduction of free primary education in no less than 16 countries, with 11 of these cases happening soon after an election. This helps to explain why democracies, and in particular elections, have so often been found to improve education and health outcomes (Wang et al., 2019).

This does not mean that either elections or democracy are a panacea, however. Another limitation of elections is that not everyone is included equally. When Alexis de Tocqueville wrote about the remarkable political equality in the United States in the 1830s in his famous book *Democracy in America*, neither Native Americans nor the 15 per cent of the population held as slaves enjoyed the vote. Although these groups now do have the ballot, they still face greater barriers to using it almost two hundred years later: '[US] states have put barriers in front of the ballot box – imposing strict voter ID laws, cutting voting times, restricting registration, and purging voter rolls. These efforts . . . have kept significant numbers of eligible voters from the polls, hitting all Americans, but placing special burdens on racial minorities, poor people, and young and old voters' (Brennan Centre for Justice 2022). Democracies may also be exclusionary in other ways. Women often face greater barriers to election than men, including prejudicial social norms, physical intimidation, and online abuse, and the vast majority of legislatures are male dominated, including those of the US and UK. The benefits of inclusion are therefore not experienced by all countries that hold elections, or by all citizens, but only by those meaningfully included in government processes.

Reflective question

Has your country moved towards or away from democracy in the last five years?

Summary and conclusion

Political institutions shape development outcomes, but not in a simplistic way that can be reduced to whether a government is democratic or authoritarian. Democracies tend to perform best on average, but often struggle to effect rapid economic transformation. While elections focus the minds of political leaders on the hopes and desires of citizens, polls can be manipulated, and the need to chase votes may lead to short-termist policies and a tendency to ignore future challenges. Authoritarian regimes may have advantages when it comes to resolving collective action problems, and have achieved some of the most remarkable developmental gains of the last fifty years. Unless authoritarian elites are disciplined and face internal constraints, however, their governments are prone to become corrupt and abusive.

It is therefore important to recognise that we need to go beyond these labels to ask how we can empower the state to promote rapid development while reducing the risk that this power will be misused. This is most likely when the government is disciplined enough to pursue a long-term vision, strong enough to build consensus around the strategy for achieving that vision – either through persuasion or coercion – and inclusive enough that developmental gains can be sustained.

Whether a political system is good at delivering growth and public services is of course only one measure of its worth. Development also includes the ability of citizens to make meaningful choices over their lives (Sen, 1999). Democracies may have mixed developmental records, but they enable citizens to learn, be creative, and speak truth to power. Many authoritarian governments, on the other hand, not only repress their citizens with force, but also practise widespread censorship and discriminate against minority groups. If you live in a democracy and do not consider yourself to be very 'political', you may think that living under an authoritarian system would be manageable. But the reality is that in the world's more repressive regimes, every aspect of your life would be different. Even politically apathetic citizens in these countries have to self-censor what they say on a daily basis because anything other than effusive support for the government can make you a target of suspicion. Imagine living in a country where you would be too scared even to read this book, because being caught with it could lead to you being thrown in prison.

The process of democratic backsliding that we have seen over the last twenty years is therefore a major concern. In 2023, only 8 per cent of the world's population lived under a fully democratic political system. If current trends continue, this figure will fall even lower, while the number of authoritarian governments increases rise. This matters, because only a small proportion of those who are forced to live under authoritarian rule will enjoy the benefits of a developmental state. For the vast majority, there will be no economic gains, only the erosion of their basic human rights. This should serve as an important reminder that it is only when the state is empowered to lead on development, while simultaneously being constrained to avoid the abuse of power, that we are likely to see transformative improvements in the quality of life enjoyed by citizens.

Discussion questions

- What kinds of goods and services do you think democracies are likely to be better at providing? And where might authoritarian political systems have an advantage?
- Is it ethically acceptable to trade off human rights for economic development? If it is, where would you draw the line between what is and is not acceptable?
- Do you think that countries benefit from having different kinds of political systems at different stages of their economic development?

Suggested further reading

Acemoglu, D., Johnson, S. and Robinson, J.A. (2005) 'Institutions as a fundamental cause of long-run growth', *Handbook of Economic Growth*, 1, 385–472.

Mkandawire, T. (2001) 'Thinking about developmental states in Africa', *Cambridge Economics*, 25 (3): 289–314.

7 Should markets rule?

Economic policy, international financial institutions, and free trade

Bizuneh Yimenu

Image 7.1 Front view of a cargo ship. Image by Alex Kolokythas Photography via Shutterstock.

> ## Learning outcomes
>
> - Trace the historical development of the concept of free trade and the contestation between free trade and interventionist policies.
> - Examine the influential ideas, interests, and institutions behind the promotion of the market by global institutions.
> - Evaluate the rationale behind the implementation of interventionist policies for economic development.

The power of markets

A market is a system that facilitates the exchange of goods and services between buyers and sellers. In simple terms, it refers to any physical location or virtual platform where transactions occur, from street vendors to established companies, to international markets and the institutions that govern them. From a global development perspective, markets matter because they help individuals meet their daily needs, companies expand their business and reach new customers, and countries access a wider range of goods and services. The resources and wealth that are produced and distributed can enable or constrain people from realising their desired future.

Classical economists have long studied markets as politically neutral, transactional structures of exchange. Adam Smith and David Ricardo argued that free trade – the international exchange of goods and services between countries – benefits every nation. In this account, all countries needed to do to benefit from this system was develop a specialisation, a comparative advantage, or an absolute advantage when trading in the market (see Box 7.1). When all states do this, they argue, free trade increases production and hence economic welfare for all.

In reality, though, markets are never neutral. From a political perspective, the opportunities to specialise, trade, and develop comparative advantage are uneven and ultimately driven by interests. Free trade was not promoted in the interests of all, but to favour wealthier states who stood to benefit more. Powerful states promoted free trade ideas as a compelling economic logic, while also using their influence and sway to force other states to accept the policies and institutions it required. Colonialism left indelible legacies which compromised the capacity of many countries to compete globally. Domestic markets, too, can be designed to include or exclude, to open or close doors to economic prosperity for all. In the classic Marxist critique, capitalist forces are responsible for the reproduction of harm in society by repressing labour, and commodifying human life. On this view, the market is not 'free' but a mechanism of enslavement.

Another critic, the economist and philosopher Amartya Sen (1999), argued that the instrumental focus of free trade arguments on economic growth should be replaced by a much broader focus on improving a wider range of human freedoms, including freedom of opportunity and freedom from poverty, suggesting that we should come to see development as freedom. These critiques point to central problems with the free market approach, but it is also important not to lose sight of the role that markets have played in enabling many people to escape poverty, and the desire of many people to work, or trade, their way to a more prosperous future.

This chapter examines the political drivers and dynamics of the market. It asks whether empowering 'the market' can bring about development, and to what extent politics should tame free trade. We begin by exploring in greater depth how markets create winners and losers, and the role that colonialism played in creating the contemporary global economic order. We ask whether free trade can really promote desired futures, or whether it is dominated by interests that will consistently reproduce inequality. The policies pursued by governments, and the considerations that shape them, are key to determining whether the potential harmful effects of the market can be curbed. We end the chapter, therefore, by asking to what extent the state should intervene in the economy.

Box 7.1 Market winners and losers

- *Comparative advantage* is an economy's ability to produce goods and services at a lower opportunity cost compared to other countries. This means that they can specialise in the goods and services that they are best placed to produce and trade with other countries to purchase what they are less efficient at producing. In theory, everyone benefits.
- *Opportunity cost* is the benefit lost when choosing one option over another from the missed opportunity of the option not being taken. So if a country produces cars, then the opportunity cost is that those same resources – labour, finance, materials – could have been used to produce, say, computer chips or sailing ships.
- *Absolute advantage* refers to a situation in which a country, individual, or organisation can produce a particular good or service more efficiently than another country, individual, or organisation.

How markets create winners and losers

Markets may sound technical, but they are institutions that also contain complex, multilayered power relations. Like any other institutions that determine who gets what, when, and how, they can create winners and losers. Take the idea of 'opportunity costs', for example (see Box 7.1). This term refers to how many units of a product a country has forgone in producing one unit of another product they intend to sell on. Suppose in South Africa that one hour of labour produces either five pairs of jeans or ten bottles of wine, while in the United States the same labour hour can produce either 20 pairs of jeans or 20 bottles of wine. This means that the US has an *absolute* advantage in making both products, because it can make them cheaper. South Africa, in this scenario, is not in a powerful position to make and trade jeans, which raises the question of why should the US bother trading with South Africa at all.

According to Ricardo, the two countries still benefit from trading with each other by producing the goods on which they have a comparative advantage. In South Africa, the opportunity cost of one pair of jeans is two bottles of wine (10 divided by 5) while the opportunity cost of one bottle of wine is half a pair of jeans (5 divided by 10). By contrast, in the United States the opportunity cost of one pair of jeans is one bottle of wine while the opportunity cost of one bottle of wine is one pair of jeans. This means that the opportunity cost of making a pair of jeans is lower in the United States, while the opportunity cost of making wine is lower in South Africa. According to comparative advantage theory, the US should produce and export clothes, while South Africa should specialise in wine exports. The situation benefits many people as both countries can enhance their overall welfare by focusing on producing and trading goods based on their respective comparative advantages, resulting in efficient resource allocation and increased economic prosperity.

These ideas subsequently became internalised, institutionalised and promoted by global actors like the World Trade Organization (WTO), World Bank, and International Monetary Fund (IMF) – highlighting the dynamic interplay between ideas and institutions (see Box 7.2 for a discussion of the theoretical foundations of free trade and the mercantilist thinking it replaced). As a result of the support and actions of these prominent actors, these arguments gained influence and recognition, solidifying the interconnectedness between the world of ideas and institutions on the global stage. This was particularly significant because while free trade principles can lead to overall economic gains, they also generate winners and losers. Advanced economies tend to benefit relatively more from free trade as they are better placed to take advantage of the opportunities it creates than poorer economies.

Box 7.2 What is free trade?

Free trade emerged to challenge the dominant economic thinking of the day: mercantilism. Mercantilism is a theory that dominated European economic thought from the sixteenth to the eighteenth centuries. It revolves around the idea that a nation's wealth and power are primarily determined by the accumulation of precious metals, particularly gold and silver. Mercantilist policies – often protectionist – aimed to promote exports, restrict imports, and achieve a favourable trade balance to strengthen economic and military might.

The origins of mercantilism can be traced back to the European Renaissance period. Key thinkers such as Thomas Mun, Jean-Baptiste Colbert, and Richard Cantillon developed and promoted mercantilist ideas. It emerged as a response to prevailing economic theories, including the 'bullionist' emphasis on metal accumulation and the 'scholastic' focus on ethical considerations.

Mercantilism has faced criticism for its exclusive focus on accumulating precious metals, neglecting productivity and innovation in economic development. Protectionist policies associated with mercantilism are viewed as limiting the benefits of free trade and global cooperation. With the rise of classical economics and free trade advocacy in the eighteenth and nineteenth centuries, mercantilism's influence diminished. Nevertheless, certain aspects, like protectionism, retain relevance in contemporary economic theories, industrial policies, and development strategies.

Free trade challenged this protectionist thinking and refers to the exchange of goods and services in the absence of protectionist measures such as import and export taxes. It is generally associated with governments that hold economically liberal positions and advocate lower levels of state involvement in the economy. Classical economists such as Adam Smith and David Ricardo argued that free trade was broadly beneficial to all. On this logic, if all states trade freely, and at the same time develop a specialisation in products that they can produce at a lower opportunity cost than their partners, more products are produced and states become wealthier.

According to the World Trade Organization, the core principles of free trade are:

1) *Trade without discrimination:* a country should not discriminate between its trading partners (giving them equally 'most-favoured-nation'), and it should not discriminate between its own and foreign products, services or nationals (giving them 'national treatment');
2) *Freer trade:* trade barriers coming down through negotiation;
3) *Predictable trade*: foreign companies, investors and governments should be confident that trade barriers (including tariffs and non-tariff barriers) should not be raised arbitrarily; tariff rates and market-opening commitments are "bound" in the WTO; and
4) *More competitive:* discouraging "unfair" practices such as export subsidies and dumping products below cost to gain market share. (WTO, 2023a).

While colonised states enjoyed some economic advantages, such as cheaper labour, they also often lacked the infrastructure, technological capacity and investment resources to compete effectively with larger, more advanced companies. This meant that firms and businesses that were exposed to fierce international competition before they grew to become large enough to generate efficiencies from operating at a larger scale were often put out of business. When this happens, advanced economies may flood developing markets with cheap goods, undercutting domestic industries before they have a chance to develop, leading to job losses and undermining processes of industrialisation. Thus, although free trade can support growth and reduce poverty over the long run, its short-term distributional impacts can be particularly harsh on vulnerable populations. Given this, the desire of wealthy states to promote free trade has been critiqued for not only maintaining, but in some cases intensifying global economic inequalities.

Latin American countries such as Brazil and Colombia, for example, were encouraged to implement trade liberalisation and import tariff cuts in the 1980s and 1990s. The tariff cuts were highest in unskilled labour-intensive industries; here, firms tried to survive competition from foreign industries by cutting wages, undermining living conditions. Indonesia's continuous reduction of and removal of import tariffs since early 1990 led to a similar reduction of workers' pay (Pavcnik, 2017). Meanwhile, in India, import tariff reduction and elimination during the 1980s and 1990s led to a decline in primary school turnout in districts with liberalised firms as compared to other areas. Edmonds et al. (2009) demonstrate that this particularly impacted on girls, who were more likely to be pulled out of school to perform tasks for families struggling to cope with the resulting pay cuts due to gender norms that favoured boys' education (for more on gender norms, see Chapter 10).

It is therefore important to consider the impact of a market-driven economy on social inequality around the world (Kantola and Squires, 2012), and to address the destabilising consequences of the kinds of economic adjustment that may occur when free trade policies are introduced. Offsetting negative side effects such as a decline in salaries or job losses is important, not just for ethical reasons, but also because pushing large sections of society into poverty can generate economic and political instability with negative consequences for a wide range of development outcomes.

The reality of free trade policies is therefore more complex than their advocates sometimes admit. In theory, open markets support overall economic growth. In practice, however, rapid trade liberalisation has uneven impacts that can exacerbate inequalities within and between countries. These problems are exacerbated by the fact that although institutions like the IMF and World Bank push developing nations to adopt free trade policies – sometimes as conditions for aid or loans (see for the power of ideas, Box 7.3) – wealthy countries do not always stay true to these principles themselves. For example, there has been a pattern of wealthy states protecting certain industries such as agricultural products, clothes, and footwear, while advocating unfettered openness to poorer trading partners (Subramanian and Wei, 2007). This often closes off opportunities for less wealthy countries to access new markets and hence to begin to overcome the colonial legacies to which we now turn.

How colonial legacies impact contemporary markets

How did colonial powers benefit from the trade institutions they created? The extractive institutions created by colonial powers and the idea of mercantilism had a profound impact on the global economic hierarchy (Box 7.2). Mercantilism was based on the notion that the global supply of wealth was limited, and it was in states' best interest to accumulate as much as possible. In line with this, European states like Britain and France focused on maximising exports and minimising imports to achieve a favourable trade balance, where exports exceeded imports. Early mercantilist states therefore pursued imperialist policies, establishing colonies to extract raw materials for processing and manufacturing, enabling them to amass wealth through a positive trade balance. Through this process, colonial powers became richer by shifting surplus value from their colonies to themselves.

In the case of Britain, trade relations were deliberately designed to enable the metropole to specialise in manufactured goods, with African and Asian economies set up to provide the primary commodities this required. This meant that the 'value added' economic activity took place in Europe (Nayyar, 2013), while colonised economies were deliberately underdeveloped, dependent on the sale of low value exports. One consequence of this was that colonised economies remained closely tied to the price of raw materials on world markets, and hence particularly vulnerable to the kind of rapid increases and decreases in these prices that can be a product of free trade. This system was so iniquitous that even the costs of constructing it were pushed onto the colonies. Consider the railways built to facilitate the transport of materials from India to Europe. The railways were built by British private investments, but with harsh regulations guaranteeing a 5 per cent return on the investment. If this target was not met, India had to generate tax revenues to cover the gap, such that the costs in effect fell on the Indian people themselves (Bogart and Chaudhary, 2019).

Once this system had been constructed, free trade policies were firmly in the interests of the European colonial powers. Although a combination of economic depression and economic nationalism contributed to the expansion of protectionist strategies during the First World War, after the Second World War states began to reduce tariffs and this process continued as countries in Africa and Asia began to gain independence. A decline in information and communication costs, technological advancement, improved productivity, the integration of Eastern Europe and East Asia into global markets, and the rise in international cooperation all contributed to increased global trade (see Figure 7.1). At the same time, powerful states and international institutions advocated for a rules-based trading system globally. The Bretton Woods institutions, the IMF, with a focus on ensuring a healthy global monetary system and macroeconomic policies, and the World Bank, with a focus on long-term investments, were formed in 1944 to promote integration, and strongly backed free trade. This was also true of the General Agreement on Tariffs and Trade (GATT), established in 1948, and its successor, the World Trade Organization, in 1995. According to Subramanian and Wei (2007), GATT/WTO facilitated global trade in an economically and statistically significant way, causing world imports to rise by approximately 120 per cent (equivalent to US$8 trillion in the year 2000 alone) compared to a scenario without the presence of the WTO. These changes

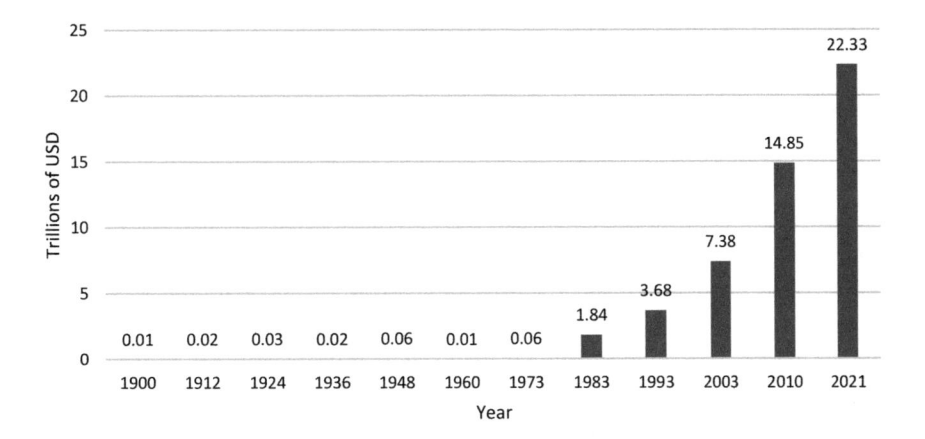

Figure 7.1 World Exports (1900–2021)
Source: Compiled from UN (1962) and WTO (2023b, 2011).

occurred due to the accession of several countries to the GATT/WTO and the organisations' active promotion of import tariff reductions.

After the 1970s, global trade flows doubled every decade and increased yearly except in the global financial crises of 2008–9, when exports declined globally by 23 per cent in 2009 compared to the previous year, but then jumped again by about 22 per cent in 2010 (WTO, 2011: 20). The impact of trade expansion, however, was uneven. Developed states witnessed a significant increase in trade, but the same was not true for many colonised economies (Subramanian and Wei, 2007). Some countries that had previously been at the 'periphery' of the world economy were able to trade their way to development, but only after empowering the state to take steps to protect infant industries and foster new comparative advantages (see Chapter 6). In many more cases, however, the governments of poorer states struggled to maximise the potential benefits of trade liberalisation because their infant industries were not competitive with those of wealthier firms and companies abroad. This has left many African and Asian countries in a similar position to the colonial era, exporting natural resources and then buying back higher value manufactured goods from wealthier states. Against this background, the kind of rules enforced by bodies such as the WTO effectively prevent historical patterns of exploitative trade from being effectively addressed, adding additional barriers to the transformation of the global economy.

Reflective question

How do imbalances in the global economy produced by colonial power dynamics shape lived realities?

Who is promoting free trade and free markets?

The central role of the IMF, World Bank and WTO in promoting free trade over the last seventy years raises a number of important questions. Who controls these institutions? What policies do they pursue, how are they formulated, and in whose interests do they operate? This section goes into greater depth on the IMF and the World Bank, while the next one addresses the role of the WTO.

With over 190 member countries, the IMF relies on funding contributions (quotas), which determine voting influence. European countries collectively hold a significant portion of the total quotas, while the United States's share of funds is 16.5 per cent, followed by Japan's 6.14 per cent and China's 6.0 per cent (IMF, 2023a). The IMF is therefore unlikely to make decisions that go against the interests of the United States, and is susceptible to pushing policies that are in its interests, such as market liberalisation. IMF officials have also been trained in orthodox economics and so tend to believe that trade liberalisation is the best way to enable Least Developed Countries (LDCs) to reduce poverty, integrating them into global markets. This combination of ideas and interests helps to explain why LDCs approaching the IMF have repeatedly been asked to engage in reforms that remove trade tariffs and duties. Many governments in Africa and Asia have been reluctant to introduce these changes, but have needed the financial and non-financial support the IMF and World Bank can offer to address issues such as high levels of debt and economic recovery. IMF approval is also important because it is often taken as a signal of a government's credibility by a slew of secondary lenders. This is where the power politics comes in. By making their support conditional on reform, the IMF and the World Bank effectively leverage the economic weakness of poorer states to drive measures that would not otherwise have been adopted. Desperate for funds, poorer countries accept the reforms in order to access the funds (Sengupta, 2009).

From the mid-1970s onwards, for example, many African states experienced economic difficulties due to an increase in the cost of oil and a fall in the value of their main export crops, which had a particularly severe impact on the imbalanced economies left by colonial rule. They therefore began to approach the IMF and the World Bank in large numbers to request economic assistance (Akinola, 2021). Frustrated with the poor performance of early investments, the IMF and World Bank increasingly began to impose conditions on financial assistance, culminating in the insistence that countries implement a policy package called a Structural Adjustment Program (SAP). SAPs included measures such as cutting public spending, devaluing the currency, liberalising foreign trade, and allowing market-based resource allocation. These policies were therefore controversial as they both caused considerable hardship and prevented governments in new democracies from responding to the demands of their electorates.

In addition to promoting free trade, SAPs sought to harness the power of the market within countries – for example, by breaking down inefficient monopolies and fostering competition between companies in order to drive innovation. To reduce government expenditure and control over the economy, the World Bank therefore advocated the privatisation of state assets. There were significant problems with this recommendation, however. First, in countries with high levels of corruption the process was often manipulated to transfer state resources into private hands at low prices, effectively making political elites rich at the expense of their citizens (Szeftel, 1998). Second, where assets were sold for their real value, a lack of local capital meant that they were often purchased by corporations in wealthier states, enabling them to expand their global reach. These trends were exemplified in Chile, which had 570 state-controlled companies in 1973 and only 24 in 1983 due to a spate of privatisation. Many of these companies ended up in the hands of a small number of 'large economic family-owned conglomerates', concentrating economic power in 'only a few hands' (Goldfajn et al., 2021: 122). Third, the need to focus on profit rather than service delivery meant that new companies faced fewer incentives than their state predecessors to be inclusive of minorities and vulnerable groups, including poorer citizens. In this way, privatisation often served not only to perpetuate inequalities, but also to exacerbate wealth disparities, both domestically and internationally.

The impact of privatisation was therefore shaped by how well designed the process was, and whether it really created more choice for consumers rather than further concentrating wealth and control (Cuervo and Villalonga, 2000). In certain cases, well-planned processes spurred economic growth. For instance, telecommunications privatisation facilitated phone and internet access expansion in parts of Africa, such as Ghana and Kenya, leading to heightened tele-density and investments. Additionally, Brazil's 1990s railroad privatisation lowered accidents, enhanced service quality, and boosted freight and passenger volumes through improved infrastructure (Sampaio and Daychoum, 2017). At the same time, however, Arnold (2022) notes that this process in Brazil also saw employees in privatised firms suffer a significant wage decline of about 25 per cent compared to state-owned enterprise counterparts, as new companies facing the pressure of competition cut wages and streamlined operations.

These examples of the potential costs and benefits of privatisation highlight the way that politics can be both an obstacle and driver of development. According to Estrin and Pelletier (2018), privatisation was more likely to work when it was meticulously planned through strong regulatory institutions in a context of effective competition law and governments determined to minimise waste and corruption while considering the need for social safeguards to protect citizens during periods of transition. The problem in the 1980s and 1990s was that these conditions did not hold in many of the countries forced to embark on painful reform processes, and without these conditions there is no guarantee that private ownership will deliver either efficiency or quality.

A lack of attention to context was also a criticism levelled at the Washington Consensus, a prescriptive set of policies that emerged in the late 1980s as a response to perceived failures of state-led development policies in developing countries during the 1970s and 1980s. In search of a new approach, international financial institutions and policy-makers advocated market-oriented reforms, economic liberalisation and budget cuts to spur economic growth and attract foreign investment (Gill and Law, 1988). Precisely because the Washington Consensus suggested a common reason for a lack of economic development, and a common solution, it has been criticised for failing to take into account the specific challenges and opportunities in different countries.

Box 7.3 The Washington Consensus

The Washington Consensus emerged in the late 1980s and early 1990s as a set of economic policy prescriptions supported by international financial institutions and the United States. The term was coined by economist John Williamson in 1989 and quickly caught on around the world. It refers to a set of policies backed by the IMF, World Bank, and the US Treasury to address the macroeconomic disorder and debt crisis in Latin American and African countries during the 1980s. The consensus was to promote economic liberalisation, market-oriented reforms, and fiscal discipline in what were called 'developing' states.

Critics argue that the one-size-fits-all approach of the Washington Consensus did not consider diverse country conditions, potentially resulting in increased inequality and social dislocation. Moreover, strict fiscal discipline undermined public investment. Over time, the influence of the Washington Consensus has diminished, in part because its policy prescriptions yielded mixed results. Policy-makers and economists now recognise the significance of institutional factors, governance, and social inclusiveness for sustainable and equitable development. The approach has therefore become more flexible and pragmatic, although civil society groups in countries that receive IMF and World Bank support continue to complain about the impact of the conditions they advocate on poverty and inequality, as in Zambia in 2023.

One factor that shaped the effectiveness of this reform agenda was the extent to which changes were actually implemented by recipient governments. In many countries, the state-led development described in Chapter 6 had been the norm and governments were reluctant to enforce policies that would make them unpopular with citizens. According to Goldfajn et al. (2021), the *Partido Revolucionario Institucional* (PRI), a party that had ruled Mexico for six decades, opposed Washington Consensus policies because they threatened their economic interests and were also viewed as an attempt by the US to increase its control over Latin America. Brazil also implemented reforms half-heartedly. Partly as a result, the impact of these measures rarely delivered economic growth and stability. For example, Mexico embarked on a period of restructuring following its 1982 economic and financial crises, but then suffered another crisis in 1987, with inflation reaching 157 per cent. There were success stories, however. Chile executed IMF and World Bank sponsored reforms more effectively, yielding macroeconomic gains. It is important to note, however, that the growth that Chile achieved through implementing liberal economic reforms brought with it the unequal distribution of these benefits, leading to disparities in access to healthcare and education, as well as uneven sectoral development.

Reflective question

Do you think that you are based in a country that was disadvantaged or advantaged by the Washington Consensus?

In summary, the effects of privatisation and free market policies in developing countries were complex and controversial. While trade liberalisation and private sector growth can aid economic development if implemented sensitively and in an appropriate institutional context, this has rarely been the case. Legally, regulatory gaps and weak oversight institutions meant that programmes of privatisation were open to abuse. Politically, legacies of state-led development, elite interests in state-owned enterprises, and perceptions of foreign imposition combined to create incentives for government to resist implementation.

The institutions of Global Trade

As previewed above, the creation of the General Agreement on Tariffs and Trade (GATT) in 1948, and its successor institution, the WTO in 1995, played an important role in promoting free trade ideas. These institutions were important because they both advocated for a specific economic vision while having the power to discipline less powerful governments and hence push them towards trade liberalisation. To fully understand the role of GATT and the WTO, however, we need to put them into their appropriate context, which is the emergence of the US as a leading actor in global trade during the First World War. The US Tariff Act of 1930, also known as the Hawley-Smoot Tariff Act, had increased import duties by about 20 per cent in a bid to protect American businesses negatively affected by the stock market crash of 1929. More than two dozen other states subsequently did the same in retaliation, significantly increasing global protectionism.

Two years later, the Tariff Act was blamed for preventing a quicker recovery from the depression, in part because it harmed US exporters. During the 1932 presidential election, presidential candidate Franklin D. Roosevelt capitalised on growing public dissatisfaction with the Tariff Act, actively campaigning against it. Once elected, Roosevelt appointed Cordell Hull, who was passionate about free trade, as secretary of state. In less than two years, Hull had prepared the Reciprocal Trade Agreements Act (RTAA), which reduced tariff levels and encouraged free trade, and Congress subsequently approved it (Gill and Law, 1988: 127–55). In this way, shifting ideas about the kind of economic policy that was most in America's interests, and the transfer of control over key political and economic institutions to a new government, led to a change in economic approach that had global ramifications.

The RTAA galvanised a new fashion for setting trade tariffs through bilateral negotiation rather than unilateral state laws, invigorating the importance of institutionalism, a global governance system based on negotiation and cooperation. The RTAA also set a precedent for trade liberalisation that became integral to world order after the Second World War. Some of the articles used to establish the GATT, for example, were taken from the RTAA, demonstrating the centrality of US leadership to the institutional apparatus that was to govern world trade. Although the Global Agreement to eliminate or reduce quotas, tariffs, and subsidies was only signed by 23 countries when it was introduced, it was subsequently expanded and refined over the years. By the time the World Trade Organization (WTO) took over from GATT in 1995, it boasted 125 signatory states that covered about 90 per cent of global trade (see Figure 7.2 for WTO members and observers). Today, the WTO plays a central role in regulating market access, government subsidies, tariffs and duties, and arbitrating commercial disputes among nations (Broome, 2014: 139–53).

One of the notable achievements of the WTO was to establish the principle of trade without discrimination, known as the Most Favored Nation (MFN) policy, which means that once a country negotiates a tariff cut with other countries, this should be automatically applied to all members. Most nations adopted the MFN principle to set tariffs steadily in rounds of subsequent negotiations, creating a more harmonised global trade system. An escape clause allows countries to negotiate exceptions, however, if tariff cuts would particularly harm their domestic producers. Meanwhile, 'special and differential treatment' provisions allow wealthier

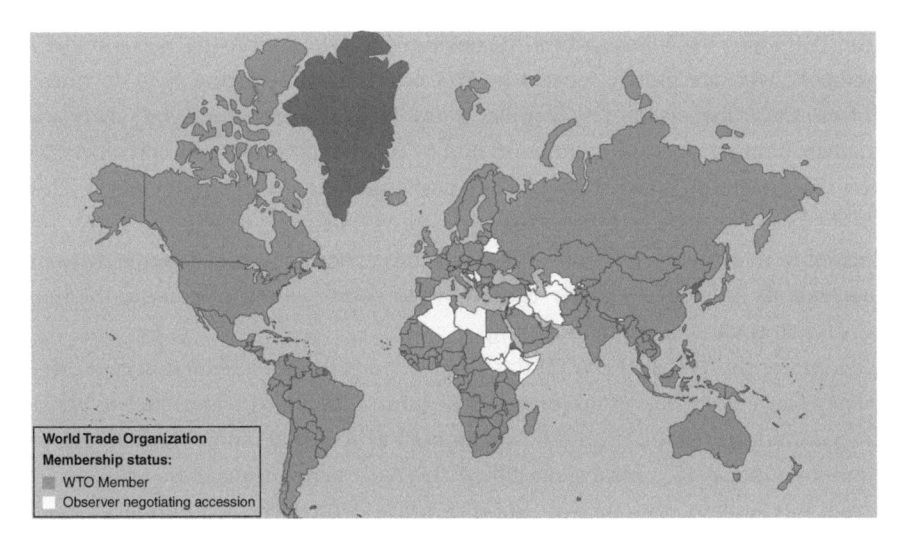

Figure 7.2 WTO members and observers
Source: WTO (2023d)

countries to treat poorer states favourably through extended agreement implementation periods, increased trading opportunities, safeguarding trade interests, and support for capacity-building in dispute resolution and technical standards implementation (WTO, 2004).

What has been the impact of this process? According to the WTO itself (2023c), there is a statistically significant relationship between free trade and economic growth. More specifically, lower trade barriers contributed to an average annual world economic growth rate of 5 per cent during the first 25 years after the Second World War. There are also other benefits – free trade can lead to lower prices for goods and services due to increased competition in a larger market. Countries can also import products they cannot produce or produce inefficiently, providing access to a wider variety of goods and services for consumers. Increased competition can encourage domestic businesses to become more efficient, innovative, and produce higher quality goods and services. When exports increase, this is also likely to create new job opportunities in those companies, while the WTO argues that the special and differential treatment provision has enabled wealthier states to actively discriminate in favour of their poorer counterparts. Additionally, trade creates interdependence among countries, which is why some liberals argue that trade promotes peace as countries become more reliant on each other economically, leading the countries to prefer trading to invading (Copeland, 1996).

Reflective question

Do you think promoting global trade relationships through trade liberalization is worth compromising on to support local industries through protectionist policies?

Yet the WTO also has many critics. An obvious limitation with the WTO model is that non-members, who are mostly located in Africa and Asia (see Figure 7.2), do not equally benefit from trade liberalisation by member states. This is for two reasons: 1) there are lower legal barriers to imposing import duties on non-WTO members relative to members; 2) WTO members often agree high tariffs on goods of particular interest to non-members. These disadvantages should provide non-members with strong incentives to join the WTO. Yet some are reluctant to do so because of concerns about the economic impact of agreeing to existing WTO agreements on reducing tariffs. Indeed, when poorer countries do join, the impact of membership on trade is often discouraging.

One reason for this is that the WTO has often failed to ensure a reduction of tariffs in sectors that are particularly important for nascent exporters in poorer states, such as agriculture, textiles, and clothing. As the US and EU retain high agricultural tariffs, for example, producers in other countries face insurmountable barriers to penetrating these markets – yet in many cases this is the main source of export earnings. Moreover, the Multi-Fiber Agreement established in 1974 imposed quotas on clothing and textiles which effectively prevented poorer states from exporting to their wealthier counterparts. This effectively 'bent' GATT rules that prohibited quantitative restrictions in order to protect jobs in wealthier states from countries in which workers were paid lower wages, and so would otherwise have been able to produce garments at a cheaper price. Such structural constraints created through negotiations among developed countries have been institutionalised and enforced by trade organisations, leading to complaints that overall the Global South often loses out. As Subramanian and Wei (2007) demonstrate, wealthier states have tended to reduce tariffs and other barriers on products produced and exported by industrial states, but not on some of the sectors of most importance to once colonised economies. As a result, other factors being equal, 'industrial countries' imports from developing countries are about 40% less than imports from other industrial countries' (Subramanian and Wei, 2007: 164).

The cumulative effect of these limitations is profound. Reflecting on the spread of free trade agreements between the European Union and the US signed during the 2000s with developing countries, such as Colombia and Peru, Stephanie Burgos, Trade Policy Advisor for Oxfam America, stated:

> Agreements such as the ones with Peru and Colombia will only exacerbate poverty in countries by imposing hardships on developing country farmers, making access to affordable medicines more difficult, and constraining the kinds of policies developing country governments should enact to protect their own citizens and fight poverty. (OXFAM, 2007)

A number of movements have emerged to try to push for changes to the system. For instance, the Group of 77 (G-77), representing the Global South developing countries, advocates for WTO reform (Toye, 2016). Similarly, the African Group brings together African countries within the WTO behind reforms designed to respond to the economic needs of the continent. Similarly, the Development Agenda Group (DAG), comprising developing nations, emphasises effective WTO reforms for trade policies to benefit the Global South. However, the fact that the most powerful international financial institutions are predominantly controlled by wealthy industrialised nations means that progress is slow, and will likely require changes in the way that such organisations are structured and run. Over the last thirty years, for example, the world's wealthiest countries have used strategies such as the 'special and differential treatment' clause to try to placate critics and defer pressure on more transformative change. The extent of the challenge was starkly illustrated during the COVID-19 pandemic, when it quickly became clear that the commitment of wealthier states to increase global access to goods and services did not extend to the distribution of vaccines (Box 7.4), despite the pressing health emergency.

Box 7.4   A pandemic of unfairness?

Following the outbreak of the global COVID-19 pandemic, scientists rushed to develop a vaccine that would protect people and enable life to return to normal. Yet despite clear evidence of a desperate need for vaccines in many countries around the world, global cooperation to make sure that they were available for all faltered at the WTO. Although India and South Africa introduced a proposal to facilitate mass production of generic vaccines at a low price that would have massively increased global access, this was blocked by wealthy countries such as Germany who effectively acted to protect the economic interests of their own pharmaceutical firms (Mercurio, 2021).

Brown and Rosier (2023) argue that despite rhetoric about vaccine equity, wealthy countries acted on their narrow self-interests by hoarding vaccine doses through direct deals with pharmaceutical companies rather than distributing equitably through COVAX, a worldwide initiative aimed at ensuring equitable access to COVID-19 vaccines. By May 2021, an apparent vaccine disparity had arisen, directly correlated with income. Dr Tedros Adhanom Ghebreyesus, the Director-General of the World Health Organization (WHO), termed this situation 'vaccine apartheid' (Reuters, 2021). The lesson of the COVID-19 pandemic was therefore that many powerful states that promote the institutions and ideas of free trade were unwilling to reduce national barriers to the distribution of key products when push came to shove.

Why markets don't work in everyone's interests

Current trade institutions go beyond traditional trade restrictions at the border, such as tariffs. They also cover wide-ranging domestic issues such as health and safety rules, investment, banking and finance, labour, the environment, and other areas with socioeconomic consequences such as exacerbating inequalities among citizens of the same country (Rodrik, 2018). Moreover, free trade creates the conditions under which Transnational Companies (TNCs) come to be global economic and political players in their own right. When these kinds of companies control similar levels of resources to state governments, and can deliver much needed jobs, they may also be able to constrain the choices available to the political leaders and citizens.

In the 1950s, for example, India wanted to build an oil refinery in partnership with international oil-producing companies. Instead, oil-producing companies conspired, demanding full ownership and rejecting state participation. The Indian government subsequently accessed some of the necessary technology from the Soviet Union in the 1960s, which enhanced its bargaining power, forcing oil companies to accept less than 100 per cent ownership (Gill and Law, 1988: 214). This example highlights the way that transnational companies can be important players in their own right. It also demonstrates the significance of countries having multiple potential foreign partners to engage with. In the 1960s and 1970s the Soviet Union, and more recently China, have offered alternative visions of economic development, pledging to impose fewer economic and political conditions in return for aid and investment.

The issue of the environment provides an excellent example of how governments, companies and international financial institutions can collude to put their own short-term interests first at the expense of sustainable development. One criticism of the WTO, for example, is that it has failed to prevent companies taking advantage of trade liberalisation to relocate their facilitates to countries with weak or rarely enforced environmental regulations. When this happens, companies benefit from being able to cut corners, the government not enforcing environmental standards benefits from an increase in investment which can be valuable come election time, but citizens and future generations can lose out as a result of environmental harms such as pollution.

Image 7.2 Pollution haze envelops the Selamat Datang statue in Jakarta, Indonesia, 2023. Image by Wulandari Wulandari via Shutterstock.

A good example is Glencore, a Swiss mining company, which Amnesty International (2020) has linked to water pollution and labour abuses in the Democratic Republic of Congo (DRC). The wealthy countries that house companies like Glencore are often complicit in this abuse because they fail to regulate their firms in order to enable them to be more competitive. Despite corporate responsibility to respect human rights under international law, no laws in Switzerland require multinational companies such as Glencore to conduct human rights and environmental due diligence, or enable them to be held accountable at home for their misconduct abroad.

Glencore is only the tip of the iceberg. Shell, the British–Dutch multinational oil company, has been accused of causing environmental damage that has undermined the livelihoods of people living in the Niger Delta, Nigeria. Although Shell has paid large sums to local communities in compensation, it has also sought to avoid being held legally responsible for the full economic cost of the environmental damage by arguing that complaints must be directed to its Nigerian subsidy, effectively insulating the head company from accountability.

In the most problematic cases, environmental damage, poor treatment of workers, and agreements in which companies pay limited taxes are facilitated by corrupt deals between companies, political leaders (in both the north and the south), and local business elites. A classic example of this is the recent scandal surrounding the billionaire French industrialist Vincent Bolloré, whose company was accused of funding the election campaigns of then Guinean President Alpha Condé and Togolese President Faure Gnassingbé in return for preferential treatment in the management of container ports. The Bolloré group, which is active in 46 African countries, ultimately agreed to pay a fine of €12 million as part of a deal with financial crime prosecutors in order to avoid a public trial after being prosecuted in France. When irresponsible businesses enter into these kinds of informal networks, reform can be particularly difficult because there are powerful veto players seeking to block it on all sides. The prosecution of Bolloré does demonstrate the potential to use the courts to punish transnational corruption, however, albeit with a fine that was a tiny proportion of the profits the company has made from its African operations.

Should governments intervene in markets?

Markets offer economic freedom and empowerment when harnessed and regulated rather than excessively controlled. They spur innovation, efficiency, and choice, benefitting entrepreneurs, small businesses, and consumers. Open markets encourage dynamism and opportunities. It is also true that state monopolies have often proved to be inefficient. We have also seen, however, how unfettered markets and collusion between businesses and political leaders can harm the public interest. Creating markets driven solely by a desire for profit maximisation can exacerbate inequality while also encouraging companies to cut corners to avoid fulfilling their environmental responsibilities. There are also other reasons for thinking that governments may wish to intervene in the market. As discussed in Chapter 6, many of the countries that made the greatest developmental gains in the 1970s and the 1980s began by protecting their infant industries. In other words, they employed tariffs to ensure that more competitive foreign companies did not put their nascent firms out of business, and over time developed a new comparative advantage based on strategic government investment. Japan safeguarded industries like automobiles and electronics, while South Korea and China maintained tariffs to protect strategic sectors and local employment (Haley and Haley, 2013).

This was also how most industrialised nations achieved their own development (Kindleberger, 1975). The United States, for example, was extremely protectionist in the nineteenth century as its manufacturing sector grew. High tariffs in the 1820s were important because they helped shield American infant industries from British competition. Moreover, as we have seen, the US still applies tariffs selectively in sectors like agriculture to protect domestic producers from imports. It is a similar story if we turn our attention to Europe, where the German Customs Union instituted tariffs to protect its fledgling industries in the nineteenth century. Thus, carefully targeted protectionism has often served to enable economies to continue to advance at vulnerable points in their development trajectory.

Protecting infant industries to enable them to grow is also important because it makes possible economic diversification. In turn, when an economy is less dependent on producing any one type of product, or exporting any one type of crop, it is less vulnerable to economic crises due to fluctuations in global demand for that export. As the then managing director of the IMF, Christine Lagarde, put it in a speech in 2017, 'We know that economic diversification is good for growth. Diversification is also tremendously important for resilience' (IMF, 2019). For instance, oil- and mineral-rich economies in Africa, Latin America, and the Persian Gulf have often attempted to strengthen their non-petroleum sectors in order to minimise their reliance on these natural resources. Doing this successfully is unlikely to be feasible in the absence of state-led interventions, not least because the high value of oil tends to lead to a country's currency accumulating, so that its other exports become less competitive.

Reflective question

In what ways can state intervention promote more equitable market outcomes?

There are other areas of economic life in which we might want governments to intervene to promote equity. Consider education, which is of critical importance both to an individual's prospects in life and to the health of the national economy. If education was only provided privately, so that children only went to school if their parents could afford to send them, this would intensify existing social inequalities because those with wealth could ensure that their children would get the best education, while the sons and daughters of poor families would not be given the skills and experiences needed to build successful careers. In cases like this, state intervention to ensure that all children receive a certain minimum standard can be viewed as distorting the market; but it could equally be said that unless the state intervenes, the market itself is distorted in a way that undermines both equality of opportunity and the skills base necessary to attract business investment. Government regulation can also generate its own challenges, of course, such as when public services are directed only at ruling party supporters, or reserved for a wealthy few. What is therefore required is for governments to strike the appropriate balance, regulating markets to promote public welfare while avoiding elite capture and corruption.

A further area in which state intervention may be beneficial is cases of market failure – i.e., situations in which private companies cannot, or have no incentive to, provide a service. To return to the case of education briefly, think about a poor rural area in which citizens have very little disposable income. Private companies delivering schooling would have little incentive to undertake the cost necessary to establish and maintain a school in such an area. It is the same for a number of important goods and services. In India, for example, the government operates the only railway network because only it can provide cheap services to taxpayers. Meanwhile, the fact that the vast majority of the millions of people who die every year due to malaria could not afford to pay the high price for a vaccine was a disincentive for pharmaceuticals companies to invest in this area. It was therefore only when private philanthropists such as the Bill and Melinda Gates Foundation stepped in to try to fill the void that hope for a scientific breakthrough began to increase.

Even those wholly committed to the free market both domestically and internationally therefore need to think carefully about the kinds of things that the market is likely to be unable to provide, or to be able to provide less effectively than the state. They also need to recognise that even the most effective markets may need to be supplemented with specific – and often state or civil society backed – mechanisms if they are to provide access to credit for those without capital, or to ensure that parents are able to take maternal or paternal leave. It is also important to keep in mind that in countries with high levels of corruption and weak regulatory systems, access to markets may depend in part on political ties with governing elites, revealing that the so-called 'free market' is actually invisibly – and iniquitously – politically regulated. All development, even the market, is political.

Summary and conclusion

This chapter has summarised the complex debate on free trade, state intervention in the market, and the influence of global economic institutions on policy-making. Classical economists argued that free trade, driven by specialisation and comparative advantage, benefits every nation by allowing them to focus on their strengths. Wealthy industrialised countries have championed these ideas through institutions like the WTO, World Bank, and IMF. Yet the reforms advocated by these bodies have often failed to generate economic prosperity, and their implementation has at times led to short-term increases in poverty and inequality, reducing people's ability to work towards their desired futures.

One reason for this is that existing free trade institutions do not protect all nations' interests equally. The continued use of protectionist measures to prevent free trade in areas such as agriculture, clothing and footwear undermines the ability of many poorer states to trade their way out of poverty. Yet they face continued pressure to implement market liberalisation because this is a precondition for financial assistance from institutions like the World Bank and the IMF. Moreover, countries that are now considered to be 'developed' used protectionist measures to safeguard their own economic interests at critical stages of their economic evolution. It is therefore easy to understand why many producers in poorer states believe that the kind of free trade model advocated by governments such as the UK and US is both unfair and hypocritical.

This does not mean, however, that the benefits of trade are not real or important. Access to both domestic and international markets has lifted millions out of poverty and facilitated economic development in countries such as Taiwan and South Korea. The choice is therefore not between free trade and a command economy, but between free trade models that sustain existing inequalities and those that allow for a redistribution of economic opportunities from North to South. Poorer countries should be encouraged to integrate into world markets, but they should also be allowed to protect their infant industries in the same way that wealthier states did in the past in order to diversify and break the cycle of exporting low-value goods. Markets should be empowered to encourage innovation and productivity gains through competition, but not at the expense of basic protections for citizens and workers, such as a minimum wage and decent working conditions. Privatisation can lead to better service delivery and reduce the ability of the government to manipulate the economy for political purposes, but is not always the answer, and must be well regulated to ensure that the benefits are not captured by a small number of politically connected individuals and families.

In other words, free trade is an important end goal, but state intervention can be beneficial to ensure that the market promotes the broader welfare of the population. Ultimately, then, the evidence of the last one hundred years suggests that neither entirely state-run nor purely private-sector models are optimal. Instead, a mixed approach that considers each country's unique context, and the challenges and opportunities for sustainable and equitable development, is likely required. The question this raises for the future is how, given the current distribution of wealth and power in the global economy, and within organisations like the IMF, World Bank and WTO, this fairer and more nuanced approach can be brought about.

Discussion questions

- How do institutions, ideas, and interests interact and shape the kinds of economic policies that a government pursues?
- What are the implications of privatisation when it comes to securing equitable access to services for all citizens?
- Some argue that a mixture of state-directed and market-driven policy is the most conducive approach to development. Do you agree?

Suggested further reading

Estrin, S. and Pelletier, A. (2018) 'Privatisation in developing countries: what are the lessons of recent experience?', *World Bank Research Observer*, 33 (1): 65–102.

Goldfajn, I., Martínez, L. and Valdés, R.O. (2021) 'Washington consensus in Latin America: from raw model to straw man', *Journal of Economic Perspectives*, 35 (3): 109–32.

Subramanian, A. and Wei, S.-J. (2007) 'The WTO promotes trade strongly but unevenly', *Journal of International Economics*, 72 (1): 151–75.

8 Power to the people?

Social movements, popular participation, and deepening democracy

Chris Lyon and Ellie Chowns

Image 8.1 People of Santiago mobilise against pereceived government indifference and repression, Chile 2019. Image by Antillanca via Shutterstock.

> ## Learning outcomes
>
> - Critically evaluate the extent to which people power can shape the pursuit of desired futures.
> - Understand the political dynamics of social movements, participation, and deepening democracy.
> - Analyse how power is claimed and contested by people through ideas, interests, and institutions.

People power: a pipe dream?

In late 1977, residents of the Vidigal neighbourhood of Rio de Janeiro began offering breakfast to street-sweepers from COMLURB, the state urban cleaning utility. The COMLURB employees would then remove, say, a single chair or bucket or some other relatively inconsequential item from the residents' houses and take it away in their rubbish-collection lorries. What was behind this strange ritual?

In the 1970s, Brazil was under a military dictatorship. Hundreds of thousands of people were evicted from Rio de Janeiro's favelas under a favela-eradication drive. The military police and COMLURB would arrive and begin destroying buildings and throwing residents' possessions into a rubbish lorry. The residents were then moved to rudimentary accommodation on the far outskirts of the city, with no access to vital services or amenities.

One day in October 1977, many of Vidigal's residents woke to find their doors marked with painted numbers indicating impending eviction and demolition. The residents' association, the AMVV, rose to the occasion (Nascimento, 2022). They secured the support of a Congressman to win a delay in the eviction. A friendly lawyer played ingenious games to obstruct the legal process. Pupils of a local school formed a human chain to block the rubbish lorries. And when the lorries got through, residents would invite the COMLURB cleaners in for *café da manhã*. Softened, the cleaners (themselves probably very low-income Brazilians) would remove the absolute minimum of possessions, technically complying with the legal order, but making the process grindingly slow.

Gradually, other supporters became involved – churches, academics, entertainers – and the AMVV became strong and well respected. It helped found similar organisations in other favelas, and carried out local development activities. Finally, in 1980, Pope John Paul II chose to visit Vidigal during his trip through Brazil, drawn by the AMVV's struggle and its relationship with the (Catholic) Favelas Pastoral Committee. This was the final straw. Even a brutal dictatorship couldn't be seen to destroy 'the Pope's favela'. The governor of Rio signed a decree halting the evictions. In the years since, the AMVV and residents have paved the streets, organised water supply, and built clinics and children's centres (Nascimento, 2022).

Of course, the years have also seen major challenges and disappointments. No human story is utopian. But the tale of Vidigal vividly illustrates the central themes of this chapter. Incredibly, an association of very poor favela residents faced down a military dictatorship – one that had little hesitation imprisoning, torturing, and killing many other opponents – and outlasted it. AMVV persists today. The regime, on the other hand, eventually crumbled under mass protests, leading – as we will see later – to an era of flourishing democratic experimentation.

The slogan 'power to the people' expresses an inspiring and evergreen rallying cry of popular mobilisations around the world and through history. As we have seen in Chapter 6 and 7, governments and markets can be unreliable in delivering inclusive systems of representation, accountability and a fair distribution of who gets what, when, and how. So can ordinary people take matters into their own hands?

While a tempting thought, the answer depends on the strength of the institutions 'the people' seek to contest, the interests vested in defending them, and the strength and embeddedness of the ideas that underlie them. 'People power' can only be won via the process of contesting *existing* power. This process might involve people taking to the streets to claim it directly, as in the case of Vidigal – power *from* the people, we could say. But it can also be written into formal institutions, devolved through participatory processes such as 'deepening democracy' – giving more power *to* the people. In this chapter we examine both forms (see table 8.1).

But is all of this just a naive and illusory pipe dream? Can social movements actually change things? Won't the powerful just manipulate orchestrated modes of 'popular participation'? To what extent can people power (re-)claim desired futures? We seek a critical understanding of when 'power to the people' rings hollow, and when it really does deliver on its exhilarating promise.

Why care about 'people power' in development?

'Power to the people' raises the prospect that more power might be held by the people. But who are they – and what is power? As we saw in Chapter 1, power can be understood in many ways: as coercive control and influence, as per Dahl (1957), or more diffusely, in the Foucauldian sense, as a micro-social force that shapes social norms and subjectivities. Particularly relevant here is Hannah Arendt's (1970) definition of power as 'the ability not just to act, but to act in concert'. This definition encourages us to recognise how power is also generated when people identify common interests and build collective strength to pursue them, including through participation in the political process.

The natural next question is: who *are* 'the people'? It's a deceptively vexing question. Ideas of who counts as 'the people' can be highly contested, or used to exclude particular social groups, as in reactionary strains of populism or xenophobic 'us and them' rhetoric. Moreover, 'the people' are, of course, not an undifferentiated mass, but rather, a population with highly diverse situations and experiences. As we will discuss in Chapters 10, 11 and 12, it would be a mistake to consider the people as a homogeneous category when not all people have equal access to resources, information, or the ability to participate in decision-making. Thus, claims to the mantle of 'the people' should always be critically scrutinised. For our purposes here, though, we understand 'power to the people' to be talking about people who are not elites. This means 'ordinary people', or 'everyday citizens', who are not already enjoying major societal power by virtue of high political office, economic resources, customary status, military roles, and so on.

History provides iconic examples where ordinary people gain or generate greater power in ways that have achieved desired futures, such as movements to expand the voting franchise, abolish the transatlantic slave trade, or gain access to food and land, resistance against caste systems, or struggles for women's rights. Inspired, in part, by such examples, 'participatory development', and related ideas such as decentralisation and citizen accountability, have been prominent agendas in contemporary development practice for several decades (Chambers, 1983; World Bank, 1999).

Both instrumental and intrinsic rationales for these things have been influential. Instrumentally, popular engagement is often seen as important to claim the material and non-material resources that people need to achieve their version of desired futures, whether in the form of land and water, or identity recognition, rights, and social justice. Advocates have touted the effects of people power on improved public services, reduced poverty, increased economic participation, and more efficient governance (Mansuri and Rao, 2013a: 1). For instance, community management of rural water supply has been widely adopted on this kind of instrumental rationale. The idea is that if communities themselves take the management of local resources into their own hands, it should be more efficient than if the state were to run them. On a very practical level, this is because communities have greater short-term (we might say, 'self-') interest in infrastructure running effectively, and, given this interest, will respond more quickly to broken pumps than bureaucrats sitting in distant regional capitals, with perhaps more pressing concerns.

Intrinsically, on the other hand, power to the people is often spoken of as something inherently valuable. People's freedoms to make meaningful choices and have a voice in how their society works is – on this view – an essential valued element of human development (Sen, 1999), and is core to the people-centred approach we apply in this book. From an intrinsic perspective, communities managing their own water might not only make the pumps run better, but also give those citizens a sense of autonomy, dignity, and empowerment. As such, the question is not simply 'are participation and deeper democracy good for development?' It's rather more complicated, because many (including the authors) would argue that such things should be part of our vision of development in the first place – an *end* as much as a *means*.

Reflective question

Is participation intrinsically valuable or only instrumentally valuable for development?

The 'participation' agenda should not be uncritically lauded. In reality, without the resources (material, financial, technical) to fix broken pumps, poorly trained volunteers on village water-point committees can struggle to maintain services. In Malawi, where community management has been the dominant framework for rural water supply for decades, local water user committees have struggled to perform their technical and financial tasks to expected standards. Data suggest that maintenance is almost never done, and repairs are slow and substandard. Part of the reason is that communities confront the kinds of collective action problem that we explored in Chapter 4: the potential value of the collective interest is diminished or diverted by individual interests. In practice, because users do not fully value the benefits of clean water, community management is not as effective as it could be. It can often take weeks or months to repair a water point, because it takes time to collect funds to pay for spare parts, which are not kept in stock by committees that are mostly dormant unless water points fail (Chowns, 2015). This reinforces the reality that participation requires resources often in short supply for marginalised groups – time, energy, interpersonal confidence, sometimes money. Think about it: would you have time and energy to run your local water supply?

In turn, we should also not assume that participation is automatically universally empowering for 'the people'. People of higher social status are more likely to participate and to exercise greater influence, often due to differences in intangible and informal aspects of power such as education, confidence, networks, and free time. In social assistance councils in Brazil, for example, a common complaint is that the homeless population – theoretically a crucial constituency – are rarely involved, and when they are, their influence is meagre (Lyon, 2018). In this way, uneven incorporation in participatory structures can simply reproduce existing inequalities (Cornwall, 2008). It can also generate new conflicts within communities if participatory mechanisms enable some to have a greater-than-before say over who gets what, when, and how. We should also beware of slipping into a simplistic binary caricature with 'people' (benign, well intentioned) on one side, and elites/the state/'politics' (malign, unscrupulous)

Table 8.1 Examples of (attempted) 'people power'

Power *from* the people ('organic' mobilisation 'from below')	Power *to* the people (opening up/ distribution of existing official power)	
	External development organisation	State political power
• Street protests • Riots, violence, trespass • Non-violent resistance • Strike (e.g., labour) • Campaign groups • Form new organisation • Form new political party • 'Capture' existing organisation/party • Co-operatives, communes, etc. • Much of the above = 'social movements'	• Participatory rural appraisal • Participatory mapping/information collection • Consultation, local priority-setting • Community selects programme recipients • Social auditing • Community resource management	*Decentralisation:* • Local elections • Public-access village councils, 'town halls', etc. *Deliberation:* • Citizens' assemblies • State–society policy councils *Participatory democracy:* • Referenda • Participatory budgeting • Citizen oversight, evaluation

on the other side. As we showed in Chapter 4, change almost inevitably involves elites, inside or outside of the state, and it would be inaccurate to assume that all elite control equates to elite capture of the benefits.

These immediate caveats mean that we need a more detailed and critical understanding of when popular mobilisation or political participation really is empowering, successful, transformative – and when it isn't. This is where we now turn, beginning with power 'from' the people, in the form of social movements.

Bottom-up social mobilisation

Why do social movements arise?

Social movements are examples of 'organic' or emergent participation: public action that emerges through the collective joining together of citizens' individual agency. They typically arise out of the perception of a problem – often coloured with a sense of injustice, grievance, or frustration – and the imagination (possibly only hazy) of something better. Such action is often called 'contentious politics' (see Box 8.1).

> ### Box 8.1   Contentious politics
>
> The book *Contentious Politics* (2007), written by the political sociologists Charles Tilly and Sidney Tarrow, was influential in analysing the factors that drive different forms of collective action, from social movements to political protests to revolutions. Social movements are distinguished in the range of contentious politics because they typically involve a more long-term, sustained effort to effect change than short-term direct action like protests (though, of course, this may be one of their tactics).
>
> The book was important in identifying 'repertoires of contention', meaning the various tactics and strategies used to challenge power. These include boycotts, protests, sit-ins, digital activism, civil disobedience, and strategic litigation.
>
> Ultimately, contentious politics is closely associated with political struggle. It implies confrontational interactions between individuals, groups, governments, corporations and institutions, involving challenges to existing power structures, policies, norms, and practices. In this sense, contentious politics is a narrower term than contestation which, as we argued in Chapter 1, may also encompass less directly confrontational forms of everyday deliberation and negotiation at the heart of the politics of development.

Interests are important to understanding social movements. There is a centuries-long history of 'bread riots', people protesting for that most basic of needs: food. Workers striking for better pay and conditions clearly have a direct personal interest, as do landless peasants mobilising through Brazil's MST or Iranian women protesting restrictions on their lives.

Aside from interests, social movements are, of course, mobilised and animated by ideas: fairness regarding the distribution of the profits of labour; equal access to land; gender equality. In fact, a classic feature of social movements is that commitment to ideas can often override immediate individual self-interest, and lead activists to face personal sacrifice or risk. Think of British suffragettes enduring injury or death; activists 'disappeared' by military juntas in Argentina and Chile; Afghan girls risking personal safety to declaim their right to education. With such potential costs, it can seem mysterious why any given individual would choose to get involved in mobilisations, rather than leaving it to others and perhaps waiting to benefit from their activism. If this thought occurs to many people, it gives us the classic 'free rider' form of collective action problem (see Chapter 4). The power of ideas is part of what explains why movements do nevertheless arise.

Reflective question

What would motivate you to join a social movement?

Ideas and interests are the 'fuel' of social movements: necessary, but not sufficient, for a movement to catch fire. For that, a spark is needed. Sometimes this is an event, as with the triggering of the Black Lives Matter movement by the killing of unarmed teenager Trayvon Martin, or the Arab Spring by the suicide of Tunisian street vendor Mohamed Bouazizi. Sometimes the spark is somebody's initiative, as with Greta Thunberg's initiating of 'Fridays for Future' climate justice protests.

Finally, 'fuel' and 'spark' also require the 'oxygen' of a sufficiently enabling context. In this regard, it is important to distinguish between political regimes according to their willingness to assimilate certain political inputs (e.g., voting, lobbying and referendums) or outputs (e.g., licensing, litigations) and to tolerate confrontation and dissent (e.g., public demonstrations, civil disobedience). Kitschelt (1986) famously described these variations in environmental conditions as 'political opportunity structures'. Opportunity structures can change, either gradually, or in critical junctures (see Chapter 3). For example, the post-Second World War context bolstered the demands of workers' and women's movements in the UK. Women's vital role in the war effort legitimised their wider push for gender quality. All else being equal, the more 'open' political space in democracies probably makes it easier for movements to mobilise. By contrast, in the most repressive environments, organic social mobilisation is extremely difficult. Even widespread famine in the 1990s in North Korea did not spark public protest, for example. In this way, forms of contestation and contentious politics are situational.

Context is not merely a fixed 'given', however. Social movements come into a world of pre-existing formal and informal power structures: nation-states, borders, economic relationships, (neo)colonial or imperial relations, institutional rules, hierarchies of gender, race, caste, and so on. Yes, these shape what social movements can do – but often these power structures, and injustices they generate, are precisely the things that movements aim to change. As in the rallying cry 'Another world is possible!', many movements seek to radically alter institutions, ideas, and material distributions, up-ending hierarchies, reclaiming spaces from which people are excluded, fighting abuses of power – typically, a very difficult task, since powerful people tend to have vested interests in upholding just those things.

However, movements can also be reactive, mobilising to protect previous gains from a threat, or, in some cases, mobilising to try to lock in social privilege in backlash against egalitarian movements. Indeed, social movements are not always a force for what most people would see as good change: 'religious fundamentalisms, neo-Nazism and ethnic nationalism have all been rooted in and propagated by social movements' (Horn, 2013: 22). Even aside from this, social movements often mobilise over visions of 'development' that others might contest – traditional 'family values' versus feminist visions of gender relations, for instance, or visions of more frugal life in harmony with nature versus visions of high-tech green industrialisation. This contestability is unavoidable when thinking about social movements.

What constitutes success or failure for a social movement?

Social movements are not linear nor predictable. They catch fire through a chance combination of interests, ideas, sparks, and contexts, and may die down then reignite over a long period. They are often informal and amorphous, rather than being highly coherent, bounded groups with a straightforward 'life history' (Tilly, 1999b). Unsurprisingly, then, they typically have very varied and complex outcomes (Tarrow, 2022: 16). How can we gauge the impact of something like this?

In one sense, simply enabling ordinary people to articulate their views is itself a success. Again, there is intrinsic value in amplifying 'the voices less heard'. By bringing people together to articulate shared interests, social movements can also build a sense of subjective personal empowerment that is both individually valuable and a foundation for future work (Horn, 2013).

Fundamentally, though, the purpose of a movement is to achieve social and political change; to change the formal and/or informal 'rules of the game' (Chapter 3). Many social movements desire formal legislative change, as with the campaigns for women's votes and abortion rights. However, legal change can always be reversed, as the overturning of the USA's *Roe v. Wade* abortion ruling illustrated. Moreover, changing the law doesn't always guarantee success. For instance, the 'water riots' in Cochabamba, Bolivia, in 2000 were successful in overturning a law privatising water-supply services, but access to water there remains a major struggle (Baer, 2015). Caste-based discrimination has been illegal in India since 1948, but prejudice remains deeply ingrained (Pew, 2021). In these ways, legal change is often 'necessary but insufficient' to achieving the aims of a movement.

Social movements may also seek less tangible, more informal impacts such as in 'framing' (see Chapter 5), public perceptions, and social norms. The Ugandan campaign for the Domestic Violence Act, for example, strategically framed the issue in terms of 'family values', rather than a (more contentious) feminist 'rights' discourse (Ahikire and Mwiine, 2019).

This example also hints at possible trade-offs in 'framing' strategies: the bill was passed but mounted little challenge to conservative gender norms. A deeper shift in social norms is an outcome that many movements covet, changing citizens' sentiments and shifting the 'Overton Window' of ideas that the public consider legitimate for discussion. Arguably, Black Lives Matter has had this kind of impact, catalysing a global examination of racism, white supremacy, and legacies of colonialism and slavery (Otele, 2023).

Sometimes, social movements fail, at least in the short term. In #EndSARS, Nigerians called for the violent Special Anti-Robbery Squad to be disbanded, which was rapidly agreed by the government (Uwazuruike, 2020). But campaigners' fears that this was a phony agreement and that the same approach would resurface under a different label were borne out. The Lekki Toll Gate massacre's flagrant state violence deterred any further mobilisation towards meaningful change in policy or practice (Amnesty International, 2021a). Movements can also become co-opted and watered down, or diverted by already powerful actors; in the Arab Spring, despite massive uprisings across 15 countries and regime changes in four, lasting democratic transition was elusive for this reason. Movements can win partial political change, but then hit stalemate, as with the 2019–20 'Estallido Social' in Chile. And they can simply run out of steam, as with the Occupy movement.

So, what constitutes 'success' is complex. Social movements don't start out with a clearly articulated 'theory of change' and 'monitoring and evaluation' procedure. Their aims may be heterogeneous or may shift over time. There may be unexpected side-effects, or seeds for future mobilisation (Gaventa et al., 2023). As such, when assessing impacts we should consider long timescales, include both formal reforms (like new laws) and informal changes (like shifts in social attitudes), and look for unexpected as well as expected changes.

What conditions enable social movements to succeed?

Since change takes time and is non-linear, and since participation involves significant costs – time, energy, and sometimes risks to livelihoods and safety – bottom-up mobilisation faces ever-present dangers: fizzling out, missing goals, facing backlash, becoming co-opted and neutralised. While people power needs an initial impetus of 'critical mass' – numbers and passion on the streets – movements and bottom-up organisations also need staying power. For that, three things are crucial: leadership, institutionalisation, and strategies.

1 *Leadership.* Some iconic social movements are clearly identified with particular leaders: Emmeline Pankhurst, Mahatma Gandhi, Martin Luther King, Nelson Mandela. To what extent is a figurehead leader necessary? This is a difficult question; inevitably, we suffer from hindsight bias, remembering individual leaders of successful movements. Nevertheless, it is very plausible that leadership that is inspirational, competent, and morally legitimate can be vital to the success of a movement. However, many social movements are highly informal and amorphous, with decentralised leadership, especially in the social media era. This can insulate against the risk of 'decapitation'; if one leader is arrested, co-opted, killed, or steps back, the movement can continue. On

the other hand, leaderless movements can also easily lose focus and fizzle out, as with Occupy or Hong Kong's 2019–20 pro-democracy mobilisations. Recent research offers a synthesis perspective: leadership in development is less a matter of individual leaders, and much more a collective phenomenon, with all kinds of leadership happening at different levels and nodes (Hudson et al., 2018).

2 *Institutionalisation*. Any movement eventually needs certain things, such as resources, funding, organisation, coordination, stability. These things require institutionalisation: setting up structures, seeking funding, and becoming a reliable, self-reproducing entity that participants know will still be there tomorrow. Social bonds between movement members can be vital in sustaining focus (Tarrow, 2022: 178), and institutionalisation provides access to resources and repertoires of power that street protests cannot. Many large, formal organisations grew out of informal mobilisations, such as Greenpeace and Slum/Shack Dwellers International. La Via Campesina, the global peasant movement, is 30 years old, with 181 member organisations in 81 countries, representing 200 million peasants (Borras, 2023). At a smaller scale, organisations like co-operatives, savings groups, or labour unions are important ways that emergent movements institutionalise. For instance, a flourishing coffee farmers' co-operative union in Western Uganda started in 1999 and now involves over 4,000 farmers, whose subgroups sit within a well-institutionalised structure of participation and devolved leadership, generating both economic and political benefits for members (King and Hickey, 2017). Alternatively, social movements might institutionalise by 'capturing' or strongly influencing existing institutions, such as political parties or NGOs. In more authoritarian political contexts, where much lower freedom of association forecloses the self-institutionalisation option, gaining a foothold in existing institutions, such as faith groups, can be an important strategy. However, institutionalisation may also, in the regularisation of processes and setting up of hierarchies, risk dampening the fire that drove the initial movement.

3 This is where *strategy* comes in. The success of a social movement depends on its ability to develop and balance what Fox (2015) calls 'voice' and 'teeth': both mobilising citizen voice and working with power-holders to build capacity to respond with real changes. This implies that social movements need to engage in 'sandwich strategies' – combining bottom-up citizen mobilisation with direct engagement with existing structures of power (sometimes called 'outsider' and 'insider' strategies). The Jubilee 2000 campaign against Third World debt combined a) large-scale demonstrations that brought hundreds of thousands of protesters on to the streets, and b) insider strategies, including high-level advocacy by celebrities to politicians, and reframing the debt issue in a range of ways (technical, religious, national prestige) more amenable to policy gatekeepers (Busby, 2007).

In summary, social movements are a crucial way for citizens to claim political space and challenge existing power structures. While it is not always easy to evaluate their success, key factors in enabling movements to flourish are effective leadership, institutionalisation (providing stability and resources), and strategies with both 'voice' and 'teeth'. 'Teeth', however, is not just about what social movements themselves do. It is also about the capacity of official power to be responsive to popular demands. Can the valuable energies of organic people power be channelled into official political power in effective and genuine ways?

Empowered participation and deeper democracy

While social movements feature the generation of people power through organic mobilisation, a different form of empowerment is where official agenda-setting and decision-making power is opened up, diffused, or shared with citizens more than it previously was. When this relates to externally led development interventions it often goes under the catch-all term 'participation' (see Box 8.2), and involves things like communities being encouraged to outline their own needs and priorities, or manage resources, or audit projects.

Box 8.2 Participation

Building on the work of writers like Robert Chambers in the 1980s, 'participation' became a catch-all term for the idea of getting ordinary people more involved and more empowered in the process of development. The idea critically responds to other approaches that heavily emphasise either the market or the state as the driver of development. Participation as both means and end finds further support in the 'capability' theories of Amartya Sen and Martha Nussbaum, on the grounds that being engaged in – rather than passive towards or excluded from – decisions that affect one's life is an inherently valuable type of human flourishing.

However, participation is also a highly contested idea. While few people disagree that participation would be desirable 'in theory', a critical debate emerged over whether international development practice was, de facto, using participation as a nice-sounding fig leaf covering over external development actors' domination over locals (Cooke and Kothari, 2001; Hickey and Mohan, 2004). A comprehensive study by Mansuri and Rao (2013a) found that it is typically very difficult to 'induce' bona fide participation by external intervention.

When participation relates to the political power of the state, it amounts to the search for 'deeper democracy' (Fung and Wright, 2003; Gaventa, 2006). Deeper democracy often involves forms of democracy that its advocates claim improve on national-level representative democracy, such as decentralisation, deliberative democracy, and participatory democracy, terms we explain in Box 8.3.

Box 8.3   Deepening democracy

Against the backdrop of the work of theorists such as Brazilian activist educator Paulo Freire, feminist Carole Pateman, and critical theorist Jürgen Habermas, early twenty-first century work offered 'deeper democracy' (Fung and Wright, 2003; Kothari, 2005) as one possible answer to lack of inclusive governance. The deepening democracy agenda has sought to enhance the quality of democracy through a range of reforms, such as:

- *Accountability.* Meaning the transparency and openness of political decision-making, to encourage governments to be more responsive and answerable to the people. This is attempted through mechanisms such as independent oversight agencies and freedom of information laws.
- *Decentralisation.* Meaning the transfer of power (political or fiscal) from more central levels to more local levels, or tiers, of government. The idea is that greater local discretion and local participation will allow development to be more closely tailored to the diversity of local needs and conditions – in effect, by bringing government closer to the people.
- *Deliberative democracy.* Meaning deliberation prior to decision-making. This puts less emphasis on the outcome of votes than the deliberative, discursive character of the process via which decisions are made, which (ideally) should have features like reasonableness, rationality, inclusivity, and respectfulness.
- *Participatory democracy.* Meaning the exercise of direct decision-making powers by citizens (ideally, large numbers of them), with the aim that decisions will be more responsive to the needs of local populations, and that a culture of political engagement and consciousness will be stimulated.

While such ideas are a mainstay of progressive thought about the quality of democracy, there is on-going debate about how such institutions operate within a variety of political landscapes, including how their formal institutional design is shaped by informal rules and norms.

To be clear, democracy and development are, of course, not the same thing. As we discussed at length in Chapter 6, democracy itself is not automatically the 'best' type of government, against certain metrics. However, there is also a means/ends question here. We, along with many others, would contend that the sorts of things involved in the vision of 'deeper democracy' ought to have the status of intrinsically valued end-goals in themselves (Sen, 1999): citizens enjoying greater 'voice' in decisions that affect their lives, participating in deliberation over social values, gaining greater sense of personal–political empowerment and capability, and so on. As such, the question of deeper democracy being 'good for' development is a complex one, because it is both end and (potential) means.

However, whether attempts at empowered participation and deeper democracy succeed – both in terms of being genuine examples of what they aim to be, and in terms of promoting development more generally – is very context-dependent. Decentralisation and citizen involvement were standard reform prescriptions of donor agencies in the 1990s and early 2000s, and 'participation' became a key part of development agency practice. However, as with many 'Good Governance' ideals, major challenges arose once the reforms began interacting with contextual factors (Johnson, 2001; Grindle, 2009).

Problems with participation?

Certainly, we can challenge both the premise and the interests behind the participation agenda. One problem is that decentralisation can make for extreme variation among different regions, with some really struggling. Indonesia, for instance, undertook major decentralisation in 2001. Many local areas show wildly divergent results in education. Some perform well. In others, children are enrolled in school but learn almost nothing (Negara and Hutchinson, 2021). Other local governments in Indonesia are unable to carry out effective economic policy and management (Nasution, 2016). In such contexts, it can seem that progressive-sounding labels of 'grassroots participation' and 'decentralisation' are either extremely naive, or, more insidiously, actively covering for a state-shrinking agenda – an abdication of state responsibility to provide services or pursue nationwide fairness, foisting 'personal responsibility' for development on to communities that are ill-equipped to deliver.

Reflective question

Is grassroots participation always helpful in achieving desired futures? Why?

A second challenge is that while there are nuances, as discussed earlier, decentralisation and newly created mechanisms of participation can be vulnerable to 'elite capture' in political contexts featuring high degrees of patronage and corruption (Bardhan and Mookherjee, 2005; see Chapter 4). In large countries such as the Philippines, Nigeria, and Pakistan, not only have local democratisation initiatives had very limited effects on touted benefits such as service delivery and poverty reduction, they have also often been easily manipulated by regional elites. In Uganda, meanwhile, a more national-level version of elite capture has taken place, whereby decentralisation has been subsumed into the patronage politics of regime survival, used to strengthen the control of President Museveni and the ruling NRM party. Particularly striking is the phenomenon of runaway 'districtisation' – the creation of irrationally large numbers of highest level subnational units by subdividing existing districts (Green, 2015). Each new district triggers the creation of new structures, and thus administrative chaos, but is a useful patronage tool for the ruling coalition. It creates new positions that can be handed out, and an opportunity to plant NRM figures down to the local level. Thus, decentralisation can easily become grist to the mill of an overall political environment of patronage, rent-seeking, and dominance by regional or central elites.

A third worry concerns when participation takes place under the auspices of external international development actors, whether alone or in collaboration with the local state. This often involves methods such as consultation, participatory mapping and information-gathering, social auditing, priority-setting, and community management of resources or services. Many critiques have alleged that such 'participatory' practices have often merely been manipulative, patronising charades designed to obscure the same old power relation of aid-provider over aid-receiver – in turn often a reverberation of the coloniser–colonised relation. Here 'participation' is little more than a performative rubberstamp on predefined donor choices. An influential book edited by Cooke and Kothari (2001) provocatively questioned whether the participation agenda was merely a 'new tyranny'. Under the auspices of international actors committed to neoliberal political economy and upholding the existing international order, participation can be both bad faith and futile; '[g]reater impact on people's empowerment [. . .] is made by decisions taken by the World Bank and the IMF on debt repayment than can be made by an infinity of face-to-face participatory events' (Cooke, 2004: 43). In general, it appears to be very difficult for outsiders to 'induce' participation that lives up to its theoretical selling-points (Mansuri and Rao, 2013b).

As such, there is a major concern that what seems like popular participation can actually be merely a fig-leaf for very unequal 'power-over', whether donor–recipient or state–citizen. If we step back and reflect, it is not hard to see why this problem arises. Why would powerful actors, like central states or international donors, ever willingly give up or dilute their own power? They seem to face many interests and incentives that push in precisely the opposite direction. This tension, then, should immediately make us suspicious – not cynical or irretrievably pessimistic, but certainly critically 'on guard' for the possibility that all is not what it seems.

A big part of the difficulty here is power relations: those between central states and peripheral citizens; between the external aid practitioner (often from the Global North, highly educated, well resourced) and the poor development 'recipient'; and those between different groups in the social context: men and women; wealthy and poor; ethnic groups or castes; education levels; owners and workers; and so on. Such pre-existing power relations or 'categorical inequalities' (Tilly, 1999a) can skew the participation process; it is, de facto, very rarely a level playing-field or neutral environment. Deep social inequalities may strongly limit who participates, and how deliberation plays out, in terms of real, effective capacity to deliberate and exercise influence (Young, 2001).

Here's the paradox, though: challenging existing power relations is precisely what needs to happen for popular participation and deeper democracy to be 'for real', and for its impact on development to be inclusive and transformative. This creates a kind of 'chicken-and-egg' problem: unequal power relations hamper attempts at deeper democracy, but mechanisms of deeper democracy are needed to recalibrate those relations. How, then, can it ever happen?

Image 8.2 Local villagers gather together to deliberate under a tree shade in Madhya Pradesh, India. Image by Subhrajit123 via Shutterstock.

When does deeper democracy really happen?

The answer combines the two things we've looked at in this chapter: experiments in deeper democracy and citizen participation ('power to the people') work best when they grow out of and retain intimate links to organic, bottom-up mobilisation ('power from the people'). This is particularly so when that linkage is made through the capture of (at least some) state power by popular movements committed to ideas of egalitarian social change that contests power relations. To some extent, this claim reiterates the finding that effective citizen empowerment and participation requires a 'supportive state' (Mansuri and Rao, 2013b) and requires sufficient state capacity to be responsive (Fox 2015). But it also goes further. Participation is most likely to be bona fide and effective when it happens as part of a wider radical political project aiming at transformative change in the direction of social justice (Hickey and Mohan, 2005).

This can be seen in cases that do appear to get closer to the ideals of power to the people, giving a tantalising vision of what deeper democracy and greater popular participation might bring to development. For example, the Indian state of Kerala has a longstanding habit of producing outcomes that confound received wisdom, with often low growth and GDP per capita, both in Indian and global comparison, co-existing with a rapid rise to India's highest HDI, highest life expectancy, lowest infant mortality, highest gender equality measures, best-performing education sector, and 100 per cent literacy. Many of these indicators are comparable to the world's wealthiest countries (see Figure 8.1).

Practices of 'deeper democracy' have played a major role in this. India's constitution – and particularly the 73rd and 74th amendments in 1993 – provides for decentralised and participatory governance with both urban and rural wings, and regular local elections. However, the important thing to understand here is that, as we've seen throughout this book, formal on-paper provisions are only one small part of the picture. Political context and culture have been crucial in Kerala's participatory mechanisms flourishing and driving action by the state government. Kerala is home to an unusually intense culture of political contestation and organisation (Jeffrey, 1992: 92–140; Kannan, 2022: 27–33), with trade unions, peasant associations, and land reform movements strong throughout the twentieth century. People engage

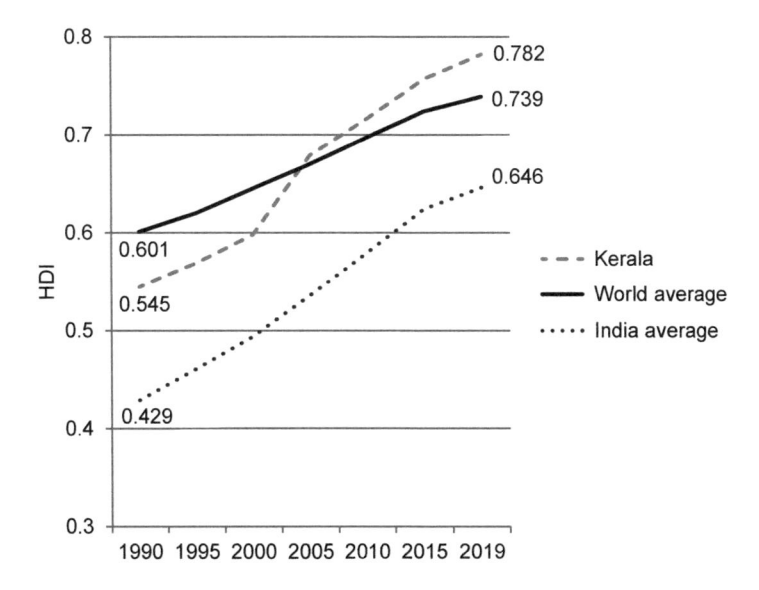

Figure 8.1 Kerala as an outlier?
Source: Based on UNDP data (HDI reports), and sub-national values from the SHDI index; see: https://globaldatalab.org/shdi/

daily in heated debate about public policy. Unions, movements, parties, and co-operatives spring up like mushrooms. At the same time, there is enough of a solidaristic subnational Keralan 'identity' to keep all of this contestation productive rather than divisive (Singh, 2016; see Chapter 10).

A great deal of this flourishing political culture has been driven by and through left political parties, particularly communist parties (Desai, 2001; Williams, 2008), which in Kerala place heavy emphasis on grassroots democracy and effective enfranchisement of the poor, more than on the central planning diktats of Soviet communism (Keefer and Khemani, 2005). For example, when the Left Democratic Front coalition took power in Kerala in 1996, it rapidly implemented its campaign pledge to further devolve decision-making authority and funding to all levels of local government, including earmarking 35–40 per cent of the state's development planning budget to initiatives generated from local bodies (Véron, 2001). Major steps were taken to facilitate public participation in decision-making mechanisms, including training and resourcing officials to administer these (Heller et al., 2007). A concerted attack on social inequalities, such as land reforms and major investments in health and education, have been the result (Franke and Chasin, 1992), and the basis of the 'Kerala miracle' in social development.

A similarly famous example is the city of Porto Alegre, in southern Brazil. From 1989, Porto Alegre pioneered an innovation known as 'participatory budgeting', where citizens have direct input into city government spending decisions. The yearly process involves mass open assemblies, elections of citizen representatives, deliberation by both the assemblies and the representatives, and citizen oversight of implementation. Participatory budgeting therefore combines elements of deliberative, participatory, decentralised, and representative democracy, in a sophisticated design. The heyday of participatory budgeting coincided with major improvements in poverty, sanitation, health services, education, and public infrastructure, as citizens used the system to prioritise these areas.

Here, too, we have an illustration of the thesis about the crucial role of links to organic mobilisation, a supportive state, and a wider radical project. Brazil exited military dictatorship in the late 1980s following mass demonstrations and civil society organising. Crucially, this heightened state of social mobilisation continued into the post-dictatorship era, leading to a time of fevered social movement activity and experimentation with new forms of democratic participation at local levels. It was as if Brazilians, having been starved of democracy for two decades, now feasted. In the flux of transition, the intrepid movements that had opposed the dictatorship played a major role in the constitutional deliberations (1985–8), and then, in the post-1988 years, played a similarly crucial role in lobbying for the constitution's many ambitiously progressive on-paper provisions to be turned into reality.

A major player in all this was the Workers' Party (PT), originally formed by trade unionists and social movements such as the landless rural worker's movement (MST), and retaining their influence. The PT eventually won national power, with the election of Lula da Silva to president in 2003, but before that the party played an almost-as-important role subnationally. The PT won the municipal elections in Porto Alegre in 1989, and, in line with social movement pressure, introduced the participatory budgeting experiment. At the national level of Brazilian politics, social movements played a similarly influential role, and the political scene was stacked with major figures of the democratic transition. Thus, the state, at both national and local levels, was predisposed to be supportive of experiments in deepening democracy. In Porto Alegre the reins of state power were taken over by an upstart leftist party that grew out of a mass movement that it was beholden to for its power. Both the interests and the ideational commitment were thus present for this PT-led city administration to support the genuine institutionalisation of popular democracy.

By contrast, for instance, Indonesia under the late twentieth-century 'New Order' was extremely centralised, with weak traditions of popular participation in politics. The decentralisation in 1999 was rather sudden, and in practice often involved the central government offloading crucial responsibilities on local governments with low capacity (Shoesmith et al., 2020). Meanwhile, in Uganda – as in many countries that adopted the formal trappings of Good Governance-era policy blueprints – the NRM's commitment to decentralisation revealed itself to be largely rhetorical. The impressive on-paper provisions for subnational participatory governance met with a public with limited prior traditions of democratic participation, and a dominant-but-threatened central regime all-too-happy to use the patronage and control opportunities that the new local government structures offered.

Moreover, Kerala and Porto Alegre are, of course, subnational entities rather than whole countries, and thus subnational contextual differences are important. Decentralised political participation has flourished to widely varying degrees, and with very different outcomes, throughout India, often because of pre-existing social conditions such as political traditions, educational levels, and inequalities (Drèze and Sen, 2002: 358–63; Prasad and Pardhasaradhi, 2020). A similar point goes for Brazil, with substantial variation and different approaches to participatory democracy (Wampler, 2008; Avritzer, 2012). Porto Alegre's model has also not yet translated into a corresponding deepening of democracy at the national level in Brazil (Baiocchi, 2005: xi), and the same is true of Kerala and India.

Reflective question

What conditions are needed for participation and deeper democracy to work?

These caveats once again underscore a main message of this book – namely, the importance of understanding the real political contexts in which policies unfold, and how this can lead to widely differential results from similar on-paper policies and formal institutions.

Does this mean 'working with the grain'?

For these reasons, it is tempting to think that within-country reformers and external advocates should refrain from promoting 'deeper democracy' institutions when there is little pre-existing cultural history of popular political mobilisation, where economic impoverishment abounds, and where the threat of elite capture or clientelism is high. Maybe, we might think, it is better to 'work with the grain' (Kelsall, 2011; Levy, 2014) – pursue developmental policies through existing institutions, and/or build institutions that align with already-existing cultural practices and political traditions. Certainly, it seems hard to argue against a motto of understanding contextual complexities rather than imposing idealised blueprints.

However, in the area of popular empowerment, there is reason to resist entirely adopting a 'working with the grain' approach. For one thing, the 'grain' of culture and politics is often inegalitarian, patriarchal, and repressive to a degree that raises a normative dilemma for external actors. For another, the preconditions for 'organic' social mobilisation often developed through centuries-long processes of socioeconomic change. If we think that popular participation is desirable, then simply being told to wait for this macro-historical process to unfold will strike many as an unsatisfying answer: it takes too long, and what if it never happens? This also reiterates the 'chicken-and-egg' dilemma at play. Successful democratic deepening may be easier under certain social preconditions, but disregarding innovative proposals for democratic deepening may spurn valuable possibilities for pushing society towards such conditions.

There is no getting away from the fact that 'power to the people' involves a vision of transformed social power relations, between citizen and state, between different social groups, and between ordinary residents of developing countries and powerful international actors – a vision that typically mounts a direct challenge to the 'grain' of the status quo. This is precisely the same kind of 'creative destruction' that organic social movements themselves aim at (Mansuri and Rao, 2013b). As Hickey and Mohan (2004: 13) argue, at least some participatory interventions can generate political space and agency, even where it was previously thin on the ground. Those that do, do so because they engage with development as a political process of underlying social change, and are 'tied into broader projects of social justice and radical political change' (ibid.).

If a surrounding culture of flourishing organic mobilisation tends to be needed for deeper democracy initiatives to succeed, then the logical next step might seem to be to support this 'demand side' of the equation. For external development partners and donors, this raises a potentially difficult question of how to navigate the contentious politics that this inevitably involves, including when to 'take sides', and when to not only use savvy 'political methods', but also to explicitly pursue 'political goals' (Carothers and De Gramont, 2013).

Summary and conclusion

The political empowerment of ordinary people can be a major driver of development, as well as being intrinsically desirable, but it is important to seek a critical understanding of when it does and does not live up to its promise. This remains an area of major debate, where it is best to retain a critical, wary, perspective.

Social movements and bottom-up organisations can play a crucial role in advancing developmental change and the expansion of real freedoms. They succeed insofar as they amplify 'the voices less heard', challenge the power of elites and hold them to account, and secure some form of tangible improvement in ordinary people's lives. Effective leadership, institutionalisation, and 'sandwich strategies' that support both mass mobilisation and engagement with the state are crucial success factors for movements.

For popular participation in development and in mechanisms of 'deeper democracy', meanwhile, efforts are most likely to be successful when they build on existing organic practice, rather than being created *ex nihilo* or imposed as an externally derived framework, and when they enjoy at least pockets of support in the state – or, even better, where the state itself is deeply marked by this history of organic mobilisation, or is even taken over by some of the movements involved. However, this shouldn't be taken as a message that new democratic mechanisms should never be experimented with where there is no precedent. The highest risk of participation being bogus arises when it happens under the auspices of international donors or predatory states with their own agendas and with meagre links to organic mobilisation. The best chance of participation in development being bona fide and effective is when it happens as part of a wider politics of transformation and social justice that doesn't flinch from challenging existing power relations. As this suggests, there is a crucial symbiotic relationship between organic social mobilisations and deeper democracy – between power from and power to the people.

Discussion questions

- Why are some social movements more successful than others?
- Is popular participation and deeper democracy a 'must have' or only a 'nice to have' in development?
- Should external development donors and organisations (sometimes) support social movements that challenge a country's political status quo?

Suggested further reading

Hickey, S. and Mohan, G. (2005) 'Relocating participation within a radical politics of development', *Development and Change*, 36 (2): 237–62.

Hossain, N. et al. (2021) 'Demanding power: do protests empower citizens to hold governments accountable over energy?', IDS Working Paper, 555.

Mansuri, G. and Vijayendra, R. (2013) 'Can participation be induced? Some evidence from developing countries', *Critical Review of International Social and Political Philosophy*, 16 (2): 284–304.

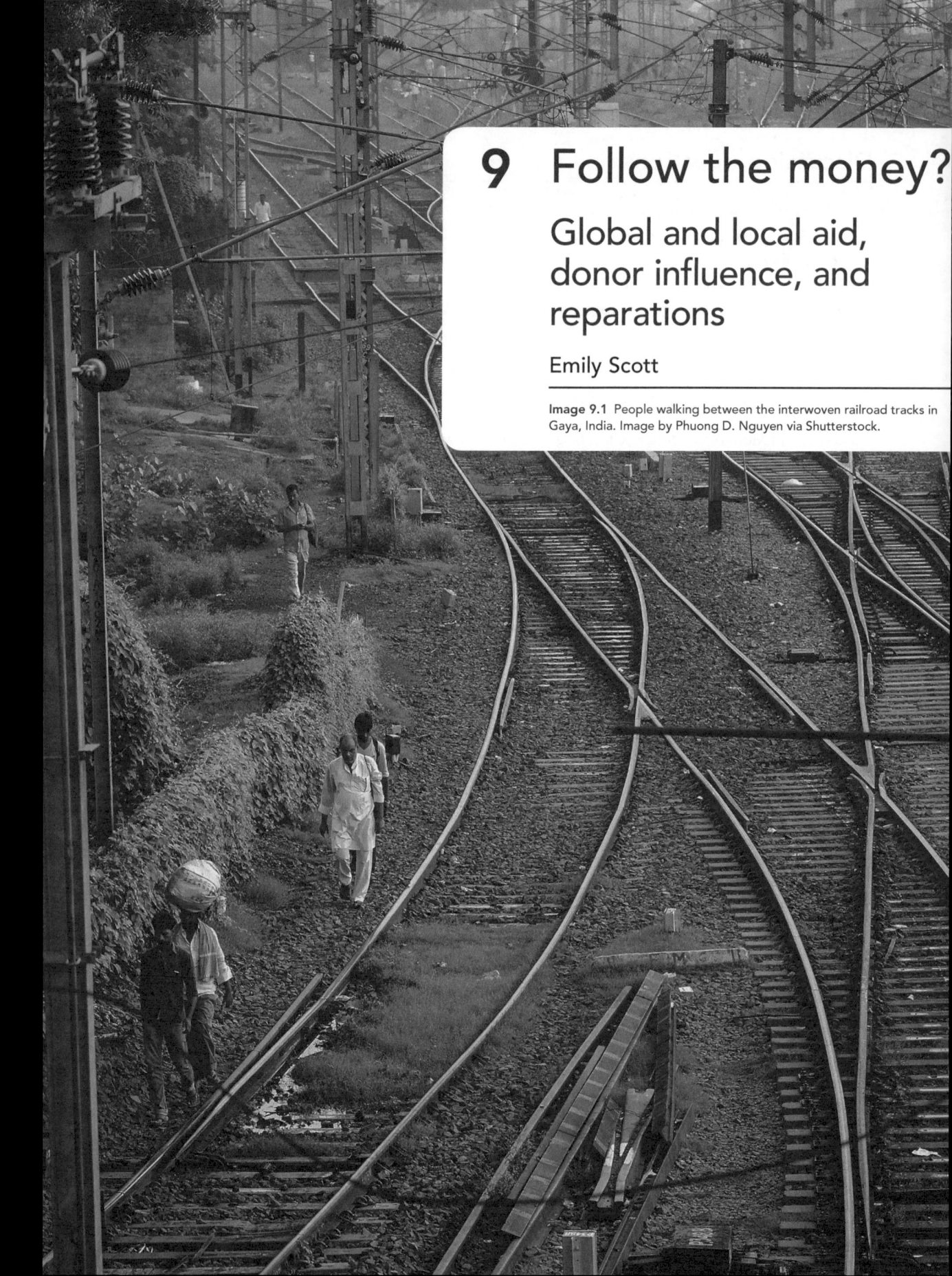

9 Follow the money?

Global and local aid, donor influence, and reparations

Emily Scott

Image 9.1 People walking between the interwoven railroad tracks in Gaya, India. Image by Phuong D. Nguyen via Shutterstock.

> ## Learning outcomes
>
> - Understand the diversity of development donors and how their interests can shape who gets what, when and how.
> - Understand how donors' ideas, values, and beliefs influence development policy and practice.
> - Discuss how the global aid architecture is being contested, including through localisation and reparations.

The limits of money power?

In the 1976 film, *All the Presidents Men*, which dramatised the downfall of United States President Richard Nixon over the Watergate scandal, the anonymous source 'Deep Throat' advises journalist Bob Woodward to 'follow the money.' The journalist does just that, uncovering bribery, corruption, and sabotage that implicates the President himself. Today, when someone says, 'follow the money,' they are reminding us that to understand power, we need to know who has money, and how they use it. In development, understood in this chapter as the practices of intervening in desired futures, donors often have that money. As a result, donors can wield a great deal of power over who gets what, when, and how. But what, really, is the extent of – but also the limit to – this power?

Understanding the ideas and interests that motivate donor agencies to give money across borders – whether it's the United Kingdom's Foreign and Commonwealth Development Office (FCDO), the European Union (EU), the United States Agency for International Development (USAID), or the China International Development Cooperation Agency (CIDCA) – is a critical part of the development puzzle. Donors represent a powerful group of states, many with histories of plundering the countries they now aid. At the same time, too, local donors – based in, or with strong ties to affected communities – also have a longstanding influence on the fates of populations. We need to understand how all of these different actors fit within the global and local aid architecture – the rules and norms of appropriate behavior, and institutions that govern how and why aid dollars move. In so doing, we can see the effects of donors on development, including on patterns of domination and control that underlie contestations over the everyday challenges we will explore in the next part of this book.

Should money shape desired futures? Why do donors give? And how are these distributions, and the interests they represent, being contested in practice?

This chapter examines these questions through the lens of the three 'I's of development: *interests, ideas*, and *institutions*. It first asks which donors are influencing who gets what, when and how, before scrutinising what shapes their interests, both stated and hidden, in doing so. We show why understanding how donors make choices and decisions also requires getting 'inside' their *ideas*, values, and beliefs. Aid is contested, not least because the legacies of slavery and colonialism, discussed in Chapters 1 and 2, continue to shape who benefits from it. Whose voices are represented in the processes via which decisions are made – whether in powerful international forums, or in local projects that claim to be 'locally owned,' but often, instead, reproduce unequal power.

Should wealth shape desired futures?

As we have seen so far in this book, and you may well know from personal experience, those who have more money can often accumulate power to influence the lives of people with less. Employees listen to employers for fear of losing their jobs or being denied a raise. The customer is 'always right' because they pay for goods and services. First-class passengers enjoy a more comfortable ride because they paid for it. And yet, the comfort of the wealthy, the right of the customer, or the control of the employer is not derived from moral superiority – these people are not inherently better than others. Nor is their power given democratically, through elections or because the people consent to their authority. No. The wealthy hold power and influence because they have – and have the potential to distribute or deny – the money others need to live, eat, access healthcare, and remain housed.

In the global fight against poverty and inequality, there is growing concern that as distributions of wealth reach new levels, an extremely wealthy few are gaining unprecedented global influence. In 2022, the world's ten richest people – all men – held more wealth than 40 per cent of humanity. During the Covid-19 pandemic, while 99 per cent of humanity lost income, these people 'more than doubled their fortunes' (Oxfam, 2022). The pandemic created 40 new billionaires from pharmaceutical profits (Ahmed et al., 2022).

The rise of the megarich raises ethical and pragmatic questions. Should Elon Musk – a CEO, engineer, and investor – be allowed to shape how information is shared on a powerful social media platform like X? Is Bill Gates – whose fortune comes from building the computer company Microsoft – qualified to act as a global aid donor, and determine the fates of millions of people, through his foundation? Who are these billionaires accountable to – their investors or the people affected by the policies they change? Are the wealthy qualified to decide people's futures simply because they have accumulated wealth? Images of billionaires like Richard Branson and Jeff Bezos spending tens of millions of dollars on private space tourism, while emitting hundreds of tons of carbon dioxide and other chemicals into the upper atmosphere, have placed these questions at the centre of public debate.

Image 9.2 Billionaires and philanthrocapitalists Melinda and Bill Gates. Image by Steve Jurvetson via Flickr.

Although less in the public eye, similar underlying questions have long animated scholarly and practitioner debates about global development assistance. Global aid has traditionally been given by wealthier nations to what have they labelled 'developing countries.' As we will see later in this chapter, this assistance has tended to come with conditions, requiring recipients of aid to follow the lead of more 'developed' nations, developing or modernising as they did (Lipset, 1959; Rostow, 1960; Rostow and Baker, 2016). But does the accumulation of capital by wealthier nations – accumulated, as we saw in Chapter 1, through colonialism (Chiba and Heinrich, 2019; Duffield and Hewitt, 2013; Goldsmith, 1997), the slave trade, extractive and exploitative industry and trade, unfair labour practices, and the degradation of our planet – qualify them to decide the futures of others? Does the wealth of some nations justify their ability to influence who gets what, when, and how in other countries?

Reflective question

Are the wealthy qualified to decide people's futures simply because they have accumulated wealth?

No matter who donors are, they are 'haves' who exercise power *over* 'have nots.' And this raises questions about whether, or to what extent, this kind of control over others is fair. When can making decisions about who receives assistance at home or abroad – who receives services, care, or compassion, on what conditions – be justified? Are those with wealth somehow more capable of making these kinds of decisions, even for peoples they do not know? To grapple with these questions, and better understand aid, we can start by asking who donors really are.

Who is influencing who gets what, and how?

Donors are individuals, groups, organisations, or countries that transfer goods, services, technical assistance or capital to development programs or projects. Notably, a donor is defined by this transfer, and not by their position within or outside of an affected population or place. There are many terms for this act of transfer, from development 'assistance' to 'co-operation,' to 'partnership,' to 'external aid' or 'foreign interference.' Regardless of how agencies themselves like to frame their actions (which shifts in line with their interests, of course), when you think of donors, *multilateral donors* like the World Bank (WB) and International Monetary Fund (IMF), or agencies like the World Health Organization (WHO) or the United Nations Development Programme (UNDP) may immediately come to mind. You might even have thought of leading philanthrocapitalist organisations, like the Gates Foundation. This makes sense. They are major financial players with significant influence on the institutions, rules, and norms that define global development. The 'super rich' play a growing role in deciding which development challenges we should face, when, and how (Bishop and Green, 2015).

There are also *bilateral* state funders, like Global Affairs Canada (GAC), or Australia's Department of Foreign Affairs and Trade (DFAT). While traditionally the world's largest bilateral donors were members of the Development Assistance Committee (DAC) – part of the Organisation for Economic Co-operation and Development (OECD) composed of 30 member countries primarily from the world's most economically advanced nations – their donations are in relative decline. Meanwhile, the relative donations of 'emerging donors,' government agencies often based in previously labelled 'developing' countries, are growing (Dreher et al., 2011). They include China, India, Turkey, and the Gulf States, among many others. These donors have the potential to reshape how aid is distributed, to who, and with what effects (Woods, 2008; Mullen, 2017). For instance, China's Belt and Road Initiative aims to develop Chinese infrastructure projects around the world, arguably extending Chinese geopolitical influence (Bird et al., 2020; Malik et al., 2021).

Reflective question

Why is the influence of 'emerging donors,' many of which were previously classed as 'developing countries,' growing?

The organisations above are likely to come to mind when you think about development donors. But for people affected by development challenges, the first line of support is often found closer to home – in local aid, and among local donors. Despite a tendency to see development aid as something that moves predominantly from the Global North to the Global South (and across borders), donors are also often local to the municipality, district, or village. These donors tend to be regrettably forgotten or left out when we talk about the global aid architecture.

Perhaps surprisingly, the amount of local development aid coming from *within* communities, including diaspora communities – community members that have migrated away from their country of origin – is believed to eclipse institutional giving. Local development aid includes remittances, local business or charity giving, faith-based or individual direct giving, as well as civil society funds, among others (Adelman, 2009; Scott, 2022). *Remittances* are cash or goods sent home by migrants, often to family members or communities in their country of origin. While not technically originating in-country or context, these are more local, people-to-people, flows as they come from individuals or groups with strong ties to a local community. Remittances to low- and middle-income countries (LMICs) alone in 2022 are estimated to have reached levels comparable to development assistance levels that year – an estimated US$626 billion (World Bank, 2021a,

Table 9.1 The landscape of 'giving'

Type of aid	Examples
Multilateral (meaning they are funded via contributions from multiple countries or organisations).	UN Agencies – e.g., United Nations Development Programme (UNDP), UN Women, the United Nations High Commissioner for Refugees (UNHCR), Food and Agriculture Organisation (FAO) – International non-governmental organisations (INGOs), Regional Development Agencies – e.g., African Development Bank (AfDB), Asian Development Bank (ADB), Arab Fund for Economic and Social Development (AFESD).
Bilateral (country to country, meaning the direct transfer of resources from one country's government to another).	Japan International Cooperation Agency (JICA), Germany's Federal Ministry for Economic Cooperation and Development (BMZ), Turkish Cooperation and Coordination Agency (TIKA), Korea International Cooperation Agency (KOICA), Saudi Fund for Development (SFD).
Philanthrocapitalism	The Bill and Melinda Gates Foundation, Chan Zuckerberg Initiative (CZI), Bloomberg Philanthropies, Emerson Collective.
Local	Local Civil Society Organizations (CSOs) or Non-Governmental Organisations (NGOs), faith-based organisations, local charities.
People to people	Remittances, faith-based giving, benefactors or patrons (see Chapter 12).

2022a; KNOMAD, 2022). These are best estimates because remittances flow through both official and unofficial channels, and so are very hard to keep track of. But this means that if official and private development aid could buy half of Google, remittances could buy the other half.

The scale and influence of people-to-people development aid goes beyond remittances. For instance, there is evidence that faith-based giving, such as almsgiving or Zakat in Muslim nations, bring in (at least) billions more dollars (Ager et al., 2015; Stirk, 2015). More money is unaccounted for because it moves through informal channels. There is also evidence that local businesses and social enterprises are essential sources of development dollars, particularly where development entrepreneurs are excluded from more traditional financing (McDade and Spring, 2005; Kuada, 2009, 2015; Bryant, 2019).

What do donors do?

In the immediate sense, donors can supply goods that sustain lives, particularly in the context of humanitarian crises. Examples of the kinds of materials that support basic human survival include blankets, lumber, and tarps for shelter, or cooking oil. Image 9.3, for example, shows Syrian women and girls at an informal tented settlement in Lebanon's Bekaa

Valley, where refugees build their own shelters out of lumber and tarps, insulate them with blankets, and weigh down their roofs with tires. Some of what builds their homes is donor given, some is found or purchased by refugees. Services can include education, healthcare, or election monitoring. When capital is transferred, money or property moves from giver to recipient.

Image 9.3 Aid as humanitarian need
Image by Russell Watkins/DFID via Flikr.

Whoever they are, donors make interventions to affect political, societal, or economic change. The aim of this, ultimately, is to alter desired futures to fit with these agencies' version (or assessment) of what those futures *should* look like.

As we saw in Chapter 7, for example, the IMF acts as a global governor of market interventions. It steps in and provides loans to a country where the cost of living is rising uncontrollably and the value of country currency might collapse. After the Covid-19 pandemic, and because of dependence on fossil fuels and the Ukraine war, you may be familiar with what it is like to see your money worth less and less each time you go to the market to buy what you need. If this is the case, goods in your country might have become more costly (this is inflation) and your wages might not have kept up. Now, imagine facing inflation of 172 per cent in Zimbabwe or 400 per cent of Venezuela as of 2023, so that goods were not just 10 per cent more expensive, but nearly two or four times more expensive (IMF, 2021). In such cases, the IMF can become a lender of last resort – able to give loans where all other options are exhausted.

The World Bank's activities look different, because it works to reduce poverty and encourage economic growth in the longer term. It is a specialised UN agency that provides financial and technical assistance across sectors of development, such as in agriculture, education, health, social protection, and energy, extractive, and financial sectors, among others. Technical assistance means giving money and dispatching international experts to advise on or build the capacity of project planners and implementers around the world.

Local donors, by contrast with hefty and complex multilateral institutions that can only operate through internal contestation and highly bureaucratic decision-making, are often more agile and responsive to evolving, local crises. They can fund projects that large institutional donors neither want, nor can have, anything to do with, for geopolitical reasons. For instance, local development donors (largely business owners) funded reconstruction efforts and development projects devised by Syrian social enterprises in rebel-held areas of north-western Syria. These were vital to local people, but considered too high risk for foreign donors, who feared reprisals from the Asad regime. There are also studies that suggest aid dollars that come from more local sources can have more positive effects on social cohesion – the strength of relationships within a community – than external sources of funding (Willitts-King et al., 2019; Alik-Lagrange et al., 2021).

Remittance flows tend to increase when times are tough, and diminish when things are more stable for affected people, making them important sources of stability and financing in developing countries (Bryant, 2019). This may be because the interests of those sending remittances are in securing the well-being of their communities, and quickly; institutional donors are often more interested in long-term development policies and outcomes and may be delayed during crises because of bureaucratic (Choudhury and Ahmed, 2002; Weaver, 2008) and accountability demands (Edwards and Hulme, 1996). Those sending remittances are not always counted as development donors but are undeniably important sources of financial aid to populations. They provide security, school fees, business start-up loans, and much more (Rapoport and Docquier 2006; Giuliano and Ruiz-Arranz 2009; Yang, 2011; Levitt and Lamba-Nieves, 2011). They are also available to many recipients not able to access capital through banks, which put up all kinds of barriers to borrowing (Watkins and Quattri, 2014). Because of these impacts, we should not assume that remittances have only individual-level effects. In fact, they made up an estimated 35 per cent of GDP in Somalia in 2021, 19 per cent in Kosovo and Lebanon, and over 5 or 10 per cent in Georgia, Vietnam, Guyana and many other places in the same year (World Bank, 2021a).

As we have seen, then, there is considerable variation in the range of donors, what they do, at what scale, and the kind of interests they have in particular outcomes; whether to maintain economic stability in the case of the IMF, or help their community through tough times in the case of remittance donors.

Why do donors give?

Because donors can influence contestations about how resources will be distributed, it is vital to understand what drives them towards certain preferred outcomes, or versions of a desired future. In other words, why do donors give?

Generally, we can say that all donors give in the hope of some kind of return on their investment (see Box 9.1). Which motivations are really driving donor decision-making, and whether these are altruistic or self-serving, can be difficult to decipher. But whatever the stated logic or rationale, aid is both a product, and a generator of, power: whether the power to enhance a donor's image, influence, and reputation on the global stage – what we might term 'soft power'; or their diplomatic leverage, stability in their own neighbourhood (reducing the spillover costs of conflict and poverty in terms of migration or terrorist threats), or direct access to resources – what we might term 'hard power,' or power that feeds into a countries' own economic or military strength.

Box 9.1 Why donors give

- *Humanitarianism.* A moral duty to alleviate suffering, respond to emergencies and help others, based in beliefs about a common humanity or humanitarian concern (Lumsdaine, 1993; Holzgrefe and Keohane, 2003; Barnett, 2011; see Box 9.4 on human rights).
- *Poverty alleviation.* To reduce poverty by providing access to water, sanitation, education, cash transfers, social insurance, or healthcare, or by protecting livelihoods or encouraging social entrepreneurship, or preserving the source of livelihoods by protecting biodiversity, and supporting sustainable management of fisheries, forests and other natural resources.
- *Promote regional or global stability.* Either by addressing the root causes of instability, such as poverty, inequality, and lack of basic services, or preventing challenges from spreading from one country to another and threatening its security – e.g., disease outbreaks, conflict, or migration. For example, when the WHO responded quickly to a cholera outbreak in Zambia to avoid it crossing into Malawi and Mozambique in January of 2023 or when the European Union promised Turkey billions of dollars in 2016 to keep migrants from travelling on to Europe.
- *Secure economic and strategic interests.* Use aid to secure policy concessions and exert geopolitical influence over recipient organisations and governments (Dunning, 2004; De Mesquita and Smith, 2009; Tierney et al., 2011). For example, the United States gives both military and development aid to many Middle Eastern nations, from Egypt, to Kuwait, to Jordan, and others, and in exchange builds military bases and houses troops there.
- *Norms promotion.* To promote norms, ideas and policies that align with domestic values, views and public opinion on what kinds of political or social systems are good for the world – e.g., to promote democracy, or human rights, or gender equality, or birth control.

To decipher when, and to what extent, these logics are present in the giving of aid, we can look more closely at the interests that aid projects serve. We can also, in turn, analyse how these interests are reflected in, and reinforce, dominant ideas about who should get what, when and how.

Giving in whose interests?

Sometimes the interests in giving reveal themselves starkly, without much need for analysis. In the 1980s, for example, the Ethiopian government diverted food aid desperately needed by victims of famine. They sent it to arid, plain areas in the south of the country, and away from fertile, high-altitude, and more defensible land in the north, to gain an upper hand in the ongoing civil war (MSF, 2015). Donors continued to give, based on their perceived responsibility to act, while knowing that some of their aid was being misused, but considered this the cost of doing business, or a necessary trade-off (Rubenstein, 2015).

In other cases, donors reveal their interests in advance, by setting conditions on loans or grants, based on their preferences about how development aid can, and should, work, and in whose interests. These are called *conditionalities* and are imposed or agreed (explicitly or implicitly) between lender (where a loan will need to be repaid) or the agency that issues a grant (money given that does not need to be paid back) and recipient (see Box 9.2).

Box 9.2 Political conditionality

Political conditionality refers to 'the allocation and use of financial resources to sanction or reward recipients' to promote certain political goals (Molenaers et al., 2015: 2). It represents a critical tool for aid donors: by imposing conditionality they can 'discipline' aid recipient states (Abrahamsen, 2000) – for example, by suspending aid following evidence of corruption, or sometimes, withdrawing aid in response to human rights abuses (see Box 9.4). However, it has often been criticised as a mechanism that promotes the interests of Western states, while undermining the agency of recipient governments.

It is not clear, however, how effective conditionality is in practice. While conditionality played a role in forcing governments in countries such as Kenya and Malawi to reintroduce multiparty elections in the early 1990s, a recent review concludes that such measures are rarely used, and that they may be less effective than has often been assumed. One reason for this is that 'recipient states have more options available to them than previous literature has allowed,' such as mobilising domestic and international support against donors by arguing that conditionality is a neocolonial infringement on their sovereignty (Cheeseman et al., 2023).

Conditionalities set forth a set of behavioural expectations, which the recipient needs to meet to remain compliant in a loan or grant agreement. These range from things like delivering X number of health consultations to women, to improving access to water and sanitation services in a particular area, to submitting receipts for transactions with vendors, to adopting policies that will promote democratic change. The IMF also has the power to 'health check' the financial policies of member countries and offers loans contingent on behavioural and policy changes. The loan will only be given and maintained if the recipient country behaves in line with their IMF loan terms (IMF, 2023b). These conditions have a lot to do with what the IMF believes is sound economic policy (its ideas) and the geostrategic and political importance the IMF places on a country's stability (the

IMF's interests) (Presbitero and Zazzaro, 2012). Like the IMF, WB financing of development projects is often contingent on national and subnational governments taking on certain World Bank-supported policy and institutional reforms (World Bank, 2023a). In this way, conditionality is a strategy that enables wealthier countries to push poorer countries towards their preferred political and economic models, such as democracy and free trade (see Chapter 6).

While some conditionalities can improve oversight, reduce risk, and increase the effectiveness and accountability of programming, others are so stringent and focused on the needs of a donor agency that is based elsewhere – perhaps in London, New York, or Geneva – that meeting them can make activities unresponsive to on-the-ground needs (Honig, 2018). Too much top-down oversight and too many centralised conditions can hurt efforts to rebuild local peace, for instance, because local needs are not incorporated into program design (Daher and Moret, 2020; Roepstorff, 2020). In Syria, anti-terror legislation in Western nations led donor agencies to ask for receipts from local actors for every little thing – from fuel to a coffee to a fee paid for a bus. But in the midst of war, it was nearly impossible to get an invoice for everything. This made doing development work costly for local actors who were not fully reimbursed or spent far too much of their time filling out reports (Daher and Moret, 2020; Roepstorff, 2020). Conditionalities can undermine local actors' power and authority and reinforce global power over local actors, undermining humanitarian and development outcomes for affected populations (Khoury and Scott, 2024).

Reflective question

What does the nature of conditionalities reveal about donor interests in giving aid?

We should not assume, though, that donor interests are entirely detached from the interests of their domestic publics. Much of the financing that goes to bilateral agencies comes from taxpayers. Governments that are members of the Organisation for Economic Co-Operation and Development (OECD), Development Assistance Committee (DAC), have repeatedly pledged to provide 0.7 per cent of their Gross Domestic Income (GDI) as Official Development Assistance (ODA). In many contexts where politicians are held accountable at the ballot box for their policies, domestic support for aid can also shape how donors conceive what is in their interests, or not, to pursue (see Box 9.3)

Box 9.3 Public opinion and aid

So how, if at all, does public opinion affect donor governments' foreign aid decisions? Researchers have established that governments are influenced by the public and that voters get what they want – when they pay attention (Mosley, 1985; Heinrich et al., 2018). So what do voters want? In general, people are more likely to support aid that does the basics: targeting water, sanitation, and hygiene (WASH), food security, and health programs (Hudson et al., 2023). Citizens tend to be most motivated by moral reasoning and the level of need (van Heerde and Hudson, 2009; Hurst et al., 2017) but worry about waste, corruption, and human rights violations (Bauhr et al., 2013; Dasandi et al., 2021). Also, cultural, diplomatic, strategic, and economic ties between donor and recipient countries influence support for aid (Heinrich and Kobayashi, 2020).

Heinrich and colleagues (2016) ask: why do aid budgets decrease in times of economic crisis (which they do)? Is it because: a) economic crises produce budgetary constraints, and therefore governments reduce aid commitments? Or b) foreign aid becomes unpopular and an easy target for politicians? Their research shows that it is b).

Finally, it is also the case that citizens seek to get involved in tackling development challenges at a personal level too – by donating money, volunteering, writing to their MP, and so forth (Hudson et al., 2020). And perceptions are often shaped by TV news coverage and international development charities' fundraising appeals – both of which tend to present people without agency and dignity – which undermines citizens' sense of being able to make a difference and therefore disengage (Hudson et al., 2019). Again – as per Chapter 2 – it underlined just how important it is to contest the representations of development and distant others.

What ideas are behind 'giving'?

Because development aid is given to affect some kind of change, the *giver's* normative ideas about what change should look like directly shape donor agendas. As we saw in Chapter 5, ideas matter, in the real world, both because they shape how we conceive of problems, and how we design appropriate solutions to them. For example, the principle of 'do no harm' has profoundly influenced discourse, policy and practices in the humanitarian aid sector. This idea, which originates in the Hippocratic Oath, was first applied to the sector in Mary Anderson's 1999 book, *Do No Harm: How Aid Can Support Peace or War*? It encouraged aid workers to appreciate that once an intervention enters a context, it becomes part of that context, and actors therefore have an ethical responsibility to consider the potential unintended consequences of their actions – ways they could inadvertently do harm while trying to do 'good.' This principle, and the 'Local Capacities for Peace' project that generated it, has spawned countless policy toolkits, conflict sensitivity approaches, and field guides that aim to translate the idea into practice.

In general, donors want to see their capital, goods, or services used in a particular way, with a particular end in mind. Those who feel they have a moral duty to care for a distant other decide when a development challenge or crisis is morally or politically important. They make a judgement based on their own values and understanding of a situation. Those who give to end poverty tend also to have a theory of how to bring an end to poverty – whether through economic policy, improving livelihoods, education, or something else. Those who aim to prevent migration from spilling over likely have ideas about what pushes people out of their home country and what draws them to a safe refuge, as well as how they can morally, legally, and strategically intervene.

When we think about what ideas influence giving, we also need to recall that some ideas are more powerful than others because of their hegemonic nature (see Chapter 5). As we discussed in Chapter 7, both the IMF and WB tend to give loans based on their own, liberal economic, and Western ideas about what is good governance and what worked to encourage development in the Global North – in Europe, North America, Japan, and South Korea, as well as Australia and New Zealand. So, for example, funds might be given to a state only if that state takes down barriers to free trade, such as tariffs that protect farmers, or demonstrates what the banks view as fiscal responsibility by reducing healthcare services it offers free to its people.

Of course, where aid is used to *promote* universalised normative ideas, these ideas may clash with the ideas communities have, themselves about what is in their own best interests. In fact, efforts to push them may generate a backlash against what is perceived to be foreign imposition. This is what happened in Tonga in response to the proposed ratification of the Convention on the Elimination of All Forms of Discrimination Against Women (CEDAW) (UN Women) (Mangisi, 2018). A vocal anti-CEDAW lobby, led by Tonga's conservative majority, succeeded in blocking its ratification after organising thousands to march in protest, and by subsequently winning a royal intervention to prevent it from being signed. In this case, CEDAW was seen to challenge existing religious and cultural values and practices. As one of Tonga's leading news outlets described it, 'CEDAW's content is contemporary colonialism … forces down the throats of signee nations … its Neo-Marxist agenda' (October 2009, Matangi Tonga, cited in Mangisi, 2018). Tonga is one of only six countries not to have signed the convention. This example illustrates a wider issue – that donor promotion of universal ideas, the basis of human rights, can generate very real dilemmas and contradictions in aid (see Box 9.4).

Box 9.4 The dilemmas of foreign aid and human rights

The international human rights regime is often studied by international lawyers and international relations scholars, but it matters for the politics of development too. The regime itself is a set of institutions: formal institutions, such as the Universal Declaration of Human Rights (1948), various international human rights treaties, regional systems, and monitoring bodies, but also informal human rights norms that are diffused internationally (Greenhill, 2010). There is evidence that aid can improve, if only in the short term, a recipient country's human rights record (Carnegie and Marinov, 2017).

This is a clear example of how international institutions and normative ideas, as well as interests, shape government actions and who gets foreign aid. Some donors, for example Norway, are explicit that human rights are an essential component of development cooperation. Many donors and other organisations use Human Rights Impact Assessments (HRIA), which are tools designed to minimise the negative human rights effects of aid activities (Danish Institute for Human Rights, 2016).

But also consider the complexity of diverging interests between donor and recipient governments, and civil society organisations, which creates contestation over desired alternative futures. As Niheer Dasandi and Lior Erez (2023) have shown in the case of anti-LGTBQ+ legislation in Uganda, while the international community may wish to punish the government and bring it into line with international norms, an overwhelming majority of Ugandans opposed homosexuality and supported the Bill. By providing aid, donors may contribute to poverty reduction, but also to rights violations by strengthening the government's position relative to other actors, such as opposition political parties and civil society (Dasandi and Erez, 2019). These political dilemmas are central to the politics of development aid.

Contesting aid

The dilemmas and contradictions within aid form the basis for people to contest it. Over the past decade, one of the ways it has been contested internally, ironically in light of the interests and power evident in its aim and ambition, is precisely for *not being political enough!* (see Box 9.5).

Box 9.5 Thinking and working politically?

Since the early 1990s, a consensus has been building around the need for aid agencies to incorporate political thinking and action into the goals and methods of development assistance (Carothers and De Gramont, 2013). This movement emerged out of a critique of the modernising idea of development as a technical exercise that merely required capital and technological investment, proper planning and logistics, in order to achieve its goals (see the Introduction to this book).

In reality, the limited effect of aid on ending poverty challenged the technocratic view, and provided strong evidence that programs were likely to fail if they did not either align with, or shift, the interests of the bureaucrats, officials, businessmen and political leaders whose support is needed for their implementation. Thinking and Working Politically (TWP) approaches, and similar strategies such as Problem Driven Iterative Adaption (PIDA), try to address this gap. They tend to promote the mainstreaming of three key elements into development practice: strong political insights and analysis, a deep understanding of local context, and flexibility to reflect and respond to developments on the ground.

Yet, while TWP has squarely entered the development lexicon, its impact has been limited in practice. The Independent Commission of Aid Effectiveness in the UK concluded the approach is yet to be mainstreamed into how development agencies operate. There are a number of reasons for this, captured in Tom Carothers and Diane De Gramont's 2013 book *Development Aid Confronts Politics: The Almost Revolution*. A key reason is that TWP requires new skills, such as political economy analysis, that not all aid officials possess, and changes to the way that aid projects are conceptualised, designed, implemented and assessed that stand in tension with existing norms and organisational ways of working.

Beyond these internal wranglings, perhaps the most important issue of direct concern to those who are affected by aid is whether the system will always be rigged to reproduce the power of those who benefit from it. Or whether some of the power to control 'the money' can be shifted to local communities who are best placed to decide their own futures (Banks et al., 2023). A related issue is whether donors should pay reparations to those countries they aim to 'aid,' the logic being that the rich countries are one of the major causes of many of the challenges that developing countries' aid is designed to address.

Can aid institutions deliver fair representation?

Both the World Bank and IMF have been widely criticised for using more restrictive and punitive economic policies where a government was non-democratic or ideologically non-Western, and for promoting neoliberal, hegemonic economic policies (Gabor, 2010; Mueller, 2011; Clift, 2018) – that is, promoting policies that maintain the dominance of already powerful states and corporations. Is it true that the IMF and the World Bank promote the powerful? Well, let's 'follow the money.'

First of all, institutional donors have an outsized influence on development work. In 2019, according to the World Bank, public sector financing (financing from governments or government-backed banks or agencies) to 'developing countries' was worth US$315 billion, while private and non-official donations made up another US$288 billion (World Bank Group, 2021: 5). The over US$600 billion these groups gave in just this one year was the equivalent of about the GDP of Sweden or Argentina, or about half the value of Google in 2022. This was also more than one hundred times the amount appealed for by the UN for humanitarian aid to Ukraine in February 2023 (UNOCHA, 2023).

Second, the IMF collects most of its funds directly from its 190 member countries, with country quota levels determined based on their relative position within the global economy (IMF, 2023b). The governance structure of the IMF also gives voting shares to member countries based on what those countries pay into the fund, based on these quotas (IMF, 2023a). The World Bank functions very similarly. Although part of the United Nations, the WB is formed by states who are shareholders with votes proportional to the funds they contribute (World Bank, 2015). This means that the richest nations in the world – mostly nations in the Global North – have the most say in setting IMF and WB policy and agendas, and can ensure that these align with their interests.

And so it goes, that some IMF and World Bank policies have forced governments to deregulate economies – particularly in the Global South (Adedeji, 1999; Balassa, 1982) – with the result that inequality has increased (Lang, 2021). Governments overturned policies that protected worker rights or dignity, population health, or education services (Homedes and Ugalde, 2005; Stuckler et al., 2011; Dreher et al., 2015; Stubbs et al., 2016), among other things. They did so often to meet the conditions set forth by the IMF and the World Bank.

It is important to note that, even as these organisations have undergone reforms in recent decades, their tendency to put growth before people and planet is persistent. A recent report by the World Bank offered guidance to governments on how to adapt to new technologies, including artificial intelligence (AI). It was widely criticised for saying little about how governments could protect workers and working conditions in the face of this new world (Anner et al., 2019). Through 'green structural adjustment' the World Bank supports investment in resilient urban infrastructure (Bigger and Webber, 2021). Yet, its lending in the agricultural and forestry sectors has, paradoxically, been associated with increased rates of forest loss (Shandra et al., 2016).

Reflective question

Can we shift the power in the global aid architecture?

Institutional donors decide based on their own ideas and interests – which are transmitted ideas and interests from their major funders – meaning that those who have gained wealth continue to play a big role in deciding how resources, rights, authority, and freedoms are enjoyed or denied in a society. And troublingly, those who have benefited from current socioeconomic and political systems are unlikely to advocate for significant changes to it because the system worked for them. For these reasons, philanthrocapitalism has been found to sustain neoliberal systems and contribute to growing inequalities (Mediavilla and Garcia-Arias, 2019), allowing a few individuals to accumulate private wealth and then use it to set public policy.

In contrast to the top-down, donor/expert-led model presented above, there is a contrary discussion asking why the money that local actors give is often excluded from discussions of a global aid architecture. In part, this is because some expect it to be more susceptible to capture by local elites or corrupt leaders. In other words, some believe that money coming from donors with ties to a community might be used for purposes other than development aid, or less impartially than money coming from global donors with fewer ties to the affected community (Gurgur and Shah, 2005). Expert-led, international donors and oversight are (rightly or wrongly) seen as increasing neutrality and impartiality – the ability to stay out of and not take a side in conflict (see Barnett, 2016). Second, global donors have long influenced who gets a seat at the table when global development challenges are up for discussion, while local actors have been systematically excluded from debate and agenda setting (Shuayb, 2022; Khoury and Scott, 2024). As a result, local actor ideas are less likely to shape development policy and practice.

Donors also sometimes give with one hand to divert attention away from something they are doing with the other. For instance, food aid or healthcare services given to a population suffering because of a war can help a state to keep fighting because the affected population has enough to survive and is less likely to protest for peace. Or, as occurred during the United Nations Climate Conference COP27 in Egypt in 2022, a state might offer to pay for the effects of climate change, to avoid dealing with its causes.

Let's look at how this works, through the snapshot below.

Box 9.6   Giving while taking away?

In 2022 at the United Nations Climate Conference COP27 in Egypt, world leaders agreed to establish a loss-and-damage fund. Its aim was to alleviate climate shocks and deal with the consequences of climate change within vulnerable nations. These countries bear the brunt of climate costs, but are also unfairly some of the world's lowest emitters. The establishment of the loss-and-damage fund was an important win in the movement for climate justice.

The idea of a loss-and-damage fund came from states traditionally excluded from global decision making – with fewer financial resources and so abilities to influence outcomes of negotiation. It was proposed three decades ago by the Alliance of Small Island States (AOSIS), which includes Nauru, Grenada, Tuvalu, Trinidad and Tobago, among others. Because they had little global influence, these states had trouble gaining global attention.

Not until the Paris Agreement of 2015 did the world's more powerful states finally agree to a provision on loss and damage. At the time, though, its mention in Article 8 was 'carefully worded to not include any liability in compensation – a condition put forward by the USA at the time' (Wyns, 2023). Four years later, in Madrid in 2019, high-income parties like the European Union and United States still refused calls for a fund requiring rich nations to pay poorer ones facing the impacts of climate change. But something was changing.

By this time, 134 low-income nations, referred to as the G77 – a group of nations created to promote developing country economic interests – had become increasingly unified around the idea that wealthy nations needed to pay for global climate damage. And, importantly, they were gaining the attention of the populations living within richer states. The murder of George Floyd by police in the state of Minneapolis in the United States in 2020 and at the height of the Covid-19 pandemic, coupled with a global movement of young people demanding climate and racial justice (people power!) meant that by 2022, the world's leaders could no longer be seen to be doing nothing.

The loss-and-damage fund was established in Egypt in 2022. While its structure, scale of payouts, and eligibility criteria are still undecided, states agreed to operationalise and distribute real funds in response to the consequences of climate change. A victory! But, while the fund was a welcome response to the needs of those most affected by climate disaster, it also allowed powerful states to distract their united and informed populations from the absence of more fundamental action on the *causes* of climate change. They avoided confronting big businesses whose practices warm the planet in the name of profit. They avoided taking radical action to address the climate emergency.

Image 9.4 Stilt house in Bangladesh. Image by DPU-UCL via Flickr. Licensed under CC BY 2.0 DEED.

People in Bangladesh are already coping with irregular monsoons, untimely rainfall, increased flooding, coastal and riverbank erosion, and more, due to climate change. Pictured here by researchers interested in how people cope with climate change, people adapt by building and living in houses on stilts.

Can aid ever be 'localised'?

The dominance of development banks, global international organisations, and international non-governmental organisations in development has historically been justified by the idea that they have global technical expertise and knowhow, and that their oversight adds value to development projects and programming. For instance, a polio vaccine rollout might require experts who can move medicines to hard-to-reach populations. Election monitoring in a nascent democracy may run more smoothly if global monitors are present to judge elections to be free and fair. And, since wealthier nations have resources that other nations need, giving aid may, on balance, be better than giving nothing. But technocratic, across-context expertise can quickly override local context-specific and political knowledge (Booth and Unsworth, 2014; Autesserre, 2016). This has been shown to undermine development initiatives, and their ability to respond to real, on-the-ground challenges (Ferguson, 1990; Ramalingam et al., 2013; Dubois et al., 2015; Tanner and Moro, 2016; Khoury and Scott, 2024).

This fact has led to calls for broad institutional change. For instance, there is evidence that a great deal of funding is lost as it moves from nations in the Global North to affected populations, through UN agencies, to INGOs, to NGOs, to contractors at project sites, and so on. Each organisation draws on funding to operate – each pays salaries, rents offices, and fuels cars – leaving less capital for the use of affected populations. Calls for the *localisation* of aid (see Box 9.7) suggest that local actors and institutions can and should be allowed to lead humanitarian and development response (Gingerich and Cohen, 2015; Sandvik and Dijkzeul, 2019). Studies show that humanitarian outcomes are improved when local responders are allowed to lead (Ayobi et al., 2017; Daly et al., 2017; Piquard and Delft, 2018) and that local actors have the right to determine their own fate, including how aid is used (Hanchey, 2020; Slim, 2021).

Box 9.7   Localisation and the grand bargain

Localisation means shifting, power and agency to local leaders and communities to ensure that aid is more responsive to their needs, and as a step toward social and racial emancipationand as a step toward social and racial emancipation. The localisation agenda is a response to critiques that aid is an externally led, top-down exercise in social engineering (Roche and Denney, 2021). The idea is that aid can achieve this through politically savvy and locally led processes.

Localisation is an official priority of *The Grand Bargain* which, launched during the World Humanitarian Summit in Istanbul in 2016, represents a commitment by some of the largest donors and humanitarian organisations to improve the effectiveness and efficiency of the humanitarian action, in order to get more means into the hands of people who need it.

Recent analysis shows that, in practice, international actors are failing to delegate power and authority to local actors as per the localisation agenda (Khoury and Scott, 2024). There is a point at which we can say that actions speak louder than words. In fact, in 2020, just 2.1 per cent of funding moved from global donors directly to local actors, down from 3.5 per cent between 2016 and 2019 (Development Initiatives, 2020). This is despite commitments made by major donors in 2016 to localise aid and send 25 per cent of funding directly to local actors by 2020, as part of the Grand Bargain.

Should donors make reparations?

In another sphere of contestation, there are also calls to shift the aims of development assistance to reparations and justice. *Reparations* are acts that make amends, repair, compensate, and atone for wrongs (Laplante, 2007; Roht-Arriaza and Orlovsky, 2009; Firchow, 2013; Balasco, 2017; Robins et al., 2022). A focus on reparations requires that we understand how structural inequalities are built into existing systems, and the way that development processes continue to create and re-create these (Bhambra, 2014; Beckles, 2019).

In 2021, the United Nations Human Rights Chief, Michelle Bachelet, released a report calling for 'transformative change for racial justice and equality' that hinged on confronting legacies of slavery and colonialism, and its formal acknowledgement by states who continue to profit from these systems (OHCHR, 2021). Wealth and opportunity gaps, the report argued, could be addressed through reparations – a move not without precedents, since they are already being tried or considered by the United States, Belgium, by the European Parliament, Argentina, Columbia, and the Caribbean.

Box 9.8 Rationales for reparations

The fact remains that many of today's problems in these countries, including the persistence, in some cases the creation, of racial and ethnic and religious tensions were the direct result of the colonial experience. So there is a moral debt that needs to be paid.

Dr. Shashi Tharoor, MP

This conversation, the call for reparations in philanthropy, requires us to confront the damning contradiction that the very existence of our sector, the sector of philanthropy, one that seeks to do good, benefits from and reinforces inequities. And it benefits from the growing wealth divide and structural racism that disproportionately impacts Black and Indigenous communities.

Nwamaka Agbo

Activists and scholars call for recognition of the ways that global donors have power and influence because they too have profited from global capitalism's extractive model, and the gains of warfare, colonialism (Tharoor, 2018; Bhambra, 2020), settlement, and slavery. Through reparations, some argue, development could work to put an end to a system designed to 'drain wealth from the Global South and channel it to the Global North,' while centring justice and human rights (Leon-Himmelstine in 'ODI Bites: Decolonising Development, Reparations and a Justice-Centred Approach to 'Aid,' 2022). How reparations through development assistance might work remains to be seen. Alternatively, some suggest that it is time to do away with development aid entirely. Degan Ali, a leader in calls to decolonise development, explains:

> We shouldn't be having aid. We should be having mechanisms for true development of global south countries, especially former colonies. ... Aid architecture is part and parcel of the design of a neo-colonial and racist structure to perpetuate economic and political hegemony of the empires. (Njambi, 2021)

Summary and conclusion

This chapter introduced a range of development donors, what they do, and how their interests and ideas shape development policy and practice. Global aid financing is as local as it is global; donors give for various reasons, from moral duty to geostrategic influence, to domestic interest. Traditional, predominantly Western donors are becoming less generous, giving less of their gross national income (GNI) to development efforts overseas, while emerging donors, such as China, India, the Gulf States, and Turkey, are increasing their influence through development aid. The chapter's last word was given to those contesting development aid through localisation and reparations, in recognition of the fact that donor power and influence today rests on the spoils of warfare, colonialism, settlement, and slavery.

Changing the global aid architecture, whether through localisation, decolonisation, or reparations will be, unfortunately, difficult. The institutions that govern wealth accumulation, how foreign aid is distributed, and why, are tied to one another. Those who 'win' in our global economic system have trouble behaving in ways that might change it. Despite having recently been on the recipient end of donor policies that aimed to constrain what they did, emerging donors have so far mostly behaved similarly to the traditional donors that came before them. The few billionaires who form philanthropic foundations set conditions on how their wealth is used by local actors, much like state funders. Meanwhile, local donors are just as complex and variously motivated as their global counterparts, and so are as likely to give out of compassion as for their own ends.

What is clear is that wealth is not accumulated because of merit or morality; it is more often the product of wealth passed down through generations and racial–colonial legacies. Nonetheless, those with it have financial resources to shape the interests, ideas, and institutions that govern development around the world. Within our global aid architecture, those with wealth – the donors – have the potential to reinforce their own power *over* others. However, they are also potential facilitators of institutional change with the power to redistribute wealth, and the power that comes with it.

Discussion questions

- Should billionaires be allowed to exist?
- Are some motivations for states to give foreign aid more justified than others?
- How do ideas and attitudes shape how interests form around the giving of aid?
- How could aid as reparations work in practice?

Suggested listening

Ali, H. (2022) '"Give us the money": Aid as reparations', *Rethinking Humanitarianism*. The New Humanitarian.

Part 4
Challenges: the politics of development from the ground up

10 How does my identity matter?

Intersectionality, positionality, and power relations

Kailing Xie, Emeka Njoku, and Merisa Thompson

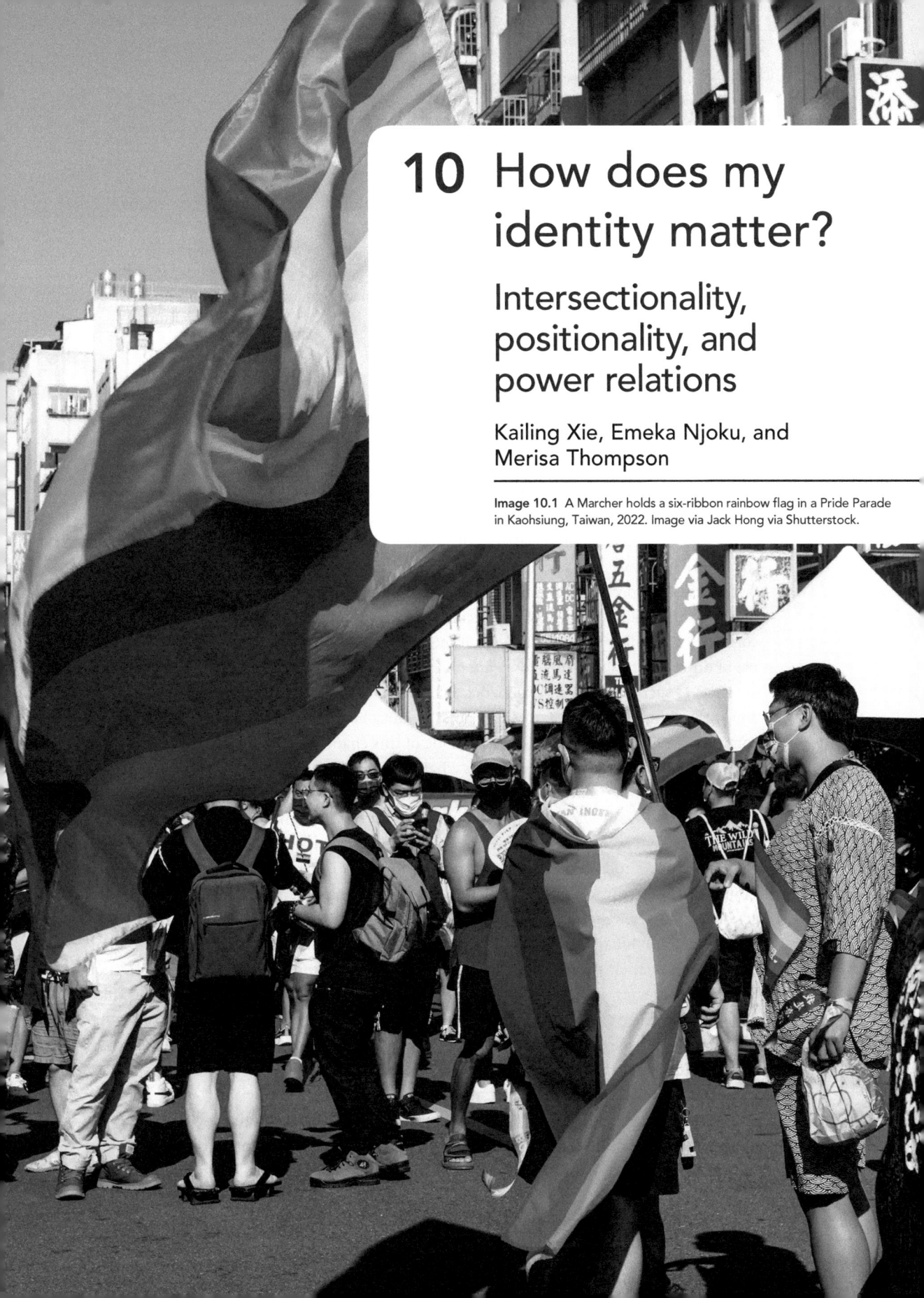

Image 10.1 A Marcher holds a six-ribbon rainbow flag in a Pride Parade in Kaohsiung, Taiwan, 2022. Image via Jack Hong via Shutterstock.

> ### Learning outcomes
>
> - Understand what identity is, how it is socially constructed, and how this is shaped by colonial legacies.
> - Critically evaluate what positionality and intersectionality add to the analysis of identity.
> - Analyse how the contestation of identities becomes developmentally consequential.

The personal is political

At the heart of the SDG agenda, there is a goal to 'leave no one behind' by combatting all forms of discrimination and inequalities that undermine people's ability to benefit from development. But there is a fundamental question underpinning this goal, and development in general – 'Development for *whom?' Who* are the winners and losers in development? Who is included and excluded in development theory, policy, and practice, when viewed through the lens of identity?

Individuals' experiences of and within development are shaped by identity categories produced by the macro social, cultural, economic, and political structures in which they are constructed. In other words, what does it mean to be a woman? How does society value people of different ethnic groups? How are migrants treated by the state, compared with native citizens? As such, individuals experience a constant tension between their individual agency and the external structural forces that foist identity-based exclusion upon individuals and communities. This tension, the central theme of this chapter, exposes the political nature of identity and how it matters for who gets what, when, and how.

In the 1960s, the feminist movement surged in the United States. One of its most inspirational slogans was 'The personal is the political', emphasising the idea that subjective experiences and choices are not just individual matters, but are shaped by larger social, political, and cultural forces. Drawing inspiration from this slogan, this chapter examines the intrinsic politics embedded within various identity categories – whether gender, ethnicity, religion, or caste, etc. – and how they are defined by external forces that shape individual experiences. It reveals the diverse political workings of these identity categories: their production through various institutions, formal and informal, such as colonial legacies, notions of citizenship, legal frameworks, and political systems, how they become salient through context specific interests, be they nationalism, ethnic mobilisation, or resource distribution, and how they are reinforced through the circulation of symbols, practices and ideas associated with certain customary systems, religious beliefs, and gender norms.

This chapter begins by introducing the concept of identity as both practice and a category of analysis. It highlights the importance of positionality and intersectionality in our understanding of the politics of identity and the role of 'identity politics' in development processes. It draws on case studies from China, the Caribbean, and Africa to highlight how political complexities converge and collide to differentially inform group and individuals' access to resources and opportunities. Consequently, the chapter shows how identity shapes people's experience of development.

What is identity and how is it produced?

We all use the word 'identity' and yet its precise definition remains slippery. It concerns a fundamental aspect of our human experience: Who am I as an individual? Who is the collective 'we'? The term 'identity' itself contains a fundamental paradox. From the Latin root *idem*, meaning 'the same', the term therefore implies both similarity and difference. On one hand, each aspect of a person's identity suggests there is something unique about this person that distinguishes them from others. Yet on the other hand, identity also implies a relationship with a broader collective or social group of some kind. Here, identity is about identification with others whom we assume share certain similarities with us, at least in some significant ways, which give us a sense of belonging and inclusion.

Our understanding of 'who we are' is subjective and multifaceted, making it a deeply personal and individual aspect of our existence. Take, for example, someone who was born in the United States to white American parents but who spent their childhood in Korea due to their parents' work. They attended a local Korean school, learned the language and customs, and developed close relationships with Korean peers. They may also have retained their American identity through their parents and occasional visits to the United States. As they grow up, they may have a unique sense of identity that incorporates cultural practices of both American and Korean societies, while also feeling different from both cultures in certain ways. Their experiences of living in multiple cultures may have shaped their worldview, values, and beliefs in unique and complex ways, resulting in a distinct sense of self. This unique sense of individual identity can be fluid and may continue to evolve throughout a person's life.

Box 10.1 Defining Identity

James Fearon posits that the term 'identity' is commonly employed in two interconnected ways, denoted as 'social' and 'personal'. Identity, as a *social* category, pertains to a group or category of individuals identified by a specific label and defined by certain rules governing membership and perceived distinctive traits. *Personal* identity, by contrast, refers to individual characteristics that a person holds dear and considers socially significant, yet are generally regarded as relatively immutable.

While some scholars emphasise the stability of identity once formed or claim that identity is natural and fixed, major scholarly works from a number of disciplines in the social sciences and humanities have contributed significantly to the contemporary understanding of identity, which acknowledge the potential for ongoing growth, transformation, and fluidity in how individuals perceive and express their identities over time. Writing in 1968, Erik Erikson's psychosocial theory *Identity: Youth and Crisis* examines identity development throughout an individual's lifespan. The groundbreaking feminist work *The Second Sex* by Simone de Beauvoir published in 1949 examines the construction of female identity within a patriarchal society, while Frantz Fanon's influential work in postcolonial studies and critical theory *Black Skin, White Masks*, published in 1952, discusses the impact of internalised racial identity and the struggle for decolonised selfhood. The last two works reveal the significant impacts of wider macro structures on how identity is experienced and perceived by individuals from certain groups. Similarly, Clifford Geertz's influential work *The Interpretation of Cultures* published in 1973 discusses how people derive meaning and identity from cultural symbols, rituals, and practices, which highlights the significance of cultural context in shaping individual and collective identities.

Erving Goffman's sociological work *The Presentation of Self in Everyday Life* published in 1959, as well as Judith Butler's influential 1990 book *Gender Trouble: Feminism and the Subversion of Identity* pinpoint the performative nature of our identities in everyday social interactions. Butler's work adds further critique to the idea of fixed identities and she argues that identities are socially constructed through performance and repetition. Identity is therefore now recognised as a complex and dynamic construct that can evolve and adapt in response to life experiences and changing social contexts.

Cultural theorist Stuart Hall (1996) points out that fundamentally, identity is about the relationships between the 'self' and others, about marking difference that draws a boundary of inclusion and exclusion. By recognising commonalities and dissimilarities with others, we assert who we are, as well as who we are not. This boundary-drawing process helps to establish our sense of self and is, in effect, a political process. For instance, as elaborated by Simone de Beauvoir in her groundbreaking work, *The Second Sex* (1949), women have been defined by their differences from men and their 'otherness' to men forms the basis for the social construction of gender roles and expectations. This boundary drawing is also evident in various nationalistic projects in their demarcation of the collective 'we' through a shared language, religion, history, as well as cultural practice. For example, the legitimacy of the Chinese government originates from its historical struggle against foreign imperialism, as opposed to being derived from democratic elections. Its foundation as a 'New China', relies on the narrative of its triumphant departure from the 'Century of humiliation' (1839–1949) as an important part in its national identity construction.

To further uncover the political nature of identities, both on individual and collective levels, we will examine how identity is produced in everyday practice through ideas, interests, and institutions, which render it as an important political category for analysis. Central to this is the importance of understanding how different categories of identity are socially constructed through everyday practices, and how the meanings ascribed to them change across time and cultures.

> ## Reflective question
>
> Do you agree that identity is not static?

Identity as practice

According to Brubaker and Cooper (2000: 4), 'As [a] category of practice, [identity] is used by "lay" actors in some (not all!) everyday settings to make sense of themselves, of their activities, of what they share with, and how they differ from others'. Understanding identity as practice means that it is not solely a fixed and inherent characteristic, but rather a fluid and dynamic process, shaped and constructed through various practices and interactions in social, cultural, and personal contexts. It acknowledges that individuals actively engage in practices that constantly influence their sense of self through shaping one's subjective understanding and perception of who they are as a unique and distinct person, as well as how they are perceived by others.

Such practices can include language use, clothing choices, cultural affiliations, social interactions, and more. Through these practices, individuals construct and communicate their identities, both to themselves and to others. For example, someone may identify as a feminist and express this identity through their participation in feminist activism, their language use, and their engagement with feminist communities. In this case, feminism becomes an active practice that contributes to the individual's sense of identity.

By exploring what people 'do' in everyday practice – instead of assuming the intrinsic characteristics of who people are – identity is shown to be a socially constructed category contingent on a specific historical, geographical, and political locality. In other words, identity is open to change. Taking gender as an example, instead of assuming that there is a shared experience of 'women' that is singular, natural and ahistorical based on biological categorisation of human genitals, interrogating the varied social, economic, and political contexts of a given space and time can reveal different realities attached to being a woman, which exposes the political nature of gender identity.

The Mosuo community, a small ethnic group living in the Lugu Lake region of southwestern China, is known for its matrilineal social structure. Lineage and inheritance in Mosuo community are traced through the female line, and property is passed down from mothers to daughters. The community practices a form of marriage known as 'walking marriage' or 'axia', where men and women do not formally marry or live together. Instead, women have the freedom to choose their partners and engage in relationships with multiple partners throughout their lives. Mosuo women are often highly respected and play a prominent role in the community's social, economic, and cultural life. Their experience and status significantly differ from the experience of women in China's mainstream Han-dominated society, which is heavily shaped by patrilineal practices and belief of male domination over women (Xie, 2021a). Critical Race Theory, which emerged in the United States in the 1970s, offers another example of the impact of the institutional distribution of power on identity. It holds that race is not only socially constructed, but that racism is so deeply embedded in society that the law and legal institutions of the United States systematically maintain and reproduce inequalities between persons of a different race (Delgado and Stefancic, 2000).

Importantly, who gets to decide how and when certain identity categories are applied and to whom is a matter of the distribution of power. In many instances, individuals and groups have little control over their ascribed identity that can significantly affect their lives. This is important in development as evidenced later in this chapter. This power is held by external forces, such as existing ideas, norms, and institutions. For example, James Scott's 1998 book *Seeing Like a State: How Certain Schemes to Improve the Human Condition Have Failed* famously critiques the ways in which states and bureaucracies use data collection, including census-taking, to impose a particular vision of order and control on society. The very process of categorising people according to certain artificial and socially constructed identity labels – such as ethnicity and race – has real-life political consequences in terms of the distribution of power and resources.

Reflective question

Can you think of a real-life example where individuals have little control over how they are categorised into certain identity groups that significantly affects their life chances?

Identity as a practice (what people do) is also intricately intertwined with discourse (what people say). In Van Dijk's critical work *Discourse and Society* published in 1985, he defines discourse as 'a type of social interaction that is basically verbal or written, broadly conceived to cover all sorts of semiotic events and phenomena in which social meaning is constructed'. Therefore, discourse encompasses both verbal and written communications and their various manifestations in society, such as visual images and gestures. The social meaning, or ideas, attached to each identity category via institutions (both formal such as the state and informal such as social norms) influences people's practice, experience and understanding of the world because they generate and distribute certain kinds of discourse. For example, Chinese national identity today is constructed through the discourse of the Century of humiliation (1839–1949), and its government relies on it to justify its political legitimacy (Xie, 2021b).

Post-structuralist thinkers like Michel Foucault (1970) and Judith Butler (1990) both reveal the power of discourse in the construction of individual and group identity, which is intricately linked to the interests of various institutions. Foucault argued that discourse shapes and governs the way we think, speak, and behave through knowledge produced by historically and socially conditioned discursive practices. These discursive practices produce and maintain knowledge, truth, and social norms, thereby exerting power over individuals and social institutions in shaping our perceptions, understanding, and construction of reality, including constructing identities and influencing power relations among groups. Such power can be employed to maintain social hierarchies, reinforce inequalities, or challenge oppressive systems through shaping societal norms and expectations.

While Foucault highlighted the oppressive nature of discourses, he also acknowledged the potential for resistance. Various interest groups may also try to generate subversive discourses that can challenge dominant power structures, and offer alternative narratives and identities that contest established norms and knowledge. For instance, the word 'queer' was historically used as a derogatory slur against individuals who did not conform to traditional gender and sexuality norms. In the 1980s and 1990s, some LGBTQ+ activists began to reclaim the term as a way of empowering themselves and rejecting the negative associations that had been attached to it. Over time, the term 'queer' has been embraced by many LGBTQ+ individuals and communities as a way of expressing a non-conforming or non-binary gender or sexual identity in many parts of the world. In Taiwan, pro-LGBTQ+ rights groups launched a campaign called 'We are all different, yet the same' releasing a series of touching real-life stories of LGBTQ+ individuals and their families who suffered because of their perceived differences in Taiwanese society. This campaign aimed to shift public discourse around the LGBTQ+ community from stigmatisation to acceptance in Taiwan, which establishes it as the first place in Asia to legalise same-sex marriage in 2019 and an emerging progressive force for LGBTQ+ rights in Asia.

Although one's sense of identity and social meaning attached to certain identity categories can and does change over time and space, it does not mean they can change easily, or without resistance. In contemporary societies facing rapid social changes, we are accustomed to hearing about 'identity crises' from the media. For example, the 'masculinity crisis' in South Korea has triggered young men to protest against feminism (Kwon, 2019) denoting a sense of unease, dissatisfaction, or conflict around how masculinity is understood, expressed, and experienced by certain groups of men. This discomfort can lead some to defend 'traditional' expectations of women to be confined to the domestic sphere.

Reflective question

Should all identities be protected by the state? Why?

Identity as a category of analysis

To help us answer important social, cultural, and political questions in various development processes thoroughly, we should also consider how to treat identity as an analytical category. The relevance of identity in understanding the politics of development are mainly twofold: first, identities are explained on individual, communal, national, and international levels, and imbued with and mediated through politics; and second and simultaneously, identities have explanatory power in deciphering the operation of politics across various interests, institutions and ideas. Thus, identity is not just a practice in terms of what people do or say, or how difference is perceived and demarcated, but an analytical category signifying broader systems of power.

Below, we first explain the concept of 'intersectionality' which we argue is a crucial point of departure when mobilising identity analytically to take into account connections between interlocking systems of oppression. We then introduce the concept of 'positionality' as an important analytical tool, both to locate and reflect upon our own position within a wider web of interests, but also to analyse how the position of actors (i.e., policy-makers or development practitioners) matters in terms of what knowledge (i.e., policy and interventions) they produce.

Major identity categories, such as gender, caste, class, and religion are mutually constitutive. As Weston (2010: 15) bluntly puts it: 'Gender is about race is about class is about sexuality is about age is about nationality is about an entire range of social relations.' Drawing on Black feminist and critical legal theories, Kimberlé Crenshaw developed the concept of intersectionality to speak to the multiple social forces, social identities, and ideological instruments through which power and disadvantage are expressed and legitimised (Crenshaw, 2017). The key to intersectionality is the idea that different categories of identity can overlap or 'intersect' and how this interaction shapes multiple dimensions of experience, and often compound experiences of inequality and discrimination (Crenshaw, 1991). For example, a Black woman at work can be discriminated against both in terms of race and gender, but when these two systems of oppression come together, they can create deeper forms of inequality that would not be experienced in the same way by a Black male or white woman.

Multiple dimensions of intersectionality can be seen to be institutionalised through the explicit and implicit incorporation of sexist, racist, homophobic, ableist and ageist discourse and ideas into formal and informal rule-making, policy-making and law-making. For example, laws that deny women access to abortion are not only discriminatory and harmful towards women in general, but are likely to disproportionally impact women of colour, rural and poorer women due to their structural position which gives them less access to safe routes for abortion – for example, lack of means to travel to abortion clinics outside of their state of residence. Intersectionality, therefore, helps us to analyse the complexity of power relations linked to identity, both structural and agential, and 'helps us to grasp the interplay between macro-level structures and institutions, and identities and lives lived at the micro level' (Thompson, 2021: 182).

The term 'intersectionality' has entered mainstream discussion and is increasingly being incorporated into development practice to describe problems of inequality and to fashion concrete solutions (see Box 10.2). Looking at identity-based exclusion, the concept is important to challenge the assumption of shared experienced merely based on one single category of identity. Take gender as an example. A rural migrant woman working in a Foxconn factory producing iPhones for the world (Pun, 1999; Pun et al., 2016) would face a starkly different reality from their urban middle-class sisters from birth (Xie, 2021a). Due to China's entrenched rural–urban divide, the One Child Policy was much better implemented in the cities, which means that girls who were born to urban families are more likely to receive a better education due to the lack of competition from male siblings. However, their rural counterparts faced abandonment at birth due to strong family pressure to have a male child. Many rural girls drop out of school to start work early to support their younger siblings. Sometimes rural girls were left unregistered to save the 'birth quota' for their future brothers. As a result,

Box 10.2   Intersectionality

The term 'intersectionality' was first penned in 1991 by Kimberlié Crenshaw, an American lawyer, civil rights activist and academic. She developed the concept in response to prior scholarship that treated 'race' and 'gender' as exclusive issues – i.e., with feminist studies focusing on women, and anti-racist studies focusing on race. Crenshaw rejected the separability of these dimensions and instead anchored her analysis in exploring their intersection and how this interaction shaped multiple dimensions of experience.

The early origins of the concept, however, predate this and are rooted in work of Black feminist theorists and activists, particularly in the US. For example, the notion of 'interlocking oppressions' is often attributed to the Kumbee River Collective, a Black feminist lesbian organisation located in Boston in the 1970s, who expanded the notion in an essay, 'The Black feminist statement', published in 1979. Other notable and influential Black US feminists working in this field at the same time who have also made significant contributions to the development of 'intersectional theory' are Audre Lorde and Patricia Hill Collins.

Despite its increasing influence and adoption across many fields, one of the key criticisms – although contested – sometimes levelled at intersectionality is that it does not constitute an actual theory as it is methodologically and ontologically unclear. Some argue that as intersectionality has travelled from activist to academic circles it has been flattened or reduced to a new buzzword (Mason, 2017) or has become 'performative' (Salem and Jibrin, 2015). Yet, this does not mean that a return to its critical origins is not possible or indeed practiced.

these individuals, mostly women, cannot access any state-provided services such as education, social welfare or healthcare (Xu, 2016). It also makes them extremely marginalised in society and vulnerable to labour exploitation. It would be naive to assume a shared experience among these two groups of women without considering the intersectional elements that shape their life experiences. Meanwhile, Chinese rural male migrants who left their families to work in urban areas often have to adapt to the new expectations and pressures of the city life. If he cannot bring enough money to the family, he might have to assume more childcare work at home to allow his wife to work, which leads to compromises of traditional ideas of masculinity (Choi and Peng, 2016). What does this context mean for developmental policy and support? It raises the question of whether a single national 'women's policy' would adequately support all women's needs in China.

Positionality reveals the social, cultural, and historical context from which an individual or group views and interprets the worlds that are shaped by various aspects of our identity, such as race, gender, sexual orientation, socioeconomic status, nationality, religion, and more (see Box 10.3). Consequently, individuals' experiences, perspectives, and understanding of reality are subjective and contain positional biases. It is pertinent, therefore, for people who occupy positions of power to consider their positional biases and how these might affect the outcomes of their decisions. In the development context, positionality emphasises the importance of reflexivity among researchers, policy-makers and practitioners, the need to reflect on and acknowledge their own position, power dynamics and potential biases in their work (Bhambra, 2007). For instance, researchers often occupy positions of privilege in relation to the communities they study, which can impact their interactions, access to data, and interpretations of findings. Therefore, they need to be mindful of potential power asymmetries that may affect research processes, practices, and outcomes.

Box 10.3   Positionality

The concept of positionality refers to recognising and understanding how researchers' sociocultural predispositions and emotional conditions can profoundly influence their perspectives and interpretations of the individuals and communities they study. The concept gained prominence through the influential work of Donna Haraway, a feminist scholar, in her essay titled 'Situated knowledges: the science question in feminism and the privilege of partial perspective' (1988). Haraway places considerable emphasis on the profound importance of historical and sociopolitical context in developing and advancing knowledge and underscores the importance of scholars recognising and embracing the influence of their perspectives and biases on the research process and the subsequent knowledge generated. Building on the works of Haraway's discourse on the positioning and contextual nature of knowledge production, Simandan (2019: 130) underscored the existence of 'epistemic gaps' that highlights the potential incompleteness of our understanding of socialcultural matters. This understanding can be influenced by the way that information is filtered through various experiences and memories.

In addition, Gayatri Chakravorty Spivak, in her notable publications *Outside the Teaching Machine* (1993) and *Can the Subaltern Speak* 1988 brings attention to the influence of power dynamics, social hierarchies, and colonial legacies on the perspectives of Western scholars when examining and comprehending communities in the Global South. Spivak emphasises the necessity for these researchers to critically reflect upon their privilege, authority, and power positions.

The idea of positionality is becoming increasingly significant in contemporary social research, highlighting the necessity for scholars to examine their subjectivity and any resulting biases that might be the product of their particular social placements. Suppose researchers have a nuanced understanding and recognition of their positionality and situatedness vis-à-vis the research subjects. In that case, they can conduct their studies in a way that upholds ethical standards, fosters empathy, and demonstrates a keen awareness of the contextual nuances surrounding their subject (Sirnate, 2014; Shaw et al., 2020).

For development practitioners, to be mindful to their own positional biases in their work means to actively examine how their privileged position might create cognitive blind spots and perpetuate harmful stereotypes, leading to the formulation of problematic or 'counterproductive' policies. For example, the common stereotype of 'Third World Women' is a product of the global power imbalance between Western dominated donor countries and other countries (Mohanty and Torres, 1991). The term was used to refer to women living in countries that were considered economically and politically marginalised, primarily in Africa, Asia, and Latin America. These women are often portrayed as victims in need of Western rescue or as exotic and oppressed Others. Such imagery might be motivated by organisations' interest in raising donations or generating media attention for a cause, but it also reveals the positional bias of actors in the Global North who strip these women of their agency. Whether or not they mean well, such erasure has been a recurring issue in various development initiatives, policies, and narratives. For example, the 'Save the Children' campaign aimed to improve children's lives in some developing countries during the mid-twentieth century unintentionally portrayed local women as passive victims in need of help, overshadowing their agency by emphasising Western donors and organisations as the main saviours and providers.

Identity politics

Identity politics refers to the practice of organising and advocating for the rights, interests, and concerns of specific social groups based on their shared identity characteristics (Bernstein, 2005). The term is widely used to describe a diverse range of phenomena from multiculturalism (see Taylor, 1994), the women's movement, civil rights, lesbian and gay movements, to violent ethnic and nationalistic conflict in postcolonial Africa and Asia (see Surucu, 2002; Yeros, 2016). Bernstein (1997) posits social movements need identity for empowerment, and to act politically (see more on social movements in Chapter 8). A social movement's collective identity is typically characterised by maintaining boundaries between group members and non-members, which help it to gather momentum to produce political claims (Taylor and Whittier, 1992). When movements diagnose problems, non-member identities are often attributed as responsible for the problems, and charged with alleviating them (Snow and Benford, 1988). This invites us to think about the role of 'identity politics' in shaping various 'desired futures', whether economic growth, poverty reduction, or freedom and voice, as perceived by different identity groups.

Identity politics can produce mixed results, proving a blessing or a curse depending on how it impacts upon individuals' and groups' social, political, and civil rights. For example, the Civil Rights Movement in the United States during the 1950s and 1960s is often considered an example of positive identity politics, as it mobilised grassroots activism, peaceful protests, and civil disobedience, and it led to significant social and legal changes, such as the Civil Rights Act of 1964 and the Voting Rights Act of 1965, to dismantle segregation and institutionalised racism against African Americans. Ethnonationalism and far-right extremism can evoke negative connotations of identity politics, being closely associated with xenophobia, racism, discrimination, violence, and intolerance towards minority groups, immigrants, and marginalised communities. For instance, in her pathbreaking work *Terrorist Assemblages: Homonationalism in Queer Times*, Jasbir K. Puar (2007) reveals how 'homonationalisms' are deployed in the US to incorporate certain queer subjects as 'properly homo' patriots to differentiate from its 'dangerous other': perversely sexualised and racialised terrorist look-a-likes – especially Sikhs, Muslims, and Arabs. It highlights even progressive moves towards sexual justice can be limited, in reality, when contradictory stances mix with various interests.

History is not short of examples of the complex connections between identity politics and the mechanics of development. China's non-plural Han identity politics (Yeh, 2013) and India's Hindutva (see Jaffrelot, 1999) are both closely tied to their states' 'developmental activities'. In these contexts, the dominant groups' exploitation of others and their mobilising of divisions were intricately tied to economic development. These and other cases, which we explore below, compel us to take identity seriously as an analytical category when examining the impacts of identity on alternative desired futures.

How does identity shape desired futures?

Below, we examine three examples of how identity shapes development in closer detail. These are identity-based inequality in the food system, the weaponisation of identity in conflict and post-conflict settings, and youth politics. Across each case, we consider how institutions, interests and ideas are constitutive of the relationship between identity and desired futures.

How identity matters in the food and agricultural system

Who gets, what, why and how in the food and agricultural system – from production through consumption – is deeply structured by gender, race, class, nation and other identity categories. The very shape of the global food system itself is deeply structured by hundreds of years of pre-colonial and colonial relations. Taking the Caribbean as an example, the European colonial conquest, settlement, slavery and indentureship, violently displaced and decimated many indigenous populations and their foodways denying them rights to land, resources and freedom based on ideologies of racial discrimination. European colonialism brought with it new systems of meaning and power, which were highly structured by hierarchical systems of gender, race, class and nation, while at the same time exploiting and accentuating pre-existing divisions (Quijano, 2000).

In the Caribbean, indigenous subsistence farming for local consumption was largely replaced by the interests of colonisers whose focus was the extractive production of cash crops – such as sugar, cocoa and later bananas – for export and profit (Best and Levitt, 2009). In order to achieve this, racialised and gendered systems of enslaved and indentured agricultural labour, from Africa and India respectively, were violently implemented. The interests of largely white, male, European colonisers, administrators, and plantation owners, therefore, took precedence over those of indigenous, enslaved and indentured populations. The latter experienced violence, impoverishment and limited or no access to equal rights. Small farmers in general, and female farmers in particular, still experience discrimination, marginalisation and lack of access to resources and power today, in part due to the low status and lack of importance given to local production for local consumption stemming from the colonial period when primacy was placed on the exportation of cash crops for profit and the importation of subsistence foods (Thompson, 2019, 2021). This often further plays out in familiar and continued policy bias that favours large-scale, agribusiness for export and consumer preferences for foreign, imported and processed foods which are seen to be more modern and of higher status (Thompson, 2020). Moreover, the very foods we eat – from the presence of bananas in Europe to Kentucky Fried Chicken in the Caribbean – continue to be influenced by neocolonial patterns of trade, which intersect with issues of identity (Wilson, 2013).

At the formal institutional level, the development and implementation of food and agricultural policy, such as international trade laws (which govern how much producers and nations are taxed by to import and export food and agriculturally related goods), national food security policies (which define policies, goals and benchmarks for ensuring populations have access to affordable, healthy food) and agricultural incentive programmes (which often define what type of food production and which producers are seen worthy of financial support) all involve decision-making processes that enable or constrain different individuals and groups to benefit depending on their structural location. For example, lack of female land ownership often means that women are less able to access credit than men. Ideas and assumptions about who does and who should farm, and indeed, who does and who should cook or prepare food, also often help or hinder access to resources and power. For example, Afro-descendant female farmers in the Eastern Caribbean have reported that Agricultural Extension Officers do not take them seriously or include them in policy and decision-making discussions due to patriarchal norms that successful farmers are male (Barry and Gahman, 2021). In Trinidad, where due to the migration of 143,939 indentured Indian labourers between 1845 and 1917, farming is often associated with Indian-descended farmers, both male and female Afro-descendant farmers report experiencing institutional biases when trying to access extension services or financial support (Thompson, 2021). The interests of large export-import companies (often linked to foreign capital or the descendants of European planters) often trump the interests of small and female farmers.

How identity matters in conflict and post-conflict settings

Despite global attempts by the United Nations (UN) to incorporate marginalised groups in policy development and implementation, gender and sexual minorities are often not included domestically in conflict and post-conflict settings. For instance, Nigerian, Gambian, Senegalese and Ugandan governments have consistently and purposefully excluded and discriminated against gender and sexual minorities, limiting their participation and involvement in political processes under the guise of protecting greater societal norms, but, in reality, are pandering to perceived popular opinion for political expediency (Pierce, 2007; Schulz and Touquet, 2020). Exclusionary policies by state actors have contributed to the persistence of conflicts due to violations of human rights and civil liberties, created resentments, and hampered peace building. As a result, developmental processes are constrained, perpetuating inequality and injustice. For example, United Nations Security Council Resolutions 1325, 4420, 2106 of the United Nations were passed to protect women and men during and after war. Despite being a signatory to UNSCR resolutions 1324, 4420, and 2106, Nigeria, a country in the Global South, still lacks comprehensive laws that address such violence, including same-sex violence. While kidnappings and sexual assaults on women and children remain common occurrences, significant numbers of men and boys are victims of sexual violence in both conflict and peacetime environments, but are frequently overlooked (Njoku et al., 2022).

Conflict-related sexual violence against men and boys functions as a weapon of war, aimed at degrading and intimidating victims through gendered subordination (Schulz, 2018). In conflict settings, male victims may be humiliated through feminisation or homosexuality, reinforcing a 'hyper-masculine hierarchy of violence' (Eichert, 2019) and impacting their standing in the community (Sivakumaran, 2007). Stereotypes linking male sexual violence to being gay exist in some African societies, erasing male victims' manhood (Njoku and Dery, 2023). Despite UN recognition of male victims in 2013 (Resolution 2106), societal norms of heteronormativity, homophobia, and toxic masculinity hinder implementation of laws and policies addressing same-sex violence. Instead, anti-homosexuality laws persist or are strengthened, as lately in Uganda, Kenya, and Nigeria, leaving a legal void in addressing such violence.

There is a substantial body of literature that delves into the idea that heteronormativity, homophobia, and toxic masculinity, as well as the acceptance or tolerance of gender and sexual minorities, are strategically employed in order to shape collective national or societal identity or to further other interests of the state (Puar, 2007; Owens, 2010). For instance, the military can be characterised as a patriarchal institution that relies on the intentional use of force to cultivate and promote a dominant hyper-masculinity in order to instil soldiers with certain qualities that often involve aggression and are considered essential during times of war (Meger, 2010; Baaz and Stern, 2013).

Gender and sexuality-based exclusion in policy formulation affects male victimisation. Scholars report physical and psychological effects among young men and boys sexually abused by militant groups in various regions like Rwanda, Liberia, Syria, the Democratic Republic of the Congo, northern Uganda, South Sudan, Sri Lanka, Uganda, the former Yugoslavia, and Bosnia (Onyango and K. Hampanda, 2011; Schulz and Touquet, 2020; Dolan et al., 2020; Njoku and Dery, 2021). Victims experience victim-blaming and gender displacement in communities (Schulz, 2018). Some male victims in north-eastern Nigeria may suffer from Stockholm syndrome due to sexual violence by Boko Haram and the Islamic State, expressing a willingness to return to the terrorist group if the opportunity arises because they have claimed that, aside from sexual violence, they were treated better in the terrorist camps than at the internally displaced persons camps, where they have faced all forms of physical anguish (Njoku, 2022). Such evidence highlights political and societal ramifications to ignoring sexual victimisation among young men and boys (Njoku, 2022).

How identity matters for youth politics

Youth social and political exclusion leads to armed conflicts and protests worldwide, fueled by resentment and marginalisation generated by resource inequities as a result of sociopolitical exclusion, and corruption, migration, and unemployment (Gurr 1970; Ismail and Olonisakin, 2021). In 2020, Nigeria, Sierra Leone, Liberia, and others witnessed 577 protests, mostly led by young people demanding socioeconomic improvement (Wilson Center, 2021: 3). These protests are driven by the exclusionary politics and practices of country governments that push young people to mass mobilise based on shared challenges, interests, or identities. Young participants develop a strong sense of solidarity by adhering to common values, beliefs, and objectives with their new shared identity bringing them closer and encouraging feelings of solidarity and inspiration to contribute to their cause (Chodak, 2016).

Reflective question

Do you agree that identity motivates political participation?

In 2020, Nigerian youths aged 15 to 35 protested against police brutality by tweeting with the hashtag #EndSARS – short for 'End Special Anti-Robbery Squad'. In 1992, the Nigerian Police Force created the anti-robbery squad, an elite police force with the sole purpose of combatting armed robberies. However, the unit went awry and abused its authority by killing, kidnapping, assaulting, and blackmailing numerous young people under the pretence of going after criminals in the state. Youth demonstrations were held throughout the country, including in Abuja, the capital, and Lagos, a major economic hub. Young people mobilised through the Twitter hashtags #ENDSARS and #Sorosoke (speak out), participating actively in debates, sharing valuable information, and making donations to support the protest. According to Abimbade et al. (2022), the hashtags have become a symbol of youth identity. The movement has fostered friendships, formed new bonds, and continued to be relevant even after the protests ended. In the eyes of many

Image 10.2 EndSars Protesters raise placards at the Lekki Toll Gate in Lagos, Nigeria, 2020. Image by Eiseke Bolaji via Shutterstock.

observers, the EndSARS protests represent more than just a backlash against police brutality; it also represents collective outrage over bad leadership, corruption, and bad governance that have dogged the Nigerian state since its independence, as well as the older generation's failure to move the nation from a developing to a developed country (*The Guardian*, 2020).

In the light of the high unemployment rate and the deteriorating infrastructure in Nigeria's education sector, scholars such as Aniche and Iwuoha (2022) argue that the EndSARs protest and other instances of the growing restiveness of Nigerian youth is a reflection of their decades long exclusion and marginalisation in governance processes, laws, policies, and practices that affect them. These exclusions extend to political recruitment; the majority of Nigerian youths are unable to run for elected office due to the high costs, millions of Naira, involved in campaigning and to pay for party tickets to be a political party's designated candidate for a constituency (*Premium Times*, 2022). Despite attempts to encourage young people to run for elected office, such as President Muhmmad Buhari's recent 'Not Too Young to Run' law, young people have labelled such initiatives hypocritical as only the children of the wealthy or political elites can buy party tickets, excluding the vast majority of young people (*Premium Times*, 2022). Such class-based exclusion further marginalises disadvantaged young people and exacerbates the gap between the wealthy and everyone else in society.

Experts and observers warned that if the EndSARS protest was not 'carefully and professionally' handled, it could have led to an implosion or unprecedented levels of violence in the country due to the lack of inclusivity in the political and governance process (Vanguard, 2020; Ojedokun et al., 2021: 1). Furthermore, the Africa report (2022: 1) stated that Nigerian youths are responding to the government's neglect and abuse over the years by using democratic channels to gain power and influence in the country's polity and politics through participation in electoral politics. The Nigerian context is a prime example of youth activism in West Africa, highlighting the importance of identity in fostering heightened political participation within a democratic framework.

Reflective question

Can political participation transform people's identity?

Summary and conclusion

This chapter has shown how identity is both a barrier and a pathway to progressive recognition. Identity categories are a complex and dynamic construct that can evolve and adapt in response to life experiences and changing social contexts. Whether individual or collective, a practice and category of analysis, identity is integral to understanding the everyday pursuit of desired futures. Institutions, interests, and ideas can inadvertently include or exclude, based on various identity aspects. How we navigate life and seize opportunities is influenced by our identity, which is shaped by, and in turn reinforced, societal structures and institutions.

The extent to which individuals or groups are able to exercise agency, and are subject to or can resist power, is determined by interactions between individual and structural identity formation. Institutions – both formal (i.e., laws, regulations or constitutions) and informal (i.e., unwritten social norms around gender, race, sexuality, disability) – determine who is protected, counted, included, as well as who is excluded from political opportunities and decision making. This involves setting the agenda, privileging certain interests, and shaping norms. Racist, sexist, ableist, ageist, sexually prejudiced, classist and religiously intolerant beliefs and ideas permeate spheres of authority, power, and decision-making. The foundations of some (or indeed most!) societies, cultures and groups are grounded in different unequal and hierarchical relations of identity, such as racism in the United States, caste in India, the racist and sexist underpinnings of European colonialism and the persistence of patriarchy on an almost universal basis (apart from the small pockets of matriarchal societies mentioned earlier in the chapter).

For this reason, it is imperative that the specific sociohistorical contexts and power relations are taken into account when we think about how identity shapes who gets what, when and how. Especially in conflict and post-conflict settings, identity-based exclusions have meant that historically, many marginalised groups' interests have been denied or jeopardised. State actors have persistently and deliberately excluded, discriminated against, and, in many cases, securitised marginalised groups to further their own political interests. These exclusions frequently result in conflicts, hamper peace-building efforts, generate abuses of human rights and civil liberties, and create resentments that violent groups frequently exploit to draw new recruits. Economically, identity-based exclusions create long-term disadvantages for marginalised groups, which can underlie political instability. Thus, development is constrained or impeded by the socioeconomic disparities and injustices generated by discrimination. This reality has persisted despite international attempts to promote the inclusion of marginalised groups in policy design and implementation.

Even when the interests of marginalised groups are included in development policy and planning, they are vulnerable to being co-opted or depoliticised, amounting to empty rhetoric and promises. Or, they can be so narrow in focus that intersectional dimensions get downplayed, such as when a focus on 'women' does not take into account the many different experiences of being a woman, and benefits women of one class, sexuality, ethnicity or ability over another. That said, as we saw with the youth politics example, identity can also play a positive role in bringing together group interests to achieve collective action, and to help overcome and transform discriminatory identity practices and social norms for the better.

Discussion questions

1 How is identity produced? Is it it is fixed over time and space? Why?

2 Can you name one empirical example each to demonstrate how interests, institutions and ideas produce identity? For example:

   a) Can you think of an example of how institutional structures produce and reproduce inequalities based on identity?

   b) Can you think of an example of how common interests based on one or more aspects of identity have brought people together to mobilise for change?

   c) Can you think of an example of how ideas about identity can either constrain or enhance a person's ability to act or access opportunities?

3 How would you respond to the following statements?

   a) Identity is an individualised personal question.

   b) Identity has been over-politicised today.

   c) Identity brings us together more than it pushes us apart.

Suggested further reading

Kreft, A.-K. (2023) '"This patriarchal, machista and unequal culture of ours": obstacles to confronting conflict-related sexual violence, social politics', *International Studies in Gender, State & Society*, 30 (2): 654–77.

Pittaway, E. and Pittaway, E. (2004) '"Refugee woman": a dangerous label'. *Australian Journal of Human Rights*, 10 (1): 119–35.

Salem, S. (2019) 'Capitalism, postcolonialism and gender: complicating development', *Gender and Development Network: Thinkpieces*, July.

11 Why doesn't everyone get the same?

Inequality, exclusion, and inclusion

Soomin Oh and David Hudson

Image 11.1 A street sweeper takes a rest in Rajasthan, India. Image by FeyginFoto via Shutterstock.

> ## Learning outcomes
>
> - Critically evaluate the politics of inequality and inclusion.
> - Define vertical and horizontal inequalities, and the constitutive and instrumental case for social inclusion.
> - Understand the role of interests, institutions, and ideas in driving exclusions, particularly the uneven distribution of public goods.

Exclusion versus desired futures

Meet Urpi, a young Quechua-speaking girl born in Bolivia. Urpi is effectively excluded from her schooling and society for speaking her own language. In Bolivia, ethnic minority Quechua-speaking women are 28 per cent less likely to complete secondary school than Spanish-speaking Bolivian men (World Bank, 2015). Meanwhile, across the border in Peru, the 2007 Census found that 13 per cent of the population decide not to teach their children the Quecha language for fear they will grow up to be rejected or mocked by the Spanish-speaking population (World Bank, 2014).

Inequalities and exclusions exist within all countries the world over, no matter how wealthy the country (see Box 11.1 defining social inclusion and exclusion). In an essay titled 'The economics of life and death', Amartya Sen (1993) famously critiqued the standard view of measuring development through national income, instead calling for more direct measures of well-being, such as life expectancy. He went on to note that Black men in Harlem, New York, were not only poorer compared to other Americans, but that they were less likely to reach the age of 65 than men in Bangladesh (see Box 11.2 on Sen's Capability Approach, inequality of opportunities and outcomes).

Why do such stark inequalities and exclusions exist and persist? To answer this question, this chapter examines who is excluded, from what, and how this influences prospects for achieving desired futures. We show how powerful formal and informal rules that exclude people have been baked into opportunity structures, often because of colonial legacies. They get stuck there because intentionally or not, they serve the interests of powerful groups. At the same time, some exclusions are also fixed because some people believe they are right or represent powerful ideas about identity and deservingness.

One of the key factors perpetuating everyday exclusions is who can and cannot access public goods such as health, education, or justice. Whether in the Andes or downtown New York, systemic and long-term exclusions from the things people need to meet their basic needs are not automatic – rather, they are generated through politics. Only politics can tell us why certain public goods and services that should in principle be provided by the government are not always distributed equitably throughout the population. While politics is at the heart of exclusion, it is also through politics that exclusions can be addressed. To understand how, we need to focus not only on the marginalised groups, but the powerful ones.

Who gets left behind?

Inequality – gaps between rich and poor – have long been a concern at the international level. A child born in Sierra Leone can, on average, expect to live to 52 years old, whereas a child born in Japan can expect to live to 84. In some countries in sub-Saharan Africa, one out of ten children will die before they are five years old (Roser, 2019). Philosophers such as Locke, Hobbes and Rawls have argued that such inequalities are effectively a birth lottery: your life prospects depend on where and when you are born. Branko Milanovic (2016), one of the foremost thinkers on global inequality, estimated the size of this birth lottery, which he calls a citizenship premium or penalty. If you are born in one of the world's richest countries, the United States, you are likely to earn 9,200 per cent more than if you were born in one of the poorest, the Democratic Republic of Congo.

Milanovic's (2016) work shows that in the twentieth century, inequalities between countries were starker than those within them, peaking in the early 1970s. But fast forward five decades, and this is shifting: now, within-country inequalities are increasingly pronounced, in part because of the rise of a new middle class in East Asia. Recognising this, a key plank of the 2030 Sustainable Development Goals (SDGs) Agenda is the principle and pledge to 'leave no one behind' (LNOB):

> As we embark on this great collective journey, … we pledge that no one will be left behind. Recognizing that the dignity of the human person is fundamental, we wish to see the Goals and targets met for all nations and peoples and for all segments of society. And we will endeavour to reach the furthest behind first (UNGA Resolution 70/1, 2015).

Critics of LNOB point out that its adoption is ideologically motivated to cover up the largely pro-business, liberal agenda of the SDGs (Weber, 2017). For example, SDG 17 has an explicit commitment to free trade and promoting the implementation of the World Trade Organization (WTO) framework. This means that, among other things, through the General Agreement on Trade in Services (GATS), there are controversial provisions for the commercialisation of water, health, and education – i.e., public goods and services. Essentially, then, in this view, the commitment to 'leave no one behind' is a strategic smokescreen designed to justify what is 'a highly problematic political project' (Weber, 2017: 399). Furthermore, many of the goals are in tension with one another – especially the planetary and environmental goals on one hand and promoting growth on the other – with few mechanisms to support deliberation and contestation over them (Waage et al., 2015).

Nevertheless, the adoption of LNOB arguably recognises that measuring progress using only national averages – as was done for the preceding Millennium Development Goals – conceals important gaps between groups (Samman et al., 2021). An income-based measure of inequality is not only too narrow to capture well-being in a wider sense, but it also doesn't tell us much about the politics of inequality – why some people and groups get more or less than others.

> ## Reflective question
>
> Do you agree that the SDGs and the LNOB agenda are an inadequate means of addressing inequality?

There are systematic patterns in who is the furthest behind. Inequalities result from structural discrimination, unequal opportunities to accumulate assets and limited political capital. For example, for the Roma people living in Europe, only one in three have a job, and 90 per cent live in poverty. Meanwhile, in the United States, the mortality rate of Black infants is 2.3 times higher than white infants. And in India, in 2012, rural women only had 4.72 years of education on average; whereas rural men had double this amount of schooling at 9.51 years on average (Samman et al., 2021: 17–18).

Distinguishing between vertical and horizontal inequalities is useful to further understand these patterns. Vertical measures of inequality are focused on individuals and rank individuals (or households or countries), whereas horizontal inequalities focus on differences between groups within a country. Groups are fundamentally important to social life: they define our identities, our affiliations, our behaviours and, crucially, how others treat us. Group identities can have multiple sources and crucially, multiple sources at the same time, such as religion, location, class, ethnicity, gender and so forth. These groupings are central to the concept of horizontal inequalities.

Frances Stewart (2008: 3), one of the foremost writers on horizontal inequalities, defines them as 'inequalities in economic, social or political dimensions or cultural status between culturally defined groups'. Basically, horizontal inequalities are the differences in well-being and life chances between groups based on a dimension of their identity, such as ethnicity or sexuality or religion. Think, for example, of the Sinhalese and Tamils in Sri Lanka, or the Tutsis and Hutus in Rwanda, the caste system in India or indeed the white and Asian communities in Bradford, or LGBTQ+ communities around the world. Horizontal inequality is the difference between one group with other groups in society. For Stewart (2008), the reason why horizontal inequalities are so important is that they are a key cause of conflict. Multi-ethnic communities are not inherently conflictual: instead, conflict only erupts when the gap between groups in terms of who gets what, when, become too large.

Excluded from what?

When we talk about inequality and exclusion, what is it in relation to? Social exclusion is defined as 'a multidimensional process of progressive social rupture, detaching groups and individuals from social relations and institutions and preventing them from full participation in the normal, normatively prescribed activities of the society in which they live' (Silver, 2007: 15). Table 11.1 shows a number of examples of the kind of things people are excluded from in their everyday lived experience. In each of these cases, the way in which institutions (state discrimination, social contract, accountability, colonial legacies), interests (getting elected), and ideas (perceptions of poverty and deservingness, social norms) work is highlighted.

Table 11.1 Exclusions

Exclusion from	Explanation	Example
• Publicly provided services	• Restricted access to publicly provided goods and services as a result of ethnicity, gender, voter identity, or geography.	• Gender: suspension in access to university education for women in Afghanistan in 2022–3. • Ethnicity: investment in education by ethnic Kongo and ethnic Mbochi leaders to their ethnic homelands in the Republic of Congo has led to a divergence in educational attainment and wealth in the two regions (study period: 1960–92) (Franck and Rainer, 2012). • Slums: public service provision in slums is higher and better in settlements that have a denser network of party workers and compete against one another to secure more followers by providing resources. Party density is itself explained by settlement size and ethnic diversity (both increase competition further!) Study: Bhopal and Jaipur in India (Auerbach, 2019).
• Labour markets	• Factors such as gender, ethnicity, and geography can limit access to labour markets.	• Lower caste groups (in particular, the 'untouchables' of Dalit) face exclusion and discrimination from certain categories of jobs due to the notion of purity and pollution associated with the caste groups. Because the 'untouchables' are traditionally considered 'impure' from birth, they perform jobs that are considered 'unclean' or menial.
• Justice and rights	• Access to justice can be limited by factors such as race, gender, geographic location, aboriginality, and economic factors.	• Indigenous women's access to justice system in Latin America.
• Political representation	• Gender, ethnicity, and race are a few factors that limit political representation.	• Ethnic Chinese population and political participation in Indonesia during the New Order.
• Public spaces and places	• Exclusion could be due to environmental barriers (physical access to the spaces/places, rural isolation, poor transportation), personal and social barriers (including lack of basic skills; low income and poverty; direct and indirect discrimination; lack of permanent address), or institutional barriers (opening hours, rules and regulations).	• Dalits of India are barred from sharing waiting spaces at hospitals with other caste members.

> ## Box 11.1 Social inclusion and exclusion
>
> Social inclusion and exclusion are the processes and outcomes that determine the participation, engagement, and well-being of individuals and groups within a society. Inclusion and exclusion arise from various factors such as socioeconomic status, gender, ethnicity, disability, age, and so on.
>
> Social exclusion refers to the systematic processes that prevent certain individuals or groups from fully participating in societal activities and accessing resources and opportunities. It often stems from discrimination, prejudice, and structural inequalities present within a society. Social exclusion can result in marginalised groups facing limited access to education, healthcare, employment, political representation, and other vital services, leading to a cycle of disadvantage and poverty. As such, addressing social exclusion is critical to achieving the Sustainable Development Goals as well as creating an environment where everyone can participate, benefit, and contribute to society.
>
> Social inclusion, on the other hand, refers to the process of ensuring that all individuals and groups, regardless of their background or characteristics, have equal access to opportunities, resources, and rights within a society. Social inclusion is normatively important because everyone deserves to feel a sense of belonging, dignity, and respect. As we will see later in this chapter, efforts to improve social inclusion means designing policies and initiatives that work to reduce the barriers that marginalise certain groups and promote their active participation in economic, social, cultural, and political life.

Who is excluded?

Groups that are consistently socially excluded are often ones that are typically – though not always – the most deprived. Indeed, exclusion is often one of the key drivers of poverty and deprivations. However, it is also possible to be rich and excluded (say, because of sexuality or religion) or someone can be included (due to race or ethnicity) and poor. So, the outcome of social exclusion is not necessarily that affected individuals or communities will necessarily be poor, but that they are prevented from participating fully in the economic, social, and political life of the society in which they live. This is what matters. And this means that people are unable to exercise basic social rights and are excluded from the basic political, economic and social functioning of society (de Haan, 1998).

Furthermore, many people are poor *not* because they are excluded but because they are *included*! This is something that's called 'unfavourable inclusion'. Many problems of deprivation arise from unfavourable terms of inclusion and adverse participation. Examples of this are unfavourable inclusion into patronage or clientelistic systems, where voters feel dutybound to participate and vote for politicians who provide them with gifts, favours or protection (see Chapter 12). Or, economically, where individuals have little option but to engage in precarious employment or, worse still, as bonded labour – which is where an individual is forced to work for someone in order to pay off a debt, which may even be a generationally inherited debt. Those in bonded labour are subject to multiple forms of coercion – such as withholding wages, physical and sexual violence, and forced confinement (ILO, 2002). Estimates put the number of people in forced labour at 27.6 million around the world, and that this number is growing not shrinking (ILO, 2022). Migrant labourers around the world are particularly vulnerable as they don't enjoy the same protections and freedoms, especially if they have travelled through irregular channels and/or were trafficked. In sum, the opposite to social exclusion is not necessarily always better.

As we have seen in the chapter on ideas (Chapter 5), social exclusion rests on (perceptions of, and ideas about) identities. Individuals and groups are excluded or included based on their group identity (Eyben, 2004) – what Charles Tilly (2007) famously calls 'categorical memberships and social connections'. This means that social exclusion is fundamentally a relational thing: it only emerges through, and is a function of, the connections and relations between individuals and groups. I cannot know who I am except through who I am not. Social exclusion is not something that is inherent or absolute to the excluder or the excluded. Identity is fundamentally relational and identities are socially constructed. Reconsider the case of Rwanda and the 1994 genocide. The cultural differences between the Hutus and Tutsis were minimal, but the actions of the German and then Belgian colonial rulers constructed a cultural mythology of the minority Tutsi's as a superior tribe (Prunier, 1997). This was then institutionalised through including ethnic identity on identity cards, imposing something that hadn't existed prior to their colonisation of the country. These identities, hierarchies and resentments were all exploited and implicated in the genocide as Hutus and Tutsis understood themselves only in relation to the 'other'.

Reflective question

In what ways does social exclusion prevent people from pursuing their desired futures?

Although ethnicity and race are often key schisms that identity divides, there are many other dimensions or axes of exclusion. For example, people are excluded because they are migrants, or because of their gender, caste, religion, or their age (both because they are too old or too young), disability status, sexual orientation being lesbian, gay, bisexual, transgender or queer (LGBTQ+), being a member of an indigenous group, medical conditions (e.g., HIV/AIDS), or because of geography – if people live in inaccessible places or are distant from the major cities. And individuals may be excluded, or included, on the basis of just one dimension of their multiple identities, such as being a wealthy, upper class Black man in London. But equally, they may be excluded because of multiple dimensions, such as a poor, rural, Dalit, woman in India.

> ## Box 11.2 Sen's Capability Approach, inequality of opportunities and outcomes
>
> Amartya Sen, an economist and philosopher known for his contributions to development economics and the study of welfare economics, developed the Capabilities Approach as a response to orthodox understandings of development as economic growth or income. This approach provides a broader perspective that emphasises people's freedom and opportunities, a multidimensional understanding of well-being that emphasises the importance of individual agency and the ability to make meaningful choices. In effect, Sen argues that true equality is not just about equalising outcomes (such as income or wealth), but also about ensuring that everyone has a fair chance to develop their potential and pursue their goals.
>
> Capabilities are the various opportunities and abilities that individuals have to function in ways that they value – to work towards their alternative desired futures. These can include access to education, healthcare, employment, social participation, political engagement, personal security, and more. Sen argues that people's well-being is not solely determined by the goods and services they possess (such as income or material possessions), but also by their capabilities to use those goods and engage in activities that contribute to a fulfilling life.
>
> Functionings are the actual activities, achievements, and states of being that individuals value and pursue. For instance, being healthy, educated, having a job, participating in community life, and experiencing personal freedom are all examples of functionings. These functionings are enabled by the various capabilities that individuals possess.
>
> The capabilities approach has been incredibly influential in development studies and the world of policy-making, offering a more holistic perspective on human well-being and development.

Why does exclusion matter?

Exclusion matters for a number of reasons. At the societal level, social exclusion is connected to a whole raft of social ills, slowing growth, increasing rent seeking, violence and crime, and insulating political elites from change. As such, exclusion matters for the politics of development in a very profound way. Recall that the Introduction to this book defined the politics of development as a process of contestation over the distribution of resources, authority, rights, and freedoms in a society. So, for this to happen effectively, fairly, to create legitimate and sustainable change, then all voices and perspective must be part of contestation (Hudson et al., 2018). Social exclusion is bad for the politics of development.

At the individual level, social exclusion matters for a number of different reasons. This is best captured by the great Amartya Sen (2000) when he writes on the constitutive (by which he means inherently or intrinsic) and instrumental relevance of social exclusion. At the individual level, social inclusion is intrinsically bad. First, the intrinsic importance or constitutive relevance of social exclusion means that those individuals are not able to participate in the life of a community. He draws Adam Smith to argue that 'the inability to appear in public without shame is an important deprivation in itself' (2000: 4). Then there is the instrumental relevance of social exclusion: 'there are relational deprivations that are not in themselves terrible, but which can lead to very bad results' (Sen, 2000: 13). For example, think about access to credit – not being able to lend and borrow isn't terrible or a disaster in itself, but it can mean that people cannot start a business or take on opportunities, such as get an education. Finally, of course, some exclusions are both constitutive and instrumental. For example, not being able to mix with others – say, in village meetings or the market place or school – is important in its own right – people are social creatures – but it may also lead to missing out on economic and other opportunities in life.

Reflective question

Can you think of exclusions in your context that have both constitutive and instrumental elements?

Is social exclusion always intentional?

As noted above, although social exclusion can and often does overlap with poverty, the two are actually quite different. But they are also quite different in another way. Poverty is an outcome; however, social exclusion is a *process as well as an outcome* (World Bank, 2013). And so this requires an analysis of the process 'through which individuals or groups are wholly or partially excluded from full participation in the society in which they live' (Sen, 2000: 26).

Amartya Sen (2000) makes the distinction between active and passive exclusion, a distinction that is crucial because it is massively important for policy reform efforts to disentangle what is the result of deliberate choices by specific actors and what effects are unintended consequences of policies. Active exclusion is when a person's right, participation, or status is granted or withheld by a government or other actor. For example, many governments do not grant equal status or rights to immigrants as to national citizens. Passive discrimination is where there is no deliberate attempt to exclude, but it happens anyway through social processes.

Consider the case of access to public libraries (Muddiman et al., 2000) bearing in mind the institutions, interests, and ideas framework. While technically, libraries are free for all to use, they still do exclude in a number of ways: institutional rules such as opening hours, stock selection policies; personal and social barriers such as lack of a permanent address; perceptions and awareness, such as the notion that 'libraries aren't for people like us'; or physical barriers, such as a lack of wheelchair access, or people who live a long way away with poor transport links. So even though people or the government or businesses might not have an interest in actively excluding people, social exclusion may still be the end result. And this is reinforced by ideas such as discrimination within society – i.e., the application of negative attributes or stereotypes to groups which are then used to legitimise exclusion, repression, and stigmatisation (Estivill, 2003).

Even when active social exclusion has stopped, exclusion may continue because of the legacies of the original active exclusion. For example, political exclusion along racial lines in South Africa continued even after the end of apartheid (Du Toit, 2004; Nevile, 2007). So, while the formal institutions had been changed, exclusion continued. The bases of the ongoing exclusion are a combination of race, poverty, historical legacies and politics. During apartheid, non-white South Africans were actively excluded from taking part in voting, elections, and the political process in general. Although now, post-apartheid, voting rights extend to everyone, political exclusion continues for particular groups – for example, agricultural workers in South Africa's Western Cape district of Ceres. They are politically excluded because they do not have a history of taking part and voting in elections because of the legacy of apartheid and racism. But political exclusion at the national level is now better characterised as passive because although government policy no longer prevents political participation, neither does it make any effort to engage these politically excluded agricultural workers. This is because:

> the national government has its power base in urban rather than rural areas, it is not sensitive to the concerns of the rural poor, a situation that does not encourage political participation among a group of people with no history of political engagement. (Nevile, 2011: 253)

Exclusion from public goods

If exclusion is a process, how does it happen? In this section, we zoom in on the processes of exclusion surrounding access to public goods and services. In particular, we explore how elections, voting and political incentives generate systems in which not everyone gets the same.

What are public goods? The classic definition is that they are non-excludable and non-rivalrous. Non-excludable means it is impossible to stop others from using the goods or services. Non-rivalrous means the goods or services can be used without reducing the consumption or use by others of the same goods or services. Government or publicly provided goods and services include public education, healthcare, and infrastructure. By definition, these goods should be provided equitably throughout the population. More often than not, however, this is distorted through the political process.

Table 11.2 Grid explaining the different types of goods

Characteristic	Rivalrous	Non-rivalrous
Excludable	• Private goods (e.g., food, clothes).	• Club goods (e.g., sports clubs, movie theatres, satellite television).
Non-excludable	• Common resource goods (e.g., fish stocks).	• Public goods (e.g. light house, public school system, public parks, clean air).

What motivates politicians to exclude?

Political elites, working with limited resources, need to make choices about what goods are provided, where, and to whom. Because these resources are geographically concentrated, they tend to have ramifications for the development of certain regions over others. For instance, in less developed contexts, public goods are primarily concentrated in urban areas where there is greater access to essential infrastructure, or clean water, etc. According to World Development Indicators (World Bank, 2020), access to basic handwashing facilities in the least developed countries (by UN classification) was 27.91 per cent in rural areas versus 43.8 per cent in urban areas. Access to basic drinking water was just over half of rural population – 56.94 per cent – versus 85.25 per cent of the urban population. Such imbalances in urban and rural areas have ramifications for basic levels of development, measures of which include infant mortality, which has close links to clean water and sanitation (WHO).

The choices that elites make about how to distribute publicly provided goods – what is sometimes termed 'distributive politics'– may depend on what interests they want to maximise (see Box 11.3. for a definition and explanation of distributive politics). Imagine a hypothetical context where leaders are elected to power. Through elections, voters can 'select leaders and then hold them accountable for the implementation of policies that benefit the broader populace' (Lindberg, 2012: 946). In theory, a representative democracy of this nature would result in politicians working to improve the welfare of the public and an equitable and needs-based distribution of public goods and services. However, this is rarely the case when elites' incentives to win elections enters the picture.

Box 11.3   Distributive politics

Publicly provided goods and services, including income redistribution and public goods and services such as education and healthcare are unequally distributed, leaving some behind and others excluded from access to such goods and services. Politics, as Harold Lasswell claimed, is all about 'who gets what, when, and how'. Distributive politics addresses the questions of who gets what, why, and how in the context of publicly provided goods and services. Publicly provided goods and services are limited in nature, so how are they distributed, to whom, and why? To understand this, studies of distributive politics look at actors – political elites, parties, and voters – and the strategies they deploy to achieve their interests within the constraints posed by institutions. For instance, political elites in democracies are assumed to want to maximise their votes and chances of re-election; with such interests, which voters or groups of voters do they target with publicly provided good and services, and why? The strategies pursued by political elites lead to patterns of distribution – at both individual, group, and geographic levels.

A number of debates exist in the study of distributive politics. A foundational and longstanding debate has been around core versus swing voters, where scholars have debated whether political elites or parties offer material incentives to their core voters or swing

> voters to maximise chances of (re-)election. Diaz-Cayeros et al. (2016) have argued that politicians do not simply target one group over the other, but diversify their 'portfolio' by pursuing mixed targeting strategies to both core and swing voters.
>
> Other studies of the provision of public goods and services also tackle the question of who gets what, why, and how, from the angle of cultural and ethnic favouritism, especially in the contexts of developing countries, as will be illustrated in this chapter. It is worth noting that even theories of ethnic favouritism of public goods and services is contested. Research by Kramon and Ponser (2013) show that not all regimes favour their co-ethnics and not all public goods and services are targeted to co-ethnics. In fact, in some countries, being a co-ethnic of the president can penalise the ethnic group from gaining access to certain public goods and services.

To win votes, one of the strategies that politicians employ is to promise, and deliver, publicly provided goods and services to specific areas or individuals with particular identities. Because such strategies are not guided by formal rules of distribution, they are what is called 'nonprogrammatic', with 'no public criteria of distribution or the public criteria is subverted by private, usually partisan, ones' (Stokes et al., 2013: 10). The question, then, is to whom or where political elites target their promises. Politicians may ask themselves 'who is more likely to support me/my party in the next election?'. Their answer may depend on partisan identities, ethnicity, religion, or socioeconomic status. Let's first look at targeting based on partisanship.

Exclusion based on partisanship

In standard (simplified) models of voting, illustrated in Figure 11.1, there are two parties – one on the left and one on the right, and three groups of voters with partisan preferences. First are the loyalists or core voters with strong partisan preference for a particular party. With these voters, the party knows them well and hence can effectively and credibly target benefits. The second group is the swing voters. These are voters who do not have partisan attachments and can 'swing' either way. The last is the opposition voters – that is, voters who have partisan loyalties for the other party. In the model, voters benefit when the party closer to their ideological preference is voted in, but also benefit from allocations of good and services promised by politicians seeking support. If a voter receives allocations that are big enough to outweigh the benefits they receive from their party being elected, they may vote for a party further away from their partisan preference. How 'big' these allocations have to be depends on their partisan attachments – core voters have greater attachments than swing voters, and hence would require more goods and services allocated to them to switch their vote.

Now that we have examined the interests of the political elites to win an election and the preferences of the different voters, who should they promise and deliver public goods to? It turns out this is not an easy question, with mixed empirical findings.

There are two large groups of theories – 'core voter theory' and 'swing voter theory'. Core voter theory begins with the premise that political elites are risk-averse – that is, they do not want to waste their resources on promising to or providing for voters that they are not sure will support them in the next election (Cox and McCubbins, 1986). As a result, politicians target core voters who have been loyal to them with promises and delivery of goods and services. In addition to loyalty, political elites have informational advantage over the core voters compared to other voters, and thus are able to target them better with the necessary goods or services.

A case for the 'core voter theory' comes from Venezuela's land grant distribution programme (Albertus, 2015). The Hugo Chavez regime expropriated private property from wealthy elites and redistributed it to his core supporters. Historically in Venezuela, land ownership had been concentrated in the hands of a small group of elites. The 2001 land law stipulated that landowners must demonstrate a consistent chain of property back to 1848 to enjoy property rights – which less than 10 per cent of the owners could do – or face expropriation. As a result, the government seized large private properties, and private citizens squatted on lands for which they knew they could not prove ownership and applied for the ownership of the land. In total, the government expropriated 4 million hectares of land and processed several hundreds of thousands of applications for land grants. To whom were the land grants given? Albertus (2015) found that the Hugo Chavez regime used land grants to reward his supporters by approving their applications and punishing its enemies, who saw their applications received less favourably.

The 'swing voter theory', on the other hand, argues that political elites target swing voters, as they are 'cheaper' to buy than other voters with stronger partisan attachments (Dixit and Londregan, 1996). The assumption here is that the party's core voters would vote for them regardless of the party's targeting strategies. Recent literature has shown that voters are not 'unconditionally loyal', and hence parties need to 'diversify their portfolio' by targeting both the core and the swing voters (Diaz-Cayeros et al., 2016).

An example of the swing voter theory comes from Peru (Schady, 2000). In 1991, the Peruvian Social Fund (FONCODES) was established by President Alberto Fujimori aimed at generating employment, alleviating poverty, and improving access to public services. An examination of patterns of distribution of FONCODES expenditures between 1991 and 1995 showed that the Fujimori government favoured 'marginal' districts – i.e., the ones in which the president came close to winning/losing in his first election and in a referendum.

Box 11.4 Interactive exercise: voting game

We illustrate a game to help understand the logic of distribution under an electoral democracy with competing parties. This exercise will help you think through the interests involved in the provision of publicly provided goods and services and the interests of the voters who are on the receiving end of the goods and services.

Imagine there are two political parties on both sides of the ideological spectrum – party 1 and party 2 (you can be either party 1 or party 2). There are five voters located in the ideological spectrum. Voters receive utility (benefits or happiness) when the party closer to them wins the election, but also receive utility when they are provided goods and services they need. Party 1 and party 2 have limited resources – 10 units of public goods each – to provide the voters. Whom should your party target, and why? What assumptions are you making about the voters? You can use examples based on your knowledge of specific cases or deduce logically why you think your strategies of targeting will win votes for your party.

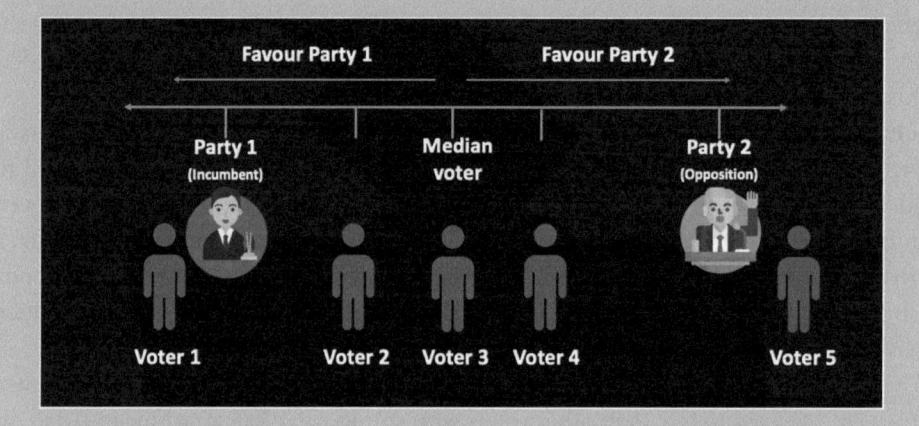

Figure 11.1   Simplified spatial model of voting

Reflective question

How do the characteristics of public goods influence political elites' interests to allocate them and *to whom*?

Beyond partisanship: exclusion from public goods based on other identities

There are other, alternative, logics through which politicians make promises and delivery of public goods and services, beyond partisanship. Particularly in the Global South, identities such as ethnicity, caste, or indigeneity are particularly salient. These identities become lines along which exclusions and favouritisms are made in resource allocation, based on their ideas about deservingness and fairness of identities. In this section, we focus on three identities to illustrate how social exclusion takes place across socially constructed identities.

First is the socially constructed identity of *caste*, particularly salient in South Asia. Lower caste members, in particular the 'untouchables', Dalits, or 'Scheduled Caste' (SC) face discrimination in accessing essential goods and services, such as education and healthcare, due to ideas of deservingness and discrimination. A case in point comes from India's national rural electrification programme, the Rajiv Gandhi Rural Electrification Scheme (RGGVY). Examination of the patterns of programme implementation at village level shows that villages with a higher proportion of Dalits have a lower likelihood of receiving the programming. Such exclusion has resulted from deliberate exclusion by officials and bureaucrats (Aklin et al., 2021).

Another example, also from India, illustrates a societal level exclusion from public goods and services. Because Dalits have traditionally been considered 'unclean', they face significant discrimination. For instance, healthcare professionals may avoid touching the individual during diagnosis, or they are forced to wait to be seen, in a separate space, until dominant caste individuals have been seen by the healthcare professional (Thorat and Sabharwal, 2015). Other societal level exclusions to Dalit communities include not being able to rent houses in a non-Dalit locality and Dalit postmen not being able to enter the streets of non-Dalits. Such exclusions based on socially constructed identities have been argued to be costly for the society – ethically, legally, and economically (Girard, 2018).

The second dimension alongside which exclusions can take place is indigeneity. Indigenous populations in countries like Guatemala and Peru have been excluded from their access to essential public goods and services. Exclusion and marginalisation have historical roots in colonisation, military dictatorships, and civil conflicts. Research from Latin American countries, including Bolivia, Nicaragua, Peru, and Guatemala show that there is evidence of exclusion of indigenous populations from government to access to basic public services. Cerón et al. (2016) document the discrimination and exclusion experienced by indigenous populations in Guatemala in accessing healthcare. They experience discrimination in access to care, receive abusive treatment in care, and experience a neglect in professional ethics at hospitals, stemming from their indigenous identity.

The final dimension of exclusion we explore is ethnicity. A wealth of evidence around favouritism in the allocation of public goods and services to the leaders' co-ethnics has emerged, in particular from sub-Saharan Africa – that is, the ethnic group in power determines where and what public goods will go to their co-ethnics. There are two key models of ethnic favouritism that may explain why ethnic leaders provide only for their co-ethnics, with little incentives to cater to other groups that are not in their power bases. These are explained in Table 11.3.

One example of ethnic favouritism in public goods comes from Congo-Brazzaville (Republic of Congo) (Franck and Rainer, 2012). In Congo, main ethnic divisions run along regional lines, with ethnic Kongo occupying the south of the country and ethnic Mbochi in the north. While the ethnic rivalry goes back to the colonial period, it was exacerbated

Image 11.2 Indigenous women from the community of Kulluchaka look out across the landscape of Ayacucho, Peru, 2022. Image by Joseycha Ramos via Shutterstock.

by the leaders who successively ruled the country after independence, each with *ideas* of their respective ethnic groups' deservingness of state resources. Fulbert Youlou (1960–3) and Alphonse Massamba-Debat (1963–8), both ethnic Kongo from the South, established a system of patronage – a form of informal *institutions* – that favoured their fellow Kongo, based on their *interests* in maximising welfare of the fellow Kongo. This is evidenced by far greater educational investments in the south than in the north, plus more positions in the civil service that were allocated mostly to fellow Kongo. In turn, this meant an increase in income of many Kongo members and an increased ability to send their kids to school, further reinforcing the Kongo's educational advantage inherited from the colonial period.

All of this was reversed in 1968, with Marien Ngouabi's coup d'etat against Massamba-Debat that brought ethnic Mbochi leaders to power (1968). It was their turn to eat. Ngouabi replaced most of the Kongo office holders with his own Mbochi appointments and under subsequent leaders ethnic Mbochi continued to hold a disproportionate number of political and administrative positions. Large investments in education (6 per cent of GDP in 1970, 8 per cent in 1979) then flowed in favour of Mbochi regions. New schools were constructed mostly in the north of the country and financial aid was distributed mostly to ethnic Mbochi students. Furthermore,

Table 11.3 Models of ethnic favouritism

Model	Assumptions	Results of the model
Ethnic altruism model	• The political leader derives direct utility from higher well-being of co-ethnics.	• The ethnic leader will provide favours, including public goods and services, to the members of their group, regardless of their actual political behaviour.
Quid pro quo model	• It may be cheaper for the leader to buy the support of co-ethnics (than the support of other groups) because they better understand their needs and can transfer benefits to them more efficiently. Further, it may be less risky for the risk-averse leader to trust the promises of their own group – namely that they will supply political support in exchange for the benefits the leader provide.	• The ethnic leader targets co-ethnics.

Mbochi members were appointed to the civil service, raising the income of many Mbochi families, which further contributed to the rise in rates of schooling of the Mbochi children, thus illustrating the stark dynamics of ethnic favouritism.

Beyond state-level policies of exclusion based on ethnicity, exclusion can also take place at local level, based on identities such as race or ethnicity (see Box 11.5 for non-identity based exclusions). When local bureaucrats are tasked with making decisions over whom to provide state resources to, their ideas of deservingness factor into the logic of allocation, thereby creating exclusions over some groups over others. This is illustrated well in the following example from the US. White et al. (2015) examine whether street-level bureaucrats managing the electoral system discriminate by race or ethnicity in their interactions with constituents about voting rules. They sent emails about ID requirements to a random sample of county or municipal election officers in 48 states in the US, randomising the names from which emails were sent – putatively, Latino or non-Latino white names. They identified a bias in email responses against Latinos; Latinos were less likely to receive a response and the responses were less accurate in information about ID requirements. This bias in responses is likely a consequence of officials' ideas about *deservingness* of certain identities of their efforts.

Recent evidence has emerged that beyond the supply-side story – i.e., ethnic leaders providing for their co-ethnics – there is also a demand-side story – in particular, around diversity of ethnic groups and their power to demand public goods and services from their leaders. There are three mechanisms that link ethnic diversity to underprovision of public goods and services, and they are illustrated in Table 11.4. An illustration of the demand-side story comes from rural western Kenya. Through an examination of the dataset of primary school committee records describing the use of sanctions against non-contributing parents, Edward Miguel and Mary Kay Gugerty (2005) find that school committees in ethnically diverse areas are less able to impose sanctions and pressurise non-contributing parents at public fundraisings, pay school fees, or contribute in other ways, due to a lack of ownership and commitment from parents to schools. As a result, ethnically diverse communities experience worse school facilities, lower levels of school funding through fundraising, and fewer community sanctions. Diversity in ethnic groups within a community can unfortunately exclude the community from (quality) public goods and services due to a lack of collective action capacity that can arise from heterogeneity in preferences and lack of technology for social sanctions.

Reflective question

How does identity influence people's power to *address* exclusions?

Table 11.4 Mechanisms linking ethnic diversity to underprovision of public goods

Mechanisms	Explanation
Diversity of preferences	• The diversity of preferences is argued to lead to disagreements over which public goods should be provided and where. This disagreement, such as over the language of instruction of schools, in turn, leads to underprovision of public goods.
Other-regarding preferences among co-ethnics	• Individuals attach positive utility to the welfare of co-ethnics but no/negative utility to the welfare of non-members. This is because people view themselves as benefitting if co-ethnics are made better off. These other-regarding preferences of co-ethnics could explain the higher rates of public goods provision in ethnically homogeneous societies.
Technology for sanctions	• Ethnically homogenous societies have a toolkit of strategies for promoting collective action. First, homogeneous communities draw on common cultural materials – language, experience, modes of interaction – that make it easier to collectively act, e.g. communicate messages. Second, there is greater 'findability' of co-ethnics in social networks. Shared membership in ethnically homogeneous communities allows co-ethnics to find and punish non-cooperators, incentivising individuals to cooperate.

Source: Adapted from Habyarimana et al. (2007)

Box 11.5 Spatial exclusion

In addition to partisan identities and socially constructed identities, such as ethnicity and caste, there are other dimensions along which exclusion takes place. One major example is exclusion based on not who you are but where you live – that is, exclusion based on geography. Individuals living in rural areas compared to urban areas could be excluded from participating in certain economic activities due to the distance or due to the stigmas associated with the certain regions (e.g., the *favelas* in Brazilian cities). Geography can also indirectly lead to exclusion. In China, the household registration system (*hukou*) registers an individual to a city or town at birth and restricts their access to welfare benefits in cities they are not registered at. This has bred immense exclusion to welfare benefits for migrant workers within China.

Demanding inclusion – (how) can everyone get the same?

Social inclusion – in opposition to social exclusion – is 'the process of improving the terms for individuals and groups to take part in society' (World Bank, 2013: 3). Building inclusion is hard! Precisely because institutions are hard to change, the existing elite rarely has strong incentives or interests in improving inclusion, and stereotypical ideas about excluded communities run deep. The electoral distributive politics described above come into play for politicians and whether they perceive benefits from using the time, energy, and political capital in supporting the kind of policy initiatives to bring about social inclusion (see Box 11.6 for some examples of the kind of policies).

But inclusion can and does happen. And it's deeply political, and involves people demanding change as they construct their interests and act collectively (see Chapter 3). Developmental social change requires contestation and collaboration between many different groups, who have many different interests, and many do not have an interest in the collective good of building inclusive institutions. The excluders use their political power to structure exclusion into institutions – to institutionalise the exclusions. Active and passive exclusions have to be addressed, which means engaging government and society. Building social inclusion is as much about creating and engaging in a political process as it is about ensuring equitable access to and share of resources and services.

Box 11.6   Examples of policies for social inclusion

- *Anti-discrimination legislation*: constitutional provisions, laws, regulations and policies explicitly outlawing discriminatory practices.
- *Affirmative action*: provide positive discrimination for preferred admissions and subsidies for education and employment, and providing mandatory political representation for marginalised groups.
- *Participation*: increase citizen participation in the political decision-making process and increase the accountability of governments – e.g., increasing electoral turnout, informing decision-makers of citizens' views and bringing citizens and decision-makers together in dialogue on policy issues.
- *Service provision*: provide access to services – e.g., education is a particularly important service because of its effect on the earning capacity of an individual, as well as on their ability to participate in social and political life.
- *Social protection*: cash transfer programmes, social services, pension systems, unemployment or disability benefits.

In a fascinating study, Judith Teichman (2016) looks at the policies most likely to bring about inclusive development across four cases with different development trajectories: Mexico, Indonesia, Chile and South Korea. Her conclusions are that the best way of creating inclusive development is through employment-generating growth with well-remunerated and secure jobs; a progressive tax system that provides the revenue base for progressive social spending; and a proactive state that pursues a combination of universal and targeted social programmes, social spending, redistributive reforms.

Teichman also describes the politics of this process, in a way that shows how interests, institutions, and ideas are critical. She argues that it is necessary to build a broad-based coalition of civil society organisation, and labour and trade unions, and agricultural and farmers' representatives – so the key here is identifying where different individuals and groups have overlapping interests and act collectively to build power (see Chapter 3). Through collective action this coalition can lobby for employment-generating industrial policy. But, Teichman continues that this coalition must also include some of the more privileged sectors of society, particularly, middle and even upper classes. Why? This is because these are the people most likely to vote and hold politicians to account. In order to stay in power and deliver what the voting public demands creates the incentives for politicians and bureaucrats to resist particularist pressures from business and interest groups to subvert policy. And finally, committed leadership is needed to create and maintain this coalition.

Reflective question

Thinking about an exclusion you are familiar with, what policies do you think could work to address this?

In sum, understanding the politics of social exclusion is about understanding the elite – politicians and middle classes – as much as the non-elite. While social exclusion is often focused on the poor and marginalised, it is not sufficient to *just* focus on the marginalised. It is clear that 'coalitions and alliances involving the powerful are necessary to bring the interests of vulnerable groups onto the political agenda which is a precondition for pro-poor changes' (Mosse, 2007). As well as the elite, the middle classes are critical as they are more likely to have a closer and functioning relationship with the state and use their voice and votes to demand services and inclusion, but also they are more likely to have the time and inclination to demand change. For example, in the Philippines, in the 1970s, President Marcos was presiding over a society characterised by corruption, human rights violations, and economic stagnation, and martial law (Kimura, 2003). The assassination of Senator Aquino, the arch political enemy of Marcos, changed this. Many middle-class citizens switched from being apolitical to leading to the 'people's power revolution', as they organised and formed an anti-Marcos Alliance. The non-violent revolution in February 1986 led to the overthrow of Marcos and the return to democracy in the Philippines. More recently, the Egyptian revolt of January 2011 and the overthrow of Mubarak was also driven by the middle classes – not the workers or peasants – as they were sick of election-rigging, corruption, and economic stagnation and it is the middle classes that can use their voice (Kandil, 2012). It is here that we can see – if coordinated – how collective interest in change can create the incentives and institutions to hold politicians and other elites to account.

Summary and conclusion

Analysing group-based or horizontal inequalities highlights dimensions of exclusion that country rankings and national averages totally miss. This is why the principle of 'leave no one behind,' at the heart of the SDGs, is important in its own right. Identities create multiple axes of exclusion and can amplify deprivations. And deprivations deny people's freedom to create their own desired futures. This chapter has introduced the different ways in which exclusion operates – exclusions can be active or passive.

Recalling the book's emphasis on how institutions, interests and ideas are the drivers of development, they are also the drivers of social exclusion and inclusion. Social exclusions can be formalised and written into the rules and laws of society, such as apartheid, or it can be informal such as the expectations that certain groups should benefit from jobs in the civil service or greater access to education. We have also seen how these social exclusions are strongly shaped by ideas, such as perceptions of poverty and deservingness, social norms, and identities. And they are exacerbated by the interests of politicians to pursue different strategies for securing support and votes. These strategies both respond to existing group identities reinforcing horizontal inequalities.

On the other hand, interests and ideas are also key to tackling social exclusions. The chapter concluded by showing how creating greater social inclusion is based on building broad-based coalitions and leadership. And this is about aligning interests around a set of ideas and a narrative that can shift and change the rules that shape societal outcomes. This underlines how deeply relational the politics of exclusion is: it's not about one group or identity, but the relations *between* individuals and groups that determines why not everyone gets the same.

Discussion questions

1 In your opinion, is it more important for public debate and policy-making to focus on inequality of opportunities or inequality of outcomes?
2 Differentiate between active and passive exclusion, and unfavourable inclusion. Use an example from your own country context to illustrate which kind of exclusion is at play and identify a suitable policy response to address the exclusion.
3 Does democratisation alter the relationship between inclusion and exclusion? Think about changes in the actors occupying decision-making roles, their incentives and interests, and their ideas on who should be included and excluded in their decisions to distribute a limited set of resources. How would the patterns of inclusion and exclusion change as a result?
4 Does everyone *want* inclusion? Are there any the conditions under which some people may not want to be included – for instance, in the allocation of publicly provided goods and services? How would the lack of demand impact the provision thereof?

Suggested further reading

Grossman, G. and Slough, T. (2022) 'Government responsiveness in developing countries', *Annual Review of Political Science*, 25, 131–53.

Sen, A. (2000) 'Social exclusion: concept, application, and scrutiny', Social Development Papers No. 1. Manila: Asian Development Bank. Available at: www.adb.org/sites/default/files/publication/29778/social-exclusion.pdf

Stewart, F. (2002) 'Horizontal inequalities: a neglected dimension of development', *Oxford Development Studies*, 30 (2), 121–38.

World Bank (2000/2001) World Development Report 2000/2001: *Attacking Poverty*. Oxford: Oxford University Press.

12 How can I jump this queue?

Petty corruption, clientelism, and other games within the rules

Claire Mcloughlin and Sameen Ali

Image 12.1 People queue to cross a small bridge to reach the city in Jembatan Pundong Imogiri, Indonesia, 2019. Image by Firmansyah Asep, via Shutterstock.

> ## Learning outcomes
>
> - Identify a range of 'games within the rules' and evaluate their developmental impacts.
> - Critically analyse the interests, institutions, and ideas behind two such games – bribery and clientelism.
> - Analyse what motivates politicians, bureaucrats and citizens to engage in games within the rules.

Getting by and getting ahead

Becoming a civil servant is a highly desirable goal for many young Indonesian graduates. More than a profession, it is a guarantee of future prosperity and a symbol of social prestige. Aspiring candidates scrutinise the entrance process which, on the surface, appears rational, and merit-based: vacancies are publicly advertised, applicants register for tests, and those achieving top scores secure the coveted prize. The high stakes nature of this admissions process was colourfully illustrated when on East Java, invigilators from the Ministry of Law and Human Rights adorned red and black suits and performed a 'Squid Game' roleplay – a playful attempt to calm nerves, they said, but also a thinly veiled metaphor for the candidates very own bid for survival.

As with many games, there is often more than one way to prevail. In the Indonesian example (and in many other countries around the world), the formal, bureaucratic rules are not the only ones in play; there are also informal, unwritten, unofficial rules, hidden beneath the surface. In this particular case, candidates may boost their prospect of recruitment by supplying envelopes containing money as 'smoothers' to key decision-makers, for example. In what becomes an informal marketplace of bids, they could deploy brokers to approach high-ranking officials on their behalf with monetary incentives in the hope of securing a favourable outcome. Alternatively, some may be lucky enough to pull levers through family connections with existing government officials (Blunt, et al., 2012).

For many people around the world, achieving something of material or symbolic value – whether it's passing a life-defining entrance exam, accessing vital public services such as medicine, clean water, or education, or maintaining a livelihood – relies on navigating the so-called 'gap' between formal laws, policies and bureaucratic procedures, and the informal rules that often determine how things really get done in practice. There are myriad ways that bureaucrats, politicians, and citizens can avoid, bend, or break the rules – by exploiting loopholes, cheating, bribery, theft, or various other practices typically labelled as 'corruption'. To use the game metaphor, if institutions are the rules of the game (North, 1990), then such behaviours are the games *within* the rules. They may be considered deviant in that they distort the way things are supposed to work, but they are also essential coping strategies for many people living in situations of precarity and scarcity.

This chapter is about how games within the rules are played, with what consequences for development. We explore how the opportunity to circumnavigate, bend, or subvert official rules arises. We identify the range of games played in the gap between formal and informal rules, before zooming in on two prevalent ones that are a daily feature of life for many: petty corruption and clientelism. We show that although such games operate at the micro-level of society, they can have dramatic structural effects on collective development prospects. So why do they exist, and persist? Whether it's a bureaucrat extracting a small bribe to quit hassling a street vendor, or a politician trading a bag of rice for a vote in a remote village, at the core of these games there are people; but are their decisions driven by institutions, incentives, or ideas?

The gap between rules and practices

The politics of development is the unavoidable process of contesting alternative desired futures. One of the livelier spaces where this happens, in practice, is wherever citizens directly encounter the state – at the so-called 'citizen-state interface'. Whether in the waiting rooms of health clinics, on street corners where traffic police stop motorists, in offices distributing social assistance or identity documents, or homes where public officials visit to read utility meters, there is potential for a clash of interests or ideas around which rules should be applied, and how. Official laws, policies and procedures are meant to determine how governments function, of course. They are typically carefully formulated in parliaments or ministries, after all. But in the real world, beyond these stuffy forums, all policies are actually *made* at the point of implementation, when bureaucrats and public servants choose how to interpret them, and whether to enforce them, or not.

In India, for example, traffic police are not technically supposed to stop and search vehicles unless a clear code violation has been committed. Nevertheless, they are routinely found at junctions, waiting to extract bribes from drivers for what may be bogus violations – in a particularly imaginative example in Kerala, for 'carrying a wash basin inside a car'.

Image 12.2 A traffic officer sits on patrol in Kolkata, West Bengal, 2022. Image by PradeepGaurs via Shutterstock.

Reflective question

Why is there a difference between official rules and how they get implemented in practice?

In all societies, to differing extents, official procedures, and the actual practices of actors at the citizen–state interface diverge, creating what has been termed 'the problem of the gap' (de Sardan, 2015). But why does this gap exist? Why don't the official rules always work as intended?

First, we might consider this a fundamental issue of the state being unable to exercise authority and control over policy implementation. To investigate this, we can scrutinise the everyday life of the state, a field of study shaped most fundamentally by the work of sociologist Joel Migdal, including in his pathbreaking book *State in Society* (2001). He encouraged us to think about the state's authority as decentred, because in practice rules made at the political centre are reinterpreted by everyday actors, themselves embedded in localised rules. The authority of the state is therefore patchy and uneven because it is ultimately entrusted to individuals with discretion to resist, subvert or appropriate the rules (White and Migdal, 2013). In this sense, the state is not separate from society, but constituted within it, through the everyday interaction of state and citizen agency.

Second, opportunities to digress from formal procedures are greater where there is a lack of transparency and accountability, or inadequate monitoring systems – in other words, where governance is weak. A key metric of good governance is the impartiality of public servants; being guided by the public interest, rather than their own (Rothstein, 2011). But in practice, bureaucrats may freely pursue their own interests where there is little or no accountability. Think about who the police should answer to in the Indian example above? Why aren't they held to account? In India, bribery by public functionaries is illegal under the Prevention of Corruption Act, and investigating cases falls under the remit of the anti-corruption ombudsmen, Lokpal. But after years of under-funding, resignations and ineffectiveness, citizens lost faith in its power, and stopped filing complaints. In this way, weak governance creates and perpetuates bureaucratic partiality and opportunities for discretion.

Third, official rules, such as codes of conduct on traffic policing, do not exist in a void. As we saw in Chapter 3, they sit alongside and are shaped by social norms, or what Christina Bicchieri (2005), a philosopher of economics, terms 'the rules we live by'. These are behaviours expected of us because of family relations, kinship, customs, traditions, or social etiquette such as deference, courtesy, or reciprocity. The result is a duality of ideas: different possible answers to the question of how things *should* get done, based on co-existing, sometimes competing, notions of what is right and legitimate. Colonisation was a major driver of duality within the state – in grafting cookie-cutter models of centralised bureaucracy onto traditional and customary systems of authority, it left a legacy of 'hybrid political orders' where formal and informal rules co-exist, sometimes in tension with one another (Boege et al., 2009). We see examples of this in the real functioning of democracies, where formal voter freedoms, political decision-making procedures and representation are profoundly shaped by pre-existing social orders, such as ethnic cleavages in Kenya, warlordism in Afghanistan, or the wantok system of kinship in Solomon Islands.

These economic, political, or social factors make it possible that formal rules may not be applied as intended (see Table 12.1). Crucially, this gap may widen in situations of scarcity, where there are insufficient resources to meet demand. Scarcity in the form of budgetary constraints and low GDP growth rates underlies what Matt Andrews and colleagues termed 'the big stuck' in their

Table 12.1 Drivers of the 'gap' between official rules and practices

Social	• State rules are filtered through social norms.
Economic	• Weak state capacity/scarcity.
Political	• Lack of accountability and monitoring.
	• Legacy of colonialism.
	• Hybrid political orders/duality of ideas.
	• Foreign aid causes 'isomorphic mimicry'.

book *Building State Capability: Evidence, Analysis, Action* (2017). Using cross-national data, they show that even after decades of investment, many governments still fail to perform basic bureaucratic functions such as paying teachers, registering births, operating a postal service, etc. In what they describe as 'isomorphic mimicry', a state may 'look' like a state, because it has all the best practice processes and systems in place, as sometimes encouraged by foreign aid actors, but these are not meaningful to how the bureaucracy actually works on the ground.

Why does any of this matter, though? Not least because of the 'big stuck' in state capability, many people live in precarious situations with no reliable electricity supply, roads in disrepair, or unsafe streets. The World Development Report 2004, *Making Services Work for Poor People,* was hugely significant in highlighting an enduring reality: services are failing the poor. Key human development outcomes – child mortality, educational attainment, access to clean water – are significantly worse for the poorest 20 per cent compared with the richest 20 per cent. Urbanisation, migration, and population growth are placing immense pressures on states' capacity to redress this injustice. As systems become overwhelmed, the capacity of bureaucrats to meet demand and provide fair and equitable distribution of vital goods and services falls. In these circumstances, achieving desired futures, or even the basic means to survive, may require finding ways to get around dysfunctional systems. In other words, to jump the 'queue'. *But how?*

Games within the rules

Where systems fail to provide for basic needs, people play 'games within the rules'. In other words, they carve out alternative ways to pursue their version of desired futures. Anyone can play, in principle – from high-level political elites, to elected representatives, and bureaucrats in positions of power and authority, to ordinary citizens. The games seek to bend, navigate, or disrupt the formal rules in the pursuit of something people value, need, or want. In effect, they are a way to realise interests in the context of scarcity.

In practice, games take many forms, and there is a fine line between them (see Table 12.2). While they are always played with the expectation of a reward, they also differ in terms of where the power lies, their level and scale, what (if anything) is exchanged and, whether the end result benefits everyone, or just the winner.

Table 12.2 Games within the rules: corruption from top to bottom?

Games	What it is	Who and what level	What is exchanged
Patrimonialism	• A type of *political system* wherein the ruler treats the state's resources as their personal possession and distributes them to family and supporters in exchange for loyalty.	• *Political elite/ruler:* Powerful political leaders, often with charismatic power and vast loyalty networks.	• Not much – the key feature is the control of resources by the ruling elite.
Grand corruption	• *High-level corruption* that involves systematic siphoning of public money.	• *Political and economic elite:* high-level officials, elites, political leaders, military.	• Large amounts of money or valuable assets, contracts for kickbacks, access money (to opportunities, decision-making processes).
Rent-seeking	• Using political connections, corruption, or manipulation to gain special government privileges.	• *Political and economic elite:* corporate elites, politicians who control policy-making.	• Subsidies, tax breaks, preferential treatment, or competitive advantage.
Clientelism and patronage	• The exchange of material goods, benefits or privileges, typically for political support.	• *Political and bureaucratic elite:* individuals or political elites (patrons) and citizens or bureaucrats (clients).	• Jobs, contracts, favours, political support, votes, access to services.
Bribery aka petty corruption	• Offering, giving, receiving, or promising something to induce an action which is illegal, unethical or a breach of trust.	• *Local level:* a person soliciting a bribe (briber), and a person in a position of trust or authority who can use their influence, power, or decision-making authority in favour of the briber.	• Something of value, such as money, gifts, favours, or benefits, is given in exchange for benefit.

Some might consider some form of rule-bending as 'corruption' – that is, dishonest or unethical behaviour that involves the abuse of power, authority, and influence for illicit gain or favouritism. Moreover, political scientists tend to view any form of rule-bending as an aberration of the proper functioning of the state apparatus – a deviation from an ideal-type 'Weberian' state, characterised by rational, rule-bound, and hierarchical bureaucracies (see Box 12.1). Of course, the counterargument is that Weber's idealised version of bureaucracy, cast in the image of Western state formation, presents a singular version of 'modernity' that is the wrong starting point for understanding the complexity and diversity of political life.

Box 12.1 The Weberian state ideal

Corruption is often considered the antithesis of the so-called Weberian state. A 'Weberian state' means:

- A highly organised and rational bureaucracy.
- Legal rules and regulations applied consistently and uniformly.
- Authority is impersonal and exercised in accordance with established rules.
- Defined hierarchies of authority and responsibility.
- Bureaucrats follow formal and transparent procedures.

In practice, there is variation across countries in terms of which games are formally classified as corruption and/or are, by extension, considered illegal. Some, such as grand theft, are usually illegal, and legislated against. Ang (2020) divides such activity into two (often overlapping) types: grand theft or access money. Access money allows for capitalist elites to bribe officials for access to government officials or to play games within the rules by lobbying for influence. Grand theft is a patently illegal activity – misappropriating government funds for personal gain. But certain forms of rent-seeking may not always be, even where they are considered unethical or immoral. Even what is ethical, or immoral, is open to interpretation. Take, for example, the pursuit of corporate interests in the political arena: while some might see such 'lobbying' as a legitimate means of influencing lawmakers, others might consider it illegitimate rent-seeking if it is untransparent and unregulated, or it privileges some groups over others.

Reflective question

Do you think corporate lobbying of governments is a form of rent-seeking?

Moreover, when games become pervasive, and embedded as social norms, it is not always clear that they could or *should* be legislated against. Based on his extensive anthropological studies across Africa, Jean-Pierre Olivier de Sardan (2015) describes these as 'practical norms', or 'the various informal, de facto, tacit, or latent norms that underlie the practices of actors which diverge from the official norms'. Examples include paying money to speed up formal bureaucratic processes, navigate around dysfunctional red tape, call in favours from people you know in the system, or exploit loopholes. If these practices are endemic and provide a valued social function, as de Sardan suggests, then can they be classed as 'corruption'? (see Box 12.2)

> ## Box 12.2 Is rule-bending always dishonest?
>
> The standard definition of corruption, as used by the World Bank and Transparency International, is 'the abuse of power for private gain'. Most definitions normatively emphasise corruption as dishonest, and detrimental to the common good. But in their book *Corruption: What Everyone Needs to Know* (2017: 4), Ray Fisman and Miriam Golden define corruption less as dishonesty, but as 'a result of interactions among individuals in which, given the choices others make, no one person can make herself better off by choosing any other course of action . . . '

Because this book is about understanding the everyday politics of development, from the ground up, we now zoom in on two games that are a feature of life for many citizens around the world: bribery and clientelism. Both games occur at the citizen-state interface, but:

- bribery happens within the *bureaucratic apparatus* of the state, when citizens encounter the civil service or other state employees.
- clientelism happens within the *political system* of the state, as people engage with (aspiring) elected representatives or their intermediaries.

Below, we explain the dynamics of these games, and analyse opposing perspectives on whether they enable or constrain development.

Bribery

Bangalore, Karnataka: 500 Indian rupees (INR) paid by an autorickshaw driver to a police officer to verify their passport and provide the necessary certification to work. Mumbai, Maharashtra: 1,000 INR paid to a government officer to be issued a Gumasta (Business) licence that had already cleared official channels. Latur, Maharashtra: only households willing to pay 500 INR to the local government officer are given a new water connection, even if they've paid their bills. These are just some of the thousands of crowd-sourced reports of bribery on IPaidABribe.com, an initiative that encourages Indian citizens to harness their collective power by sharing individual experiences of corruption.

These experiences are neither exceptional nor unusual: they are a common feature of everyday life for many people as they seek to eke out a decent living. Indeed, surveys across 34 African countries between 2019 and 2021 reveal an upward trend. While perceptions of bribery and corruption in key public institutions (justice, utilities, services) vary across countries, the police are universally considered to be the worst offenders, with nearly a third of citizens paying them a bribe (Afrobarometer, 2021).

The term 'bribery' means the abuse of power by public officials working on the front-line of distributing public services – famously termed 'street-level bureaucrats' (see Box 12.3). Crucially, these agents of the state may exercise discretion by bypassing the rules or giving preferential treatment, allowing people or organisations to effectively 'jump the queue' for vital goods and services. Inducements may be financial (illegal payments, paying for services that should be free, or facilitation payments), offering gifts (gratitude payments, in cash or kind) or exchanges (a public sector job or protection from accountability), or indirect (promise of future favours, credit).

Box 12.3 Dilemmas of street-level bureaucrats

Street-level bureaucrats are the face of government. They can have considerable discretion over decisions about how to implement rules and distribute state resources. In doing so, though, they face dilemmas that affect who gets what, when and how, such as:

- Balancing discretion (flexibility) with adherence to rules (consistency).
- Allocating limited resources fairly when there are not enough for everyone.
- Focusing on quality of services, or meeting targets.

It is important to remember, though, that corruption, petty or otherwise, takes a village. A street-level bureaucrat accepting a bribe will not be the only one to benefit; the revenue from the bribe may be shared with colleagues, superior bureaucrats, perhaps even local politicians. Olken and Pande (2012: 501) refer to this as a 'market' where identifying 'strategic interactions' among bureaucrats, and between them and other actors, is crucial for understanding not only amounts paid in bribes, but also what reforms would effectively disincentivise and reduce corruption.

Bribery is a tacit bargain that takes place in the context of power asymmetry. The capacity of each party to exercise agency and secure favourable outcomes depends on their relative power. A stark illustration of this is the fact that the poorest in society are up to twice as likely to pay a bribe as the richest. Why? On the surface, this may appear irrational: surely a traffic officer would target the people most likely to be able to pay, to maximise financial return. But powerlessness can render the poorest in society an 'easy target' if bureaucrats perceive they lack the knowledge or social connections to avoid paying. Low-income groups are, compared to more advantaged ones, also relatively powerless in their ability to 'opt-out' of using public services and must pay for private healthcare or education. In other words, inequality in susceptibility to bribery is also a function of *contact* with the state. In relying on the state more often, the poor become more vulnerable to it (Peiffer and Rose, 2016).

Reflective question

How does power influence which groups are more or less susceptible to bribery?

Does bribery enable or constrain development?

While bribery is usually referred to as 'petty' corruption, owing to the small-scale sums exchanged, its cumulative effects on development can be devastating. Consider the impact of petty corruption in the education sector, for example. In Malawi, where education is supposed to be free, bribery is rife in schools. A 2017 Afrobarometer survey found 57 per cent of people had paid a bribe for grades, gratitude payments, or informal fees for extra lessons, books, meals, or exams. When teachers can earn informal income via bribes, they may be less committed to their educational work, for which they are unlikely to be predictably paid anyway (owing to the 'big stuck' in state capability). If children leave school with fake and fraudulent qualifications, bought via bribes, they are not learning. The system therefore does not produce teachers to educate the next generation either. This chain of consequences shows how the effects of bribery can be systemic and long term.

The effects of bribery are also uneven, though, at the individual level. Not everyone can afford to pay bribes, meaning some children are forced to drop out, robbing them of their right to free education. Where bribery reinforces exclusion from accessing vital services in this way, it can widen the gap between the rich and poor. That said, new research suggests the effects of petty corruption on income inequality are sometimes more nuanced. In the context of otherwise very slow and ineffective bureaucracies, bribery may be the only system that works. Certain forms of bribery, such as unblocking laborious government regulations or avoiding paying taxes, may enable people to pursue their livelihoods and increase their share of income (Nel, 2020).

This raises the wider question of whether petty corruption 'sands' or 'greases' the wheels of economic growth (see Table 12.3). On one hand, some economists have shown that it may hinder (sand) economic growth where it stunts private sector development and curbs innovation. Bribing public officials can be costly for firms. It may also deter foreign investment in industry by reducing certainty that profits are secure from theft and increasing the costs of doing business.

On the other hand, bribery may enable (grease) economic growth where it promotes innovation and profit by enabling firms to overcome bureaucratic obstacles (see Nur-tegin and Jakee, 2020 for a review of the evidence). These debates are difficult to resolve, not least

Table 12.3 Bribery and development: enabler or constraint?

Constraint to development?	Enabler of development?
• Reproduces unequal access to goods and services based on who can afford to pay. • Undermines effective delivery of state goods by weakening bureaucratic performance incentives. • Costly for people and firms to pay bribes. • Undermines perceptions of state legitimacy. • Undermines tax morale.	• Firms can bypass cumbersome red tape. • May speed up access to goods and services for some. • Tax avoidance may boost livelihoods prospects in the short term.

because of the methodological challenges of measuring what is often a hidden phenomenon. At the macro-level, corruption can clearly coexist with economic growth, as we see in India, China, or Brazil, but we may also ask what growth *potential* is lost because citizens' interactions with public officials in these countries are frequently mired by cumbersome and laborious informal procedures.

The other cost of repeatedly encountering the hassle of petty corruption is that it may affect citizen's perception of the state, and their willingness to comply with its rules. From a sociological perspective, front-line encounters with bureaucracy convey the state's commitment to human rights, equality, freedom, and fairness: in effect, they shape the social contract from the bottom up. In an in-depth study of this dynamic in Argentina, Auyero (2012: 9) described the act of subjecting people to extended wait times for vital state services as a way of moulding 'a particular submissive set of dispositions among the urban poor'. Where everyday experiences of authority are negative, it can erode confidence in state institutions, and reduce 'tax morale' – people's willingness to pay taxes (Jahnke and Weisser, 2019). Without a viable tax base, a country cannot deliver quality services that would in turn enhance confidence in their institutions.

In this way, countries can become locked into vicious cycles of petty corruption and weak governance. A brief return to the case of Malawi, ranked 110th out of 180 countries on Transparency International (TI) Corruption Perception Index (CPI), 2021, is instructive. On a scale of 0 (highly corrupt) to 100 (very clean), it scored 32 points. It also exhibits some of the highest tolerance of non-compliant taxpayers in cross-country surveys in Africa (Jahnke and Weisser, 2019). Here, bribery is fuelling a vicious cycle of state ineffectiveness: people do not receive quality education; as their rights diminish, they become more forgiving of tax avoidance, meaning that the government has a limited tax base (revenue), hindering its capacity to run public services such as schools effectively – hence, the cycle continues.

Clientelism

Sewage and water problems, road paving and streetlights, hospital admissions and fees: just some of the reasons people queue at the roadside to see Pravin Dalal, a municipal councillor, on an average day in urban Gujarat, India (Berenschot, 2010). People turn to this street-level politician because they trust that with his attention, stamp, and signature, their complaints about public services will be addressed. Mercifully, they might avoid long queues, or being pushed around by arrogant officials demanding speed money. As a 'street-level' politician, Pravin spends substantial time providing this 'constituency service' – facilitating access to jobs, assisting funerals, or brokering access to state goods. In return, Pravin takes credit for getting things done, rewards loyal supporters and attracts new ones. A seemingly win–win situation ensues: citizens win favours, while Pravin wins political support.

But why does brokerage exist and persist? Most political systems rely on the exchange of goods and services in return for votes. But there is a fundamental distinction in how this exchange happens in 'programmatic' versus 'clientelist' political systems. In *programmatic systems*, political parties set out their policies and ideological positions on matters of public interest and people vote based on how they perceive policies will affect them or their community. In *clientelist systems*, such as the one in which Pravin operates, individual politicians target specific groups (villages, individuals, towns) and promise specific benefits to them, in exchange for political support. In such settings, party systems may be fluid and fragmented, and parties lack clear programmatic agendas (see Box 12.4).

Box 12.4   Clientelism as a form of queue-jumping?

Clientelism, sometimes referred to as patron–client relations, is a form of distributive politics in which individual 'clients' seek favours, resources, or benefits from more powerful individuals or 'patrons' in exchange for their political support or loyalty. In effect, patrons offer 'queue-jumping' rewards in exchange for votes.

Brokers (or intermediaries) can be an essential point of contact in clientelist relationships. Powerful brokers were at the heart of what came to be known as 'machine politics' in the UK and the US in the nineteenth and twentieth centuries. In these countries, the rise of programmatic politics – parties offering voters policy choices – led to the decline of the political machine.

Research across diverse settings has revealed (2006) how historical, cultural, and contextual factors, including legacies of colonialism, have shaped the dynamics of clientelism. Contemporary examples include Enrique Arias's (2006) research on drug trafficking and clientelism in Rio de Janeiro's shanty towns, or Claire Bénit-Gbaffou's (2011) research on the impact of clientelism on accountability relationships in Johannesburg.

Clientelism takes different forms across different spaces, and periods in the electoral cycle, of course. As in the Indian case, it can exist and thrive alongside democracy. Indeed, countries where elections and clientelism are deeply entwined are sometimes classed as 'competitive clientelism'. An example is Ghana, where successive elections have incentivised elites to use public institutions to secure short-term political gains (Abdulai and Hickey, 2016). But clientelism also adapts to its wider institutional setting in other ways. In some countries, it is formalised into the 'rules of the game', via Constituency Development Funds (CDFs). Prevalent in parts of Africa, Asia and the Pacific, these funds allocate often substantial amounts of discretionary funding to individual MPs, ostensibly to carry out projects in their constituencies, but often used to fund clientelist relationships. In Kenya, for example, the rising costs of clientelism under the Harambee Movement – an informal system of 'self-help' in which aspiring politicians showcase their ability to privately fund development – precipitated the creation of CDFs (Ochieng' Opalo, 2022).

Reflective question

Do you agree that clientelist systems can supplement democratic processes?

The nature of patron–client relations also adapts to scale, or 'smallness'. In microstates across the Caribbean and Pacific with less than one million inhabitants, where politics is hyper-personalised, the need to acquire a relatively small number of votes means that politicians can perform their political work in direct interactions with clients (Veenendaal and Corbett, 2020). Logically, these interactions intensify in the run-up to elections. In the Solomon Islands, where clientelism is rife and also institutionalised in the form of a CDF, the night before the polls open is known locally as 'Devil's Night' because candidates' campaign fervently, handing out gifts, bags of rice or cash in a last-ditch bid for votes.

Does clientelism enable or constrain development?

The impact of clientelism on who gets what, when, and how has been extensively studied. Does clientelism help the neediest, or does it reinforce their exclusion? Does it support or undermine democratic accountability?

The picture is decidedly mixed (see Table 12.4). For some citizens living in remote or excluded communities, or fragile polities, clientelism may bring the *only* tangible rewards from the state that they are likely to receive. In low-income urban settlements across Latin America, for example, where many people live in squalid and destitute conditions, clientelism

Table 12.4 Clientelism and development: enabler or constraint?

Constraint to development?	Enabler of development?
• Undermines the principle of universal entitlements. • Weakens incentives to strengthen state bureaucracy (because it bypasses it). • Reduces incentives for programmatic politics. • Weakens political party development.	• May improve the responsiveness of state machinery to citizens otherwise excluded from power. • May be the only way excluded groups can access certain vital goods and services. • May actually *increase* the immediate accountability of politicians.

is an essential form of 'survival politics' (Deckard and Auyero, 2022). Residents otherwise frequently given the run-around by municipal authorities can gain quicker access to material goods (jobs, food, clothes), and state welfare via brokers (Auyero, 2000).

But even if it can sometimes reach otherwise marginalised groups, is clientelism good for equality overall? Here there is a principled argument that however goods are distributed, clientelism distorts the uniform application of policies in pursuit of personal advantage. Entitlements become favours. And the personalisation of the state opens possibilities for reproducing inequality, if politicians favour their own ethnic groups, village, caste, or religion in their handouts. But do they, always? While we might assume so (see Chapter 4), some research suggests otherwise. In her extensive, mixed-method research, Bussell (2019) shows that politicians often provide clientelist 'constituency' services on a non-contingent basis, meaning without bias towards any political or identity group. Some argue that clientelism is not necessarily anti-democratic where it allows for local and immediate accountability of politicians (Bénit-Gbaffou, 2011). Likewise, we should not assume that citizens are universally powerless or meek in clientelist relationships: they can often *choose* their brokers, sometimes with the effect of inducing beneficial competition between them, to their own personal advantage (Auerbach and Thachil, 2018).

How do these individual experiences of clientelism impact the pursuit of desired futures at the national level? Jean-François Bayart (1989) famously described clientelism, or the 'politics of the belly', as a dominant explanation for the failure of African countries to promote long-term economic development. Why? Because when political elites are focused on short-termism, as in the case of Ghana, they are distracted from building a broad political consensus on any national development issues. But all may not be lost because even in this hyper-clientelist environment, politicians still need to appeal to 'swing-voters' with long-term policies that benefit wider society (Odijie and Imoro, 2021).

In the end, much of this comes back to individual incentives. How invested is Pravin, the municipal councillor, for example, in strengthening the state bureaucracy, when he seemingly benefits from its disarray? Consider the cumulative effects of the substantial time and effort politicians give to addressing individual requests at the national level. Constituency Development Funds divert resources from state systems into the pockets of MPs with little accountability or oversight, producing limited developmental gains. The personalised nature of the goods provided (e.g., funeral costs, food) detracts from investment in *public* or *common* goods, such as street lighting, or local infrastructure, the benefits of which are shared. In this sense, clientelism may short-circuit the incentives to pursue programmatic policies that could achieve broader, community developmental goals and deliver better services for all: deficiencies which motivate clientelism in the first place.

Why games persist

Whatever forms they take, informal games within the rules are ultimately dependent on the choice, agency, and power of individuals. To understand why they exist and persist, we can scrutinise what motivates these actors to behave in such ways. Bribery and clientelism involve formal and informal rules, being contested by rational actors with competing interests, who hold a set of ideas about what is right and fair. But how do these three I's influence motivations in practice? (see Table 12.5).

Table 12.5 Why games persist: the three 'I's as motivations

	Clientelism	Petty corruption
Institutions	• Breakdown of political marketplace. • Democratic scepticism and backsliding.	• Weak or low-capacity bureaucracy. • Weak monitoring and accountability.
Interests and incentives	• Targeted vote buying. • Tangible cash handouts are favoured over untrustworthy political promises.	• Low (or not existent) wages create incentives to supplement income. • Street-level bureaucrats find shortcuts under pressure to deliver.
Ideas	• Moral economy of demonstrating capacity to deliver or 'service' as a leader. • Fits with traditional 'big men' models of leadership.	• Social norms of reciprocity and gifting. • Beliefs that others will/will not follow the rules.

Why do politicians 'buy' votes?

Fundamentally, political actors operate within the formal and informal rules that govern the political marketplace. But in many countries, the formal political 'market' in which politicians are meant to build programmatic political agendas and execute them in return for votes, crumbles. In an influential study, economists Phil Keefer and Stuti Khemani (2005) provide three reasons why:

1 *Lack of information* among voters means that citizens cannot easily assess or attribute the quality of public goods and services to certain politicians. This 'information asymmetry' is particularly acute in the health and education sectors, where it is especially difficult for voters to assess quality and efficiency (e.g., to observe infection in hospitals, or judge teacher performance).

2 Voting often takes place in the context of *social fragmentation*, where people often vote along ethnic, linguistic, or religious rather than programmatic lines, and identity trumps performance.

3 All of this *undermines the credibility of political promises*. If citizens are not voting based on services, politicians are unlikely to build credible political manifestos around their delivery, and citizens will not have confidence in their delivery anyway. These institutional conditions disincentivise programmatic platforms, making direct favours to the electorate a more predictable and efficient way to secure votes.

Even under these institutional constraints, though, elected officials can still make choices about whether and how to provide goods in exchange for political support. What are their incentives in doing so? We may assume that the self-serving goal of political elites is always re-election, and that they provide gifts or favours to this instrumental end. But this is not always the case. In Kenya, for example, gift giving performs a clear social function. Candidates see it as essential for establishing their credibility as a viable leader because gifts convey information about the kind of politician you are (Kramon, 2019), and a commitment to *serving* voter interests. Research in villages in South Asia similarly revealed patronage as embedded into the social fabric of what people expect their leaders to deliver (see Mohmand, 2019).

Purely transactional, rational-choice accounts of patron–client relations miss these moral dimensions. They cannot explain, for example, why politicians sometimes provide 'constituency services' regardless of political affiliations, as noted earlier (Bussell, 2019). From this, alternative perspective, 'the local logic of patronage is not about profiteering. On the contrary, it is a radical denial of individual self-advancement' (Piliavsky, 2014: 22).

Why do citizens 'sell' their votes?

In the Solomon Islands and Papua New Guinea – two countries that are poorly governed, and some of the most linguistically diverse and socially fragmented countries on earth – political parties are weak and difficult to distinguish in terms of specific programmes or ideologies. In these contexts, people vote along ethnic or clan lines for candidates who they believe will reward them materially for their electoral support. But why? From a rational-choice perspective (see Chapter 4), this appears a calculated response to incentives – given the scarcity of resources, there is more tangible value in a cash handout, food stamp or a bag of rice today than in the diffuse promise of improved living tomorrow. Or does the explanation lie in Melanesian culture? Perhaps people's expectations are a continuation of the traditional, pre-colonial 'big man' model of leadership, whereby people followed leaders who could provide certain benefits and protection (Wood, 2016). Or is it both?

These two cases are useful in indicating that certain institutional conditions may need to be in place for people to vote for parties and programmes, rather than short-term rewards. First, that political promises are credible, and programmatic alternatives *will* be effective, both of which may be dependent on trust that bureaucracies will be impartial and fair. People would need to believe that others would do the same, so that they do not sacrifice their own individual rewards for a greater good that is not collectively pursued. It is important to recognise that these conditions may be in jeopardy everywhere, not just in cases where the state has historically been weakly institutionalised. Even in the US, a self-styled bastion of democracy, a reported 20 per cent of Americans would sell their vote for US $100 – a barometer of democratic sceptism and backsliding (Gans-Morse and Nichter, 2021).

Where voters accept gifts or bribes, why do they then vote how they promised? Is it the mercenary threat of punishment or the removal of future benefits if political representatives or their brokers discover their defection? Perhaps. But what if there were no such monitoring or enforcement mechanisms? Voters still accept goods and services in return for their political support in places where the ballot is secret, so what then stops them from 'taking the money and running'? Is it a passive normalisation of habitual practices, embedded in the institution – socially embedded rules – around voting, such that deviations become unthinkable? Or is there a more active social driver of compliance? To try to understand this, political scientists conducted surveys of voter compliance in Mexico. They found that clientelism is also sustained by reciprocal obligation: feelings of indebtedness are activated when people are helped with gifts, favours, or protection in times of need, and these actions are embedded into a moral economy (Lawson and Greene, 2014).

Why do bureaucrats extract bribes?

For those who follow the Weberian model (see Box 12.1), bribery is born out of a deficiency in formal institutions – it is not how the state is *supposed* to function. A variety of institutional configurations might contribute to a permissive environment for corrupt behaviour, such as extractive institutions (see Chapter 3). Lack of transparency, high levels of administrative discretion, elite monopoly of power and decision making, and difficulty in enforcing laws all result in the underlying informal 'rules of the game' (North, 1990) around the distribution of power and resources becoming more significant than formal processes and regulations. Routine opportunities to demand and expect bribes open up as avenues of accountability breakdown (Hoffman and Patel, 2021), causing systemic weaknesses in public services.

How can we explain bribery from an interest's perspective? One answer is principal–agent theory (see Box 12.5). From a principal–agent perspective, corruption is a fundamental betrayal by those who hold the power and agency to make decisions that affect our lives. Reforms that demand greater transparency of street-level bureaucrats are hindered by the self-interest of those who benefit from them: there is little incentive for bureaucrats to implement them (Persson, et.al., 2013). For example, implementation of India's National Rural Employment Guarantee Act, 2005, has been stymied by street-level bureaucrats' unwillingness to implement systems that would expose and close off their avenues for '"eating of money" (*paisa khana*)' (Mathur, 2017).

Box 12.5 Principal–agent theory

The principal–agent model, popularised in the work of Susan Rose-Ackerman (1978) and Robert Klitgaard (1988), has been a dominant way of understanding how interests and incentives produce rule-breaking behaviours.

At the heart of the theory there are two actors: 'agents' (someone who controls access to a service or good), and 'principals' (someone who seeks access to that service or good). The theory says that corruption happens when an agent acts in their own self-interest, rather than that of a principal. For example, when a politician or a bureaucrat, as the agent, behaves in a way that maximises their own gains, rather than those of a citizen, or the principal.

> This problem is exacerbated under two conditions:
>
> 1 When the agent and the principal have different interests – for example, when a politician seeks to pursue their own private, rather than public, interests.
> 2 Where there is an information asymmetry between the agent and principal – for example, when a politician has greater access to information than citizens about how government is operating.

More recent work has challenged the principal–agent model, however. Anna Persson, Bo Rothstein and Jan Teorell (2013) argue, instead, that corruption is a collective action problem (introduced in Chapter 4). So what's the difference? Crucially, if we view corruption as a collective action problem, then everyone, not only the agent but also the principal, is seeking to maximise their own, individual interests. And because people believe that everyone else is maximising their own interests, no one is willing to forego them. Hence, even when citizens think corruption is morally wrong, they may continue to engage in it because they expect others to keep doing it. In other words, as Caryn Peiffer and Linda Alvarez (2016) put it, fighting corruption also needs 'principled principals'.

Reflective question

Should bribery be analysed as a principal–agent problem or a collective action problem?

Another reason that bureaucrats may extract bribes relates more keenly to social norms. Actors mediating access to vital services are invariably embedded within networks of reciprocity and exchange (Barbalet, 2022). For some public servants, preserving their networks is an essential means of survival. Gift-giving and exchange maintains and extends these networks. Hence, bureaucrats may extract bribes not out of venal self-interest, but out of social pressure, based on their embeddedness in society (Pepinsky et al., 2017). Perceiving corruption as 'socially embedded' (de Sardan, 1999) in this way, allows for the possibility that ideas about fairness, reciprocity, family obligations, and deservingness shape attitudes to corruption as much as incentives do. Such social motivations may only be revealed, methodologically, by applying a behavioural lens. When Baez-Camargo et al. (2020) applied this in Rwanda, Uganda and Tanzania, using focus groups, interviews and surveys, they found, among other dynamics, that the imperatives of helping out and sharing with the family are particularly high when a relative is a service provider or public official.

Why do citizens pay bribes?

As we have seen, from the perspective of many citizens, petty corruption is the only way to survive: it is sometimes in people's *interest* to pay a bribe to make state actors more responsive to their needs. Citizens often report experiences of hostility, dismissal, or harassment at the citizen–state interface. It is, of course, possible for the state to redesign its services to shift these 'administrative burdens' where there is will (Herd and Moynihan, 2018). The Biden administration in the United States has sought to do this by simplifying application forms and procedures for student loan repayment waiver programmes, for example. However, where states are unwilling to do so, people pay bribes to 'grease the wheels', to move labyrinthine bureaucratic processes faster and to get them to the front of the queue.

To really capture the diversity of who is willing to pay a bribe, when and why, we also need to look beyond interests, and take a moral economy perspective. Doing so can sometimes challenge our assumptions. For example, you might assume, rightly or wrongly, that women act more ethically than men do, because they are socialised to be caring and nurturing, and because the consequences of rule breaking – of playing games outside the rules – are heavier for women than for men. However, Ahmad's 2020 research among female police officers in Pakistan reveals that it is not that women are intrinsically less corrupt, but that their gender constrains the type and extent of corruption they can engage in. In this way, ideas about gender and gender roles both shape worldviews about bribery, as well as its gendered dynamics in practice.

Appreciating the nuances around why people pay bribes, and the institutional and ideational framework within which they do so, is essential to developing anti-corruption strategies that work. In countries with weak rules of law, enforcement and widespread corruption, it is important to understand the 'power, capabilities and interests' of actors (corrupt or not) in the system (Roy et al., 2022). As we saw in Chapter 5, well-intentioned anti-corruption strategies can backfire if they do not carefully consider the power of ideas about who else is engaging in corruption, and whether it is considered the norm (Cheeseman and Peiffer, 2022). Mental models that normalise corruption not only perpetuate corruption but impact people's views of the state and its credibility to act to fight it (Baez-Camargo et al., 2020).

If we approach corruption and bribery as a collective action rather than principal–agent problem, the key implication is that to refrain from engaging in corruption, people need to trust that others do the same (Rothstein, 2021). The efforts of the Janaagraha Centre for Citizenship and Democracy, the small, non-profit organisation (NPO) based in Bangalore that runs ipaidabribe.com, is an example of how this kind of trust can be built in practice: specifically, by aggregating interests and making the issue visible. A copycat effort in China – a very different institutional environment – fizzled out after a few months (Ang, 2014). This was the direct result of websites being shut down, but also the indirect effect of authoritarian rule in terms of weakening the autonomy and professional capacity of Chinese NGOs (Ang, 2014). In this way, the prospects for collective action that could overcome trust deficits also depend on how permissive the wider institutional environment is of collective action.

Summary and conclusion

This chapter has shown that policies get distorted at the citizen–state interface because of the discretion of bureaucrats, low quality of governance, and a duality of ideas. This creates a so-called gap, whereby the formal state and its policies and regulations become a façade, behind which real power politics plays out in people's daily lives. Where there is scarcity, competition, and inequality, accessing public or private goods may incentivise or indeed necessitate bending or breaking the rules. These activities are the 'games within the rules'.

Games within the rules invariably take place in the context of power asymmetries, meaning they can disproportionally disadvantage the poorest in society, who may lack resources to exercise agency and choice in the same way as those at the top of the socioeconomic ladder. In turn, games have significant implications for equality, growth, the quality of governance and the nature of state–society relations.

These games are born of necessity; they are essential survival strategies for many. But they ultimately persist because of the motivations of individual actors whose actions may be enabled by the breakdown in formal systems of accountability and control. A purely interests-based interpretation of motivations is unlikely to fully capture the choices people make within these systems, however. Activities to bend or break the rules might be considered corruption, or aberrations of the way things are supposed to work, but they are also situated within a moral economy that can legitimise them. Ultimately, the degree to which games within the rules are likely to continue depends on understanding not only institutional or instrumental but social motivations for behaviour, including the power of ideas.

Discussion questions

- Should we view 'games within the rules' as corruption or survival strategies?
- In what ways are games with the rules the product of weak formal institutions?
- Under what conditions does corruption support development?
- In your particular context, what motivates politicians, bureaucrats, and citizens to engage in 'games within the rules'?

Suggested further reading

Ang, Y.Y. (2016) *How China Escaped the Poverty Trap*. Ithaca and London: Cornell University Press.

Berenschot, W. (2010) 'Everyday mediation: the politics of public service delivery in Gujarat, India', *Development and Change*, 41 (5): 883–905.

Cruz, C. and Keefer, P. (2015) 'Political parties, clientelism, and bureaucratic reform', *Comparative Political Studies*, 48 (14): 1942–73.

Grindle, M. (2016) 'Democracy and clientelism: how uneasy a relationship?', *Latin American Research Review*, 51 (3): 241–9.

13 Can the planet cope with development?

Sustainability, justice, and transformational political change

Fiona Nunan, Harriet Croome, and Chukwumerije Okereke

Image 13.1 Flooding destroys houses in rural Bandladesh. Image by Saigh Anees via Shutterstock.

Learning outcomes

- Analyse who pays the price of environmental degradation from a political perspective.
- Understand the interests, institutions, and ideas behind the commodification of nature.
- Evaluate how environmental protection and justice are contested.

How did we get here?

Climate change is not something for the future, but is already a lived reality. From devastating floods in Pakistan, to wildfires in North America, North Africa and Europe, and melting Arctic Sea ice, the climate crisis is being experienced across the globe. In August 2022, a third of Pakistan was under water, having received unprecedented monsoon rainfall, affecting 33 million people, with more than 1,700 lives lost and four million hectares of agricultural land destroyed. Yet, despite this, the United Nations' convened meeting on climate change, COP27, held in Cairo, Egypt, in the same year, was a site of contestation, with more lobbyists from the oil and gas industry present than ever before, preventing adequate action on fossil fuels.

The politics of environment and development are further illustrated by the failure of the Convention on Biological Diversity to reverse loss in biodiversity and habitats. Despite the Convention being agreed by the political leaders of hundreds of countries at the 1992 Earth Summit, wildlife populations have continued to decline, at an average of 69 per cent over the past 50 years (WWF, 2022). The extinction rate of species is estimated to be 1,000 to 10,000 times the natural rate, suggesting that anywhere between 200 and 100,000 species are being lost each year. Plants, insects and mammals are becoming extinct even before people know about them. This matters – for the species themselves and the complex ecosystems they are part of; for people everywhere, dependent on ecosystem security for clean air, soil nutrients and food; and for future advancements in medicine, crop diversity and adaptation to climate change.

The world is experiencing climate and biodiversity crises, affecting everyone – now and in the future. However, they affect poorer people much more: people who do not have the resources to cope with change, such as increased droughts and floods, who live in parts of the world that are already warmer and warming faster, and whose lives and livelihoods are directly dependent on natural resources, including agriculture, forests and fisheries.

How have we got here? And why? These crises cannot be explained solely by understanding what is going on in the environment. What lies beneath them are powerful interest groups, seeking wealth and profit ahead of clean air and protected natural forests; political ideology that puts markets and economic value before the well-being of people and the planet; and institutions that prevent radical change in how we produce, benefit from and dispose of goods and services to protect or serve some interests, above others.

This chapter seeks to answer key questions at the environment and development nexus that preoccupy global debates: can the world develop and save the environment at the same time? Who is paying the price of environmental damage and why? How have affected communities responded to environmental threats and with what success? How can more radical transformation be made possible? In exploring these questions, we introduce a diverse and diffuse literature on the interplay between environment, development, and politics. We identify key concepts that help explain why the environment is political, and review contemporary responses to the climate emergency and biodiversity crisis to grasp at hopeful endeavours for a fairer, greener future.

Can the world develop and save the environment at the same time?

Until at least the late 1980s, the perceived wisdom was that countries need to develop and should address environmental pollution once they had reached a 'Western level' of development. This 'develop first, save the environment later' approach is illustrated by economists using an Environmental Kuznets Curve (see Figure 13.1), where pollution increases until it plateaus at a level of per capita income and then begins to reduce as a country has the funds available to reduce pollution and clean up the environment (Okereke and Massaquoi, 2018). This classical economic thinking fitted with political prioritisation of economic growth, supported by powerful business interest groups, particularly associated with the oil and gas industry. However, this thinking has been challenged by at least two alternative concepts and observations in the intervening years.

The first of these is the concept of sustainable development (see Box 13.1). The idea of 'sustainable development' came to prominence with the publication of the World Commission

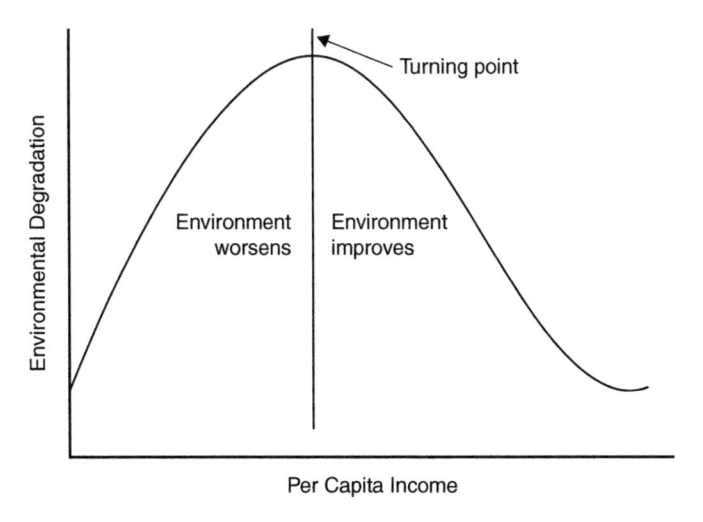

Figure 13.1 The environment-development Kuznets Curve

on Environment and Development's (WCED) *Our Common Future Report* in 1987. This is often referred to as the 'Brundtland Report' after the then Chair of WCED, Gro Harlem Brundtland. WCED was brought together by the Secretary General of the United Nations (UN), following a decision by the General Assembly that recommendations were needed on how the global community can better protect the environment while at the same time pursue social development objectives, particularly poverty reduction. Sustainable development is founded on the concept of sustainability, drawing principally on its ecological roots, referring to maintaining or restoring the components of ecosystems. The definition from the WCED report is referred to as the 'Brundtland' definition, which reads: 'development that meets the needs of the present without compromising the ability of future generations to meet their own needs' (WCED, 1987: 43).

Sustainable development challenged previous thinking that environmental protection could not be achieved at the same time as economic growth, on which development was seen to depend. Instead, the concept reflected the idea that environment and the economy can be reconciled, as demonstrated by its three pillars of environment, economy and social sustainability. However, different interpretations of what is meant by sustainable development and how it should be pursued has meant that politicians, businesses, international organisations and others have adopted contrasting definitions and approaches, resulting in slow progress and limited positive change (Baker, 2016).

Box 13.1   Sustainability and sustainable development

Within sustainable development, sustainability is seen as the objective being pursued, in three forms, often referred to as pillars – environmental, economic and social. These three pillars are often portrayed in a Venn diagram to emphasise that they need to come together for sustainable development to be realised. In addition to sustainable development having three pillars, it is also considered to have underlying principles, such as intra- (within) and inter- (between) generational equity, giving sustainable development its ethos of poverty alleviation, gender equality, justice, participation and common but differentiated responsibility. The last principle recognises that everyone has a responsibility to pursue sustainable development, but their level of responsibility differs according to how responsible they were for unsustainable development and what means they have to pursue sustainable development. Seeking sustainable development is therefore not a technical exercise, but one of seeking fairness, making sustainable development a political pursuit.

This concept of sustainable development was revolutionary in the late 1980s, as it implied that economic development and environmental protection do not need to be in conflict. Rather, the right kinds of economic development could enhance environmental protection and forms of 'green growth' could be part of an economic development plan. Not everyone accepts this and certainly there are critics of the concept of sustainable development. Critics range from those who believe the concept is both too human-centred and too vague (i.e., anything and everything fits within its mandate) to those who believe that it is unnecessary and that technology – given enough economic investment – will provide the solutions needed.

The concept and theory of sustainable development remain relevant, though new ideas and approaches have built on the concept, bringing in greater recognition of ecological limits to growth, such as through the idea of Planetary Boundaries and Doughnut Economics (see section on 'Old interests and institutions, but new ideas?', below).

The second challenge to the 'develop first, clean up later' approach was the idea that we can leapfrog or tunnel through the bell-shaped Kuznets curve by adopting clean technology and avoiding polluting technology – whether that is associated with industrial processes or avoiding fossil fuels for electricity generation. Such 'leapfrogging' has contributed to ideology centred on technology providing solutions to environmental challenges, such as 'ecological modernisation', an attractive proposition to politicians as it avoids measures requiring undesirable lifestyle changes for the electorate that are likely to make politicians unpopular (Carter, 2018).

Thinking on whether we can afford to protect the natural environment and develop at the same time has changed over the years. Not everyone has accepted that we can do both, and progress on environmental protection is too often slow and piecemeal, reflecting politicians' prioritisation of economic growth and the interests of big business. A case in point is the heavy burden of air pollution across many cities, particularly in the Global South. The air quality in Delhi fell within the category of 'unhealthy' in the US Air Quality Index for the whole of 2019, with several months in the 'very unhealthy' category (IQAir, 2023). High levels of particulate matter, soot and black carbon have been associated with an estimated 54,000 premature deaths in the city and an economic cost of US$8.1 billion (Greenpeace, 2023).

In response to the situation in Delhi and other Indian cities, the National Clean Air Programme aims to see a reduction of 20–30 per cent in the air pollution of 102 of the most polluted cities by 2024 (IQAir, 2023). While improvements have been realised in Delhi in terms of better monitoring and communication of air quality information, political tensions between state and national government, and lack of coordination between the city government and surrounding states, means that realising improvements is slower than needed. Institutions set up to tackle air pollution have been inadequate in terms of power and resources, with political and business interests continuing to keep measures in check. In other words, as explored extensively in Chapters 3 and 4 of this book, institutions have been unable to rein in the pursuit of self-interests and overcome collective action problems. One response to slow and inadequate progress has been a range of protests – members of the Legislative Assembly of the Bharatiya Janata Party (BJP) wore masks and carried oxygen cylinders into the Delhi Assembly and a citizens' protest at Delhi Gate demanded more action from national and state government.

> ### Reflective question
>
> Is environmental protection a constraint on development for the world's poorest countries?

The politics of environmental choices

The example of the contestation around the clean air programme in Delhi shows that avoiding the Environmental Kuznets Curve and moving to sustainable development is far from easy, and always political. Contestation over the measures and slow progress reflects differing interests and the exercise of power. Protests are driven by economic interests seeking to protect their profit, but also from poorer communities unable to adapt to costly alternatives such as cleaner transport. Ultimately, political choices have to be made.

An example of positive political choices for the environment and for the rights of Indigenous Peoples comes from the re-election of Lula da Silva as president in Brazil. Under the presidency of Jair Bolsonaro (2019–22) deforestation of the Amazon rainforest was encouraged, clearing land for cattle ranching and soy cultivation, benefitting wealthy business interests and politicians at the expense of Indigenous Peoples living in and around the rainforest. Since Lula's inauguration in January 2023, deforestation rates have plummeted, attributed to enforcement of environmental regulations and bringing back protected status for designated areas (Mongabay, 2023).

What these examples all show is that to understand the power relations at play within and around environment-development concerns, and how they affect decision-making, we need to combine the study of economic and political factors. The key approach to this is called 'political ecology' (see Box 13.2).

> ### Box 13.2   Political ecology
>
> Political ecology brings together ecological concerns with the political economy. Within development studies, Blaikie's (1985) investigation into the experience of and response to soil erosion in Africa and Asia laid the foundations for political ecology. He argued that technical explanations for and responses to soil erosion would never be sufficient; instead, political and economic factors led to soil erosion and so political and economic responses were needed. These factors included how political decisions made in other parts of the world, such as maintaining or introducing agricultural subsidies, affected commodity prices and therefore the investment farmers make.
>
> Political ecology provides a strong argument against neo-Malthusian ideas of overpopulation, resource scarcity and environmental limits. Instead, the distribution and

exercise of power is a central component of political ecology analysis aimed at exposing the racial, class-based and patriarchal lines along which resource use and access is divided. Other characteristics of political ecology approach include analysis at multiple levels and scales, in recognition of the interconnections along a chain of social and economic relations, leading Blaikie (1985) to refer to 'chains of explanation', and recognition of multiple sources and forms of knowledge, including local ecological knowledge. Recognition of multiple sources and forms of knowledge reflects the politics of knowledge creation and use, with certain sources and forms of knowledge prioritised over others.

The practice of political ecology has been criticised for insufficiently investigating politics, not involving adequate ecological analysis and failing to provide practical policy recommendations. Such limitations reflect the critical perspective of the approach, seeking to identify alternative explanations for environmental degradation, particularly from the perspective of people dependent on natural resources, rather than offer practical solutions. Application of political ecology analysis remains pertinent and, given its strong concern with delivering on social justice, is closely aligned with literature and theory associated with environmental justice.

Political ecology helps us to analyse why politicians face a range of challenges in deciding which policies to adopt when it comes to the environment. Which policies will be more acceptable to their voters? Who bears the costs of pollution and environmental degradation and the costs of tackling pollution and protecting the environment? As argued in Chapter 3 of this book, the ideas that elites hold about the nature and causes of problems shape how they decide what, if anything, should be done to address them. Neoliberalism has dominated the political and economic ideology of many democratic countries and institutions, including international financial institutions, of the Global North, such as the World Bank, since the 1980s (Potter et al., 2018).

How has neoliberal ideology dominated responses to environmental problems?

Political decision making on environmental problems have been dominated by the ideology of neoliberalism since the 1980s. As discussed extensively in Chapter 8, this is characterised by reducing the role of the state, leaving markets to respond to pollution and encouraging technological innovation (Islam, 2013). Such neoliberal ideology has led to an increasing use of market-based instruments to address environmental concerns and to the neoliberalisation or commodification of nature (see Box 13.3) in pursuit of both development and environmental outcomes (Carter, 2018; Igoe and Brockington, 2007).

Box 13.3 Neoliberalisation and commodification of nature

The commodification of nature is associated with the influence of political and economic neoliberal ideology on how nature is portrayed and accessed. Neoliberalism asserts that markets can provide more efficient and effective solutions, including to conservation issues, than state regulation. Examples of how nature has been commodified include interactive experiences with elephants in Botswana and South Africa, where elephants are used to attract tourists to the region, with little attention given to the wider social–ecological context in which the elephants exist. Such an approach leads to a fragmented view of social–ecological systems rather than taking a holistic perspective, and encourages nature to be seen in terms of how much money it can generate rather than recognising its intrinsic value or value to local communities.

Image 13.2 African elephants swimming across the Chobe River, Botswana, watched by tourists on safari. Image by THP Creative via Shutterstock.

What are some of the key policy instruments chosen by political elites, and how has neoliberalism influenced them? In practice, the kinds of measures adopted by governments to implement political decisions fall into four general categories (Carter, 2018): 1) Command and control (CAC); 2) government expenditure; 3) market-based instruments (MBIs) and 4) voluntary instruments. CAC instruments include policies such as setting minimum standards or maximum pollution levels and have remained the dominant policy response to environmental issues. MBIs, by contrast, include taxes (such as on fossil fuel use and carbon emissions) that more deliberately target and attempt to penalise those contributing to pollution. Although MBIs have not been as widely adopted as envisaged, they have been widely promoted in responding to climate change and biodiversity loss. One example of a market-based measure is the establishment of emissions trading schemes in which industry bids for, or are provided with, permits to pollute up to a certain 'cap'. Companies can buy more permits if they wish to pollute more or change their technologies to reduce pollution. These types of measures are attractive to economists and politicians as firstly they follow the 'polluter pays' principle – that is, polluters pay to pollute – and secondly, they are believed to incentivise innovation in how businesses, industry and individuals respond – those not willing to pay to pollute should invest in technologies to reduce pollution.

> ## Reflective question
>
> Why are politicians attracted to neoliberal solutions to environmental challenges?

Despite the political attractiveness of these types of measures, evidence is mixed as to how effective they are. Findings show that the low price of carbon, for example, means that the effectiveness of emissions trading is linked more to regulatory measures, such as vehicle emission standards, than MBIs (Cullenward and Victor, 2020). This is because the pricing of carbon is not providing the financial incentive expected of an MBI, and so MBIs cannot be assumed to necessarily encourage innovation in industry to avoid paying to emit (Mazaheri et al., 2022).

One of the observations that Cullenward and Victor (2020) make is that the politics of different sectors – energy, roads, agriculture, etc. – differ greatly and therefore a range of policy packages and approaches are needed for effective climate responses that transcend sectoral differences. For example, these sectors differ in terms of the type and aims of interest groups, how many key stakeholder groups there are, and how power is shared. Agriculture, for example, may be more fragmented, with a greater diversity of interests, than a sector such as building and maintaining roads, where there are fewer companies involved, meaning that the businesses that are involved may develop close relationships with politicians and civil servants, creating opportunities for games within the rules, such as collusion (see Chapter 12).

Who is paying the price?

Biodiversity conservation and climate change negotiations (see Box 13.4) have so far not succeeded in saving the planet or protecting people – particularly the poorest and most marginalised – from the negative impacts of these crises. Record-breaking droughts and floods are increasing in frequency and severity with almost every year that passes, destroying lives and livelihoods in their path. Particularly in least economically developed countries, events such as these cause acute malnutrition and a lack of clean water, put serious strain on already underfunded healthcare systems and require governments to direct significant funding to recovery efforts. Why are the costs and consequences of the climate and biodiversity crises particularly felt by the poor, paying the ultimate price for crises they did not cause?

An historical perspective is needed to understand the power relations that have produced wide-scale land use change and precipitated biodiversity loss and climate change. Deep-rooted racial inequality and enduring colonialities have shaped climate change and related climate (in)justice with implications for climate change negotiation, policy and action (Okereke and Coventry, 2016). Specifically, the commodification and over-exploitation of natural resources in the colonial era fuelled industrialisation in Europe and the

United States through the late nineteenth and early twentieth centuries. Industrialisation, including of farming, and attendant land-use changes are the greatest contributors to climate change. Even still, prevailing economic, political and scientific conditions are shaped by colonial continuities in nations both formerly colonising and colonised. Such enduring and institutionalised coloniality in part explains why the impacts of climate change continue to be felt most keenly by the most marginalised and least responsible.

The continuing dominance of powerful Western interests and institutions are evident in the outcomes of the United Nations Framework Convention on Climate Change (UNFCCC) negotiations in recent decades. Initial UNFCCC frameworks focused on carbon dioxide mitigation over adaptation or reversal strategies, despite advocacy by low-income countries to move beyond a focus on mitigation (see Box 13.4 for an explanation of mitigation and adaptation). As early as 1995, this approach was seen as too little, too late – the harmful effects of climate change to land, lives and livelihoods already apparent in those countries. Even following the issuing of the Delhi Declaration in 2002 by low-income countries, which reiterated the need for global resources to be focused on adaptation, countries of the Global North promoted a limit of two degrees global temperature rise above pre-industrial levels. This target, presented as the safe limit of temperature rise, was really a political choice aimed at protecting the economic interests of nations of the Global North, as opposed to protecting the most people, or the environment (Klein, 2015).

Box 13.4 Responding to climate change

International negotiations on how the world should respond to climate change are led by the UNFCCC, which has an Executive Secretary and Secretariat which convene the meetings of the Conference of Parties (COP). The 'parties' are those countries that signed the UNFCCC, which was agreed at the 1992 United Nations Conference on Environment and Development. The negotiations include actions that should be taken to reduce further human-induced climate change and actions to adapt to the consequences of climate change.

Mitigation: climate change mitigation refers to activities aimed at reducing or altogether avoiding greenhouse gas emissions. For example, using renewable energy technologies to provide clean energy and therefore avoiding carbon dioxide emissions.

Adaptation: climate change adaptation refers to activities aimed at helping people or nonhuman nature adapt to the impacts of climate change already being experienced. For example, building flood barriers to protect communities at higher risk and developing drought resistant crop varieties.

Both mitigation and adaptation responses are important and urgently needed. However, for those whose lives and livelihoods are already threatened by the impacts of climate change, the focus on adaptation takes on increased importance.

Fast forward more than a decade, and similar interests could be seen in key decisions resulting from COP27 in 2022. On one hand, the COP27 agreement represented breakthrough progress, for the first time establishing a loss-and-damage fund, discussed earlier in this book, in Chapter 9. This fund made developed nations obligated to financially assist developing countries that are worst affected by climate change (UN, 2022). In spite of these gains, though, many have argued that the summit fell short in terms of a plan to phase out fossil fuels (peak GHG emissions only by 2050) and limit global temperature rises (1.5C above pre-industrial levels). The lack of ambition evident in the agreed targets, which will knowingly cause hunger, freshwater scarcity, drought and flooding across vulnerable countries, has been attributed to stonewalling by the interests of big emitters and oil-producing companies who were strongly represented at the conference (Deutsche Welle, 2022).

How does power undermine the interests of poorer and marginalised countries and communities in climate adaptation? In terms of everyday lived realities, communities with little political power cannot easily resist the siting of destructive industrial infrastructure or the disposal of pollutants in the vicinity of their communities. But also, powerful institutions and interests may combine to exclude those less powerful from the decision-making process. For example, in the Niger Delta, the commercial interests of global oil and gas corporations have combined with the state's desire to secure wealth and powerful geopolitical alliances, resulting in widespread environmental and social abuses. An environmental justice lens (see Box 13.5) illustrates how distributional injustice (fossil-fuel powered increases in industrialisation and economic expansion for some in return for near-complete fisheries collapse, loss of productive lands, illness, and death for people in the Niger Delta) is perpetuated through procedural injustice (see Chapter 14 for a discussion of the relationship between procedural justice and authority). Traditional institutions are often not recognised by major oil companies and the judicial process is prohibitively bureaucratic, lengthy and costly for affected communities (BSOEC, 2019). Powerful economic, political and commercial interests work together to retain procedural injustice.

Box 13.5   Environmental justice

Environmental justice is concerned with how social difference influences a person or community's relationship with, and lived experience and use of, the natural environment. It is also concerned with how powers to change these relations or experiences are not fairly distributed between individuals and institutions. The origins of environmental justice are associated with social movements and civil rights activism in the US, protesting about the spatial location of toxic waste sites and how people of colour are disproportionately affected by multiple forms and sources of pollution. Literature and thinking on environmental justice is therefore not only informed by academic research, but by campaigning, political debate and policy making. Three forms of environmental justice are often identified and investigated: distributive, procedural and recognition.

Distributive justice describes the fair and equitable distribution of either benefits or burdens across a group of individuals, communities or nations. Procedural justice describes

> fair and equitable participation in the decision-making process about issues connected to the environment and people's relationship with it, and equality of access to legal representation and recourse in matters relating to the environment. It is important to consider equity within groups as well as between groups, and whether people have the knowledge and practical means to participate, not merely the legislative right. Environmental justice as recognition refers to analysis of who is and who is not valued, or recognised, within decision-making.
>
> Environmental justice analysis recognises how politics affects how issues are understood and portrayed – how they are 'framed' – and how politics influences 'claim-making', referring to claims made about environmental issues, who is affected, how and why. Analysis of how issues are framed or presented, and what claims are being made and by whom is central to environmental justice analysis. The approach has been criticised for the breadth of how the term is used, with many approaches and empirical examples being placed within its remit. Application of an environmental justice lens to climate change has led to the pursuit and analysis of 'climate justice', recognising the inherent unfair origins and experience of climate change, associated with colonial legacies of production, wealth and power.

Poorer communities do not only often end up paying the price of destructive environmental activities, but also for remediation. For example, REDD+ (Reducing Emissions from Deforestation and forest Degradation) projects have attempted to usher in a new era of sustainable development globally, promising local people increased income generation from the protection of carbon and biodiversity-rich forests. However, the win–win goals of REDD+ are hotly contested. Far from being the panacea it purports to be, critics of REDD+ in countries including Indonesia, Brazil and Cameroon, look upon projects as yet another highly politicised example of development serving the interests of the developed world. Units of carbon – protected through restricting local people's access to forests – are traded with developed nations to offset emissions from the extraction and use of fossil fuels. The revenues from traded units of carbon are meant to go to local people, but instead are often diverted through corruption or politically motivated self-interest (Transparency International, 2021).

Many diverse examples of this are documented in Transparency International's 'Corruption and Climate Atlas' (see: www.transparency.org/en/projects/climate-governance-integrity-programme/climate-corruption-atlas). In Indonesia, for example, there is evidence that Suharto's military dictatorship used reforestation funds to boost crony business. In the post-Suharto era, corporations or individuals encroach on the areas that are supposed to be protected under REDD+ to run illegal logging, mining, or palm oil operations. Rather than take action to prevent this, the incentives and interests of local authorities, including the police, are to takes bribes from these rich companies to allow their illegal activities to continue. As discussed in Chapter 12, these actions may well be motivated both by self-interest, but they are also part of a moral economy, with many officials having family or personal ties to those who run and manage the extractives.

Whatever the motivation behind collusion and rent-seeking, funds diverted by corruption result in desired futures not being fully realised. In addition, diverse forms of knowledge and social organisation connected to forests are lost through restricted access models. In the Indonesian case, as in many countries, the financial incentives of REDD+ are weak when compared to the riches promised by increasing demand for oil palm, timber and metal ore (Irawan et al., 2013). The extractive industries include powerful lobbyists, often in receipt of political support as jobs creation and economic growth are of central importance to many politicians' election manifestos (Dermawan and Sinaga, 2015). An investigation by Indonesian NGO Jatam concluded that up to 86 per cent of donations to the 2019 presidential candidates' campaign came from extractive industries and were connected to land-use change and deforestation (Jatam, 2019). The combined interests of commercial institutions and politicians impeded the progress of REDD+ in Indonesia to the detriment of environmental and development outcomes, as local people have been denied promised revenue.

Campaigners fear that Indigenous Peoples and local communities will also end up paying the price of biodiversity loss. A key reason for this is the global adoption, in 2022, of the idea that 30 per cent of the planet's land and ocean should be set aside to conserve biodiversity – e.g., through establishing Protected Areas, by 2030. This is referred to as '30 x 30' – a target included in the Kunming–Montreal Global Biodiversity Framework. This catchy slogan, while highly accessible from a public relations perspective and spearheaded by the EU and other countries in the Global North, has been heavily criticised as a threat to the lives of millions of Indigenous Peoples, who may be evicted from their ancestral lands or have their rights to use and benefit from natural resources curtailed as a result. Evidence suggests that levels of biodiversity in Indigenous managed lands are equal to, if not higher than, those in Protected Areas (Schuster et al., 2019), meaning that such a policy could potentially undermine both human and environmental well-being. Many argue that through the enclosure of Indigenous land and resources, the agreement actually stands to benefit those countries in the Global North the most. How so? By enabling the world to reach targets without changing production and consumption levels and norms. It remains to be seen whether 30 x 30 will be the new paradigm of equitable conservation it is heralded to be, or another neocolonial project that undermines human rights and social justice.

Reflective question

Could an environmental justice lens inform fairer and more effective political decisions on environment and development dilemmas?

How have people contested environmental decision making?

Given that more marginalised, poorer people tend to carry the cost of a degraded environment, how have people most affected contested decisions and decision-making powers? There are at least two key areas of action involving local people in responding to environmental degradation, beyond engaging in formal politics.

Direct action for environmental justice

The first is direct action and the formation of, or participation in, social movements. As discussed in chapter 7, 'power to the people' can provide spaces where agency and power are used to question and challenge dominant interests and their agendas. Environmental groups and connected social movements are very diverse, ranging from less radical groups such as the Royal Society for the Protection of Birds (RSPB) in the UK and the Sierra Club in the USA, to grassroots groups, including the global Fridays for Future movement inspired by climate change activist, Greta Thunberg.

The strategies of environmental movements across the world vary greatly in terms of their aims and beliefs, the resources available to them, and how close they are to governments. Some groups may be close to government and use strategies associated with 'insider' pressure groups. These include encouraging members to write to their MPs, lobbying governments through submissions and closed meetings. In contrast, 'outsider' pressure groups either do not want to be close to government or cannot be because of their size or stance. These groups are more associated with direct action, such as Extinction Rebellion blocking roads or Greenpeace protestors scaling oil platforms.

The effectiveness of these strategies is difficult to measure, as the scope for impact is affected by so many factors, including how protests are reported by the media (itself political in many respects), what point the government is in the election cycle, and how salient the issues are to the electorate. Carter (2018) suggests that many kinds of impact can be associated with environmental campaigning action, such as raising awareness of the issues among the public, getting issues onto the political agenda, and raising the profile of the group, be it among potential members or with relevant decision-making authorities.

Many environmental groups and movements are strongly associated with social justice. This implies that in fighting against actual or potential environmental degradation or pollution, grassroots activists have also fought for local voices to be heard and their rights upheld – if not in securing the demanded protections, then in the form of reparations. Key examples include the Chipko movement of the 1970s in India, in which women villagers hugged trees over days and nights to prevent deforestation; the Narmada Bachao Andolan movement, formed with the aim of stopping the construction of the Sardar Sarovar Dam on the Narmada River in 1985; Dena'ina community-led activism to stop advances to the Alaska pebble mine in 2022; and Navdanya, a more recent movement formed by the eco-activist Vandana Shiva to encourage preservation and use of native plant varieties.

All these movements achieved some success, with the Chipko movement gaining international recognition and a 15-year ban on the cutting of trees in the area, the action of Narmada Bachao Andolan contributing to the formation and investigations of the World Commission on Dams (Mallick, 2021) and Dena'ina community activism securing the protection of 44,000 acres of land and water, including a globally important salmon fishery (Conley, 2022). While such movements may not have been successful in achieving all their aims – for example, the Sardar Sarovar Dam was constructed and adequate compensation, including through resettlement, had to be pursued for many years – they were, and are, very successful in galvanising global interest and awareness, and inspired grassroots action across the world.

Community-based natural resource management

The second key area of local action in response to environmental degradation is in participating in collaborative or community-based natural resource management (CBNRM) governance arrangements. Since at least the 1980s, communities, particularly in rural areas, have been involved in making and enforcing decisions on how renewable natural resources, such as forests and fisheries, are governed. In some areas, traditional customary systems are still in place – for example, traditional authorities in Ghana formed the Wechiau hippo sanctuary and nomadic pastoralists in Ethiopia move their livestock according to traditional routes, timings and agreements with other groups. CBNRM tends to be more associated with government and/or project-led introduction of participatory and collaborative governance, where local communities work with government and other stakeholders.

CBNRM and collaborative governance approaches to managing forests and fisheries have had mixed success. Nepal, for example, is renowned for its vast network of Forest User Groups which have contributed to considerable reforestation. Even here, though, in some locations powerful interests have captured the community-level committees, reflecting the widespread practice of 'elite capture' of natural resource governance, where more powerful actors capture power and monetary benefits by, for example, using their status and power to be elected onto committees and awarding themselves allowances (Gurung et al., 2013).

There are other examples where many factors have contributed to governance systems struggling to keep going and deliver on sustainable management. This includes fisheries co-management on Lake Victoria, the second largest freshwater body in the world and therefore a key resource to the countries bordering the lake: Kenya, Tanzania and Uganda. The community-based fisheries management groups formed in the 2000s across the approximate 1,500 landing sites have struggled to keep going and be effective. This is at least partly due to political intervention at local and national levels, systemic corruption in society reflected within the sector and governments being unwilling to really share power with fishing communities (Nunan, 2020).

Endeavours to prevent environmental degradation, secure compensation or sustainably manage environmental resources, particularly in the Global South, are strongly linked to maintaining rights, well-being and livelihoods. The intricate links between the environment and development inevitably mean that local action is bound up with power relations within and beyond local communities, and with politics at local, national and international levels. Above all, the pursuit of environmental protection and sustainable management of natural resources is also the pursuit of justice, including recognition of the rights to life, good health and sufficient livelihood.

Old interests and institutions, but new ideas?

For the planet to be able to cope with development, then, radical transformation is needed – transformation of the kind that restores the living environment, reverses climate change, and eradicates multidimensional poverty globally. Throughout the chapter, it has been evident that tension between the environment and development remains, despite the emergence of sustainable development in the late 1980s. At the heart of this is the divergence of interests and preferences that ultimately define *alternative* desired futures. The political and economic interests of people, governments and businesses of the Global North continue to influence global responses to the climate and biodiversity crises. These are seen in the international institutions through which negotiations take place on climate change and biodiversity protection, in the ideas that dominate those negotiations and in the interests that have greater power and influence. There are, however, new ideas making their way into global economic, environment and development policy vocabularies with renewed vigour, including Green Growth, Post-Growth and Doughnut Economics.

The Organisation for Economic Cooperation and Development (OECD) defines Green Growth as 'fostering economic growth and development, while ensuring that natural assets continue to provide the resources and environmental services on which our well-being relies' (OECD, 2011: 9). We know what you're thinking . . . sounds a bit like sustainable development, right? Absolutely. In essence, green growth is touted as sustainable development's renewable energy powered, bright-futured, younger sibling. It purports that economies can keep on growing in terms of GDP, while reducing greenhouse gas emissions and unsustainable extraction of material natural resources by using and continuing to invest in renewable and emission-gobbling technologies.

Post-growth is an approach to thinking about what comes after (what it views to be) the inevitable collapse of the economic growth-centred capitalist system. For post-growth thinkers, current rates and patterns of economic growth, natural resource extraction, and mass production and consumption constitute an 'impossibility theorem' for development economics (Daly, 1993: 27). Any notions of leapfrogging or tunnelling through are by now ecologically, socially and financially impossible. The only way to decouple development from environmental degradation is to rethink the relationship between people, the economy and the non-human environment, and work towards a future where economies do not grow infinitely and are not measured by GDP.

The idea of planetary boundaries is central to a post-growth agenda (Rockström et al., 2009; Steffen et al., 2015). Planetary boundaries are deemed to be the limits within which 'humanity can operate safely' (Rockström et al., 2009: 1). The nine interdependent boundaries relate to atmospheric carbon dioxide levels; ocean acidification; stratospheric ozone; biogeochemical nitrogen and phosphorus cycles; global freshwater use; land system change (e.g., conversion to cropland); extinction rates; chemical pollution and atmospheric aerosol loading (Rockström et al., 2009). For the planet to be able to cope with development, the path to development must not overstep any one of these boundaries. In developing on the idea of planetary boundaries, Rockström et al. (2023) report on the development of Earth System Boundaries, which are identified in terms of being safe and just. Earth System Boundaries (ESBs) build on planetary boundaries by bringing in distributional concerns, both within current generations (between countries, communities and individuals) and between current and future generations. They report that of the eight ESBs, seven have already been crossed, providing strong evidence of the need for transformational change that addresses distributional concerns. As impacts are unfairly distributed, within and between generations, globally negotiated solutions are essential.

Doughnut Economics (Raworth, 2012, 2017) is a model for economic transition which reflects many principles of post-growth thinking. Under doughnut economics, planetary boundaries are the outer edge of the doughnut – think glazed ring doughnut with a hole in the middle, not a filled jammy centre. The inner edge of the doughnut represents minimum standards of human health and well-being. This includes economic well-being, but extends also to education, water and food security, political voice and social equity (Raworth, 2017). The space between the 'ecological ceiling' and 'social foundations' (the doughnut) balances ecological security with social justice – it is the space where the planet can theoretically cope with development (Raworth, 2017). City economies, including Amsterdam, Brussels and Nanaimo in Canada, have been among the first to adopt the principles of Doughnut Economics, formally putting well-being and environmental protection above GDP and demonstrating that – to an extent and in certain contexts – there is political will to support such transformative change (e.g., see: https://amsterdamdonutcoalitie.nl/).

Reflective question

Could the ideas of post-growth, planetary boundaries and doughnut economics challenge entrenched interests, institutions and ideas for a fairer, greener future?

Summary and conclusion

A recurring theme runs through literature, policy and practice of whether the environment can be protected or improved at the same time as growing an economy. But whether environmental protection and economic development are compatible or mutually exclusive depends on their form, scale and interpretation – all influenced by the ideas, institutions and interests involved, manifested in political responses to the environment and development.

The key to this is the influence of neoliberal ideology. Assumptions and beliefs that markets will create the incentives needed for less polluting behaviour and prevent further deforestation has led to a significant reliance on market-based solutions, such as carbon pricing, emissions trading and payments for the conservation of forests. Neoliberal ideology reflects the interests of corporate interests and limits demand for more transformational change.

It is clear that environmental issues are political. Yes, they are technical, with understanding and responses needed from many disciplines and professions, from engineers to ecologists. However, how environmental issues are understood and explained, what sources of knowledge are recognised and prioritised, and who is involved in making decisions in relation to environmental resources are all political matters and often a site of contestation. Political ecology encourages analysis of how environmental issues are framed, which sources of knowledge are drawn on to explain and respond to environmental issues, and of the power relations at play within and around environment–development concerns. The analysis of social movements and collaborative and community-based governance of natural resources demonstrates that environmental management and protection often also concerns social justice, inequity and power imbalances.

Momentum for more transformational change is gaining pace, through recognition of there being planetary boundaries, which, if overshot, will undermine the achievement of desired futures. What is clear is that political action is needed at all levels, from grassroots activism and environmental defenders to international climate negotiations. Politicians, the private sector, activists and the electorate all have a role to play, but power and the longstanding predominance of neoliberal ideology mean that it remains a struggle to secure the commitment and investment needed in a just transition to a greener future.

So, can the planet cope with development? The answer will depend on what form development takes, how the benefits of development are shared, and who bears the environmental costs of development. This chapter has demonstrated, however, that political decision-making is and will continue to be central to the answer. For the planet to cope with development, we need politics that delivers on greater equity and faster action in response to the climate change and biodiversity loss emergencies.

Discussion questions

- How are institutions, interests and ideas evident in approaches to protecting the environment that also enable development?
- Can bottom-up responses to social and environmental injustice challenge dominant ideas, interests and institutions at scale for positive change?
- Which theoretical approach – sustainable development and sustainability, political ecology or environmental justice – provides the most useful lens for understanding the political dimensions of environment and development dilemmas?

Suggested further reading

Bjork-James, C., Checker, M. and Edelman, M. (2022) 'Transnational social movements: environmentalist, indigenous, and agrarian visions for planetary futures', *Annual Review of Environment and Resources*, 47: 583–608.

Maslin, M.A., Lang, J. and Harvey, F. (2023) 'A short history of the successes and failures of the international climate change negotiations', UCL Open, *Environment*, (5): 8.

Raworth, K. (2012) 'A safe and just space for humanity', Oxfam Discussion Paper, Oxford: Oxfam.

Scoones, I., Leach, M. and Newell, P. (2015) *The Politics of Green Transformations*. London: Routledge.

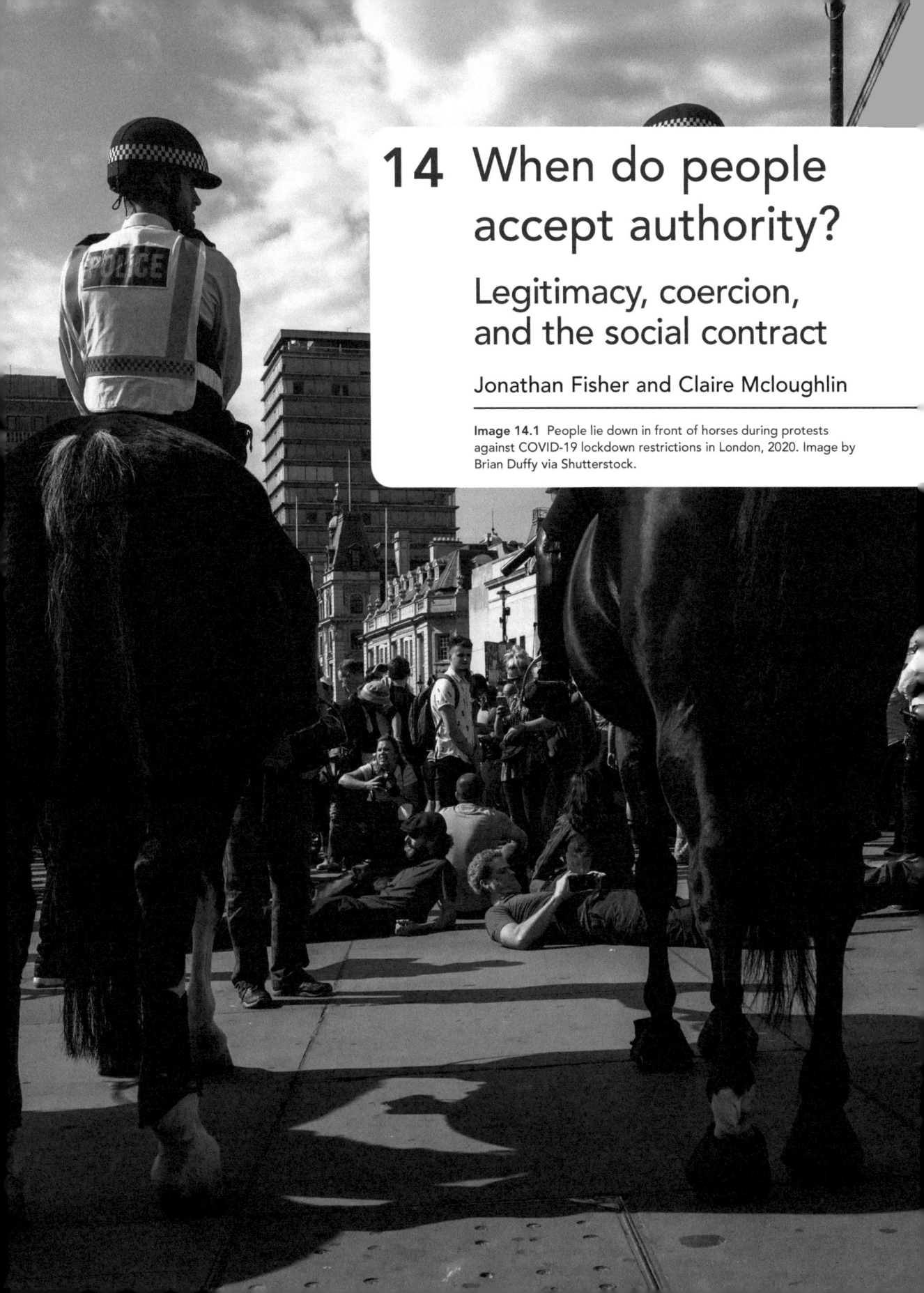

14 When do people accept authority?

Legitimacy, coercion, and the social contract

Jonathan Fisher and Claire Mcloughlin

Image 14.1 People lie down in front of horses during protests against COVID-19 lockdown restrictions in London, 2020. Image by Brian Duffy via Shutterstock.

> ## Learning outcomes
>
> - Define authority and explain why compliance with authority matters for development.
> - Analyse how interests, institutions, and ideas affect whether people accept authority, or not.
> - Critically evaluate what drives contestation over authority beyond the state.

Contesting authority

Whether in our private homes or our public lives, each of us conforms to or exercises some form of authority. Authority – the power to make and enforce rules – matters because without it, neither individuals, nor families, nor societies can generate stability, or make decisions that benefit the greater good. Self-evidently, though, authority cannot be made to order. Even in stable institutional environments, people rarely accept the ability of powerful decision makers to dictate their lives without question. In the real world, this power is more often resisted, sometimes violently, in divided societies or unstable political regimes. The paradox, then, is that authority is decisive for achieving desired futures, but is often actively contested.

This paradox was starkly revealed at the height of the COVID-19 global pandemic, when states were compelled to take citizens on an uncomfortable but essential journey: restricting individual freedoms in the interests of protecting lives and safeguarding the collective good. Citizens' responses to inconvenient rules, from mask wearing, to lockdowns, social distancing, and vaccination programmes, ranged from passive acquiescence to active resistance. While the majority of New Zealanders complied with public health guidelines, protests erupted in Johannesburg's Alexandra township, where the police used rubber bullets and stun grenades to disperse the crowds, leading to several injuries and arrests.

What explains why some people follow the rules, while others resist them? In the case of the pandemic, some complied out of a sense of duty, or obligation. Others assumed that authorities knew best, because, after all, they had access to crucial information. Some conformed more passively because, well, everyone else was. Fear was also central for many: fear of catching the virus or passing it to a loved one or vulnerable person, or fear of being punished, like the protestors in the South African townships, for disobeying the rules. Particularly in contexts where states failed to help people whose livelihoods were threatened by lockdowns, many feared that *obeying* the rules would have devastating consequences for themselves and their families.

In parts of the world where the state is distant, predatory, or neglectful, a long history of mistrust in government led some to ignore or resist the rules. 'There is nothing like government in Nigeria', water vendor Dan Sadi told journalist Idris Mohammed in May 2020, 'I can only hear from them [Nigerian political leaders] when they need our vote so why will I even waste my time on the issue of corona[virus]?' (Mohammed, 2020). In other contexts, like parts of the United States, mistrust of the idea of 'big state' government provoked resistance – among conservative Republicans in particular – while elsewhere, people followed the rules because they trusted that their leaders had their best interests at heart.

These diverse responses tell us that there are no universal criteria for predicting when people will accept or resist authority. But, at the same time, social science can provide clues – from the power of interests and incentives, to the role of ideas, to the trade-offs we make in our minds about the costs and rewards. This chapter investigates these themes, to reveal the inner workings of authority. It asks whether authority is good for us, before dissecting the key explanations for when people obey or resist it. Finally, it explores what this means for the dynamics of contestation between the state and actors 'beyond the state'.

Is authority good for us?

Any power-seeking entity – whether a political leader, community elder, ambassador or rebel group – benefits from authority. The right to claim or exercise authority is itself an *outcome* of contesting alternative desired futures. In turn, it can be decisive in deciding whose version of who gets what, when and how, wins. Authority can reproduce the kinds of unjust hierarchies and exclusions we have already explored in this book. After all, it is primed to reproduce itself in its own image. As we saw in Chapter 4, political elites have vested interests in preserving existing structures of domination. Incumbency – already being in a position of authority – gives them a tangible head-start in doing so: governments may have greater influence over the media agenda, legislators may amend laws that determine who can vote, or how constituencies are formed, men may exclude women from gaining access to traditional decision-making forums that they already dominate.

If authority is capable of (re-)producing harms, such as inequality, exclusion, or patriarchy, this begs the question, do we need it?

Some say no. Radical libertarians, writing in the philosophical tradition of John Locke, Immanuel Kant and others, fundamentally rejected any form of authority that encroaches on individual freedoms. In the contemporary era, prominent anarchists Noam Chomsky and Edward Herman (1988) continue to draw on Gramsci's ideas of 'manufactured consent' (see Chapter 5) to reject the power vested in capitalist domination and state-controlled mass media. This may seem radical to some, but intrinsically, all forms of authority, everywhere, do limit freedoms to some degree. When people accept a particular way of organising power, they relinquish certain powers and freedoms of their own. For example, when they consent, tacitly or implicitly, to majoritarian rule, they may forego their own preferences for which policies are pursued, and how far they serve their own interests.

When is authority good for us, then? Conventionally, political theory draws a line between legitimate authority and that which is coercive, predatory, collusive or corrupt (see Box 14.1). Legitimate authority is morally justified, based on popular consent and voluntary compliance (Beetham, 1991). It implies that people accept the state's rules of the game as morally appropriate, true and right (Migdal, 2001). By contrast, coercion involves either the application of physical force or the use of threats, whether explicit or implied. It can have no substantive justification, since it only endures via them. This binary distinction

> ## Box 14.1   What is legitimate authority?
>
> Legitimacy scholars seek to understand the grounds on which people accept the author-
> ity or 'right to rule' of a government or ruling entity. The legitimacy of a political system is
> essential for its stability, as it determines whether citizens comply with its decisions and laws.
>
> Early theories of political legitimacy can be traced back to the ancient Greek philoso-
> pher Plato. In his work *The Republic*, he argues that the legitimacy of a government stems
> from its commitment to promoting the common good and acting in the best interest of
> the people. In *Politics as a Vocation*, published in 1919, Max Weber famously later defined
> legitimacy as the belief or perception that a government, ruler, or institution has the right
> to exercise power and make decisions.
>
> More recently, political scientists have emphasised the dynamic nature of legitimacy. In
> his State in Society approach, Joel S. Migdal underlines that legitimacy is rooted in diverse
> perspectives and interests within a society. Margaret Levi's work highlights that legitimacy
> is not a fixed attribute but subject to contestation, over time. To appreciate this dynamic,
> we must study the process of legitimation. This is because, as David Beetham argues in
> his book, *The Legitimation of Power*, authority does not become legitimate by chance;
> instead, legitimacy is continually engineered by powerful elites who seek to justify their
> dominance.

echoes Western regime classifications that classify democracy as legitimate and 'good', and
autocracy as coercive and 'bad' (see Table 14.1). Western donors, in particular, tend to argue
that legitimate states are more sustainable, more effective and, ultimately, more capable of
bringing peace and stability, whereas illegitimate or authoritarian regimes are drivers of so-
called 'state fragility', posing a threat to security everywhere (OECD, 2010; International
Growth Centre, 2018).

Table 14.1   Legitimacy versus coercion: good versus bad?

	Legitimate 'good' authority	Coercive 'bad' authority
Basis:	• Moral justifiability, rightfulness.	• Power imbalance between coercer and coerced.
Goal:	• Gain popular consent.	• Manipulate or control the choices and actions of individuals or groups.
Sustained via:	• Voluntary compliance.	• Use or threat of force.

Is there such a clear distinction between good and bad authority, though? Empirically,
the boundaries between authority that is violently imposed versus legitimately won are
sometimes blurry. In her ethnographic inquiries in India, for example, Khanikar (2018)
explored how legitimacy and democracy can coexist alongside periodic state offensives
against ethnic groups, and routine, everyday violence against slumdwellers. The Indian

state seeks to resolve these apparent contradictions by justifying violence against 'outsiders' as a way of protecting the nation from further contestation. Stepping back from this example, the key point is that outside observers should not assume that authority is automatically considered illegitimate, or rejected, when it contravenes universal rights or, in this case, when it does harm to others. Paradoxically, even a legitimate, democratic state can (re-)produce violence and exclusion.

Reflective question

Is 'good' authority always 'legitimate', and is 'bad' authority always illegitimate?

The empirically blurry lines between good or bad authority challenge us to fundamentally question assumptions about the way that authority works, and whether people accept it, which we return to later. But first we must ask, why does compliance with authority matter for the pursuit of alternative desired futures?

Why compliance with authority matters for development

No institution can tackle urgent development challenges such as public health epidemics or the climate crisis without the authority to ask – and expect – people to comply with its rules. Compliance with authority is particularly vital to the functioning of the state: a complex system of institutions that seeks territorial control and centralised decision-making. Whether it's abiding by laws and regulations, or paying taxes, the state needs people to willingly follow its directives, ideally without having to resort to the threat or use of force (Tsai, 2015).

At the street level, for example, the police need voluntary compliance, and ideally the *active* co-operation of communities, in order to provide security and control crime. Very practically, they need citizens to be willing to report crimes, provide the location of criminals, and help identify causes of insecurity (Tyler, 2011). As Jackson et al. (2022) show in neighbourhoods in São Paulo, Brazil, otherwise police–citizens relations can become locked into a vicious circle of violence and non-compliance; the police use force even in mundane interactions, voluntary compliance is withdrawn, police resort to more extreme forms of control that, in turn, exacerbate high levels of fear and violence among certain groups.

This pivotal nexus between compliance, order and effectiveness can also be seen if we zoom out from the local to the macro-level challenges of governing. To fund vital public services such as the police, many states rely on domestic resource mobilisation in the form of taxation. But in order to tax citizens, bureaucracies need to encourage as much *voluntary* compliance with the rules as possible (meaning without the need for direct enforcement or coercion). Imagine the alternative: the sheer scale and costs of training and paying tax officers to travel door to door, or business to business, to collect returns. In most countries, even high-income ones, it simply would not be feasible or affordable to orchestrate such an elaborate enforcement operation. As we saw in Chapter 12, too, there would inevitably be a gap between the intention of the rules, and how they are implemented in practice, by street-level bureaucrats. The problem, as Joel Migdal (2013) put it, is that 'any authority wannabees, from a parent to a boss to a state, cannot constantly monitor those whom it wants to obey the rules. In the end, they depend on the acceptance of the rules – and the spirit of the rules . . . '.

As in this taxation example, voluntary compliance matters because it makes governing more efficient by reducing enforcement costs and avoiding bureaucratic discretion. Political scientists refer to this positive relationship between the laws, regulations, and rules set down by the state and more efficient governing as the 'virtuous circle' (Schmelzle and Stollenwerk, 2018). But how does the virtuous circle work? The theory goes that when individuals and businesses voluntarily comply with laws and regulations, this creates a predictable and stable environment. This predictability fosters stability and allows governments to plan and implement policies, such as taxation, more effectively. When compliance is high, governments can allocate fewer resources to costly enforcement mechanisms (think about the cost of militarising the police in São Paulo) and more to other critical areas such as public services, infrastructure, and welfare programmes. When people's everyday well-being subsequently improves, and when they perceive that the rules are fair, consistently applied, and transparent, they are more likely to trust the government and judge its decisions as legitimate. Enhanced legitimacy, in turn, means that people become generally more inclined to voluntarily comply with the rules laid down by the state, including paying more taxes. In this way, the virtuous circle continues (see Figure 14.1).

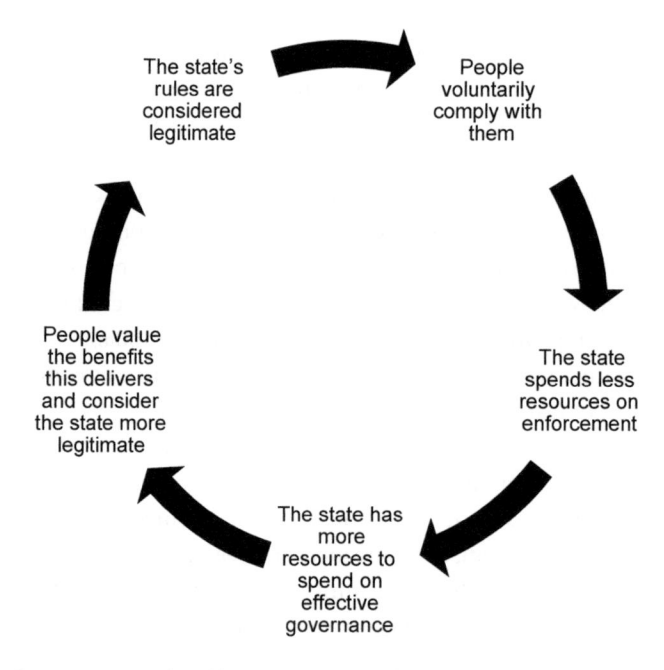

Figure 14.1 The virtuous circle of legitimacy and effectiveness

Sounds good, in theory. But is it really so straightforward to kick-start a virtuous circle of governance? Cross-national trends suggest that in practice, no. Intrinsic willingness to pay taxes, or 'tax morale', is actually in decline, globally (OECD, 2019). On the African continent, popular support for taxation has generally weakened over the last decade, alongside a growing public perception that other people are avoiding paying their taxes (Isbell, 2022; recall how, in Chapter 5, we discussed how perceptions of what other people think can shape how we think). Similar downward trends are observed in one of the key drivers of compliance – trust in government. In 2021, the OECD's inaugural *Trust Survey*, carried out in twenty-two countries, found that the proportion of people who said they trust their government varied from between 30 and 60 per cent, and just over one in four overall. Citizens raised serious concerns about government responsiveness, integrity, and access to equal opportunities. The virtuous circle has seemingly broken down, then, in many countries around the world. But why? What is going on here? How can we make sense of trends and variations in when people do, or do not, feel inclined to voluntarily comply with rules that, in theory at least, could benefit them?

When do people follow the rules?

The only way to make sense of compliance with authority is to study it in the context of people's own lived experience, political histories, ideologies, beliefs and world views. In other words, to examine what makes authority legitimate or objectionable, in situ, within its own system of meaning. To really get beneath the skin of authority, we must interrogate its justification – its substantive reason to be obeyed.

To think about this, imagine for a moment you're driving along a deserted road in the middle of the night. There is no one around. You've been working or studying late, and you're desperate to get home. The traffic light turns to red. No other cars are on the road and no pedestrians are in sight. Do you stop? And if so, why?

There are many reasons why people would follow the rules in this situation. Of course, it may be sheer habit to stop. But why are we socialised into those habits? And if we do consciously decide, what drives our decision making? Broadly, there are three reasons frequently advanced for why people would accept authority and stop:

1 *Coercion (or the threat of punishment)*. You might fear there will be consequences from disobeying the law, if you are caught violating it. Maybe there's a hidden camera, or perhaps a police car is waiting out of sight.
2 *Interests*. Stopping serves what people perceive to be in their interests – perhaps they don't want to risk an accident if someone's lurking in the dark, or a car suddenly came out of nowhere, so stopping is a way of ensuring their safety and that of others. This, too, is an interest-based, or instrumental, motive.
3 *Ideas*. People stop because they believe it's the right thing to do – in other words, they believe that the laws are fair; they support the collective good, and people *should* obey them, even if it is not in their immediate self-interest.

Of course, these are heuristics, and their meaning and significance must be understood in context. For example, in some unsafe cities, people might *avoid* stopping at traffic lights at night for fear of being robbed, car-jacked, or kidnapped. Nevertheless, these three themes help us to systematise the range of possible logics behind, and consequences of, rule-following (see Table 14.2). Below, we explore these in greater depth.

Table 14.2 Logics and consequences of rule following

	Coercion	Interests	Ideas
Logics	• Fear of punishment for non-compliance. • Fear of personal harm. • Lack of alternative/no choice.	• Valued, instrumental rewards. • Cost-benefit, rational calculation.	• Shared beliefs and norms. • It's the right thing to do.
Consequences	• Cannot produce voluntary compliance. • Expensive and unstable.	• Quasi-voluntary compliance. • At the heart of the 'virtuous circle' argument.	• Voluntary compliance. • The core basis of all legitimate authority.

Coercion

A common reason why people obey the rules, particularly in authoritarian settings, is fear of punishment – or, as it is often described – of the coercive power of the state. Indeed, some of the classical Western texts that analyse the emergence of state authority in Europe argue that the control and deployment of violence were actually central to state-building efforts across the continent (Tilly, 1993; Weber, [1919] 2015).

More recently, scholars have pointed to the durability and resilience of coercive governance institutions in some postcolonial states and societies. As we have explored throughout this book, European colonial administrations focused principally on establishing forms of rule which protected European interests and harshly punished those perceived to be challenging those interests. This embedding of violence and intimidation into core state institutions continues to cast a long shadow over policing and public order management in particular, from West Africa to South Asia (Tankebe, 2009; Jauregui, 2016; Aubyn, 2019).

Attempting to 'rule through fear' is, however, highly resource-intensive, and costly, both literally and metaphorically. Most states therefore use force selectively, albeit with different degrees of intensity, and do so for two main reasons. First, to target perceived transgressors, which, depending on the nature of the state, can range from murderers to protestors, and from fraudsters to opposition candidates. Second, and often more importantly, to deter others from following their example.

Consequently, even in authoritarian states, the coercive side of the state is experienced very unequally and can often depend on a person or community's wider relationship with state and society. Anthony Pereira (2015) notes, for example, that following the introduction of military rule in Brazil in the 1960s, 'if you weren't overtly political, your life might have gone on more or less as the same'. Marginalised communities and those living in poverty also tend to experience the state as a more violent and abusive actor than those who are in the majority and/or economically prosperous, including in Western democracies like the US and UK (Soss and Weaver, 2017; Koch, 2019). Indeed, it is striking how some citizens' association of state authority with 'punishment' can be found in recent work on both teachers in Eritrea – one of the world's most authoritarian states – and residents in local authority housing in the UK (Riggan, 2016; Koch, 2019).

Reflective question

Why is coercive authority experienced unevenly *within* countries?

It is difficult to argue that continued exposure to coercion – directly or indirectly – leads to voluntary 'acceptance' of authority. It can in many circumstances, though, make people feel powerless and ultimately submit to the state's authority, albeit usually in the shallow, resigned manner which Justice Tankebe (2009) has characterised as 'dull compulsion'. Equally, states that rely too heavily on coercion – or that blatantly tolerate the violent, everyday abuses of their police and other officials – can ultimately find their rule challenged, sometimes violently, by a range of actors, from protestors and social movements to rebel groups (Fisher, 2020). In other words, coercion is very rarely sufficient as a 'legitimation strategy' – a way to persuade citizens of a state's right to rule (Dukalskis and Patane, 2019).

This is particularly so in the era of the Internet and social media. Very few states today are in a position to insulate their populations from the views of one another and of wider global society for more than a brief period, with the partial exception of North Korea (Lee, 2015). Any and all forms of state coercion cannot only be documented, but also spread across the country and the world almost instantly, mobilising and connecting peoples, organisations, and movements which may previously have been entirely independent of one another. The 'Arab Spring'

Image 14.2 Anti-government protests take place in downtown Beirut during the so-called '17 October revolution', 2019. Image by Ali Chehade via Shutterstock

– a series of protests, insurgencies and revolutions that took place across the Middle East and North Africa during the 2010s – is perhaps the most recent powerful example of this in the digital era. Another are the 2022 protests in China against draconian Covid-19 lockdown regulations (Perrigo, 2022). This 'A4 Revolution' in reference to the blank sheets of paper protestors held up to taunt the police, led to a swift reversal of policy by the Chinese government, underlining how fragile legitimation strategies built on coercion can be.

Indeed, as Cherian George (2007) notes, a state that relies on coercion to rule is ultimately weak and vulnerable. Using the case of Singapore under the People's Action Party (PAP), George explains how the PAP – in power since Singapore's independence in the 1960s – has governed through a form of 'calibrated coercion'. This strategy entailed more subtle, less visible measures to gain control of – in this case – the press than the outright violence sometimes seen in other (semi-) authoritarian states. He contrasts Singapore's use of oppressive legislation and regulations with more flagrant displays of coercion such as the arbitrary arrests of journalists or the raiding and closure of media houses. 'Calibrated coercion', he writes, 'is recognized by [some] authoritarian rulers as a governance skill required for the consolidation of their power'.

Interests

Singapore is, nonetheless, perhaps best well-known internationally for the high quality of life experienced by its citizens. Number 12 in the Human Development Index, its health, education, and other development indicators are assessed by UNDP – at the time of writing – to be superior to those of New Zealand, Canada, Luxembourg, and the United Kingdom. This is a consequence of Singapore's longstanding and extensive investment in public service delivery, identified by a range of scholars as an important source of its government's domestic legitimacy (Chang et al., 2013). This is the second way in which scholars often explain why people follow the rules – because they feel that it is in their interests to do so. In this scenario, people stop at traffic lights because they are rewarded with something they value – social order, justice, or protection of their own safety.

The provision of quality services – including healthcare, education, justice, and security – is a frequently-advanced reason for compliance in a range of states, including (semi-)authoritarian states where elections play little role in determining who is in power. Indeed, as we covered in Chapter 6 there is an extensive literature that charts the course of the so-called 'developmental state', whereby authoritarian states from Rwanda to Cuba deploy economic and social development gains to induce support from their populations ('output legitimacy'), at the expense of allowing democratic participation ('input legitimacy') (Booth and Golooba-Mutebi, 2012; Routley, 2014; Brown and Fisher, 2020).

Indeed, the idea of 'trading democracy for governance', in the words of Lu and Chu (2021), has been a legitimation strategy used by many authoritarian states across the world, including that of China. The promise of 'development' or economic growth also continues to be a powerful rallying cry in election campaigns across the world, including even by parties and politicians whose time in power has manifestly underdelivered.

Interest-based reasons for following the rules may not, of course, necessarily be based on the provision of benefits across a territory or society. It is much more commonplace for governments to selectively distribute resources to particular regions, communities, or economic/political elites whose support they rely on to maintain power. Scholarship on political 'clientelism' and 'patronage' has argued that African states especially have historically been structured around the corrupt allocation of state resources (from scholarships to jobs to government contracts) to (principally ethnic) allies and groups who, consequently, can be counted on to support the government in a range of political settings, although this literature has increasingly been challenged as simplistic or essentialising (Mkandawire, 2015).

But do people really evaluate authority based simply on the output it delivers? Over the past decade, a key focal point of this debate has been the thorny question of whether the provision of vital goods and services, such as health, water and education, is key to unlocking insecurity and building legitimate states. Contrary to the original received wisdom that it should, the evidence is much more mixed. While some studies find robust correlations between public goods performance and legitimacy perceptions at particular junctures – for example, during the Ebola outbreak in West Africa (Flückiger et al., 2019), more generally, there is no linear relationship between the two. Whether institutions produce outcomes that go in our favour (outcome favourability) does not necessarily determine our choice to support them or not. For example, a cross-country study in sub-Saharan Africa found that negative individual experiences with police and courts do not tend to change citizens' perceptions of the rightful authority of rule-of-law institutions (Dreier and Lake, 2019). So what is going on here?

Reflective question

Do the services on your doorstep influence whether you think the state is legitimate or not?

The explanation for these divergent findings lies in the texture of state–society relations. Material rewards are always evaluated in wider political context, expectations and perceived intentions. For example, foreign aid may or may not influence state legitimacy, depending on the degree to which people expect their government to deliver certain goods and rewards itself (Blair and Winters, 2020). Material rewards alone cannot mend broken trust, either. In post-war Nepal, bringing improvements to electricity to rural communities marginalised by the state failed to erase the past (Krampe, 2016). This tapestry of findings underpins the need to look beyond a purely instrumental account of the services–legitimacy relationship, and engage with the normative criteria by which citizens judge them, such as fairness, justice, and deservingness (Mcloughlin, 2015).

Ultimately, when people comply due to fear or material rewards, these are instrumental reasons for compliance that logically follow an interest-based calculation. As we have argued extensively throughout this book, though, people are not purely rational. Social motivations also drive our choices and how we exercise agency (Tyler, 2011). For instance, people may evaluate outcomes not only in terms of whether they are favourable to them, but the process via which they were arrived at – what is known as 'procedural justice' (see Box 14.2). In theory at least, procedural justice is a foundational premise of liberal democracy. What stabilises it as an institutional arrangement, is that citizens trade their individual preferences to majority rule – they will accept election results even if their preferred candidate does not win – because at least in principle, the rules around candidate nomination, voting and political appointment are accepted as predictable and fair.

Box 14.2   What is procedural justice?

Procedural justice refers to the perceived fairness and transparency of the decision-making processes and rules used by authorities. A key insight from this theory is that the processes via which decisions are made are as important as the actual decisions for determining whether people will accept them or not. In effect, the most important social determinant of acceptance of decision-making power is the 'how' in who gets what, when and how.

We can see the importance of procedural justice from the ground up if we return to the challenge of community compliance with the police. Studies of everyday encounters with police officers show that people are more willing to accept decisions when they consider the police to be acting fairly. Research by Tom Tyler and Yuen Huo (2002) in the US context was particularly important in revealing that judgements of procedural fairness are distinct from, but may be equally as important as, perceptions of the *effectiveness* of police in discharging their duties, or the favourability of outcomes. In other words, people evaluate whether the police are entitled to be obeyed against certain normative criteria. These criteria may include impartial and objective rules for decision-making, the perceived motives of authorities, or being treated with dignity and respect (Tyler, 2011).

But does the theory of procedural justice, which originated in the West, travel across contexts where authority is contested? Some studies of people's willingness to obey the police in postcolonial Africa have concluded not. In Ghana, Justice Tankebe (2009) found that public co-operation with the police was based solely on utilitarian assessments of effectiveness – i.e., whether the police could guarantee safety and protect property. Ordinary people felt powerless in the face of police reprisals, producing the sense of 'dull compulsion' to comply noted earlier. A later study in Nigeria similarly found that people were more likely to comply with laws when they had personally experienced police abuse (Akinlabi and Murphy, 2018). These divergent findings caution us to think about individual and collective decision making in situ, and a crucial aspect of this is understanding the ideas that people have about how authority *should* be exercised.

Ideas

Even when we consider interest-based explanations for compliance, such as material goods and services, the influence of these things tends to boil down to how far they align with prevailing *ideas* about what is fair and right for society (Mcloughlin, 2015; 2024). In other words, it is not just that material goods serve interests, but that they reflect and (re)produce a wider social good, such as order, justice or fairness. To return to our traffic lights example above, the idea is that people stop because they consider it the right thing to do. David Beetham's book *The Legitimation of Power* (1991) made an important contribution to breaking down how legitimacy influences our decision making, in practice. He identified how legitimacy works based on rules, justifiability and consent (see Box 14.3). Applied to the traffic lights example, people stop because there is a *set of rules* that they believe are *justifiable*. And when they actually *do* stop at traffic lights, they are reinforcing and reproducing their *consent* to that rule.

> ### Box 14.3 Criteria of legitimate authority
>
> David Beetham (1991) argued that power can be considered legitimate to the extent that it fulfils three criteria:
>
> 1 *Rules*. It conforms to established rules (written or unwritten) governing the acquisition and exercise of power.
> 2 *Justifiability*. Legal validity is insufficient, and the rules must be justified by reference to shared ideas and beliefs.
> 3 *Evidence of consent*. What counts as consent is culturally specific, but may include public acts such as voting, taking part in traditional ceremonies, or attending weddings.

Beetham's work was significant in showing that with legitimacy comes shared beliefs, either about the qualities of the power holder, or the degree to which the power arrangement serves a recognisable common interest (Beetham, 1991). But what kinds of shared beliefs justify the exercise of power, in practice? In an influential classification, Max Weber ([1919] 2015) distinguished three sources of legitimate power: legal–rational, traditional, and charismatic. Each of these is justified by recourse to different ideas (see Table 14.3). Legal–rational legitimacy denotes a system of rules that are applied judicially in accordance with agreed principles and procedures. For example, when elections are run according to the law, or public officials are subjected to rules that separate their private lives from official duties. This system of power is

Table 14.3 Legitimising ideas?

Legal–rational authority	Traditional authority	Charismatic authority
• Principles and procedures should be agreed. • Private and public lives should be separate. • Decisions are faithfully executed under law.	• History is worth protecting. • History is vested in people who inherit certain roles.	• People are carriers of ideas. • Authority can be earned via personal qualities.

legitimised by the predictability of decision making, and the assumption that decisions are reliably fair because they are faithfully executed according to laws and regulations.

Traditional authority is more often underpinned by cultural and inherited ideas – systems of rule-making that are legitimate because they are long-standing, historically rooted, and a continual feature of social organisation. This includes customary institutions, tribal structures, and patriarchal or monarchical systems of government. Under such systems, the right to rule is often vested in individuals who inherit certain roles. We can see this, for example, in the succession of leaders with family ties that have ruled dynastic dictatorships such as North Korea. In many postcolonial societies, traditional leaders have often retained their local legitimacy because they represent the values and ideas passed down from generation to generation.

Legal–rational and traditional authority are institutions, in the sense they are anchored in established norms and rules. *Charismatic legitimacy* is, by contrast, vested in individuals. Here we can think of the ways in which leaders make appeals for support based on their personal qualities, cultivating cults of personality by promoting an exaggerated or idealised version of their unique claim to authority – in effect, mythologising themselves. In the extreme, we see this in the claims of leaders to superhuman or mystical qualities. Joseph Kony, the notorious warlord who founded the Lord's Resistance Army in Uganda, cultivated his following by proclaiming himself the spokesperson of God and a spirit medium. More routinely, charismatic legitimation is increasingly seen in the personalisation of politics and the rise of populist leaders, such as former US President Donald Trump, who present macho images of themselves as heroes or saviours. Because it is vested in an individual rather than an institution, this form of authority is brittle, though. It does not lend itself to succession in the way that, for example, traditions do. Moreover, shifts towards personalist legitimacy claims may be a warning sign of a deterioration of democratic quality – or 'democratic backsliding' – manifested in the expansion of executive power (Brunkert and von Soest, 2022).

Weber's threefold classification has been an important point of departure for most contemporary analyses of authority and legitimacy. It is important to remember, though, that Weber was writing more than a century ago, during a period when much of the Global South was under European colonial rule and when most European states were monarchies rather than republics. Although Weber's work remains useful for thinking about the role of ideas in upholding political authority, it is therefore also important to reflect on some of its limitations. For example, it is valid to 'match' different states, governments, and leaders to one of Weber's three forms of authority, when in reality, most contemporary regimes exist at the intersection of two, or all three?

At the same time, diifferent forms of authority rarely exist independently of, or in opposition to, the rational–legal authority of the modern state. In a range of contexts, including in parts of West Africa, some contemporary traditional rulers owe their titles to decisions taken by colonial powers around which the candidate of a ruling house was likely to be the most cooperative 'local' collaborator and, therefore, which should be recognised – and supported – as emir or sultan (Yakubu, 1993). Traditional rulers also enjoy particular constitutional status in a range of polities, such as South Africa, and in cases like Uganda, lines of traditional monarchs have 'returned', re-emerged or (re)gained significance because of legal decisions made by the – republican – state (Mamdani, 1996; Tangri and Mwenda, 2010). In other words, the authority of elders, in this context, is understood to derive from their holding of *both* traditional and rational–legal legitimacy.

Another example is the authority of traditional 'elders' in north-west Uganda – men (usually) who enjoy significant influence over the management of a range of disputes and other aspects of community life. During research on experiences of (in)security in this region, where elders play a major governance role, we discussed (with elders and others) what determines the authority of an elder. Seniority, descent, and knowledge of the community's history and traditions was an integral part of many answers. In addition, though, many emphasised how most elders had at some point held a government role, as a councillor, civil servant, tax collector, or other kind of official, and that this too undergirded their legitimacy (Storer et al., 2021).

This points to the key contemporary puzzle, which is *how* social scientists can determine whether a political system is legitimate. Is it sufficient for the people to believe an authority is legitimate, as per Weber, or should there be an objective set of criteria against which all authority is evaluated as legitimate or not? In other words, should legitimacy be studied as an *empirical* phenomenon, based on what people believe or how they act, or *normatively* as against universal standards, such as human rights? Many argue for the empirical approach, because even regimes that appear overtly repressive or inimical to democratic governance may nevertheless enjoy a high degree of legitimacy and resilience in practice.

Understandings, experiences, and perceptions of the state and its authority vary enormously across the world – and, indeed, *within* societies themselves. Even in the same city, marginalised communities may experience a much more coercive and fearsome state than those from the majority ethnic or political grouping – as research on policing in the United States underlines (Soss and Weaver, 2017). A critical way of interpreting this disaggregation is via a 'social contract' lens.

Contesting the social contract

(Mis)trust and (il)legitimacy may rest on a much more longstanding and enduring set of relationships and histories linking those seeking to rule with those whose obedience they seek – in other words, the social contract. Markus Loewe and colleagues (2021) define the social contract as 'the entirety of explicit or implicit agreements between all relevant societal groups and the sovereign (i.e., the government or any other actor in power) defining their rights and obligations towards each other'.

A social contract lens (see Box 14.4) encourages us to interpret contemporary state–society bargaining and contestations in historical perspective. In some cases, the fact that a particular form of authority has an established record of *delivering* prosperity and development may be a key plank of the state's contemporary legitimacy, and may help preserve continued trust in it when shifting circumstances mean that it underperforms. In many cases, the fundamental evaluative criteria for state legitimacy was embedded during critical junctures of state formation, most notably anti-colonial struggle (Mcloughlin, 2024). In an influential account, Alex de Waal (1996) argued that because the postcolonial Indian nationalist movement used famine to discredit the colonial government, famine prevention thereafter became a key pillar of its legitimacy.

Box 14.4 Social contract theory

Social contract theory is a political philosophy that seeks to explain the mutually agreed roles and responsibilities of states and societies. According to this theory, people voluntarily enter into a tacit agreement with the state, surrendering certain freedoms and rights in exchange for their protection, security, and the promotion of their collective interests. In this way, the social contract creates a moral obligation for the people to consent to state authority, and in turn, expectations that the state should enhance their well-being.

Social contract theory originated from the thinking of several influential philosophers of the seventeenth and eighteenth centuries, including Thomas Hobbes, John Locke, and Jean-Jacques Rousseau. Although the theory continues to resonate in contemporary debates, many have critiqued its normative foundation and its application to modern societies. Scholars such as Achille Mbembe (2001) argue that the theory ignores the complex cultural and social dynamics of non-Western countries.

While the social contract is often seen to promote stability and cooperation, it can also potentially hinder development where certain elites or powerful groups secure special privileges at the expense of the marginalised, including women and girls. Carole Pateman's *The Sexual Contract*, published in 1988, offered a feminist critique of the social contract as a foundation of patriarchy that institutionalises male power and subordinates women.

In other cases, legacies of abusive and extractive rule may mean that mistrusting the state and its institutions is natural, even rational, for many citizens, even when that state appears to be governing well. This is a particular challenge in postcolonial societies where the damaging and traumatic period of European colonialism continues to exact a major toll. Colonial legacies had a dramatic effect on relationships between police and citizens in the cases of Nigeria and Ghana, mentioned above. During the colonial period, the police used fear, intimidation, and force to seek compliance, with the effect that into the contemporary period, police abuse is considered an inevitable fact of life. Police in both countries suffer an acute legitimacy deficit as a result.

While the concept of the social contract provides a powerful and persuasive framework through which to understand authority and legitimacy, it should not be applied uncritically, or universally. Contractarian thought emerged out of philosophical debates in Europe in the seventeenth and eighteenth centuries, and its assumptions and frames of reference were founded in Western experience. In his book *On the Postcolony* (2001), Achille Mbembe argued that the theory does not apply on the African continent, because the idea of consensual social contract is often undermined by historical legacies of colonialism, ongoing struggles for power, and complex sociopolitical dynamics. This reflects a wider critique, made by anthropologists Burnyeat and Johansson (2022) among others, that the social contract begins with a set of flawed assumptions about the nature of state–society relations in other countries that flattens lived realities and denies the messy realities of power (see Table 14.4).

Table 14.4 Flawed assumptions of social contract theory?

Social contract assumption	Alternative lived reality
• Individuals are autonomous agents, free to make such agreements.	• Citizens are not equal or free, women in particular.
• Consent is voluntary.	• Consent is coercively enforced.
• Power is ultimately devolved to the people.	• Power is concentrated in the hands of the elite.
• Governing is a mechanism of representation and protection of citizens' interests.	• Governing is an instrument of control.
• There is a clear separation between state and society.	• The state is indistinguishable from the ruling elite.

In some cultures, the idea of the individual, the central unit of social contract theory, resonates much less than that of the community. Across South Asia, for example, the concept of kinship/biraderi is the central organising principle in politics, above and beyond the state. Moreover, particularly for those living in places with a long history of authoritarian and/or colonial rule, little consideration may be given to the legitimacy of the governing authority, at least in these terms. In some communities, there is a single word which in English could be translated as 'government', 'state', 'power', or 'authority'; those in authority are simply 'there', whatever form they take.

Reflective question

Does the idea of the social contract apply beyond the Western context?

These problematic universalising tendencies are also evident in the way that contractarian thinking has travelled from the academic into the international development policy world. In the aftermath of the global financial crisis of 2008 and the Arab Spring of 2011, for example, the World Bank began to apply a social contract framing to its country diagnostics, ostensibly to identify how seemingly 'broken' contracts could be renewed. It modelled the social contract as a process of citizen–state bargaining, developing indicators to measure it, including state and civic capacity, inclusion and openness (Cloutier et al, 2021). Alhough this framework suggests a willingness to take social contracts seriously, it simultaneously instrumentalises them, reducing a relational process to a policy tool aimed at diagnosing blockages to development and explaining outbreaks of unrest.

Authority beyond the state

Legitimacy is not a static property of institutions. Rather, it is 'constantly being negotiated and questioned by those whose obedience and support is demanded' (Levi, 2018: 603). This is why the legitimation process – the process via which any actor or institution convinces an audience of their justifiability (Beetham, 1991) – is a key arena of contestation in the politics of development. All actors seeking popular support need to cultivate their legitimacy. But authority is rarely absolute or uncontested in any setting. A misplaced concreteness about the state system can deny the reality of multiple competing organisations: there is never one source of authority, but many.

The authority – even presence – of the state itself, for example, cannot be taken for granted. Legacies of colonialism and postcolonial authoritarianism and misrule have led to the 'formal' state being largely non-existent in some regions, meaning that governance (including the provision of security and other public services) is undertaken by non-state actors ranging from traditional authorities and elders to NGOs and UN agencies. Indeed, so absent was the formal state in Southern Sudan during the 1983–2005 civil war, and so significant was the role of international NGOs in providing services and other forms of support that analysts like Volker Riehl came to muse whether the region – at the time, the southern part of the Republic of Sudan – was 'the first NGO-istan (Riehl, 2001).

Civil wars, by definition, often focus on a fundamental – and violent – contestation of state authority; rebel movements frequently seek not only to remove the current government but to *replace* it. In many cases, then, insurgencies – at least, once they come to hold territory – set themselves up as alternative governments, even adopting flags and minting currency, as a symbolic and aspirational 'performance' of state authority (Mampilly, 2015). This can also involve, in some cases, implementing some of the governance practices the rebel movements has pledged to introduce when it takes power. During the 1981–6 Ugandan civil war, for example, the National Resistance Army (NRA) introduced 'Resistance Councils' in the region north of the capital, Kampala, where it held territory. These councils, a form of local democracy that contrasted with the authoritarian model of the ruling Milton Obote regime, were later introduced across Uganda – eventually renamed as 'Local Councils' – when the NRA took power (Kasfir, 2005).

Analysing the success of some rebel movements can often help us to understand how populations judge, or judged, the legitimacy and performance of the existing, or previous, polity. The Taliban in Afghanistan, for example, are often characterised internationally as violent, oppressive, misogynist extremists who took Kabul in 1996 and, again, in 2021 through force of arms and a ruthless pursuit of power at any cost. We do not contest these representations of the Taliban as vicious, uncompromising, brutal, and reactionary. Their capture of power twice within two decades, the second time in opposition to a US-led counter-insurgency campaign, nonetheless requires us to reflect on whether their success can be explained by factors beyond coercion.

Research examining the group's gradual recapturing of territory during the 2010s underscores how important the provision of services became in the areas that the Taliban came to control. Described by Niels Terpstra as 'pragmatic legitimacy', the Taliban's delivery of public services – in particular security and justice – not only brought it popularity with some of those it now governed, but also contrasted with the record of the Afghan state itself, widely viewed as corrupt and ineffective (Terpstra, 2020). The Taliban could also, of course, marshal support through positioning itself as a nationalist group in opposition to a foreign-backed 'proxy' government, a legitimation strategy also employed by the Islamist militant group Al-Shabaab in Somalia (Solomon, 2014).

Summary and conclusion

Authority – the power to make and enforce rules – is decisive for development because it generates compliance with laws, rules and tax regimes that are, in turn, crucial for effective governance, stability and prosperity. This 'virtuous circle' of authority and effectiveness, in this way, is an enabler of desired progress. But authority must be earned through an implicit bargain between those who seek and confer it. This chapter has shown that people may choose to obey the rules for a variety of reasons – ranging from individual, to social, and psychological factors, but there are three overall categories of explanation – coercion, material rewards, and ideas.

People accept state authority voluntarily, without coercive enforcement, when they view it as legitimate, or rightful. Trust is a critical element of establishing, and sustaining, legitimacy. Neither are gained or lost through the actions of a single politician or the implementation of a policy, though. There is a difference between not trusting a president and campaigning for their removal in an election on one hand, and leading an insurgency to overthrow the entire system on the other.

Citizens accept or reject state authority because of the nature of the 'social contract', and the history of state–society contestation over rights and power that it embedded. Contestations between would-be authorities must be read in this historical context. Wherever state or non-state actors compete for authority, there will be attempts to persuade and legitimate, coerce, or distribute goods and favours. In this way, who gets what and when, fundamentally reflects who wins the continual contest for authority.

Discussion questions

- Why does authority matter for development prospects?
- What prevents the 'virtuous circle' of legitimacy–compliance–effectiveness from working in some contexts?
- Which of the three explanations for compliance – coercion, interests, ideas – do you find most compelling?
- Do you agree that the process (i.e. procedural justice) is as important as the outcome in determining whether people accept authority?

Suggested further reading

Cloutier, M. et al. (2021) 'Social contracts for development: bargaining, contention, and social inclusion in sub-Saharan Africa', AFD and World Bank.

Levi, M., Sacks, A. and Tyler, T. (2009) 'Conceptualizing legitimacy, measuring legitimating beliefs', *American Behavioral Scientist*, 53 (3): 354–75.

Mcloughlin, C. (2015) 'When does service delivery improve the legitimacy of a fragile or conflict-affected state?', *Governance*, 28 (3): 341–56.

15 When does contestation turn violent?

Conflict and peacebuilding

Jonathan Fisher and Paul Jackson

Image 15.1 A UN peacekeeper on patrol in Lebanon during the 2006 war. Image by Sadik Gulek via Shutterstock

> ## Learning outcomes
>
> - Critically evaluate the politics of defining and analysing conflict.
> - Understand major reasons why contestation turns violent, including the impact of ideas, institutions, and interests of domestic and international actors in shaping conflict dynamics.
> - Evaluate the roles that identity and inequalities play in sustaining conflict and undermining the chances of peace.
> - Assess the evolving politics of peacebuilding and evaluate how power and interests underlie prospects for resolving conflict and addressing its underlying causes.

From contestation to violence

This book has shown why contestation sits at the heart of the politics of development. In societies where institutions function and enjoy popular acceptance, contestation over the rules, resources, or even the power to shape and distribute them, is managed through formal and informal institutions that ultimately resolve the diversity of preferences inherent in all societies. These institutions may include, for example, democracy, customary governance, or traditional courts. But when such institutions are absent, powerless, or illegitimate, mechanisms for deliberation and disagreement can be abandoned in favour of violent conflict. Whether it be all-out interstate war or local armed disputes, conflict is an acute, ever-present global challenge. The World Bank estimates that by 2030, up to two-thirds of the world's extreme poor could live in conflict-affected settings. Conflicts also drive 80 per cent of all humanitarian needs globally, making conflict a key reason why people struggle to achieve desired futures (World Bank, 2022).

If conflict is so devastating and costly, why is it so endemic? Is it a failure of institutions, or the epitome of the selfish pursuit of interests? For many marginalised people around the world, conflict is the last resort: a means to redress structural inequality and grievance when all other options are exhausted. Particularly in more authoritarian, oppressive and deeply unequal polities, violent conflict – whether in the form of uprising, or revolution – may be viewed by some as the only way to meaningfully change a system stacked against them.

The 'Arab Spring' revolutions that swept North Africa and parts of the Middle East in the early 2010s, for example, began as protests against entrenched dictatorships that had been in power for many decades and were no longer operating – if they ever had – in the interests of the people. The spark for Tunisia's 2010 revolution – which catalysed protest across the region – came from a street vendor, Mohamed Bouazizi, who set himself on fire after local officials confiscated his vegetable cart, depriving him of his livelihood. This followed years of Bouazizi facing harassment and abuse from the Tunisian police, and public outrage at his treatment soon led to wider anger and protest against the autocratic and repressive Tunisian state (Ryan, 2011).

We might assume that violent conflict, such as that witnessed during the Arab Spring, undermines development, but it might also be argued that conflict can be productive where it can force a more just distribution of public goods and a more inclusive political system. All violent conflict, however, comes with a human cost – often severe, and invariably borne most heavily by the poor and the marginalised, particularly women. Conflict can also exacerbate existing societal tensions and generate new divisions and grievances which can prolong or intensify fighting. This reproductive capacity is why the highest risk factor for a country to experience civil war is a recent history of emerging out of one (Marks, 2016).

When does contestation turn violent, though? And how can we understand this, politically? In this chapter, we unpack the political drivers of violent conflict (hereafter 'conflict'), and consider how it is defined and understood, the reasons why it occurs, and how it can be addressed. We apply the political lens of the three 'I's – interests, institutions and ideas – to encourage critical reflection on who fights whom, how conflict is fought, who is affected, and why it breaks out. In doing so, we bring to bear key conceptual debates on the causes of conflict and why conflicts sometimes take very different forms.

The ultimate reason to understand the politics of conflict, though, is to understand how conflicts can be brought to an end, peacefully – a debate we also unpack in this chapter. 'Peacebuilding' has been the solution to conflict argued for by many scholars, policy-makers, and practitioners in recent decades. As we underline, however, lasting peace cannot be forged unless those seeking to build it take the politics of contestation, and what lead to conflict in the first place, seriously. As we explain, past generations of peacebuilding efforts – often championed by Western aid agencies and international organisations such as the UN – have been criticised for failing to consider the central role of ideas, interests (including those of international 'peacebuilders' themselves), power, and inequalities in sustaining conflict, or undermining peace. While peacebuilding approaches have evolved, and are increasingly more appreciative of the complex politics of contestation, there remains a long way to go to realise the ambitions of the peacebuilding enterprise.

The politics of conflict

Even the act of defining and analysing conflict is inherently political. The language and frameworks used can often underplay key dynamics or betray wider political or ideological biases, including deeply held ideas and worldviews. Governments of all stripes, for example, have often used the language of 'terrorism' to characterise movements or insurgencies that others may view as progressive revolutionaries. This was common practice by European colonial administrations with nationalist and independence movements, and has also been used frequently in the contemporary era by governments, and their allies, seeking to delegitimise their opponents. Governments in countries as diverse as Uganda, Nigeria and Colombia, for example, have all branded a wide variety of opposition movements as 'terrorists' (Fisher and Anderson, 2015). Of course, this also had the advantage of allying the government with the interests of Western powers. The Ugandan government, for example, generally referred to the Lord's Resistance Army (LRA), a brutal domestic rebel movement, as 'bandits' or 'ordinary lawbreakers' until the 9/11 Al Qaeda attacks on New York and Virginia. Subsequently, the LRA were increasingly characterised as 'terrorists' by Ugandan policy-makers, in part to tie the insurgency to the wider US-led 'Global War on Terror' (Fisher, 2013: 16–19).

Reflective question

What are the differences between a 'terrorist', a 'criminal', and a 'revolutionary'?

The terminology used around a particular conflict can imply a particular interpretation of its nature, cause, justification, or of who the main aggressor is; the UK government, for example, euphemistically referred to its 30-year counter-insurgency campaign in Northern Ireland between the 1960s and 1990s as 'The Troubles' (a term with a particular heritage in British and Irish history). Language used in relation to the Arab–Israeli conflict since 1948 is also particularly sensitive, to the extent that the International Press Institute has produced a 60-page 'vocabulary handbook' for journalists across the globe which highlights terms related to the conflict which 'may be regarded as loaded, biased . . . or misleading' and suggests 'reasonable alternatives . . . to serve as a tool for journalists trying to find their way in the typically complicated terminology of the conflict' (International Press Institute, 2021: 5). One example of this, they suggest, is the use of the words 'riots' and 'rioters', which they note is sometimes used as a 'blanket term to describe any protests or demonstrations by Palestinians against Israel . . . impl[ying] violence and disorder . . . even if the protestors are not violent'. The handbook suggests 'protests' and 'protestors' as a preferable alternative (International Press Institute, 2021: 46).

In international arenas, defining a conflict as 'internal' may tie the hands of institutions such as the UN or African Union, whose rules and bylaws often limit the ability of member states to intervene in the internal affairs of other member states. This is less the case for wars *between* states. More prosaically, the quantitative criteria scholars and researchers use to define and measure conflict – from duration and actors involved, to number of people killed – can sometimes mean that particular conflict situations do not even appear in major indices or databases, or, therefore, on the radar of policy-makers and activists. This is especially so with 'low-intensity' conflicts, where smaller numbers are killed annually (although across the lifetime of the conflict the total number may be high), or where sometimes widespread violence – for example, that associated with drug cartels in Mexico – is classified as 'criminal' activity, or is not easily attributed to specific actors (UCDP, 2022).

In the same way that defining conflict is a political process, all conflict is, in practice, political in nature. Even when it does not overtly seem the case, there are interests, institutions and ideas at play within the conflict dynamic – from who is fighting whom, how the conflict is being fought, who is affected, and the conflict's underlying causes. All four are necessary to understand in order to appreciate the politics of conflict.

Who is fighting whom?

Conflict is often analysed by focusing on the key actors directly involved, or the main 'belligerents'. Here, a distinction is typically drawn between conflicts fought *within* a country or territory – intrastate conflict or civil war – and conflicts fought *between* countries or territories, sometimes referred to as interstate war. Although interstate wars have historically been more devastating than civil wars in terms of numbers of lives lost, civil wars have been much more common since the end of the Second World War, and have, consequently, collectively accounted for a significantly higher number of deaths, as Figure 15.1 illustrates.

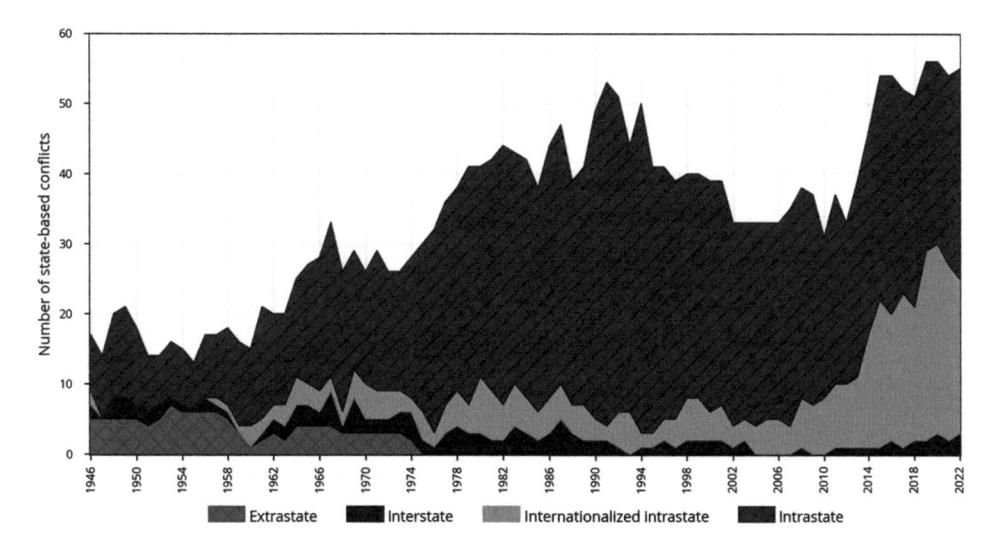

Figure 15.1 State-based armed conflicts by type of conflict (1946–2022)
Source: 'Armed conflicts by type of conflict' (Davies et al., 2023). This graph draws on data compiled by the Uppsala Conflict Data Program (UCDP). UCDP distinguishes between intrastate wars (civil wars), which include 'troop support from other governments' and those 'with no interference from other countries' – a distinction which, as we note below, is not always clear in practice.

There are a number of limitations to the interstate/intrastate analytical lens, though. First, few conflicts are wholly internal, or which are not impacted by wider global dynamics. International actors, including the US, UK, EU, Gulf states and a number of East African states, have, for example, played a major role in driving Somalia's long-running civil war since 1991 through arming, funding, or in other ways supporting some of the key belligerents (Williams, 2018). The governments of both Ukraine and, to a lesser extent, Russia have also relied on international allies to sustain their defence and offensive respectively since Russia's invasion of Ukraine in 2022 (House of Commons, 2023; Lvovskiy, 2023). In addition, the economic and political conditions which lead to internal conflict are often at the very least exacerbated by global forces, and the political interests of powerful states. These include, for example, the wider unequal access to resources across the globe discussed earlier in this book – in Chapters 2 and 11, for example.

Moreover, civil wars also take a number of distinctive forms, as Box 15.1 outlines.

> ## Box 15.1 Varieties of Civil War
>
> Most civil wars tend to take one of four different forms:
>
> 1 Wars of national liberation – fought between nationalist forces and colonial regimes.
> 2 Wars of secession, such as those which occurred in Nigeria during the 1960s, the Horn of Africa during the 1970s and 1980s, and the former Yugoslavia during the 1990s.
> 3 Wars aimed at establishing – often highly repressive – theocratic states, such as that fought by the Taliban in Afghanistan during the 1990s and 2001–2021 or by Boko Haram in West Africa since 2002.
> 4 Wars fought indirectly by powerful states through arming and/or financing politically aligned rebels or governments – usually known as proxy wars.

If this distinction between 'interstate' and 'intrastate' conflict is simplistic and obtuse, why does it endure? In sum, because of the interests and institutions that drive global politics. The Westphalian basis of the international system, whereby a state is understood to exercise complete sovereignty over its territory, means that, under international law, there are (at least in theory) significant political and legal repercussions when one state invades, or seeks to intervene illegally in, another. In practice, of course, powerful states can block or frustrate the implementation of international law. The UN Security Council, for example, is theoretically the supreme international body when it comes to authorising (or withholding authorisation for) the use of force against member states. In 2003, however, when it became clear to the US and its allies that key members of the Council would veto a resolution authorising a military intervention in Iraq (aimed at dismantling the country's supposed weapons of mass destruction programme), the US withdrew this resolution. Days later, a US-led coalition invaded Iraq without UN authorisation, setting in train a series of conflicts that would endure for over a decade and lead to hundreds of thousands of deaths (Bennett, 2008).

> ## Reflective question
>
> Is every contemporary conflict 'international' to some extent?

How is the conflict being fought?

An exclusive focus on belligerents provides limited insight into how conflict is actually experienced on the ground in people's lived realities. The nature and spread of violence during conflict can vary profoundly. In some cases, the intensity of violence can be felt dramatically in some regions and barely at all in others, depending on the epicentre or focus of the conflict and the relative military strength of the different parties involved. For example, many insurgencies operate principally in remote, marginalised, or difficult-to-reach areas, meaning that while populations in these areas may be living in a conflict zone, their counterparts in urban settings, including the capital city, may experience little disruption to their lives. This is increasingly the case in parts of North and West Africa, where more than half of conflict-related violence in the early 2020s has taken place in rural areas compared to barely a fifth ten years' previously (Radil et al., 2022).

This happens for many reasons: as noted below, insurgencies often stem from longstanding grievances relating to inequality and poor governance, and remote and marginalised regions are often particularly impacted in this regard. Equally, operating from isolated or inaccessible areas can provide an additional layer of protection for rebel groups from usually better-armed and -resourced government forces. Examples of such areas include jungles, which have been particularly popular areas of operation for rebels such as Colombia's FARC guerrillas and Uganda's LRA, and mountainous regions, which have provided a base for movements like Ethiopia's TPLF/TDF or Afghanistan's Taliban.

In other conflicts, particularly those centred around ethnic or other identity markers (see Chapter 10), almost everyone in a territory is likely to be impacted by the fighting, directly or indirectly. South Sudan's devastating 2013–2022 civil war, which included, according to the UN Commission on Human Rights, the use of ethnic cleansing by all sides (UN, 2016), is an especially shocking example. The war led to $c.4.5$ million of South Sudan's $c.11$ million people fleeing their homes, around 2.3 million of whom became refugees (UNHCR, 2023). In 2023, three years after the conflict's official end, the World Bank estimated that over 75 per cent of South Sudan's population was in need of humanitarian assistance, with women and children most affected (World Bank, 2023).

Critically, though, conflicts evolve. Many rebel movements begin, for example, as small, lightly-armed groups carrying out 'hit-and-run' guerrilla attacks on military and government facilities in remote, rural areas. As they become more successful and acquire more support and advanced weaponry, however, these movements may shift their focus to capturing cities and, ultimately, the capital, requiring a switch to more conventional forms of warfare. Moreover, in cases of inter-state war where an invasion or intervention encounters an unanticipated degree of resistance from insurgents – as occurred in Iraq and Afghanistan during the 2000s and 2010s – the nature of the conflict may move into a protracted counter-insurgency phase. In other words, a military campaign initially marked by a large-scale invasion, troop deployment, and aerial bombardment may shift to street-to-street fighting as insurgents target the intervention forces with ambushes and 'homemade' bombs, often called 'improvised explosive devices' (IEDs).

Who is affected?

When it comes to the impact of all of this on populations and, ultimately, the pursuit of desired futures, there is a key debate about the extent to which civilians or 'non-combatants' are actively targeted by belligerents as part of their campaigns. The intentional targeting of civilians – often along ethnic or gendered lines – has been a tragic feature of many recent conflicts from West and Central Africa to the Balkans, while governments such as the US, Russia, and Israel have been accused of targeting civilians – or failing to minimise civilian casualties – in their operations in Pakistan, Ukraine and Palestine respectively (Amnesty International, 2021b; Kreps et al, 2022; UN OHCHR, 2022).

An influential body of research, most associated with Mary Kaldor, has suggested that this deliberate and mass targeting of civilians is a particular feature of modern, post-Cold War conflict. In her 1999 book *New and Old Wars*, Kaldor argues that civilians have become the principal target of violence in contemporary conflict, describing this – and other phenomena – as part of a 'new type of organized violence developed . . . during the last decades of the twentieth century' (Kaldor, 1999, 2013). While it is true that civilian-targeting is a common part of warfare today, and that nearly 90 per cent of contemporary wartime casualties are civilians (UN Security Council, 2022), it is nonetheless misleading to suggest that this is a recent development.

In their 2019 analysis of civilian populations across the history of South Sudan's conflicts, for example, Nicki Kindersley and Øystein Rolandsen trace how civilians there have used as 'strategic assets to be managed and exploited' by colonial armies, post-colonial governments, and rebel movements since at least the nineteenth century (Kindersley and Rolandsen, 2019). Indeed, in general critics of the 'new wars' thesis also point to the theory's lack of historical context and reflection (Newman, 2004).

The impact of conflict on civilians is not just a question of those killed or injured by government soldiers or rebels, though. Conflicts can have a devastating impact on the provision of services and maintenance of infrastructure. From destroying roads, railways, bridges, and airports, to disconnecting regions from electricity grids and Internet servers, to damaging schools and hospitals, and/or forcing teachers, nurses, and doctors to fight or flee, it is not uncommon for belligerents to deliberately target infrastructure as a political strategy aimed at breaking down the resolve of populations and alienate them from the existing authority, often the state. Particularly in protracted conflicts, this can destroy livelihoods, disrupt food and fuel supply chains, deprive whole generations of a formal education, and force those in need to rely on humanitarian support for even basic medical needs.

Conflict also causes sometimes huge population movements, as people and families run from the violence. These internally displaced persons, or refugees, which can sometimes number in the millions, are often accommodated in crowded, unsanitary camps where, in some cases, perpetrators and criminals prey on the vulnerable. Violent conflict is often, therefore, experienced through famine, sickness, and impoverishment. Indeed, in some conflicts more ultimately die from these causes than from being caught up in the violence itself. Although establishing reliable numbers remains very challenging, it is estimated, for example, that by March 2022, of the c.500,000 people who had died during the then on-going war in Tigray, northern Ethiopia, 150,000–200,000 of these were the result of starvation and a further 100,000+ from a lack of healthcare. This was, to a significant degree, the result of the Ethiopian state (one of the key belligerents) shutting-off access to the region, including, it is alleged, that of humanitarian agencies (York, 2022).

When does contestation turn violent?

As we saw in Chapter 1, political drivers of contestation include manufactured scarcity, diversity of interests and preferences, and the inequalities baked into who gets what, when, and how, via legacies of colonialism. But while the drivers of contestation have to be understood as both structural and politically-engineered, two overall, empirical trends stand out clearly about the likelihood that contestation will turn violent:

1 Countries with higher levels of poverty and slow economic growth are much more likely to experience violent conflict.
2 Conflict is frequently associated with major social, political, and economic change, and vice versa.

Often, uprisings and civil wars are launched in order to reform or overthrow an authoritarian and/or deeply unequal political system. Such systems are usually characterised by unequal distribution of limited resources. When a transfer of power from such a regime occurs, violently or otherwise, the successor administration then has the challenging task of both building a more participatory, just, legitimate, and equitable state while also accommodating or neutralising those political and economic elites who benefitted from the previous system.

New and transitional democracies – particularly those with higher levels of poverty and inequality – are, therefore, particularly vulnerable to conflict. Many African states, and a number in South Asia, the Middle East, and Central America, fall into this category and, indeed, according to the Geneva Academy, 80 of the 110 conflicts it was monitoring in 2023 were taking place in the Middle East or the African continent (Geneva Academy, 2023).

Conflicts can begin when access to decent employment and services (including justice and security), and economic and/or political power is unevenly distributed, usually across identity lines. As discussed at length in Chapter 11, these are what Frances Stewart calls 'horizontal inequalities'. Where these are extensive, and deep, structurally excluded groups may ultimately feel their grievances cannot be addressed peacefully within the system, because the system is effectively set up *in order to* exclude them. States themselves may not be inclusive or represent all of those who may have become combatants; for example, access to state power and resources may be determined largely by ethnic or other ties with the ruling elite.

Image 15.2 An aerial view of a camp for displaced people in war-torn Northern Syria. Image by Ammar Alzeer via Shutterstock.

But even where horizontal inequalities are evident, conflict may not always turn violent. In fact, as Chris Blattman (2022), a political economist, argues in his book *Why We Fight: The Roots of War and the Path to Peace*, resorting to conflict remains rare, because the costs are too high. The reason for this lies in the interests of would-be combatants. A classic interests-based, or rational choice approach, to the motivation of combatants derives from a game-theoretic model (see Box 15.2).

Box 15.2 Blattman's theory of why people fight

Chris Blattman's book *Why We Fight: The Roots of War and the Path to Peace* outlines five reasons why conflict may start:

1 Unchecked rulers and interests: unaccountable leaders, dictators or oligarchs who might gain from war but bear none of the costs.
2 Intangible incentives: human desire for vengeance, status, freedom or combatting injustice.
3 Uncertainty: calling a bluff.
4 Commitment problems – e.g., pre-emptive strikes on a rising enemy because you do not trust it not to attack you, so you get in there first before it becomes too strong.
5 Misperceptions: over-confident leaders, mistaken beliefs about enemy weakness or your own strength, or even 'war by mistake'.

Blattman argues that there are a number of 'false causes' of conflict, including: poverty, scarcity, natural resources, climate change, ethnicity, injustice, and social polarisation. Of course, while none of these elements may themselves lead to conflict, as opposed to a more localised insurgency, they change the cost–benefit calculation of those who may end up fighting. You are far more likely to fight if you are alienated, unemployed, poor, from an oppressed group and subject to perceived injustice. In this way, the 'false causes' and the reasons why people fight are closely entwined.

People living in poverty may also feel that they have less to lose – and more, potentially, to gain – from taking up arms than wealthier groups, many of whom will benefit in some way through their relationship with the existing politico-economic system. The middle classes can nonetheless come to mobilise, and lead protests and insurgencies when they feel that the political structure prevents them from realising their full potential. Students, for example, played a key role in the Arab Spring protests mentioned in the introduction to this chapter, a number of which led to the ultimate removal of longstanding authoritarian regimes like that of Hosni Mubarak in Egypt in 2011.

We should not, however, reduce the causes of the Arab Spring – or any conflict – to an instrumental calculation on the part of those opposing the status quo. Indeed, one of the more influential, albeit contested, bodies of literature on this topic is that which has sought to distinguish between those participating in conflict because of 'greed' (economic, political or other reward from participation) versus 'grievance' (political or other non-economic motivation) (Collier and Hoeffler, 2004; Murshed and Tadjoeddin, 2009; Keen, 2012; see Box 15.3).

Box 15.3 Rational choice theory, interests, and the drivers of conflict

The 'greed versus grievance' approach mentioned above is most associated with the work of Paul Collier and Anke Hoeffler (2004). Using a statistical model, they conclude that economic motivations ('greed') can better explain the onset and durability of conflict than motivations based in social or political inequalities, ideas, or identities ('grievance'). This draws on a theoretical understanding of human motivations based in rational choice theory, an approach which has its foundations in economics.

As we discussed in Chapter 4, rational choice theorists view people as 'rational' actors who make choices based on a systematic evaluation of the pros and cons. In the context of conflict, this entails people deciding whether or not to join an insurgency, for example, after weighing up the costs and benefits of doing so for their interests; in particular, whether this will increase ('maximise') their access to economic resources.

While influential, rational choice perspectives on conflict drivers have been criticised from a range of perspectives. In particular, critics argue that the theory oversimplifies conflict landscapes and overlooks the complex and often context-specific set of factors that lead to participation in conflict. They also contend that a narrow, individualist understanding of human behaviour is misleading since people can and do make choices that are *against* their economic or other interests out of ideological conviction or solidarity with a wider group or community (Cramer, 2002; Keen, 2012).

In reality, even proponents of relatively strong versions of rational choice arguments acknowledge that the opposing argument has some merit in explaining reasons for conflict. Keen (2012) argues that conflicts should be seen as multifaceted and complex, drawing on a significant list of different elements. This non-binary idea has been adopted by most international agencies. 'Complex emergencies' are officially defined by the InterAgency Standing Committee (IASC) as:

> A multifaceted humanitarian crisis in a country, region or society where there is a total or considerable breakdown of authority resulting from internal or external conflict and which requires a multi-sectoral, international response that goes beyond the mandate or capacity of any single agency and/or the ongoing UN country program. Such emergencies have, in particular, a devastating effect on children and women and call for a complex range of responses.

The identity–inequality nexus

Treating ideology and identity as being at opposite ends of a spectrum, as some of the 'greed and grievance' and 'new wars' debates arguably do, is problematic, and often serves to reinforce tired notions of European wars as noble battles of ideas, while relegating contemporary conflicts in the Global South to parochial ethnic clashes (Dexter, 2007). Ideas, ideologies, and beliefs, as argued earlier in this book (Chapter 10, in particular), can rarely be easily detached from notions of identity and, indeed, of how political and economic resources should be fairly distributed – who should get what, when and how. In many Western states, these debates take place along class or regional lines for a range of historical reasons, whereas in many postcolonial states, ethnicity or religion tend to be more powerful differentiators.

This is in many respects a legacy of colonial rule, whereby European colonial administrations governed through privileging particular ethnicities for positions of political and economic power and marginalised others (see Box 15.4). Indeed, some colonial powers were virtually obsessive in their pseudo-scientific use of racist stereotyping to determine which ethnic groups in a colony were suited, for example, to agriculture versus politics versus military service (Ochonu, 2014). This served to institutionalise political, economic, and social inequalities in many countries – including, importantly, land ownership – along ethnic lines. While some postcolonial governments have sought to pull apart this legacy, many others have leant into it. Mobilising populations along ideas of belonging and divisionism – as populist politicians from the US and Brazil to India and Italy have demonstrated in the twenty-first century – can often be more electorally rewarding than appealing to ideas of a shared future and common good.

Box 15.4 'Communalizing colonial policies' and contemporary conflict

Matthew Lange, Tay Jeong, and Emre Amasyali (2021) have introduced the concept of 'communalizing colonial policies' (CCPs) to help explain one way in which European colonial rule has precipitated conflict in the postcolonial era. CCPs, they explain, involved colonial governments recognising, or in some cases 'inventing', ethnic boundaries between colonised communities. Some of these groups would then be privileged over others in the distribution of political, military, and economic power as a means to govern and control sometimes vast territories. Indirect rule – where day-to-day governance would effectively be 'delegated' by colonial officers to local leaders – is a key example of this, particularly across the British Empire. These ethnic and communal distinctions and, critically, their linkages to resources and power, have endured into the present day in a range of cases, structuring conflict and contestation along these identity-based lines (Mamdani, 2001; Lynch, 2011).

How inequality, exclusion, identity, and ideas come together to produce conflict obviously varies across contexts, and can tie into other forms of exclusion. The uneven costs of environmental degradation, discussed in Chapter 13, is an increasingly significant driver of conflict, particularly in regions where resources are becoming more scarce because of climate pressure or deforestation. The systematic exclusion of women and young people from politics in many regions is also a key driver of protests and uprisings; indeed, a photo of female student Alaa Salah standing on top of a car leading a crowd of demonstrators in Khartoum quickly became a symbol of Sudan's 2019 revolution, given the centrality of women and young people to that struggle.

The identity–inequality nexus can also be critical in explaining some interstate conflicts, particularly when the ethnic, linguistic or other identities of different states' border communities overlap, but where these communities possess different political and economic statuses in their respective polities. Somalis, for example, have been historically marginalised in Ethiopia, leading to successive interventions in that country by Somali rebel groups and, between 1977 and 1978, the Somali army itself. Addressing the treatment of Russian speakers in a number of post-Soviet states has also been one of a number of justifications that Moscow has provided for political and military involvement in its western neighbourhood since the 1990s, including its 2022 invasion of Ukraine.

Nationalist ideas of protecting or defending co-ethnics or co-nationals can, therefore, sometimes partly undergird what are ultimately wars of imperial aggression and expansion, with the aggressor even suggesting (and possibly even believing) that it is acting in self-defence. Russian president Vladimir Putin, for example, claimed that Russia's 2022 invasion of Ukraine was undertaken in 'self-defence against the threats posed to us' by, according to him, the Ukrainian government and its allies (*The Spectator*, 2022). Other forms of external intervention, particularly those involving external involvement in more distant polities, tend to be more informed by calculations around foreign policy and security – sometimes the security of the intervenor's population (e.g., Western interventions in Afghanistan and Iraq) and sometimes of a domestic population viewed as under threat (this was the rationale for the 2011 NATO-led intervention in Libya).

Even some of these conflicts, however, ultimately reflect global inequalities. As Martin Shaw, Mark Duffield, Mahmood Mamdani and others have argued, in recent decades, some Western states – notably the US and its European allies – have increasingly sought to protect the security of their own populations through a form of containment. This has involved 'transferring' the frontlines of conflict far beyond their borders through military intervention in the Global South, and securitised approaches to humanitarianism and migration (Shaw, 2005; Duffield, 2007; Mamdani, 2010). In other words, Western states have 'moved' the frontier of what they view as a global crisis of, in this case, terrorism well beyond their own borders.

Reflective question

What leads civilians to take up arms and participate in violent conflict?

So how can we build peace?

Given the dreadful costs for those affected by conflict, dealing the consequences of conflict and trying to prevent further conflict is a central concern of communities, governments and international agencies. The core approach to addressing the effects of violent conflict is known as peacebuilding, defined by the United Nations as efforts by a range of actors, from NGOs and local citizen groups to governments and international organisations, to assist societies, states, and regions in their transitions from war to peace, and to reduce a country's risk of lapsing or relapsing into conflict by strengthening capacities for peaceful conflict management, and by laying the foundations for sustainable peace and development (UN, 2023). Ideas of what actually constitute peace usually revolve around the idea of positive and negative peace. Negative peace is the absence of direct violence. This can be achieved through peacekeeping, ceasefires, or through oppression. Positive peace implies an absence of indirect or structural violence and held to be sustainable. The idea of positive and negative peace was popularised by Galtung (1969), but is an old idea mentioned by, among others, Martin Luther King in the 'Letter from Birmingham Jail' in 1953, in which he wrote about 'negative peace which is the absence of tension' and 'positive peace which is the presence of justice'.

Activities associated with peacebuilding are very broad-ranging and inherently political. At its most basic, peacebuilding is really about developing relationships across societal boundaries where there has been violence. This may include demobilisation of combatants, establishing transitional justice processes, human rights hearings and courts, conflict prevention, conflict management, conflict resolution and transformation, reintegration of combatants and post-conflict reconciliation of divided communities. In addition, interventions around continuing poor mental health, societal stress and ongoing injustice are often critical, as are tackling the significant environmental consequences of conflict (Kaplan and Nussio, 2018).

The main institutions of the international community, including the UN and the World Bank, are organisations of states that therefore see the world as a network of states. Most peace interventions aim to create a functioning and democratic state within an international system premised on the state. In particular, the UN system, for example, along with subsystems like the African Union, have found it difficult to intervene in substate conflicts including civil wars, secession or insurgency. This has been seen as undermining sovereignty and remains controversial. Seeing the state as the key actor, rather than one of the key actors, has therefore been an issue in a context where intrastate conflict has increased rapidly.

Reflective question

Whose interests operate for or against peacebuilding, and how?

The context of peacebuilding has, however, changed radically over the lifetime of this set of approaches. An increasing number of conflicts have not ended well, by which we mean that there has been no clean break between peace and war, or violence and non-violence.

Violence itself may continue as a result of weak governance, a state's inability to provide security, broken peace agreements, political manoeuvring by different actors, and a failure to build representative institutions.

Moreover, most conflict actors are closely linked to global challenges, particularly illegal activity (e.g., drugs in Colombia), regional politics (e.g., external political sponsors in Lebanon) or even climate change (e.g., illegal resource exploitation in Sierra Leone). This adds to violent conflicts becoming complex, international and protracted (Nitzschke, 2003). A continuation of war economies created to benefit fighters may reduce incentives for peace as, for example, with drugs in Colombia or diamonds in Angola. War economies can be part of complex international networks that include some important and influential members that may lack an incentive to give up access to resources. For example, conflict in Sudan following the 2019 overthrow of autocratic President Omar al-Bashjr has been dominated by two warlords he himself brought to prominence – one in charge of the military and one running a paramilitary. The paramilitary Rapid Support Forces (RSF) was supported by international Russian mercenaries from the Wagner Group, which generated funding by smuggling diamonds from mines in Darfur, through Syria and into Russia (*Al Jazeera*, 2023; Malik, 2023). All of these layers had an interest in not disbanding this network, until its leader, Yevgeny Prigozhin, spearheaded an aborted mutiny on Russia in 2023.

Some scholars go further, suggesting that the international aid system itself can be used as a political instrument supporting the war economy by subsidising state spending in places like South Sudan (Duffield, 2014). Large influxes of aid, for example, may allow states engaged in war to shift their own spending into weaponry rather than service provision, relying on the international community to provide those basic services. The mutation of violence also creates new grievances through targeting new groups, including civilians, women and youth, as well as specific ethnic or regional groups. In this way, violence constantly reinvents itself, making it increasingly difficult for peacebuilding efforts to deal with the underlying causes of conflict, leading ultimately to conflict relapse, or recidivism (returning to illegal or violent activity).

Criticisms of peacebuilding

One of the core issues with peacebuilding currently, therefore, is that the transition from war to peace is not a linear, or predictable process. As peacebuilding has expanded and the contexts of peacebuilding have become more violent, a core question becomes how far can one pursue peacebuilding during conflict itself?

Most approaches to peacebuilding tend to assume some degree of coherence across contexts, discourses and practices. The development of peacebuilding industry has, for example, led to the codification of associated language (see below, and Mac Ginty, 2014). Ironically, peacebuilding itself as a discipline, however, suffers from the same malady that affects its policies: a tension between the international and the local (Mac Ginty and Richmond, 2013) – in particular, the failure to adequately account for the politics of the 'local' in peacebuilding efforts aimed at state level where there may be considerably different dynamics between the international, the national and the local (Jackson and Bakrania, 2018; see Box 15.5).

> ## Box 15.5 The 'Local Turn' and Hybridity in Peacebuilding
>
> A significant criticism of peacebuilding programmes has been their failure to adequately involve and empower local communities, instead imposing 'top down', externally devised agendas. This led to the emergence of a so-called 'local turn' in peacebuilding scholarship during the 2000s. (Mac Ginty and Richmond, 2013). The 'local turn' places emphasis on the views, perspectives, and desires of conflict-affected communities themselves – in effect, *local* understandings of desired futures. Effective peacebuilding, local turn scholars argue, requires peacebuilding efforts to be locally developed and 'owned'. These efforts must also be based in a deep understanding and appreciation of local political, historical, social, and cultural context rather than follow a standardised, 'off-the-shelf' approach.
>
> Local turn scholars have struggled, however, to clearly define where the 'local' ends and the external or international begins. The approach has also been criticised for romanticising the 'local', and for not problematising some 'local' processes which reinforce or amplify exclusionary perspectives or practices (Randazzo, 2016). Increasingly, then, critical peacebuilding scholars have adopted a 'hybridity' lens which focuses on the ways in which different norms, ideas, interests, and institutions emerge and interact in peacebuilding contexts, rather than on clearly distinguishing the 'local' from the non-'local' (Uesugi, 2020).

Language is really important here. The international community tends to act as if everyone accepts the international language of peacebuilding. However, language itself can be politicised within conflict and some forms of language are clearly biased. Most of the language of 'post-conflict', for example, assumes that there is a state and a rebel group and the rebel group needs to be rehabilitated and integrated in to the state. In Nepal, several Maoist combatants left meetings on demobilisation because of the language used: 'why do we need to be rehabilitated? We didn't lose.' In a world where increasingly there are very few clean endings to conflicts, though, the identification of winners and losers is extremely difficult, if not impossible. In this context, who then needs to be rehabilitated? Lack of understanding can lead to unwillingness to participate in discussions through being identified in this way and through careless use of language and labels. The language also reflects the bigger set of assumptions that the state is right and opponents of the state need to be brought in, rather than aiming at the reform of the state itself.

This illustrates the increased politicisation of everything within conflict contexts, but also international hubris. The complexity of most conflicts means that simplistic solutions are unlikely to have much positive effect. Simplification, along with almost everything within peacebuilding, is politically sensitive and the use of language requires careful consideration. Politically complex conflicts require politically complex approaches encompassing pragmatism and an inclusive approach, including local and everyday approaches and concerns.

Discontents and ways forward

Given the criticisms of approaches to peacebuilding outlined above, how can political complexity be accommodated in the reinvention of peacebuilding? Peacebuilding actors have been evolving to more complex approaches and are incorporating more local voices into approaches, non-state voices like civil society, youth and gender. Some challenges to peacebuilding concentrate on its linearity and short time frames, while others concentrate on further refinement of the programmes, including end goals, processes and methods. While there are many different policy approaches within these critiques, three main responses to these challenges are common: reduction of aims; denial of failure; and the reassertion of peacebuilding.

The reduction of aims of peacebuilding and a series of approaches that are more targeted, limited interventions that are, in many ways, less ambitious than the all-encompassing liberal democratic transitions that were seen as the eventual outcome of peacebuilding as a process (Chandler, 2017). The issues and challenges coming out of international interventions in Iraq and Afghanistan have led to a reassessment of what can actually be achieved in violent contexts and a set of more realistic expectations of outcomes that are far less ambitious.

Arguably the most influential of these approaches has been 'stabilisation', or the strengthening of state institutions and achieving quick wins in peacebuilding in areas affected by violence. This represents a long-overdue recognition that peacebuilding frequently takes place within contexts of violence and not afterwards. Part of this is in the emphasis on the state in situations where the state may itself be implicated in violence, and whether this can itself lead to anti-democratic outcomes. It should be noted that stabilisation is not a fixed model and recognises the need for pragmatism, evolution and realistic expectations rather than what 'should be' and, as such, it concentrates on what is possible rather than what is desirable (UK Government, 2019).

A second approach, primarily taken by critical scholars, is to assert that peacebuilding is not actually failing in what it was originally designed to achieve (Duffield, 2014; Sabaratnam, 2017). The idea that peacebuilding is actually a neo-colonial imperialist project, bringing a new form of civilising mission categorised by a particular view of the state, leads one to conclude that peacebuilding is doing exactly what you expect in relaunching the Eurocentric Weberian state. This narrative holds that deviant states are held to have 'failed' when held against an array of indices based on successful states predominantly in Europe or North America. In this critique, such failed states, unsurprisingly need external intervention since they are incapable of building themselves – e.g., Afghanistan (Ghani and Lockhart, 2008). In this way, peacebuilding manages to simultaneously separate functioning and failing states while simultaneously placing the blame for failure on societies that live in those states. Peacebuilding is therefore not failing, but is reproducing imperial orders based on Eurocentric ideas of institutions and societies. Taking this neo-orientalist view, it is the Europeans who impose order on the unruly locals (Tuastad, 2003).

> **Reflective question**
>
> Is what ways is the language and practice of 'peacebuilding' political?

The third approach is essentially continuing to evolve through incorporating increasing complexity into peacebuilding approaches (de Coning, 2018). This worldview has found its way into global approaches through the UN recognising that societies themselves evolve through collapsing and reconstructing, and thinking about how the resilience of society can be supported over time. This approach also rejects linearity, concentrating instead on how societies can manage conflict and prevent societies falling into violence. This implies a number of things in relation to peacebuilding. If societies are able to re-form themselves and are constantly evolving, then peacebuilding is a continuous process with no clear end-state. It also implies that there are no universal laws that can be applied to peacebuilding, and international intervention should be seen as an additional layer, not the whole solution. This has profound implications for the politics of how to engage with post-conflict societies, and in particular recognising that peacebuilders are, and peacebuilding is, deeply political.

Moreover, applying models that are too rigid can actually prevent societies naturally re-forming and could undermine peacebuilding in the larger sense. This approach relies on the peace industry taking a more humble approach to its own capabilities. In this narrative, there is no constant peace, or peace as something that is programmable, since peace itself is constantly being remade and is an integral part of society itself. In many ways, this is back to the original idea of peacebuilding rather than the programmable version developed by the international community, but it requires an admission that the international community is not omnipotent and peace itself is not linear or predictable.

A fourth approach considers the post-Anthropocene, 'more-than-human', or 'environmental' peacebuilding. We (humans) are a remarkably narcissistic species and to most of the other species in the world we are the threat to peace. There is an increasing acknowledgement that the environment and climate change are likely to have a significant influence on conflict and human security, but also conflicts themselves significantly affect the environment (Ide et al., 2021). Climate migration, reducing livelihoods due to climate change, predatory behaviour by armed groups around resources alongside the exploitation of resources by political elites, can all contribute to conflict in different ways, or themselves be a result of conflict. Including non-human aspects in peacebuilding as either a focus for society itself through, for example, sharing resources, or as a focus of peace management through ongoing stewardship of resources may be a potential way to make peace with nature as well as each other. For example, forest management in Kenya comprises co-operation over the management of forestry resources themselves, but also of the elephant population in terms of their migration patterns.

Summary and conclusion

This chapter has outlined a critical approach to analysing the politics of conflict and peace, violence and development. It has considered major political reasons why contestation turns violent, including the impact of ideas, inequality, identity, resources and external interests (past and present) in shaping conflict dynamics. It has also assessed and analysed the politics of peacebuilding, and explained how power and interests underlie prospects for resolving conflict and addressing its underlying causes.

This is an extremely complex area of the politics of development and, indeed, is highly politicised in terms of the language used, for example. It draws on a lot of 'big' political ideas, including the nature of the state itself and relationships to international institutions and approaches, as well as to subnational movements, many of which may be violent. It also touches on the interaction between inequality – national, regional and global – and identity, a term that we understand to include ideas on politics and governance, as well as feelings of ethnic, religious or other forms of belonging.

A focus on the nexus between inequality and identity remains a helpful way to understand the drivers of conflict. Conflict is most likely to turn violent, we underline, when societal inequalities are structured along the lines of identity. Often these structures are, at least in part, a legacy of racialised colonial-era approaches to governance, although in many cases these have been reinforced in the post-colonial era by political parties and leaders and, indeed, by aid donors and other external actors to varying degrees.

Finally, we have examined how conflict can be resolved, and societies rebuilt – underlining the challenge of determining when a conflict has 'ended' or, indeed, what 'peace' looks like. Using the lens of peacebuilding as a generic term for most post-conflict interventions, we demonstrate how these activities have increasingly broadened out and are starting to embrace broader ideas of positive peace, as well as the negative peace of 'just' stopping violence. The perspective of everyday peace arguably aligns with the people-led approach to development we have applied throughout this book, and links the resolution of conflict more closely to the pursuit of desired futures.

Discussion questions

- What best explains why some conflicts turn violent and others do not?
- Does lack of development drive conflict or does conflict lead to lack of development?
- Are some conflicts more about ideas than others?
- Under what circumstances can peacebuilding be effective?

Suggested further reading

Jackson, P.J. and Beswick, D. (2018) *Conflict, Security and Development: An Introduction* (3rd edn). London: Routledge.

Mac Ginty, R. (2021) *Everyday Peace: How So-Called Ordinary People Can Disrupt Violent Conflict*. Oxford: Oxford University Press.

Podder, S. (2022) *Peacebuilding Legacy: Programming for Change and Young People's Attitudes to Peace*. Oxford: Oxford University Press.

Stewart, F. (ed.) (2008) *Horizontal Inequalities and Conflict: Understanding Group Violence in Multi-Ethnic Societies*. Basingstoke: Palgrave Macmillan.

References

Abdulai A.-G. and Hickey S. (2016) 'The politics of development under competitive clientelism: insights from Ghana's education sector', *African Affairs*, 115 (458): 44–72.

Aberbach, J.D., Dollar, D. and Sokoloff, K.L. (1994) *The Role of the State in Taiwan's Development*. New York: M.E. Sharpe.

Abers, R.N. and Keck, M.E. (2013) *Practical Authority: Agency and Institutional Change in Brazilian Water Politics*. Oxford: Oxford University Press.

Abimbade, O., Olayoku, P., Herro, D. (2022), 'Millennial activism within Nigerian Twitterscape: From mobilization to social action of #ENDSARS protest', *Social Sciences & Humanities Open*, 6 (1).

Abrahamsen, R. (2000) *Disciplining Democracy: Development Discourse and Good Governance in Africa*. London: Zed Books.

Acemoglu, D. and Robinson, J.A. (2012) *Why Nations Fail*. London: Profile Books.

Acemoglu, D. and Robinson, J.A. (2002) 'The political economy of the Kuznets Curve', *Review of Development Economics*, 6 (2): 183–203. Available at: https://doi.org/10.1111/1467-9361.00149

Acemoglu, D., Johnson, S. and Robinson, J.A. (2005) Institutions as a fundamental cause of long-run growth, in P. Aghion and S. Durlauf (eds), *Handbook of Economic Growth*, London: Elsevier. pp. 385–472.

Adams, K. and Kreiss, D. (2021) *Power in Ideas: A Case-Based Argument for Taking Ideas Seriously in Political Communication*. Cambridge: Cambridge University Press.

Adebanwi, W. (2016) *Nation as Grand Narrative: The Nigerian Press and the Politics of Meaning (Rochester Studies in African History and the Diaspora)*. Martlesham: Boydell & Brewer.

Adedeji, A. (1999) 'Structural adjustment policies in Africa', *International Social Science Journal*, 51 (162): 521–28.

Adelman, C. (2009) 'Global philanthropy and remittances: reinventing foreign aid', *The Brown Journal of World Affairs*, 15 (2): 23–33.

Adeney, K. (2007) 'Federalism and ethnic conflict regulation in India and Pakistan', Basingstoke: Palgrave Macmillan.

Adesina, J.O. (2021) 'Social policy in the African context', Dakar: CODESRIA.

Africa Centre for Strategic Studies (2021) 'Autocracy and instability in Africa', Africa Centre for Strategic Studies. Available at: https://africacenter.org/spotlight/autocracy-and-instability-in-africa/

African Report, The (2022) 'Nigeria: how #EndSARS figures are transforming into an 'Obidient' army'. Available at: www.theafricareport.com/222267/nigeria-how-endsars-figures-are-transforming-into-an-obidient-army/ (accessed 28 March 2023).

Afrobarometer (2021) *Africans see growing corruption, poor government response, but fear retaliation if they speak out*, Afrobarometer Dispatch.

Ager, J.E. Fiddian-Qasmiyeh and Ager, A. (2015) 'Local faith communities and the promotion of resilience in contexts of humanitarian crisis', *Journal of Refugee Studies*, 28 (2): 202–21. Available at: https://doi.org/10.1093/jrs/fev001

Ahikire, J. and Mwiine, A. (2019) 'Contesting ideas, aligning incentives: the politics of Uganda's Domestic Violence Act (2010)', in S. Nazneen, Hickey, S. and Sifaki, E. (eds), *Negotiating Gender Equity in the Global South*. New York: Routledge. pp. 67–87.

Ahmad, S. (2020) 'Pakistani policewomen: questioning the role of gender in circumscribing police corruption', *Policing and Society*, 30 (8): 890–904.

Ahmed, N., Marriott, A., Dabi, N., Lowthers, M., Lawson, M. and Mugehera, L. (2022) 'Inequality kills: the unparalleled action needed to combat unprecedented inequality in the wake of COVID-19', Oxfam. Available at: https://doi.org/10.21201/2022.8465

Akanle, O. and Adésìnà, J.O. (2018) *The Development of Africa*. Springer.

Akinlabi, O. and Murphy, K. (2018) 'Dull compulsion or perceived legitimacy? Assessing why people comply with the law in Nigeria', *Police Practice and Research*, 19 (2): 186–201.

Akinola, A.O. (2021) 'The Bretton Woods Institutions and economic reforms in Africa', *Oxford Research Encyclopedia of African History*. Available at: https://doi.org/10.1093/acrefore/9780190277734.013.754

Aklin, M., Cheng, C.Y. and Urpelainen, J. (2021) 'Inequality in policy implementation: caste and electrification in rural India', *Journal of Public Policy*, *41* (2): 331–59.

Al Jazeera (2023) 'Russian mercenaries in Sudan: what is the Wagner group's role?', 17 April. Available at: www.aljazeera.com/news/2023/4/17/what-is-the-wagner-groups-role-in-sudan (accessed 1 May 2023).

Alam, N. (2015) 'How Lee Kuan Yew transformed Singapore from small town into global financial hub', *The Conversation*, 23 March.

Albertus, M. (2015) 'The role of subnational politicians in distributive politics: political bias in Venezuela's land reform under Chávez', *Comparative Political Studies*, 48 (13): 1667–710.

Albertus, M. (2021) *Property without Rights: Origins and Consequences of the Property Rights Gap*. Cambridge: Cambridge University Press.

Albiston, C.R. and Fisk, C.L. (2021) 'Precarious work and precarious welfare: how the pandemic reveals fundamental flaws of the US social safety net', *Berkeley Journal of Employment and Labor Law*, 42: 257.

Alesina, Al, and David, D. (2000) 'Who gives foreign aid to whom and why?', *Journal of Economic Growth*, 5 (1): 33–63. Available at: https://doi.org/10.1023/A:1009874203400

Ali, S.A.M. and Altaf, S.W. (2021) 'Citizen trust, administrative capacity and administrative burden in Pakistan's immunization program', *Journal of Behavioral Public Administration*, 4 (1). Available at: https://journal-bpa.org/index.php/jbpa/article/view/184

Alik-Lagrange, A., Dreier, S.K., Lake, M. and Porisky, A. (2021) 'Social protection and state–society relations in environments of low and uneven state capacity', *Annual Review of Political Science*, 24 (1): 151–74. Available at: https://doi.org/10.1146/annurev-polisci-041719-101929

Alkire, S. (2005) 'Why the capability approach?', *Journal of Human Development*, 6 (1): 115–33.

Amnesty International (2020) 'Multinationals seem too big for accountability. Switzerland may change that'. Available at: www.amnesty.org/en/latest/news/2020/11/multinationals-seem-too-big-for-accountability-switzerland-may-change-that/

Amnesty International (2021) 'Nigeria: cover up of Lekki Toll Gate massacre continues, 100 days after killings', 28 January. Available at: www.amnesty.org.uk/press-releases/nigeria-cover-lekki-toll-gate-massacre-continues-100-days-after-killings

Amnesty International (2021) 'Pattern of Israeli attacks on residential homes in Gaza must be investigated as war crimes'. Available at: www.amnesty.org/en/latest/press-release/2021/05/israelopt-pattern-of-israeli-attacks-on-residential-homes-in-gaza-must-be-investigated-as-war-crimes/ (accessed 5 April 2023).

Amsden, A.H. (2001) *The Rise of the Rest: Challenges to the West from Late-Industrializing Economies*. New York: Oxford University Press.

Amsden, A., H. (1989) *Asia's Next Giant: South Korea and Late Industrialization*. Oxford: Oxford University Press.

Amsden, A.H., DiCaprio, A. and Robinson, J.A. (eds) (2012) *The Role of Elites in Economic Development*. Oxford: Oxford University Press.

Andersen, B. (1983) *Imagined Communities: Reflections on the Origin and Spread of Nationalism*. New York: Verso Books.

Andersen, J.J., Johannesen, N. and Rijkers, B. (2022) 'Elite capture of foreign aid: evidence from offshore bank accounts,' *Journal of Political Economy*, 130 (2): 388–425.

Andrews, M., Pritchett, L. and Woolcock, M. (2017) 'Building state capability: evidence, analysis'. Action. Oxford Scholarship Online.

Ang, Y.Y. (2014) Authoritarian Restraints on Online Activism Revisited: Why "I-Paid-A-Bribe" Worked in India but Failed in China. Comparative Politics, Volume 47, Number 1, October 2014, pp. 21-40(20).

Ang, Y.Y. (2016) *How China Escape the Poverty Trap*. Ithaca, NY: Cornell University Press.

Ang, Y.Y. (2020) 'Unbundling corruption: revisiting six questions on corruption', *Global Perspectives*, 1 (1). Available at: https://doi.org/10.1525/gp.2020.12036

Aniche, E.T. and Iwuoha, V.C. (2022) 'Beyond police brutality: interrogating the political, economic and social undercurrents of the #EndSARS protest in Nigeria', *Journal of Asian and African Studies*.

Anner, M., Pons-Vignon, N. and Rani, U. (2019) 'For a future of work with dignity: a critique of the World Bank Development Report, the changing nature of work', *Global Labour Journal*, 10 (1): 2–19.

Archer, M. (2003) *Structure, Agency and the Internal Conversation*. Cambridge: Cambridge University Press.

Arendt, H. (1970) *On Violence*, Orlando, FL: Harcourt Brace Jovanovich.

Arias, E.D. (2006) 'Trouble en route: drug trafficking and clientelism in Rio de Janeiro shantytowns', *Qualitative Sociology*, 29: 427–45. Available at: https://doi.org/10.1007/s11133-006-9033-x

Arnold, D. (2022) 'The impact of privatisation of state-owned enterprises on workers', *American Economic Journal: Applied Economics*, 14 (4): 343–80.

Aspinall, E. and Berenschot, W. (2019) *Democracy for Sale: Elections, Clientelism, and the State in Indonesia*. Ithaca, New York: Cornell University Press.

Aubyn, F. (2019) 'Understanding variations in police performance in UN peacekeeping and domestic policing in Ghana'. Presentation at International Studies Association Conference, Accra, Ghana, 3 August.

Auerbach, A.M. and Thachil, T. (2018) 'How clients select brokers: competition and choice in India's slums', *American Political Science Review*, 112 (4): 775–91.

Auerbach, A. (2019) *Demanding Development: The Politics of Public Goods Provision in India's Urban Slums (Cambridge Studies in Comparative Politics)*. Cambridge: Cambridge University Press.

Autesserre, S. (2016) *'Paternalism and peacebuilding: capacity, knowledge, and resistance in international interventions'*. Columbia Academic Commons: Columbia University.

Auyero, J. (2000) The Logic of Clientelism in Argentina: An Ethnographic Account. *Latin American Research Review*, 35 (3), 55–81. http://www.jstor.org/stable/2692042

Auyero, J. (2001) *Poor People's Politics: Peronist Survival Networks and the Legacy of Evita*, Durham: Duke University Press.

Auyero, J. (2012) *Patients of the State: The Politics of Waiting in Argentina*. Durham: Duke University Press.

Avritzer, L. (2012) 'The different designs of public participation in Brazil: deliberation, power sharing and public ratification', *Critical Policy Studies*, 6 (2): 113–27.

Ayobi, Y.A., Black, A., Kenni, L., Nakabea, R. and Sutton, K. (2017) 'Going local: Achieving a more appropriate and fit-for-purpose humanitarian ecosystem in the Pacific. Melbourne: Centre for Humanitarian Leadership, Fiji National University, Humanitarian Advisory Group.

Bachrach, P. and Baratz, M.S. (1962) 'Two faces of power', *The American Political Science Review*, 56 (4): 947–52. Available at: https://doi.org/10.2307/1952796

Bachrach, P. and Baratz, M.S. (1970) *Power and Poverty*. New York: Oxford University Press.

Baer, M. (2015) 'From water wars to water rights: implementing the human right to water in Bolivia'. *Journal of Human Rights*, 14 (3): 353–76.

Baez-Camargo, C. Bukuluki, P., Sambaiga, R., Gatwa, T., Kassa, S. and Stahl, C. (2020) 'Petty corruption in the public sector: a comparative study of three East African countries through a behavioural lens', *African Studies*, 79 (2): 232–49.

Baiocchi, G. (2005) *Militants and Citizens: The Politics of Participatory Democracy in Porto Alegre*. Standford, CA: Stanford University Press.

Bajo-Rubio, O. and Yan, H.D. (2019) 'Globalization and populis', in F.L.T. Yu and D.S. Kwan (eds). *Contemporary Issues in International Political Economy*. New York: Springer. 229–52.

Bajpai, R. and Brown, G.K. (2013) 'From ideas to hegemony: ideational change and affirmative action policy in Malaysia, 1955–2010', *Journal of Political Ideologies* 18 (3): 257–280.

Baker, S. (2016) *Sustainable Development* (2nd edn). London: Routledge.

Balasco, L.M. (2017) 'Reparative development: re-conceptualising reparations in transitional justice processes', *Conflict, Security & Development*, 17 (1): 1–20.

Balassa, B. (1982) 'Structural adjustment policies in developing economies', *World Development*, 10 (1): 23–38.

Baloch, B.A. (2021) 'When ideas matter: democracy and corruption in India'. Cambridge: Cambridge University Press.

Banks, N., Bukenya, B., Elbers, W., Kamya, I., Kumi, E., Schulpen, L., van Selm, G., van Wessel, M. and Yeboah, T. (2023) 'Transforming power inequalities between development NGOs'. Manchester: Manchester University.

Barbalet, J. (2022) 'Conceptualising informal institutions: drawing on the case of guanxi', *The British Journal of Sociology*.

Bardhan, P. and Mookherjee, D. (2005) 'Decentralizing antipoverty program delivery in developing countries', *Journal of Public Economics*, 89 (4): 675–704.

Barkey, K., & Parikh, S. (1991) *Comparative Perspectives on The State. Annual Review of Sociology*, 17, 523–549. http://www.jstor.org/stable/2083353

Barnett, M.N. (2011) *Empire of Humanity: A History of Humanitarianism*. Ithaca, NY: Cornell University Press.

Barnett, M.N. (ed.) (2016) *Paternalism Beyond Borders*. New York: Cambridge University Press.

Barry, T., Gahman, L., Greenidge, A. and Mohamed, A. (2020) 'Wrestling with race and colonialism in Caribbean agriculture: toward a (food) sovereign and (gender) just future. *Geoforum*, 109: 106–10, February. Available at: https://doi.org/10.1016/j.geoforum.2019.12.018

Batley, R. and C. Mcloughlin (2015) 'The Politics of Public Services: A Service Characteristics Approach', *World Development*, 74: 275–285.

Bauhr, M., Charron, N. and Nasiritousi, N. (2013) 'Does corruption cause aid fatigue? Public opinion and the aid-corruption paradox,' *International Studies Quarterly*, 57 (3): 568–79.

Bayart, J.F. (1993) *The State in Africa: the Politics of the Belly*. (London and New York, Longman, 1993)

BBC (2018) 'Argentina notebook scandal: driver details "decade of bribes"' 2 August.

BBC (2020) 'Mali coup: thousands take to Bamako streets to celebrate', 21 August. Available at: www.bbc.co.uk/news/world-africa-53868236

Beckles, H. McD. (2019) 'The reparation movement: greatest political tide of the twenty-first century', *Social and Economic Studies*, 68 (3/4): 11–30.

Beetham, D. (1991) *The Legitimation of Power*. Basingstoke: Palgrave Macmillan.

Behuria, P., Buur, L. and Gray, H. (2017) 'Studying political settlements in Africa', *African Affairs*, 116 (464): 508–25, July.

Béland, D. and Cox, R.H. (2016) 'Ideas as coalition magnets: coalition building, policy entrepreneurs, and power relations', *Journal of European Public Policy*, 23 (3): 428–45.

Béné, C. (2022) 'Why the Great Food Transformation may not happen – A deep-dive into our food systems' political economy, controversies and politics of evidence.' *World Development*, 154: 105881.

Benček, D. and Strasheim, J. (2016) 'Refugees welcome? A dataset on anti-refugee violence in Germany', *Research & Politics*, 3 (4): 2053168016679590.

Bénit-Gbaffou, C. (2011) '"Up close and personal" – how does local democracy help the poor access the state? Stories of accountability and clientelism in Johannesburg.' *Journal of Asian and African Studies*, 46 (5): 453–64.

Bennett, R. (2008) 'Ten days to war', *The Guardian,* 8 March. Available at: www.theguardian.com/world/2008/mar/08/iraq.united nations (accessed 1 May 2023).

Berenschot, W. (2010) 'Everyday mediation: the politics of public service delivery in Gujarat, India'. *Development and Change*, 41 (5): 883–905.

Bernstein, M. (1997) 'Celebration and suppression: The strategic uses of identity by the lesbian and gay movement', *American journal of Sociology*, 103 (3), 531–565.

Bernstein, M. (2005) 'Identity politics', *Annual Review of Sociology*, 31: 47–74.

Besley, T. and Ghatak, M. (2006) 'Public goods and economic development', *Understanding Poverty*.

Besley, T. and Ghatak, M. (2010) 'Property rights and economic development', *Handbook of Development Economics*, 5 (C), 4525–95.

Besley, T. and Persson, T. (2009) 'The origins of state capacity: property rights, taxation and politics', *American Economic Review*, 99 (4): 1218–44.

Best, L. and Levitt, K. (2009) *Essays on the Theory of Plantation Economy: A Historical and Institutional Approach to Caribbean Economic Development*. Kingston, Jamaica: University of West Indies Press.

Beswick, D. and Jackson, P. (2013) *Conflict, Security and Development: An Introduction*. New York: Routledge.

Bhambra, G.K. (2014) 'Postcolonial and decolonial dialogues', *Postcolonial Studies*, 17 (2): 115–21.

Bhambra, G.K. (2007) 'Sociology and postcolonialism: another 'missing' revolution?' *Sociology*, 41 (5): 871–84.

Bhambra, G.K. (2020) 'Colonial global economy: towards a theoretical reorientation of political economy', *Review of International Political Economy*, 28 (2): 307–22.

Bicchieri, C. (2005) 'The rules we live by' in C. Bicchieri, *The Grammar of Society: The Nature and Dynamics of Social Norms*. Cambridge: Cambridge University Press. pp. 1–54.

Bicchieri, C. (2012) *The Grammar of Society: The Nature and Dynamics of Social Norms*. Cambridge: Cambridge Core All Books.

Bicchieri, C. (2017). *Norms in the Wild: How to Diagnose, Measure, and Change Social Norms*. New York: Oxford Academic.

Biewener, C. and Bacque, M.-H. (2015) 'Feminism and the politics of empowerment in international development', *Air & Space Power Journal–Africa & Francophonie*, 6 (2), 58–75.

Bigger, P. and Webber, S. (2021) 'Green structural adjustment in the world bank's resilient city', *Annals of the American Association of Geographers*, 111 (1): 36–51.

Bird, J., Lebrand, M. and Venables, A.J. (2020) 'The belt and road initiative: reshaping economic geography in Central Asia?', *Journal of Development Economics*, 144 (May): 102441. Available at: https://doi.org/10.1016/j.jdeveco.2020.102441

Bishop, M. and Green, M. (2015) 'Philanthrocapitalism rising', *Society*, 52 (6): 541–8.

Bittker, B. (2021) 'The ethical implications of clinical trials in low-and-middle-income countries', *Human Rights Magazine*, 46 (4).

Blaikie, P. (1985) *The Political Economy of Soil Erosion in Developing Countries*, London: Longman.

Blaikie, P. (2010). Introduction: The Tsunami of 2004 in Sri Lanka: An Introduction to impacts and policy in the shadow of civil war. Chapter 1 in Blaikie and Lund (eds). The Tsunami of 2004 in Sri Lanka: Impacts and Policy in the Shadow of civil war. London: Routledge.

Blair, R. and Winters, M. (2020) 'Foreign aid and state–society relations: theory, evidence, and new directions for research', *Studies in Comparative International Development*, 55: 123–42.

Blattman, C. (2022) *Why We Fight: The Roots of War and the Paths to Peace*. London: Viking.

Blunt, P. Turner, M. and Lindroth, H. (2012) 'Patronage, service delivery, and social justice in Indonesia', *International Journal of Public Administration*, 35 (3): 214–20.

Blyth, M. (2003) 'Structures do not come with an instruction sheet: interests, ideas, and progress in political science', *Perspectives on Politics*, 1 (4): 695–706, December.

Boege, V., Brown, M.A. and Clements, K.P. (2009) *Hybrid Political Orders, Not Fragile States, Peace Review*, 21:1, 13–21.

Bogart, D. and Chaudhary, l. (2019) 'Extractive institutions? Investor returns to Indian railway companies in the age of high imperialism', *Journal of Institutional Economics'*, 15: 751–74.

Booth, D. and Golooba-Mutebi, F. (2012) 'Developmental patrimonialism? The case of Rwanda', *African Affairs*, 111 (444): 379–403.

Booth, D. and Unsworth, S. (2014) 'Politically smart, locally led development', Research Report. Overseas Development Institute. Available at: www.odi.org/publications/8800-politically-smart-locally-led-development

Borras, S.M. (2023) 'La Via Campesina – transforming agrarian and knowledge politics, and co-constructing a field: a laudation', *The Journal of Peasant Studies*.

Brennan Centre for Justice (2022) 'Voter suppression: why it matters', Brennan.

Botella-Ordinas, E. (2013) 'Colonialism and Post-Colonialism.' In *Oxford Bibliographies in Atlantic History*. Ed. Trevor Burnard. New York: Oxford University Press.

Centre for Justice. Available at: www.brennancenter.org/issues/ensure-every-american-can-vote/vote-suppression

Briggs, R.C. and Weathers, S. (2016) 'Gender and location in African politics scholarship: the other white man's burden? *African Affairs*, 115 (460): 466–89.

Broome, A. (2014) *Issues and Actors in the Global Political Economy*. Basingstoke: Palgrave Macmillan.

Brown, S. and Fisher, J. (2020) 'Aid donors, democracy, and the developmental state in Ethiopia', *Democratization*, 27 (2): 185–203.

Brown, S. and Rosier, M. (2023) 'COVID-19 vaccine apartheid and the failure of global cooperation', *British Journal of Politics and International Relations*, 25 (3): 535–54.

Brubaker, R. and Cooper, F. (2000) 'Beyond identity', *Theory and Society*, 29 (1): 1–47.

Brubaker, R. and Stern, M. (2020) 'What is sexual about conflict-related sexual violence? Stories from men and women survivors', *International Affairs*, 96 (5): 1151–68.

Brunkert, L. and von Soest, C. (2022) 'Praising the leader: personalist legitimation strategies and the deterioration of executive constraints', *Democratization*, 30 (2): 1–21.

Bruns, B., Filmer, D., and Patrinos, H., (2011) *Making Schools Work: New Evidence on Accountability Reforms*. Washington: The World Bank.

Bryant, J. (2019) 'Mapping local capacities and support for more effective humanitarian response'. London: Overseas Development Institute. Available at: www.alnap.org/help-library/mapping-local-capacities-and-support-for-more-effective-humanitarian-responses

BSOEC (The Bayelsa State Oil and Environmental Commission) (2019) *November 2019 Interim Report*. Available at: www.bayelsacommission.org/wp-content/uploads/2019/11/BSOEC-Public-Interim-Report-ONLINE-VERSION-29.10.19.pdf

Bueno de Mesquita, B. and Downs, G.W. (2005) 'Development and democracy', *Foreign Affairs*, 84: 77.

Burnyeat, G. and Johansson, M. (2022) 'An anthropology of the social contract: the political power of ideas', *Critique of Anthropology*, 42 (3): 221–37.

Busby, J.W. (2007) 'Bono made Jesse Helms cry: Jubilee 2000, debt relief, and moral action in international politics', *International Studies Quarterly*, 51 (2): 247–75.

Bush, S.S. (2015) *The Taming of Democracy Assistance: Why Democracy Promotion Does Not Confront Dictators*. Cambridge: Cambridge University Press.

Bussell, J. (2019) *Clients and Constituents: Political Responsiveness in Patronage Democracies*. Oxford University Press.

Butler, J. (1990) *Gender Trouble: Feminism and the Subversion of Identity*. London: Routledge.

Cairney, P. (2009) 'The role of ideas in policy transfer: the case of UK smoking bans since devolution', *Journal of European Public Policy*, 16 (3): 471–88.

Campbell, S.P. (2018) *Global Governance and Local Peace: Accountability and Performance in International Peacebuilding*. Cambridge: Cambridge University Press.

Campbell, J.L. (1998) Institutional analysis and the role of ideas in political economy. *Theory and Society*, 27 (3): 377–409.

Campbell, J. (2020) *Causation in Psychology*. Cambridge: Harvard University Press.

Canen, N. and Wantchekon, L. (2022) 'Political distortions, state capture, and economic development in Africa', *Journal of Economic Perspectives*, 36 (1): 101–24.

Capoccia, G. (2015) 'Critical junctures and institutional change', in *Advances in Comparative-Historical Analysis*. Cambridge: Cambridge University Press.

Carnegie, A. and Marinov, N. (2017) Foreign Aid, Human Rights, and Democracy Promotion: Evidence from a Natural Experiment. *American Journal of Political Science*, 61: 671–683. https://doi.org/10.1111/ajps.12289

Carothers, T. and De Gramont, D. (2013) *Development Aid Confronts Politics: The Almost Revolution*. Washington, DC: Brookings Institution Press.

Carstensen, M.B. (2011) 'Ideas are not as stable as political scientists want them to be: a theory of incremental ideational change', *Political Studies*, 59 (3): 596–615.

Carstensen, M.B. and Schmidt, V.A. (2016) 'Power through, over and in ideas: conceptualizing ideational power in discursive institutionalism', *Journal of European Public Policy*, 23 (3): 318–37.

Carter, N. (2018) *The Politics of the Environment: Ideas, Activism, Policy* (3rd edn). Cambridge: Cambridge University Press.

Cerón, A., Ruano, A.L., Sánchez, S., Chew, A.S., Díaz, D., Hernández, A. and Flores, W. (2016) 'Abuse and discrimination towards indigenous people in public health care facilities: experiences from rural Guatemala', *International Journal for Equity in Health*, 15 (1).

Chambers, R. (1983) *Rural Development: Putting the Last First*. Upper Saddle River, NJ: Prentice Hall.

Chambers, R. (1994) 'Paradigm shifts and the practice of participatory research and development'. Academia.

Chambers, R. (1997) 'Responsible well-being: a personal agenda for development, world development', 25 (11): 1743–54.

Chandler, D. (2017) *Peacebuilding: The Twenty Years' Crisis, 1997–2017*. Cham: Springer International Publishing.

Chandra, R. (2010) *Knowledge as Property: Issues in the Moral Grounding of Intellectual Property Rights*. Oxford: Oxford University Press.

Chang, A., Chu, Y-H. and Welsh, B. (2013) 'Southeast Asia: sources of regime support', *Journal of Democracy*, 24 (2): 150–64.

Chang, E. and Golden, M.A. (2010) 'Sources of corruption in authoritarian regimes', *Social Science Quarterly*, 91 (1): 20.

Chang, H.J. (2002). *Kicking Away the Ladder: Development Strategy in Historical Perspective*. London: Anthem Press.

Chang, H.J. (2011) 'Institutions and economic development: theory, policy and history', *Journal of Institutional Economics*, 7 (4): 473–98.

Chant, S. and Sweetman, C. (2012) 'Fixing women or fixing the world? "Smart economics", efficiency approaches, and gender equality in development', *Gender & Development*, 20 (3): 517–29.

Cheeseman, N., Swedlund, H. and O'Brien-Udry, C. (2023) 'Foreign aid withdrawals and suspensions: why, when and are they effective?' *World Development*.

Cheeseman, N. (2015) *Democracy in Africa: Successes, failures, and the struggle for political reform*. Cambridge University Press.

Cheeseman, N., and Fisher, J (2019) *Authoritarian Africa: Repression Resistance and the Power of Ideas*. Oxford: Oxford University Press.

Cheeseman, N. and Klaas, B. (2019) *How to Rig an Election*. New Haven, CT: Yale University Press.

Cheeseman, N., and Peiffer, C. (2022) The Curse of Good Intentions: Why Anticorruption Messaging Can Encourage Bribery. *American Political Science Review*, 116 (3), 1081–1095.

Cheeseman, N., Fisher, J., Hassan, I., Hitchen, J. (2020) 'Social Media Disruption: Nigeria's WhatsApp Politics,' *Journal of Democracy*, 31 (3): 145–159.

Chemouni, B. (2018) 'The political path to universal health coverage: power, ideas and community-based health insurance in Rwanda', *World Development*, 106: 87–98.

Chenery, H.B. (1960) 'Patterns of industrial growth', *The American Economic Review*, 50 (4): 624–54.

Chiba, D, and Heinrich, T. (2019) 'Colonial legacy and foreign aid: decomposing the colonial bias', *International Interactions*, 45 (3): 474–99. Available at: https://doi.org/10.1080/03050629.2019.1593834

Chodak, J. (2016) 'Symbols, slogans and taste in tactics: Creation of collective identity in social movementsi, in V. Yevtukh et al. (eds), *Identities of Central-Eastern European Nations*. Kyiv: Interservice Ltd. pp. 277–297.

Choi, S.Y.P. and Peng, Y. (2016) *Masculine Compromise: Migration, Family, and Gender in China*. Oakland, CA: University of California Press.

Chomsky, N. and Herman, E. (1988) *Manufacturing Consent: The Political Economy of the Mass Media*. London: Random House.

Choudhury, E. and Shamima A. (2002) 'The shifting meaning of governance: public accountability of third sector organizations in an emergent global regime', *International Journal of Public Administration*, 25 (4): 561–88. Available at: https://doi.org/10.1081/PAD-120013256

Chowns, E. (2015) 'Is community management an efficient and effective model of public service delivery? Lessons from the rural water supply sector in Malawi'. *Public Administration and Development*, 35: 263–76.

Christensen, A. and Jensen, S.Q. (2012) 'Doing intersectional analysis: methodological implications for qualitative research'. *NORA – Nordic Journal of Feminist and Gender Research*, 20 (2): 109–25. Available at: https://doi.org/10.1080/08038740.2012.673505

Clark, K. and Rogers, H. (2019) 'Corrupting influence: Purdue & the WHO'. *Report: 'Exposing dangerous opioid manufacturer influence at the World Health Organization'*, 22 May.

Clift, B. (2018) *The IMF and the Politics of Austerity in the Wake of the Global Financial Crisis*. Oxford: Oxford University Press.

Climate Knowledge and Development Network (2022) 'Mobilising finance for community-based resilience: Insights from the voices from the frontline initiative', *Climate Knowledge and Development Network*. Available at: https://cdkn.org/resource/mobilising-finance-community-based-resilience-insights-voices-frontline-initiative

Cloutier, M. et al. (2021) *Social Contracts for Development: Bargaining, Contention, and Social Inclusion in Sub-Saharan Africa*. AFD and World Bank.

Colagrossi, M., Rossignoli, D. and Maggioni, M.A. (2020) 'Does democracy cause growth? A meta-analysis (of 2000 regressions)', *European Journal of Political Economy*, 61, 101824.

Collier, P. and Hoeffler, A. (2004) 'Greed and grievance in civil war', *Oxford Economic Papers*, 56 (4): 563–95.

Collier, R.B. and Collier, D. (1991) *Shaping the Political Arena: Critical Junctures, the Labor Movement, and Regime Dynamics in Latin America*. Princeton, NJ: Princeton University Press.

Collins, P.H. (2019) *Intersectionality as critical social theory*. New York: Duke University Press.

Conley, J. (2022) '"Huge News": Alaska native group secures protections for land eyed by Pebble Mine developers'. *Common Dreams*, 22 December. Available at: www.commondreams.org/news/pebble-mine-alaska (accessed 20 February 2023).

Conn, D. (2022) 'Revealed: Tory peer Michelle Mone secretly received £29m from "VIP lane" PPE firm', *The Guardian*, 23 November. Available at: www.theguardian.com/uk-news/2022/nov/23/revealed-tory-peer-michelle-mone-secretly-received-29m-from-vip-lane-ppe-firm

Cooke, B. (2004) 'Rules of thumb for participatory change agents', in S. Hickey and G. Mohan (eds), *Participation: From Tyranny To Transformation?*, London: Zed Books.

Cooke, B. and Kothari, U. (2001) *Participation: The New Tyranny?* London: Zed Books.

Cooper, F. and Packard, R.M. (1997) *International Development and the Social Sciences: Essays on the History and Politics of Knowledge*. Berkeley, CA: University of California Press.

Copeland, D.C. (1996) 'Economic interdependence and war: a theory of trade expectations', *International Security*, 20 (4): 5–41.

Cornwall, A. (2008) 'Unpacking "participation": models, meanings and practices', *Community Development Journal*, 43 (3): 269–83.

Cox, G.W. and McCubbins, M.D. (1986) 'Electoral politics as a redistributive game', *The Journal of Politics*, 48 (2): 370–89.

Cramer, C. (2002) 'Homo Economicus goes to war: methodological individualism, rational choice and the political economy of war', *World Development*, 30 (11): 1845–64.

Crawford, G., Mai-Bornu, Z. and Landström, K. (2021) 'Decolonising knowledge production on Africa: why it's still necessary and what can be done', *Journal of the British Academy*, 9 (s1): 21–46.

Crenshaw, K. (1991) 'Mapping the margins: intersectionality, identity politics, and violence against women of color', *Stanford Law Review*, 43 (6): 1241–99.

Crenshaw, K.W. (2017) *On Intersectionality: Essential Writings*. New York: The New Press.

Cuervo, A. and Villalonga, B. (2000) 'Explaining the variance in the performance effects of privatisation', *Academy of Management Review*, 25 (3): 581–90.

Cullenward, D. and Victor, D.G. (2020) *Making Climate Policy Work*. Cambridge: Polity Press.

Dados, N. and Connell, R. (2012) 'The Global South'. *Contexts*, 11 (1): 12–13. Available at: https://doi.org/10.1177/1536504212436479

Daher, J. and Moret, E. (2020) 'Invisible sanctions: how over-compliance limits humanitarian work on Syria, challenges of fund transfer for non-profit organizations working on Syria',

IMPACT. Available at: https://impact-csrd.org/reports/Invisible_Sanctions_IMPACT _EN.pdf.

Dahl, R.A. (1957) 'The concept of power', *Systems Research*, 2: 201–15.

Daly, H. (1993) 'Sustainable growth: an impossibility theorem', in H.E. Daly and K.N. Townsend (eds), *Valuing the Earth: Economics, Ecology, Ethics*. Cambridge, MA: The MIT Press. pp. 267–8.

Daly, P., Ninglekhu, S. Hollenbach, P., Barenstein, J.D. and Nguyen, D. (2017) 'Situating local stakeholders within national disaster governance structures: rebuilding urban neighbourhoods following the 2015 Nepal earthquake'. *Environment and Urbanization*, 29 (2): 403–24. Available at: https://doi.org/10.1177/0956247817721403

Danish Institute for Human Rights (2016) *Human Rights Impact Assessment Guidance and Toolbox*. Copenhagen: The Danish Institute for Human Rights.

Daron, A. and Robinson, J.A. (2012) *Why Nations Fail: The Origins of Power, Prosperity, and Poverty*. New York: Crown Business.

Dasandi, N. and Erez, L. (2019) 'The donor's dilemma: international aid and human rights violations', *British Journal of Political Science*, 49 (4): 1431–52.

Dasandi, N. and Erez, L. (2023) 'The flag and the stick: aid suspensions, human rights, and the problem of the complicit public', *World Development*, 168: 106264.

Dasandi, N., Fisher, J., Hudson, D. and van Heerde-Hudson, J. (2021) 'Human rights violations, political conditionality and public attitudes to foreign aid: evidence from survey experiments, *Political Studies*, 70 (3): 603–23.

Dasandi, N., Laws, E., Marquette, H. and Robinson, M. (2019) 'What does the evidence tell us about "thinking and working politically" in development assistance?', *Politics and Governance*, 7 (2): 155–68.

Dasgupta, A. and Beard, V.A. (2007) 'Community driven development, collective action and elite capture in Indonesia', *Development and Change*, 38: 229–49.

Davies, S., Petterson, T. and Öberg, M. (2023) 'Organized violence 1989–2022 and the return of conflicts between states?', *Journal of Peace Research*, 60 (4): 691–708.

de Beauvoir, S. (1949) *Second Sex*. Paris: Librairie Gallimard.

de Coning, C. (2018) 'Adaptive peacebuilding', *International Affairs*, 94 (2): 301–17.

De Mesquita, B.B. and Smith, A. (2009) 'A political economy of aid', *International Organization*, 63 (2): 309–40.

de Sardan, J.P.O. (1999) A Moral Economy of Corruption in Africa? *The Journal of Modern African Studies*, 37(1), 25–52. http://www.jstor.org/stable/161467

De Sardan, J. P. O. (2015) Chapter 2: Practical norms: informal regulations within public bureaucracies (in Africa and beyond). In, Tom De Herdt, Jean-Pierre Olivier de Sardan (eds.), Real Governance and Practical Norms in Sub-Saharan Africa: The game of the rules. Routledge.

De Waal, A. (1996) 'Social contract and deterring famine: first thoughts', *Disasters*, 20 (3): 194–205.

Deckard, F.M. and Auyero, J. (2022) 'Poor people's survival strategies: two decades of research in the Americas', *Annual Review of Sociology*, 48 (1): 373–95.

Decker, C. and McMahon, E. (2020) *The Idea of Development in Africa: A History*. Cambridge: Cambridge University Press.

Delgado, R. and Stefancic, J. (eds) (2000) *Critical Race Theory: The Cutting Edge*. Philadelphia, PA: Temple University Press.

Dell, M. (2010) 'The persistent effects of Peru's mining mita', *Econometrica*, *78* (6): 1863–1903.

Dendere, C. (2021) 'Financing political parties in Africa: the case of Zimbabwe', *The Journal of Modern African Studies*, 59 (3): 295–317.

Dercon, S. (2022) *Gambling on Development: Why Some Countries Win and Others Lose*. NewYork: Hurst & Co.

Dermawan, A. and Sinaga, A.C. (2015) 'Towards REDD+ integrity: opportunities and challenges for Indonesia'. Bergen: Chr. Michelsen Institute, U4, 5: 1–46. Available at: www.cmi.no/publications/5371-towards-redd-integrity-indonesia

Desai, M. (2001) 'Party formation, political power, and the capacity for reform: comparing left parties in Kerala and West Bengal, India, *Social Forces*, 80 (1): 37–60.

Deutsche Welle (2022) 'EU: COP27 agreement "not enough" for the planet' (accessed 30 March 2023).

Development Initiatives (2020) *Global Humanitarian Assistance Report 2020*. Development Initiatives.

Dexter, H. (2007) 'New war, good war, and the war on terror: explaining, excusing, and creating Western neo-interventionism', *Development and Change*, 38 (6): 1055–71.

Diaz-Cayeros, A., Estevez, and Magaloni, B. (2016) 'The political logic of poverty relief', in A. Diaz-Cayeros, F. Estevez and B. Magaloni, *The Political Logic of Poverty Relief: Electoral Strategies and Social Policy in Mexico*. Cambridge: Cambridge University Press.

Dixit, A. and Londregan, J. (1996) 'The determinants of success of special interests in redistributive politics', *The Journal of Politics*, 58 (4).

Dodsworth, S. and Cheeseman, N. (2018) 'The potential and pitfalls of collaborating with development organizations and policy makers in Africa', *African Affairs*, 117 (466): 130–45.

Dolan, C., Baaz, M.E., Barry, T., Gahman, L., Greenidge, A. and Mohamed, A. (2019) 'Wrestling with race and colonialism in Caribbean agriculture: toward a (food) sovereign and (gender) just future', *Geoforum*, 109: 106–10.

Dolan, C., Baaz, M.E., & Stern, M. (2020) 'What is sexual about conflict-related sexual violence? Stories from men and women survivors', *International Affairs*, 96 (5): 1151–1168.

Domar, E.D. (1946) 'Capital expansion, rate of growth, and employment', *Econometrica, Journal of the Econometric Society*, 14 (2): 137–47.

Downs, A. (1957). *An Economic Theory of Democracy*. New York: Harper and Row.

Dreher, A., Sturm, J.-E. and Vreeland, J.R. (2015) 'Politics and IMF conditionality', *Journal of Conflict Resolution*, 59 (1): 120–48.

Dreher, A., Nunnenkamp, P. and Thiele, R. (2011) 'Are "new" donors different? Comparing the allocation of bilateral aid between nonDAC and DAC donor countries', *World Development*, 39 (11): 1950–68.

Dreier, S. and Lake, M. (2019) 'Institutional legitimacy in sub-Saharan Africa', *Democratization*, 26 (7): 1194–215.

Drèze, J. and Sen, A. (2002) 'The practice of democracy', in J. Drèze and A. Sen (eds.), *India: Development and Participation*. Oxford: Oxford University Press.

Dubois, M., Wake, C., Sturridge, S. and Bennet, C. (2015) 'The Ebola response in West Africa: exposing the politics and culture of international aid'. London: Overseas Development Institute. Available at: www.odi.org/publications/9956-ebola-response-west-africa-exposing-politics-culture-international-aid.

Duffield, M. (2007) *Development, Security, and Unending War: Governing the World of People.* Cambridge: Polity.

Duffield, M. (2014) *Global Governance and the New Wars: The Merging of Development and Security.* London: Zed Books.

Duffield, M. and Hewitt, V. (2013) *Empire, Development & Colonialism: The Past in the Present.* Martlesham: Boydell & Brewer.

Duffy, R. (2014) 'Interactive elephants: nature, tourism and neoliberalism', *Annals of Tourism Research*, 44: 88–101.

Dukalskis, A. and Patane, C. (2019) 'Justifying power: when autocracies talk about themselves and their opponents', *Contemporary Politics*, 25 (4): 457–78.

Dunning, T. (2004) 'Conditioning the effects of aid: cold war politics, donor credibility, and democracy in Africa', *International Organization*, 58 (2): 409–23.

Dutta, N., Leeson, P.T. and Williamson, C.R. (2013) 'The amplification effect: foreign aid's impact on political institutions', *Kyklos*, 66 (2): 208–28.

Eaton, J., Krishna, A., Sudi, C., George, J., Magomba, C., Eckman, A., Houck, F. and Taukobong, H. (2021) Gendered Social Norms Change in Water Governance Structures Through Community Facilitation: Evaluation of the UPWARD Intervention in Tanzania. *Frontiers in Sociology*, 6, 672989.

Edmonds, E.V., Topalova, P. and Pavcnik, N. (2009) 'Child labor and schooling in a globalizing world: some evidence from urban India', *Journal of the European Economic Association*, 7 (2–3): 498–507.

EDMW FTW (2019) *LKY – 'Whoever governs Singapore must have that iron in him'*, EDMW FTW. Available at: www.youtube.com/watch?v=O_cS1T65B5g

Edwards, M. and Hulme, D. (eds) (1996) *Beyond the Magic Bullet: NGO Performance and Accountability in the Post-Cold War World.* Kumarian Press Books on International Development. West Hartford, CT: Kumarian Press.

Eichert, D. (2019 'Homosexualization revisited: an audience-focused theorization of wartime male sexual violence'. *International Feminist Journal of Politics*, 21 (3): 409–433.

Elliott, J.A. (2013) *An Introduction to Sustainable Development* (4th edn). London: Routledge.

El Nour, S., Elaydi, H., and Hussein, H. (2021) 'Thirst revolution: practices of contestation and mobilisation in rural Egypt.' *Contemporary Levant*, 6 (2): 169–184.

Engels, F. and Marx, K. (2004) *The Communist Manifesto.* London: Penguin.

Erikson, E.H. (1968) *Identity Youth and Crisis* (No. 7). London: W.W. Norton & Company.

Escobar, A. (2011) *Encountering Development: The Making and Unmaking of the Third World.* Princeton, NJ: Princeton University Press.

Estivill, J. (2003) 'Concepts and strategies for combating social exclusion: an overview'. Geneva: International Labour Organisation.

Estrin, S. and Pelletier, A. (2018) 'Privatisation in developing countries: what are the lessons of recent experience?', *The World Bank Research Observer*, 33 (1): 65–102.

Eyben R., (2004) 'Inequality as Process and Experience' in Eyben R., and Lovett J., *Political and Social Inequality: A Review*, IDS Development Bibliography 20, Institute of Development Studies, Brighton, pp 32–39.

Feng, K., Davis, S.J., Sun, L., Li, X., Guan, D., Liu, W., Liu, Z. and Hubacek, K. (2013) 'Outsourcing CO2 within China', *Proceedings of the National Academy of Sciences*, 110 (28): 11654–11659.

Ferguson, J. (1990) *The Anti-politics Machine: Development, Depoliticization, and Bureaucratic Power in Lesotho*. Minneapolois, MN: University of Minnesota Press.

Ferraz, C. and Finan, F. (2011) 'Electoral accountability and corruption: evidence from the audits of local governments', *American Economic Review*, 101 (4): 1274–1311.

Firchow, P. (2013) 'Must our communities bleed to receive social services? Development projects and collective reparations schemes in Colombia', *Journal of Peacebuilding & Development*, 8 (3): 50–63.

Fischer, A.M. (2018) *Poverty as ideology: Rescuing social justice from global development agendas*. Bloomsbury Publishing.

Fisher, J. (2013) 'Some more reliable than others: image management, donor perceptions and the global war on terror in East African diplomacy', *Journal of Modern African Studies*, 51 (1): 1–31.

Fisher, J. (2020) *East Africa after Liberation: Conflict, Security, and the State since the 1980s*. Cambridge: Cambridge University Press.

Fisher, J. and Anderson, D.M. (2015) 'Authoritarianism and the securitization of development in Africa', *International Affairs*, 91 (1): 131–51.

Fisma, R. and Golden, M. (2017) *Corruption: What Everyone Needs to Know*. Oxford: Oxford University Press.

FLIGSTEIN, N. (1997) Social Skill and Institutional Theory. *American Behavioral Scientist*, 40 (4), 397–405.

Flückiger, M., Ludwig, M. and Önder, A.S. (2019) 'Ebola and state legitimacy', *The Economic Journal*, 129 (621): 2064–89.

Foucault, M. (1970) 'The archaeology of knowledge', *Social Science Information*, 9 (1): 175–85.

Foucault, M. (1982) 'The subject and power', *Critical Inquiry*, 8, 777–95.

Fox, J.A. (2015) 'Social accountability: what does the evidence really say?', *World Development*, 72: 346–61.

Franck, R., and Rainer, I. (2012) Does the Leader's Ethnicity Matter? Ethnic Favoritism, Education, and Health in Sub-Saharan Africa, *The American Political Science Review*, 106 (2): 294–325.

Franke, R. and Chasin, B. (1992) 'Kerala state, India: radical reform as development', *International Journal of Health Services*, 22 (1): 139–56.

Freedom House. (2023) 'Rwanda: Freedom in the World 2023'. https://freedomhouse.org/country/rwanda/freedom-world/2023

Fukuda-Parr, S. (2019) 'Keeping Out Extreme Inequality from the SDG Agenda – The Politics of Indicators', *Global Policy*, 10 (S1): 61–69.

Fukuyama, F. (2011) *The Origins of Political Order*. New York: Farrar, Straus and Giroux.

Fukuyama, F. (2014) *Political Order and Political Decay: From the Industrial Revolution to the Globalization of Democracy*. London: Profile Books.

Fung, A. and Wright, E.O. (eds) (2003) *Deepening Democracy: Institutional Innovations in Empowered Participatory Governance*. New York: Verso.

Gabor, D. (2010) 'The international monetary fund and its new economics', *Development and Change*, 41 (5): 805–30.

Galtung, J. (1969) 'Violence, peace, and peace research', *Journal of Peace Research*, 6 (3): 167–91.

Gani, J.K. and Marshall, J. (2022) 'The impact of colonialism on policy and knowledge production in international relations', *International Affairs*, 98 (1): 5–22.

Gans-Morse, J., & Nichter, S. (2021) *Would You Sell Your Vote? American Politics Research*, 49 (5), 452–463. https://doi.org/10.1177/1532673X211013565

Gaventa, J. (1980) *Power and Powerlessness: Quiescence and Rebellion in an Appalachian Valley*. Oxford: Clarendon Press.

Gaventa, J. (2006) 'Triumph, deficit or contestation? Deepening the "deepening democracy" debate'. Institute of Development Studies. IDS Working Paper, 264.

Gaventa, J., Joshi, A., Anderson, C. (2023) 'Citizen action for accountability in challenging contexts: what have we learned?', *Development Policy Review*, 41 (1).

Geertz, C. (1973) *The Interpretation of Cultures* (Vol. 5019). New York: Basic Books.

Geertz, C. (1994) 'Ideology as a cultural system', in T. Eagleton (ed.), Ideology. London: Routledge.

Geneva Academy (2023) *Today's Armed Conflicts*. Available at: https://geneva-academy.ch/galleries/today-s-armed-conflicts (accessed 5 April 2023).

George, C. (2007) 'Consolidating authoritarian rule: calibrated coercion in Singapore', *The Pacific Review*, 20 (2): 127–45.

Ghani, E. and Iyer, L. (2010) *Conflict and Development: Lessons from South Asia*, Economic Premise No. 31. Washington, DC: World Bank. Available at: https://openknowledge.worldbank.org/entities/publication/e263c247-34fa-59f9-8ff9-7c2b1af97323 (accessed 5 April 2023).

Ghani, A. and Lockhart, C. (2008) *Fixing Failed States: A Framework for Rebuilding a Fractured World*. Oxford: Oxford University Press.

Gibbs, J.P. (1965) 'Norms: the problem of definition and classification', *American Journal of Sociology*, 70: 586–94.

Giddens, A. (1984) *The Constitution of Society: Outline of the Theory of Structuration*. Cambridge: Polity Press.

Gill, S. and Law, D. (1988) *The Global Political Economy: Perspectives, Problems, and Policies*. Baltimore, MD: Johns Hopkins University Press.

Gingerich, T.R. and Cohen, M.J. (2015) 'Turning the humanitarian system on its head: saving lives and livelihoods by strengthening local capacity and shifting leadership to local actors', Oxfam Research Reports. Washington, DC: Oxfam.

Giuliano, P. and Ruiz-Arranz, M. (2009) 'Remittances, financial development, and growth', *Journal of Development Economics*, 90 (1): 144–52.

Goffman, E. (1959) *The Presentation of Self in Everyday Life*. New York: Anchor Books.

Golden, M. and Min, B. (2013) 'Distributive politics around the world', *Annual Review of Political Science*, 16 (1): 73–99.

Goldfajn, I., Martínez, L. and Valdés, R.O. (2021) 'Washington consensus in Latin America: from raw model to straw man', *Journal of Economic Perspectives*, 35 (3): 109–32.

Goldsmith, E. (1997) 'Development as colonialism', *The Ecologist*, 27 (2): 69–77.

Goopta, N. (2000) 'Sex Workers in Calcutta and the Dynamics of Collective Action: Political Activism, Community Identity and Group Behaviour', Working Papers No. 185, Helsinki: UNU World Institute for Development Economics Research (UNU/ WIDER).

Green, E. (2015) 'Decentralization and development in contemporary Uganda', *Regional & Federal Studies*, 25 (5): 491–508.

Greenfeld, L. (2003) *The Spirit of Capitalism: Nationalism and Economic Growth*. Cambridge, MA: Cambridge University Press.

Greenhill, B. (2010) 'The company you keep: international socialization and the diffusion of human rights norms', *International Studies Quarterly*, 54 (1): 127–45.

Greenpeace (2023) 'Tracking the cost of air pollution'. Available at: www.greenpeace.org/southeastasia/campaign/tracking-cost-air-pollution/ (accessed 17 January 2023).

Grindle, M. (2001) 'In Quest of the Political: The Political Economy of Development Policy Making' in G. Meier and J.E. Stiglitz, eds., *Frontiers of Development Economics. The Future in Perspective*. New York: Oxford University Press, pp. 345–380.

Grindle, M. (2009) *Going Local: Decentralization, Democratization, and the Promise of Good Governance*. Princeton, NJ: Princeton University Press.

Grossman, S., Phillips, J. and Rosenzweig, L.R. (2018) 'Opportunistic accountability: state–society bargaining over shared interests', *Comparative Political Studies*, 51 (8): 979–1011.

Guardian, The (2020) '#EndSARS: youths reshaping protest as tool for socio-political change'. Available at: https://guardian.ng/saturday-magazine/endsars-youths-reshaping-protest-as-tool-for-socio-political-change/ (accessed 28 March 2023).

Gurgur, T. and Shah, A. (2005) *Localization and Corruption: Panacea or Pandora's Box?* Vol. 3486. World Bank Publications.

Gurr, T.R. (1970) *Why Men Rebel*. Princeton: Princeton University Press.

Gurung, A., Bista, R., Karki, R., Shrestha, S., Uprety, D. and Oh, S-E. (2013) 'Community-based forest management and its role in improving forest conditions in Nepal', *Small-scale Forestry*, 12: 377–88. DOI 10.1007/s11842-012-9217-z

Haan, A.d. (1998), 'SocialExclusion': An Alternative Concept for the Study of Deprivation?. *IDS Bulletin*, 29: 10–19.

Habermas, J. (1989) The Structural Transformation of the Public Sphère: An Inquiry into a Category of Bourgeois Society. Cambridge: MIT Press.

Habyarimana, J, Humphreys, M., Posner, D., and Weinstein, J. (2007) Why Does Ethnic Diversity Under- mine Public Goods Provision?, *American Political Science Review*, 101 (4): 709–25.

Haley, U.C.V. and Haley, G.T. (2013) *Subsidies to Chinese Industry: State Capitalism, Business Strategy, and Trade Policy*. New York: Oxford University Press.

Hall, P.A. (2010) *Historical Institutionalism in Rationalist and Sociological Perspective: In Explaining Institutional Change: Ambiguity, Agency, and Power*. New York: Cambridge University Press.

Hall, P.A. and Taylor, R.C.R. (1996) 'Political science and the three new institutionalisms', *Political Studies*, 44 (5): 936–57.

Hall, S. (1996) 'Who needs "identity"?, in S. Hall and P. Du Gay (eds), *Questions of Cultural Identity*. London: Sage. pp. 15–30.

Han, F.K., Fernandez, W. and Tan, S. (2015) *Lee Kuan Yew: The Man and His Ideas*. Singapore: Singapore and Straights Times Press.

Hanchey, J.N. (2020) 'Decolonizing aid in *Black Panther*', *Review of Communication*, 20 (3): 260–8. Available at: https://doi.org/10.1080/15358593.2020.1778070

Hanlon, J., Barrientos, A., & Hulme, D. (2012) *Just give money to the poor: The development revolution from the global South*. Boulder, Colarado: Kumarian Press.

Hansen, B., T., and Stepputat, F. (eds) (2001) *States of imagination*. Durham [N. C.]: Duke University Press.

Hardin, G. (1968) 'The tragedy of the Commons', *Science*, 162 (3859): 1243–8.

Harding, R. and Stasavage, D. (2014) 'What democracy does (and doesn't do) for basic services: school fees, school inputs, and African elections', *The Journal of Politics*, 76 (1): 229–45.

Harrod, R.F. (1939) 'An essay in dynamic theory', *The Economic Journal*, 49 (193): 14–33.

Hasan, Z., Huq, A.Z. and Nussbaum, M.C. (eds) (2018) *The Empire of Disgust: Prejudice, Discrimination, and Policy in India and the US*. Oxford: Oxford University Press.

Hay, C. (2002). *Political Analysis*. Basingstoke: Palgrave.

Hay, C. (2011) 'Ideas and the construction of interests', in D. Béland and R.H. Cox (eds), *Ideas and Politics in Social Science Research*. Oxford: Oxford University Press.

Hay, C., and Wincott, D. (1998) 'Structure, Agency and Historical Institutionalism', *Political Studies*, 46 (5) p51–957.

Heckscher, E.F. (1995) *Mercantilism*. London: Routledge.

Heinrich, T., Kobayashi, Y. and Bryant, K.A. (2016) 'Public opinion and foreign aid cuts in economic crises', *World Development*, 77: 66–79.

Heinrich, T., & Kobayashi, Y. (2020) How Do People Evaluate Foreign Aid To 'Nasty' Regimes? *British Journal of Political Science*, 50 (1), 103–127.

Heinrich, T., Kobayashi, Y. and Long, L. (2018) 'Voters get what they want (when they pay attention): human rights, policy benefits, and foreign aid', *International Studies Quarterly*, 62 (1): 195–207.

Heller, P., Harilal, K.N. and Chaudhuri, S. (2007) 'Building local democracy: evaluating the impact of decentralization in Kerala, India', *World Development*, 35 (4): 626–48.

Helmke, G., and Levitsky, S. (2004) 'Informal Institutions and Comparative Politics: A Research Agenda', *Perspectives on politics*, 2 (4), 725–740.

Herd, P. and Moynihan, D. (2018) *Administrative Burden: Policymaking by Other Means*. New York: Russell Sage Foundation.

Hicken, A. (2011) 'Clientelism', *Annual Review of Political Science*, 14: 289–310.

Hickey, S. and Mohan, G. (2004) Participation–From Tyranny to Transformation? *Exploring New Approaches to Participation in Development*. London: Zed Books.

Hickey, S. and Mohan, G. (2005) 'Relocating participation within a radical politics of development,' *Development and Change*, 36 (2): 237–62.

Hilgers, T. (ed.) (2012) *Clientelism in Everyday Latin American Politics*. New York: Palgrave Macmillan.

Hobbes, T. (2017) *Leviathan*. London: e-book. Available at: https://ebookcentral.proquest.com/lib/bham/detail.action?docID=5302410

Hoffman, L.K. and Patel, R.N. (2021) 'Pass-mark bribery in Nigerian schools: strong incentives and weak consequences for corruption', *Chatham House Briefing Paper, Africa Program*, September. Available at: www.chathamhouse.org/sites/default/files/2021-09/2021-08-27-pass-mark-bribery-nigeria-hoffmann-patel.pdf

Hogendorn, J.S. and Scott, K.M. (1981) 'The East African groundnut scheme: lessons of a large-scale agricultural failure', *African Economic History*, 10: 81–115.

Holifield, R., Chakraborty, J. and Walker, G. (eds) (2017) *The Routledge Handbook of Environmental Justice* (1st edn). Abingdon: Routledge. Available at: https://doi.org/10.4324/9781315678986

Holzgrefe, J.L. and Keohane, R.O. (2003) *Humanitarian Intervention: Ethical, Legal and Political Dilemmas*. Cambridge: Cambridge University Press.

Homedes, N. and Ugalde, A. (2005) 'Why neoliberal health reforms have failed in Latin America', *Health Policy*, 71 (1): 83–96.

Honig, D. (2018) *Navigation by Judgment: Why and When Top down Management of Foreign Aid Doesn't Work*. Oxford: Oxford University Press.

Horn, J. (2013) *Gender and Social Movements: Overview Report*. BRIDGE, UK. Institute of Development Studies.

Horner, R. (2020) 'Towards a new paradigm of global development? Beyond the limits of international development', *Progress in Human Geography*, 44 (3): 415–36.

Horner, R. and Hulme, D. (2019), Global Development, Converging Divergence and Development Studies: A Rejoinder. *Development and Change*, 50: 495–510. https://doi.org/10.1111/dech.12496

Hossain, N. and Hickey, S. (2019) The problem of education quality in developing countries. *The Politics of Education in Developing Countries: From Schooling to Learning*. S. Hickey and N. Hossain. Oxford, Oxford University Press.

Haraway D (1988) 'Situated knowledges: the science question in feminism and the privilege of partial perspective', *Feminist Studies*, 14(3): 575–599.

House of Commons (2023) *Military Assistance to Ukraine since the Russian Invasion*. London: House of Commons.

Hudson, D. and Dasandi, N. (2014) 'The global governance of development: development financing, good governance and the domestication of poverty', *Handbook of the International Political Economy of Governance*. Cheltenham: Edward Elgar. pp. 238–58.

Hudson, D. and Leftwich, A. (2014) 'From political economy to political analysis, research paper 25'. Developmental Leadership Program, Birmingham, UK.

Hudson, D. and vanHeerde-Hudson, J. (2012) 'A mile wide and an inch deep': surveys of public attitudes towards development aid. *International Journal of Development Education and Global Learning*, 4 (1), 5–23.

Hudson, D., McLoughlin, C., Marquette, H. and Roche, C. (2018) *Inside the Black Box of Political Will*. DLP Report.

Hudson, D., Laehn, N.S., Dasandi, N. and vanHeerde-Hudson, J. (2019) 'Making and unmaking cosmopolitans: an experimental test of the mediating role of emotions in international development appeals'. *Social Science Quarterly*, 100 (3): 544–64.

Hudson, J.D., Morini, P., Clarke, H. and Stewart, M.C. (2020) 'Not one, but many "publics": public engagement with global development in France, Germany, Great Britain, and the United States', *Development in Practice*, 30 (6): 795–808.

Hudson, D.J., Hudson, F., Raposo, T., Oh, S., Morini, P. (2023) 'Explaining public support for foreign aid projects: evidence from France, Germany, Great Britain and the United States'. Paper presented at the American Political Science Association 2023, Los Angeles, CA.

Hurst, R., Tidwell, T. and Hawkins, D. (2017) 'Down the rathole? Public support for US foreign aid', International Studies Quarterly, 61 (2): 442–54.

Ibrahim, M. (2005) 'The securitization of migration: a racial discourse 1', *International Migration*, 43 (5): 163–87.

ICCCD. (n.d.). *Locally Led Adaptation (LLA) Programme*. International Centre for Climate Change and Development. Retrieved May 3, 2023, from https://www.icccad.net/programmes/lla-programme/

Ide, T., Bruch, C., Carius, A., Conca, K., Dabelko, G.D., Matthew, R. and Weinthal, E. (2021) 'The past and future(s) of environmental peacebuilding', *International Affairs* 97(1): 1–16.

Igoe, J. and Brockington, D. (2007) 'Neoliberal conservation: a brief introduction', *Conservation and Society*, 5 (4): 432–49. Available at: www.jstor.org/stable/26392898

ILO (International Labour Organization) (2022) Walk Free and the International Organization for Migration (2022) *Global Estimates of Modern Slavery: Forced Labour and Forced Marriage*. ILO: Geneva.

ILO (International Labour Organization) (2022) *Global Estimates of Modern Slavery Forced Labour and Forced Marriage*. ILO: Geneva.

IMF (International Monetary Fund) (2019) 'Benin: harnessing the power of economic diversification', speech by Christine Lagarde, IMF Managing Director Chamber of Commerce. Available at: www.imf.org/en/News/Articles/2017/12/11/sp121117-md-benin-speech

IMF (2021) 'International monetary fund: inflation rate: average consumer prices'. Available at: www.imf.org/external/datamapper/PCPIPCH@WEO/WEOWORLD/VEN/MEQ/LBN

IMF (2023) *'IMF executive directors and voting power'*. Available at: www.imf.org/en/About/executive-board/eds-voting-power

IMF (2023a) 'IMF members' quotas and voting power, and IMF Board of Governors. Available at: www.imf.org/en/About/executive-board/members-quotas

IMF (2023b) 'International Monetary Fund Lending'. Available at: www.imf.org/en/About/Factsheets/IMF-Lending

Independent Commission on Aid Effectiveness (2022) 'Review of the UK's approach to democracy and human rights: literature review'. ICAI.

International Growth Centre (2018) Collier, C., Besley, T. and Khan, A. (2018) 'Escaping the fragility trap'.

International Press Institute (2013) 'Use with care: a reporter's glossary of loaded language in the Israeli–Palestinian conflict'. Available at: https://ipi.media/use-with-care-reporters-glossary-of-loaded-language-in-the-israeli-palestinian-conflict/ (accessed 1 May 2023).

International Rescue Committee (IRC) (2007) *Mortality in the Democratic Republic of Congo: An Ongoing Crisis*. New York: IRC.

IQAir (2023) 'Air quality in Delhi'. Available at: www.iqair.com/india/delhi (accessed 17 January 2023).

Irawan, S., Tacconi, L. and Ring, I. (2013) 'Stakeholders' incentives for land-use change and REDD+: the case of Indonesia', *Ecological Economics*, 87: 75–83.

Isbell, T. (2022) 'Footing the bill? Less legitimacy, more avoidance mark African views on taxation', Afrobarometer Policy Paper No. 78. Available at: www.afrobarometer.org/wp-content/uploads/2022/02/pp78-pap6-less_legitimacy_more_avoidance_mark_africans_views_on_taxation-afrobarometer_policy_paper-28jan22.pdf (accessed 5 April 2023).

Islam, Md. S. (2013) *Development, Power, and the Environment: Neoliberal Paradox in the Age of Vulnerability*. New York: Routledge.

Ismail, O. and Olonisakinm F. (2021) 'Why do youth participate in violence in Africa? A review of evidence, conflict, security & development', *Conflict, Security & Development*, 21 (3): 371–99.

Jackson, J. et al. (2022) 'Fear and legitimacy in São Paulo, Brazil: police–citizen relations in a high violence, high fear city', *Law & Society Review*, 56 (1): 122–45.

Jackson, P. and Bakrania, S. (2018) 'Is the future of SSR non-linear?', *Journal of Intervention and Statebuilding*, 12 (1): 11–30.

Jaffrelot, C. (1999) *The Hindu Nationalist Movement and Indian Politics: 1925 to the 1990s: Strategies of Identity-building, Implantation and Mobilisation'*. Delhi: Penguin Books India.

Jahnke, B. and Weisser, R.A. (2019) How does petty corruption affect tax morale in Sub-Saharan Africa? *European Journal of Political Economy*, Volume 60, December 2019, 101751. https://doi.org/10.1016/j.ejpoleco.2018.09.003

Jakimow, T. (2016) 'Clinging to hope through education: the consequences of hope for rural laborers in Telangana, India, *Ethos*, 44 (1): 11–31.

Jalal, A. (1995) *Democracy and Authoritarianism in South Asia: A Comparative and Historical Perspective (Contemporary South Asia)*. Cambridge: Cambridge University Press.

Jatam (2019) '2019 election is driven by mining and energy's business interests'. Available at: www.jatam.org/2019-election-is-driven-by-mining-and-energy-s-business-interest/

Jauregui, B. (2016) *Provisional Authority: Police, Order, and Security in India*. Chicago: University of Chicago Press.

Jefferson, T. (2020) 'Sponsorship bias in clinical trials: growing menace or dawning realisation?', *Journal of the Royal Society of Medicine*, 113 (4): 148–57.

Jeffrey, R. (1992) *Politics, Women and Well-Being: How Kerala Became a Model*. Basingstoke: Palgrave Macmillan.

Jewett, C. (2023) 'Sacklers gave millions to institution that advises on opioid policy', *The New York Times*, 23 April.

Johnson, C. (1995) *Japan, Who Governs?: The Rise of the Developmental State*. W.W. Norton & Company.

Johnson, C. (2001) 'Local democracy, democratic decentralisation and rural development: theories, challenges and options for policy', *Development Policy Review*, 19 (4): 521–32.

Jordan, W.D. (1974) *The white man's burden: Historical origins of racism in the United States*. New York: Galaxy Books

Kabeer, N. (1999) 'Resources, agency, achievements: reflections on the measurement of women's empowerment', *Development and Change,* 30 (3): 435–64.

Kagawa, R.C., Anglemyer, A., & Montagu, D. (2012). The scale of faith based organization participation in health service delivery in developing countries: systemic review and meta-analysis. *PloS one*, 7 (11), e48457.

Kaldor, M. (1999) *New and Old Wars: Organized Violence in a Global Era*. Stanford, CA: Stanford University Press.

Kaldor, M. (2013) 'In defence of new wars', *Stability*, 2 (1): 1–16.

Kandil, H. (2012) 'Why did the Egyptian middle class march to Tahrir Square?', *Mediterranean Politics*, 17 (2): 197–215.

Kannan, K.P. (2022) 'Kerala "model" of development revisited: a sixty-year assessment of successes and failures', Centre for Development Studies Thiruvananthapuram, Working Paper #510.

Kantola, J. and Squires, J. (2012) 'From state feminism to market feminism?', *International Political Science Review*, 33 (4): 382–400.

Kaplan, O. and Nussio, E. (2018) 'Explaining recidivism of ex-combatants in Colombia', *The Journal of Conflict Resolution*, 62 (1): 64–93.

Kasfir, N. (2005) 'Guerrillas and civilian participation: the national resistance army in Uganda, 1981–1986, *Journal of Modern African Studies*, 43 (2): 271–96.

Keefer, P. and Khemani, S. (2005) 'Democracy, public expenditures, and the poor: understanding political incentives for providing public services', *The World Bank Research Observer*, 20 (1): 1–27, Spring. Available at: https://doi.org/10.1093/wbro/lki002

Keen, D. (2012) 'Greed and grievance in civil war', *International Affairs*, 88 (4): 757–77.

Keeves, J.P., Lietz, P., Gregory, K. and Darmawan, I.G.H. (2006) 'Some problems with analysing cross-national survey data', *International Education Journal*, 7 (2): 110–126.

Kelsall, T. (2011) 'Going with the grain in African development?', *Development Policy Review*, 29: 223–51.

Kelsall, T., Schulz, N., Ferguson, W.D., vom Hau, M., Hickey, S. and Levy, B. (2022) *Political Settlements and Development Theory, Evidence, Implications*. Oxford: Oxford University Press.

Khan, M. (2017) 'Political settlements and the analysis of institutions', *African Affairs*, 117 (469): 636–55.

Khanikar, S. (2018) *State, Violence, and Legitimacy in India*. Oxford: Oxford University Press.

Khetpal, V. (2021) 'The U.S. needs to stop hoarding vaccines immediately', *Slate*. 12 March. Available at: https://slate.com/technology/2021/03/covid-variants-vaccine-nationalism-us-share-supply-now.html

Khoury, R.B. and Scott, E.K.M. Scott (2023) 'Going local without localization: power and humanitarian response in the Syrian War', *Review and Resubmit*.

Kuhn, T.S. (1962) The structure of scientific revolutions. Chicago: Chicago University Press.

Kim, H. (2022) 'The emotional dimensions of North Korean politics through the lens of historical institutionalism', *Journal of Contemporary Eastern Asia*, 21 (2).

Kim, H.J., Ahn, Y.S. and Lee, S.G. (2001) 'Health development experience in North and South Korea', *Asia Pacific Journal of Public Health*, 13: S5–S57.

Kimura, M. (2003) 'The emergence of the middle classes and political change in the Philippines', *The Developing Economies*, 41 (2): 264–84.

Kindersley, N. and Rolandsen, Ø. (2019) 'Who are the civilians in the wars of South Sudan?', *Security Dialogue*, 50 (5): 383–97.

Kindleberger, C.P. (1975) 'The rise of free trade in Western Europe', *The Journal of Economic History*, 35 (1): 20–55.

King, S. and Hickey, S. (2017) 'Building democracy from below: lessons from Western Uganda', *Journal of Development Studies*, 53 (10): 1584–99.

Kitschelt, H.P. (1986) 'Political Opportunity Structures and Political Protest: Anti-Nuclear Movements in Four Democracies.' *British Journal of Political Science*, 16 (1): 57–85.

Kitschelt, H. and Wilkinson, S. (2007) 'Patrons, clients and policies: patterns of democratic accountability and political competition', Cambridge: Cambridge University Press.

Klein, N. (2015) *This Changes Everything: Capitalism vs. the Climate*. London: Penguin Books.

Klitgaard, R. (1988) *Controlling Corruption*. University of California Press. http://www.jstor.org/stable/10.1525/j.ctt1pnj3b

KNOMAD (2022) 'Remittances brave global headwinds, special focus: climate migration. Migration and development brief'. Available at: www.knomad.org/publication/migration-and-development-brief-37

Koch, I. (2019) *Personalizing the State: An Anthropology of Law, Politics, and Welfare in Austerity Britain*. Oxford: Oxford University Press.

Kohli, A. (2004) *State-directed Development: Political Power and Industrialization in the Global Periphery*. Cambridge: Cambridge University Press.

Kohn, M. and McBride, K. (2011) *Political Theories of Decolonization: Postcolonialism and the Problem of Foundations*. Oxford: Oxford University Press.

Kothari, R. (2005) *Rethinking Democracy*. New Delhi: Orient Longman.

Kothari, U. (2006) 'An agenda for thinking about "race" in development', *Progress in Development Studies*, 6 (1): 9–23.

Kothari, U. and Klein, E. (2023) *Advanced Introduction to Critical Global Development*. Cheltenham: Edward Elgar.

Kramon, E. (2019) Ethnic group institutions and electoral clientelism. *Party Politics*, 25 (3), 435–447. https://doi.org/10.1177/1354068817728212

Kramon, E., and Posner, D., (2013) Who Benefits from Distributive Politics? How the Outcome One Studies Affects the Answer One Gets, *Perspectives on Politics*, 11 (2): 461–474.

Krampe, F. (2016) 'Empowering peace: service provision and state legitimacy in Nepal's peace-building process', *Conflict, Security & Development*, 16 (1): 53–73.

Krauss, J. (2018) 'Decolonising development – what, how, by whom and for whom?', *Decolonising Development*, 20 November. Available at: http://blog.gdi.manchester.ac.uk/decolonising-development/

Kreps, S., Lushenko, P. and Raman, S. (2022) 'Biden can reduce civilian casualties during US drone strikes. Here's how'. Washington, DC: Brookings Institution. Available www.brookings.edu/articles/biden-can-reduce-civilian-casualties-during-us-drone-strikes-heres-how/ (accessed 5 April 2023).

Kuada, J. (2009) 'Gender, social networks, and entrepreneurship in Ghana', *Journal of African Business*, 10 (1): 85–103.

Kuada, J. (2015) *Private Enterprise-Led Economic Development in Sub-Saharan Africa: The Human Side of Growth*. Springer.

Kwon, J. (2019) CNN: 'South Korea's young men are fighting against feminism'. 23 September. Available at: https://edition.cnn.com/2019/09/21/asia/korea-angry-young-men-intl-hnk/index.html

Lang, V. (2021) 'The economics of the democratic deficit: the effect of IMF programs on inequality', *The Review of International Organizations*, 16 (3): 599–623. Available at: https://doi.org/10.1007/s11558-020-09405-x

Langdon, J. (2013) 'Decolonising development studies: Reflections on critical pedagogies in action', *Canadian Journal of Development Studies/Revue Canadienne d'études Du Développement*, 34 (3): 384–99.

Lange, M., Jeong, T. and Amasyali, E. (2021) 'The colonial origins of ethnic warfare: re-examining the impact of communalizing colonial policies in the British and French empires', *International Journal of Comparative Sociology*, 62 (2): 141–65.

Laplante, L.J. (2007) 'On the indivisibility of rights: truth commissions, reparations, and the right to develop', *Yale Human Rights & Development. Law Journal*, 10: 141.

Lasswell, H.D. (1958) *Politics: Who Gets What, When, How*. Cleveland: World Publishing Company.

Laws, E. and Marquette, H. (2018) 'Thinking and working politically: reviewing the evidence on the integration of politics into development practice over the past decade', *TWP Community of Practice*. University of Birmingham.

Lawson, C., & Greene, K.F. (2014) Making Clientelism Work: How Norms of Reciprocity Increase Voter Compliance. *Comparative Politics*, 47 (1), 61–77. http://www.jstor.org/stable/43664343

Lee, H. (2015) *The Girl with Seven Names: A North Korean Defector's Story*. Glasgow: William Collins.

Leeson, P.T. (2014) 'Pirates, prisoners, and preliterates: anarchic context and the private enforcement of law'. *European Journal of Law and Economics*, 37: 365–379.

Leftwich, A. (2010) 'Beyond institutions: rethinking the role of leaders, elites and coalitions in the institutional formation of developmental states and strategies', *Forum for Development Studies*, 37 (1): 93–111.

Levi, M. (2006) 'Presidential address: why we need a new theory of government', *Perspectives on Politics*, 4 (1), 5–19.

Levi, M. (2018) 'The who, what, and why of performance-based legitimacy', *Journal of Intervention and Statebuilding*, 12 (4): 603–10.

Levi, M., Sacks, A. and Tyler, T. (2009) 'Conceptualizing legitimacy, measuring legitimating beliefs', *American Behavioral Scientist*, 53 (3): 354–75.

Levitsky, S. and Way, L.A. (2002) 'Elections without democracy: the rise of competitive authoritarianism', *Journal of Democracy*, 13 (2): 51–65.

Levitt, P. and Lamba-Nieves, D. (2011) 'Social remittances revisited', *Journal of Ethnic and Migration Studies*, 37 (1): 1–22.

Levy, B. (2014) *Working with the Grain: Integrating Governance and Growth in Development Strategies*. Oxford: Oxford University Press.

Liberman, R., C. (2000) 'Ideas, Institutions, and Political Order: Explaining Political Change', *American Political Science Review*, 96 (4) 697–712.

Lijphart, A. (1999) *Patterns of Democracy: Government Forms and Performance in Thirty-six Countries*. New Haven, CT: Yale University Press.

Lindbeck, A. and Weibull, J.W. (1987) 'Balanced-budget redistribution as the outcome of political competition', *Public Choice*, 52 (3): 273–97.

Lindberg, S.I. (2013) 'Have the cake and eat it: the rational voter in Africa', *Party Politics*, 19 (6): 945–61.

Lipset, S.M. (1959) 'Some social requisites of democracy: economic development and political legitimacy 1', *American Political Science Review*, 53 (1): 69–105.

Lipsky, M. (1980) *Street Level Bureaucracy Dilemmas of the Individual in Public Services'*, New York: Russell Sage Foundation.

Liu, M., Feng, X., Wang, S. and Qiu, H. (2020) 'China's poverty alleviation over the last 40 years: successes and challenges', *Australian Journal of Agricultural and Resource Economics*, 64 (1): 209–28.

Locally Led Adaptation (LLA) Programme (n.d.) International Centre for Climate Change and Development. *'Locally led adaptation (LLA) programme'*. Available at: i (accessed 3 May 2023).

Loewe, M., Zintl, T. and Houdret, A. (2021) 'The social contract as a tool of analysis: introduction to the special issue on framing the evolution of new social contracts in Middle Eastern and North African countries', *World Development*, Vol. 145, 104982.

Loewe, M., Zintl, T. and Houdret, A. (2021) 'The social contract as a tool of analysis: Introduction to the special issue on framing the evolution of new social contracts in Middle Eastern and North African Countries', *World Development*, 145.

Lu, J. and Chu, Y-H. (2021) 'Trading democracy for governance', *Journal of Democracy*, 32 (4): 115–30.

Lucas, B. (2022) 'Lessons learned by the K4D Helpdesk Service: delivering evidence synthesis for policy and practice'. GSRDRC.

Lukes, S. (1974) *Power: A Radical View*. London: Red Globe Press.

Lumsdaine, D.H. (1993) *Moral Vision in International Politics: The Foreign Aid Regime, 1949–1989*. Princeton, NJ: Princeton University Press.

Lund, J.F. and Saito-Jensen M. (2013) 'Revisiting the issue of elite capture of participatory initiatives', *World Development*, Vol. 46, June, pp. 104–12.

Lvovskiy, L. (2023) 'Has Belarus's support for Russia's war gone unrewarded?'. Washington, DC: Carnegie Endowment for International Peace. Available at: https://carnegieendowment.org/politika/89276 (accessed 5 April 2023).

Lynch, G. (2011) *I Say to You: Ethnic Politics and the Kalenjin in Kenya*. Chicago: Chicago University Press.

Lyon, C. (2018) 'Towards a relational approach to social justice – liberals, radicals, and Brazil's "new social contract"'. Ph.D. thesis, University of Manchester.

Mac Ginty, R. (2014) 'Everyday peace: bottom-up and local agency in conflict-affected societies', *Security Dialogue*, 45 (6): 548–64.

Mac Ginty, R. and Richmond, O.P. (2013) 'The local turn in peace building: a critical agenda for peace', *Third World Quarterly*, 34 (5): 763–83.

Madariaga, A., et al. (2021) 'Multilevel business power in environmental politics: the avocado boom and water scarcity in Chile', *Environmental Politics*, 30 (7): 1174–1195.

Mahoney, J. and Rodríguez-Franco, D. (2018) 'Dependency theory', *The Oxford Handbook of the Politics of Development*, 22–42.

Mahoney, J. and Thelan, K. (2009) 'A theory of gradual institutional change' in J. Mahoney and K. Thelan (eds), *Explaining Institutional Change: Ambiguity, Agency and Power*. Cambridge: Cambridge University Press.

Malik, A.B. et al. (2021) 'Banking on the belt and road: insights from a new global dataset of 13,427 Chinese development projects'. Williamsburg, VA: AidData at William & Mary.

Malik, R. (2023) 'The seeds of Sudan's conflict were sown decades ago', *The Guardian*, 23 April. Available at: www.theguardian.com/commentisfree/2023/apr/23/sudan-conflict-power-struggle-darfur-genocide (accessed 1 May 2023).

Malinowski, B. (1921) 'The primitive economics of the Trobriand Islandees', *The Economic Journal*, 31 (121): 1–16.

Mallick, K. (2021) *Environmental Movements of India: Chipko, Narmada Bachao Andolan, Navdanya*. Amsterdam: Amsterdam University Press.

Mamdani, M. (1996) *Citizen and Subject: Contemporary Africa and the Legacy of Late Colonialism*. Princeton, NJ: Princeton University Press.

Mamdani, M. (2001) *When Victims Become Killers: Colonialism, Nativism, and the Genocide in Rwanda*. Princeton, NJ: Princeton University Press.

Mamdani, M. (2010) *Saviors and Survivors: Darfur, Politics and the War on Terror*. New York: Crown Publishing Group.

Mamdani, M. (2020) *Neither Settler nor Native: The Making and Unmaking of Permanent Minorities*. Cambridge, MA: Harvard University Press.

Mampilly, Z. (2015) *Rebel Rulers: Insurgent Governance and Civilian Life During War*. New York: Cornell University Press.

Mangisi, M. (2018) CEDAW in Tonga: global social policy analysis. Conference Presentation, 2018 Pacific update. Development Policy Centre, Canberra: Australian National University.

Mann, M. (1984) 'The autonomous power of the state: its origins, mechanisms and results'. *European Journal of Sociology/Archives Européennes de Sociologie/Europäisches Archiv für Soziologie*, 25 (2): 185–213.

Mason, C.L. (2019) 'Buzzwords and fuzzwords: flattening intersectionality in Canadian aid', *Canadian Foreign Policy Journal*, 25 (2), 203–219.

Mansuri, G. and Rao, V. (2013a) *Localizing Development: Does Participation Work?* Washington, DC: The World Bank.

Mansuri, G. and Rao, V. (2013b) 'Can participation be induced? Some evidence from developing countries', *Critical Review of International Social and Political Philosophy*, 16 (2): 284–304.

Maravall, J.M. (1994) 'The myth of the authoritarian advantage', *Journal of Democracy*, 5 (4): 17–31.

March, J.G., & Olsen, J.P. (1984) The New Institutionalism: Organizational Factors in Political Life. *The American Political Science Review*, 78 (3), 734–749. https://doi.org/10.2307/1961840

March, J.G. and Olsen, J.P. (1996) 'Institutional perspectives on political institutions', *Governance*, 9 (3): 24–64.

Marks, Z. (2016) *Conflict and Poverty*. GSDRC Professional Development Reading Pack No. 52. Birmingham: University of Birmingham. Available at: https://assets.publishing.service.gov.uk/media/5980670a40f0b61e4b00003e/Poverty-and-conflict_RP.pdf (accessed 5 April 2023).

Marx, K. and Engels, F. (2023) 'The German ideology', in W. Longhofer and D. Winchester (eds), *Social Theory Re-Wired*. Basingstoke: Routledge. pp. 123–7.

Masaki, T. and Van de Walle, N. (2015) 'The impact of democracy on economic growth in sub-Saharan Africa 1982–2012, in C. Monga and J.Y. Lin (eds) *The Oxford Handbook of Africa and Economics*, Vol. 2: *Policies and Practices*. Oxford: Oxford University Press.

Maschietto, R.H. (2020) 'Integrating subjectivities of power and violence in peacebuilding analysis', *Third World Quarterly*, 41 (3): 379–96.

Maslow, A.H. (1943) 'A theory of human motivation', *Psychological Review*, 50 (4): 370–96.

Mathur, N. (2017) 'Eating money: corruption and its categorical "other" in the leaky Indian state', *Modern Asian Studies*, 51 (6): 1796–817.

Mayer, F., (2014) *Narrative Politics: Stories and Collective Action*. Oxford: Oxford University Press.

Mazaheri, M., Roca, J.B., Markus, A. and Walrave, B. (2022) 'Market-based instruments and sustainable innovation: a systematic literature review and critique', *Journal of Cleaner Production*, 373: 133947. Available at: https://doi.org/10.1016/j.jclepro.2022.133947

Mbembe, A. (2001) *On the Postcolony*, Vol. 41. Berkeley, CA. University of California Press.

McDade, B.E. and Spring, A. (2005) 'The "newgeneration of African entrepreneurs": networking to change the climate for business and private sector-led development', *Entrepreneurship & Regional Development*, 17 (1): 17–42.

Mcloughlin, C. (2015) 'When does service delivery improve the legitimacy of a fragile or conflict-affected state?', *Governance*, 28 (3): 341–56.

Mcloughlin, C. (2018) 'When the virtuous circle unravels: unfair service provision and state de-legitimation in divided societies', *Journal of Intervention and Statebuilding*, 12 (4): 527–44.

Mcloughlin, C. (2024) "Public services as carriers of ideas that (de-) legitimise the state: The illustrative case of free education in Sri Lanka." *World Development* 173: 106439.

Mediavilla, J. and Garcia-Arias, J. (2019) 'Philanthrocapitalism as a neoliberal (development agenda) artefact: philanthropic discourse and hegemony in (financing for) international development, *Globalizations*, 16 (6): 857–75.

Mehta, J. (2010) From 'whether' to 'how': the varied roles of ideas in politics, in D. Beland and B. Cox (eds), *How Ideas Matter: Reframing Political Research*. Oxford: Oxford University Press.

Mehta, L., et al. (2019) 'The New Politics and Geographies of Scarcity, *Geoforum*, 101: 222–230.

Menzies, K. (2019) 'Understanding the Australian Aboriginal experience of collective, historical and intergenerational trauma.' *International Social Work*, 62 (6): 1522–1534.

Mercurio, B. (2021) 'WTO waiver from intellectual property protection for COVID-19 vaccines and treatments: a critical review', *Virginia Journal of International Law*, 62: 9–32. Available at: https://doi.org/10.2139/ssrn.3789820

Meger, S. (2018) 'The political economy of sexual violence against men and boys in armed conflict' in Zalewski, M., Drumond, P., Prugl, E., & Stern, M. (eds), *Sexual violence against men in global politics*. London: Routledge. pp. 102–116.

Migdal, J. (2001) *State in Society: Studying how States and Societies Transform and Constitute one Another*. Cambridge: Cambridge University Press.

Migdal, J. (2013) *The Everyday Life of the State: A State-in-Society Approach*. Seattle, WA: University of Washington Press.

Miguel, E., and Gugerty, M. (2005) Ethnic diversity, social sanctions, and public goods in Kenya, *Journal of Public Economics*, 89 (11–12): 2325–2368.

Mignolo, W.D. (2007) 'Delinking: The rhetoric of modernity, the logic of coloniality and the grammar of de-coloniality', *Cultural Studies*, 21 (2–3): 449–514.

Mignolo, W.D. (2009) 'Epistemic disobedience, independent thought and decolonial freedom', *Theory, Culture & Society*, 26 (7–8): 159–81.

Mignolo, W.D. (2021) *The Politics of De-colonial Investigations*. Durham, NC: Duke University Press.

Milanovic, B. (2016) *Global Inequality: A New Approach for the Age of Globalization*. Cambridge, MA: Harvard University Press.

Mitlin, D. (2022) 'Understanding the politics of shelter in three African cities; the contribution of political settlements', *Cities*, 128: 103797.

Mitova, V. (2020) 'Decolonising knowledge here and now'. Philosophical Papers, 49 (2): 191–212.

Mitra, D. (2020) *Indian Sex Life: Sexuality and the Colonial Origins of Modern Social Thought*. Princeton, NJ: Princeton University Press.

Mkandawire, T. (2001) 'Thinking about developmental states in Africa', *Cambridge Journal of Economics*, 25 (3): 289–314.

Mkandawire, T. (2005) 'Targeting and universalism in poverty reduction', Social Policy and Development Programme Paper No. 23, United Nations Research Institute for Social Development: Geneva.

Mkandawire, T. (2015) 'Neopatrimonialism and the political economy of economic performance in Africa: critical reflections', *World Politics*, 67 (3): 563–612.

Moe, T. (2005) 'Political control and the power of the agent', *The Journal of Law, Economics, and Organization*, 22 (1): 1–29.

Mohai, P., Pellow, D., Timmons Roberts, J. (2009) 'Environmental Justice', *Annual Review of Environment and Resources*, 34 (1): 405–30.

Mohammed, I. (2020) 'Covid-19: government's negligence and the mistrust of the masses', *Daily Trust*, 10 May. Available at: https://skydaily.ng/2020/05/covid-19-governments-negligence-and-the-mistrust-of-the-masses-by-idris-mohammed/ (accessed 5 April 2023).

Mohanty, C.T. and Torres, L. (eds) (1991) *Third World Women and the Politics of Feminism*, Vol. 632. Bloomington, IN: Indiana University Press.

Mohmand, S. (2019) 'Crafty oligarchs, savvy voters: democracy under inequality in rural Pakistan'. Cambridge: Cambridge University Press.

Molenaers, N., Dellepiane, S. and Faust, J. (2015a) 'Political conditionality and foreign aid', *World Development*, 75: 2–12.

Mongabay (2023) 'Amazon deforestation continues to fall under Lula'. Available at: https://news.mongabay.com/2023/08/amazon-deforestation-continues-to-fall-under-lula/ (accessed 8 August 2023).

Moore, M. (2004) 'Revenues, state formation, and the quality of governance in developing countries', *International Political Science Review/Revue Internationale de Science Politique*, 25 (3): 297–319.

Mosley, P. (1985) 'The political economy of foreign aid: a model of the market for a public good', *Economic Development and Cultural Change*, 33 (2): 373–93.

Mosse, D. (1997) 'The symbolic making of a common property resource: history, ecology and locality in a tank-irrigated landscape in South India', *Development and Change*, 28: 467–504.

Mosse, D., (2007). Power and the durability of poverty: a critical exploration of the links between culture, marginality and chronic poverty, CPRC Working Paper 107, SOAS: Chronic Poverty Research Centre.

Mosse, D. (2018) 'Caste and development: contemporary perspectives on a structure of discrimination and advantage', *World Development*, 110: 422–36.

Moyo, D. (2018) 'Why democracy doesn't deliver', *Foreign Policy*.

MSF (Medecins Sans Frontières) (2015) *Speaking Out case studies*. Available at: www.msf.org/speakingout/all-case-studies

Muddiman, D., Durrani, S., Dutch, M., Linley, R., Pateman, J. and Vincent, J. (2000) *Open to All? The Public Library and Social Exclusion*, Vol. 1. London: Resource: The Council for Museums, Archives and Libraries.

Mueller, J.L. (2011) 'The IMF, neoliberalism and hegemony', *Global Society*, 25 (3): 377–402.

Mugambiwa, S.S. (2018) 'Adaptation measures to sustain indigenous practices and the use of indigenous knowledge systems to adapt to climate change in Mutoko rural district of Zimbabwe', *Jàmbá* (Potchefstroom, South Africa), 10 (1): 388.

Mukhongo, L.L. (2020) 'Participatory Media Cultures: Virality, Humour, and Online Political Contestations in Kenya.' *Africa Spectrum*, 55(2): 148–169.

Mullen, R.D. (2017) *'India in Afghanistan: understanding development assistance by emerging donors to conflict-affected countries'*. JSTOR. Available at: www.jstor.org/stable/pdf/resrep10798.pdf

Mullis, I., Martin, M., Behuria, P., Kelly, D. and Fishbein, B. (2019) 'Highlights: TIMSS 2019 international results in mathematics and science', Lynch School of Education. Available at: https://timssandpirls.bc.edu/timss2023/

Murshed, S.S. and Tadjoeddin, M.Z. (2009) 'Revisiting the greed and grievance explanations for violent internal conflict', *Journal of International Development*, 21 (1): 87–111.

Musgrave, M. and Wong, S. (2016) 'Towards a more nuanced theory of elite capture in development projects: the importance of context and theories of power', *Journal of Sustainable Development*, 9 (3).

Naim, M. (2000) 'Washington consensus or Washington confusion?' *Foreign Policy*. 118: 87–103, Spring.

Nair, S. (2017) 'Introducing postcolonialism in international relations theory', *E-International Relations*, 8 (12).

Nascimento, B. (2022) '45 years ago, mid-dictatorship, Vidigal resisted evictions, paving the way for resistance that endures'. RioOnWatch.com, 20 November.

Nasution, A. (2016) 'Government decentralization program in Indonesia', Working Paper No. 601, October. Asian Development Bank.

Nayyar, D. (2013) *The Great Divergence and The Great Specialization, in Catch Up: Developing Countries in the World Economy*. Oxford: Oxford University Press. pp. 11–32.

Nazneen, S. and Mahmud, S. (2015) 'The gendered politics of securing inclusive development', in S. Hickey, K. Sen and B. Bukenya (eds), *The Politics of Inclusive Development: Interrogating the Evidence*. Oxford: Oxford University Press.

Ndlovu-Gatsheni, S.J. (2012) 'Coloniality of power in development studies and the impact of global imperial designs on Africa', *Australasian Review of African Studies*, 33 (2): 48–73.

Ndlovu-Gatsheni, S. (2018). *Epistemic Freedom in Africa: Deprovincialization and Decolonization*, London: Routledge

Negara, S.D. and Hutchinson, F. (2021) 'Special issue: the impact of Indonesia's decentralization reforms two decades on: Introduction', *Journal of Southeast Asian Economies*, 38 (3).

Nel, P. (2020) 'When bribery helps the poor', *Review of Social Economy*, 78 (4): 507–31.

Nevile, A. (2007) 'Amartya K. Sen and social exclusion', *Development in Practice*, 17 (2): 249–55.

New York Times, The (2010) 'Singapore's Lee Kuan Yew, in his own words', 29 March. Available at: www.nytimes.com/interactive/2015/03/26/world/asia/29leekuanyew-quotes.html

Newman, E. (2004) 'The new wars debate: a historical perspective is needed', *Security Dialogue*, 35 (2): 173–89.

Ngũgĩ wa Thiong'o, (1986) Decolonising the Mind: The Politics of Language in African Literature. London: Heinemann.

Ning, L. (1945) *A Daughter of Han: The Autobiography of a Chinese Working Woman*. Eastford: Martino Fine Books.

Nitzschke, H. (2003) 'Transforming war economies: challenges for peacemaking and peacebuilding'. Report of the 725th Wilton Park Conference in Association with the International Peace Academy (27–29 October), Wiston House, Steyning, West Sussex.

Njambi, E. (2021) 'Can aid be decolonized? – With power shifter Degan Ali. Equals'. Available at: https://equalshope.org/index.php/2021/08/10/can-foreign-aid-be-decolonized-with-power-shifter-degan-ali/.

Njoku, E.T. (2022) 'Queering terrorism', *Studies in Conflict & Terrorism*.

Njoku, E.T. and Dery, I. (2021) 'Spiritual security: an explanatory framework for conflict-related sexual violence against men'. *International Affairs*, 97 (6): 1785–803.

Njoku, E.T. and Dery, I. (2023) 'Gendering counter-terrorism: Kunya and the silence of male victims of CRSV in Northeastern Nigeria', *African Studies Review*.

Njoku, E.T., Akintayo, J. and Mohammed, I. (2022) 'Sex trafficking and sex-for-food/money: terrorism and conflict-related sexual violence against men in the Lake Chad region', *Conflict, Security & Development*, 22 (1): 79–95.

North, D.C. (1990) *Institutions, Institutional Change, and Economic Performance*. Cambridge: Cambridge University Press.

North, D.C. (2003) 'The role of institutions in economic development'. Discussion Paper Series No. 2003.2, United Nations Economic Commission for Europe. Available at: www.malaysia-today.net/wp-content/uploads/2011/08/www3.unisa.it_uploads_3366_north.pdf (accessed 8 August 2023).

Nunan, F. (2015) *Understanding Poverty and the Environment: Analytical Frameworks and Approaches*. London: Routledge.

Nunan, F. (2020) 'The political economy of fisheries co-management: challenging the potential for success on Lake Victoria', *Global Environmental Change*, 63: 102101.

Nunn, N. and Wantchekon, L. (2011) 'The slave trade and the origins of mistrust in Africa', *American Economic Review*, 101 (7): 3221–32.

Nur-tegin, K. and Jakee, K. (2020). Does corruption grease or sand the wheels of development? New results based on disaggregated data. *The Quarterly Review of Economics and Finance*, Volume 75, February 2020, Pages 19–30. https://doi.org/10.1016/j.qref.2019.02.001

Nussbaum, M. (2011) *Creating Capabilities: The Human Development Approach*. Cambridge, MA: Harvard University Press.

Ochieng' Opalo, K. (2022) 'Formalizing clientelism in Kenya: from Harambee to the Constituency Development Fund', *World Development,* Vol. 152.

Ochonu, M. (2014) 'Colonialism by proxy: Hausa imperial agents and middle belt consciousness in Nigeria. Indianapolis, IN: Indiana University Press.

ODI (2022) '*ODI bites: decolonising development, reparations and a justice-centred zpproach to 'aid'*. Available at: https://odi.org/en/events/odi-bites-decolonising-development-towards-a-justice-centred-approach-to-aid-can-reparations-help/ Odijie, M.E. and Imoro, M.Z. (2021) 'Ghana's competitive clientelism and space for long-term stable policies', *SAGE Open*, 11 (3). Available at: https://doi.org/10.1177/21582440211031513

OECD (2022) *Education at a Glance*. OECD. Available at: https://doi.org/10.1787/3197152b-en

OHCHR (2021) 'High commissioner: acknowledging and confronting historical legacies crucial for racial justice'. Available at: www.ohchr.org/en/stories/2021/07/high-commissioner-acknowledging-and-confronting-historical-legacies-crucial-racial

Ojedokun, U.A, Ogunleye, Y.O. and Aderinto, A.A. (2021) 'Mass mobilization for police accountability: the case of Nigeria's #EndSARS protest', *Policing: A Journal of Policy and Practice*, 15 (3): 1894–1903.

Okereke, C. and A-B.S. Massaquoi (2018) 'Climate change, environment, and development', in P. Haslam, J. Schafer and P. Beaudet (eds) *Introduction to International Development: Approaches, Actors and Issues* (3rd edn). Don Mills: Oxford University Press.

Okereke, C. and Coventry, P. (2016) 'Climate justice and the international regime: before, during, and after Paris', *Wiley Interdisciplinary Reviews: Climate Change*, 7 (6): 834–51. Available at: https://doi.org/10.1002/wcc.419

Olken, B.A. and Pande, P. (2012) 'Corruption in developing countries'. *Annual Review of Economics*, 4 (1): 479–509.

Olson, M. (1965) *The Logic of Collective Action: Public Goods and the Theory of Groups*. Cambridge, MA: Harvard University Press.

Onah, C.C., et al. (2022) 'Dynamics of the politico-administrative conflicts of resource control in Nigeria: Exploring the oil politics of who gets what, when, and how.' *Natural Resources Forum*, 46 (2): 245–259.

Öniş, Z. (1991) 'The logic of the developmental state', *Comparative Politics*, 24 (1): 109–26.

Onyango, M.A. and Hampanda, K. (2011) 'Social constructions of masculinity and male survivors of wartime sexual violence: an analytical review', *International Journal of Sex Health*, 23 (4): 237–47.

Opalo, K.O. (2019) *Legislative Development in Africa: Politics and Postcolonial Legacies*. Cambridge University Press.

Opalo, K. (2020) 'Constrained presidential power in Africa? Legislative independence and executive rule making in Kenya, 1963–2013', *British Journal of Political Science*, 50 (4): 1341–58.

Oreskes, N. and Conway, E.M. (2011) *Merchants of Doubt: How a Handful of Scientists Obscured the Truth on Issues from Tobacco Smoke to Global Warming*. New York: Bloomsbury Publishing.

Organisation for Economic Co-operation and Development (OECD) (2011) *Fostering Innovation for Green Growth*, Paris: OECD.

Organisation for Economic Co-operation and Development (OECD) (2010) *The State's Legitimacy in Fragile Situations: Unpacking Complexity*. Paris: OECD.

Organisation for Economic Co-operation and Development (OECD) (2019) *What's Driving Tax Morale? An Empirical Analysis on Social Preferences and Attitudes Towards Taxation*. Paris: OECD.

IMF (2021) 'International monetary fund: inflation rate: average consumer prices'. Available at: www.imf.org/external/datamapper/PCPIPCH@WEO/WEOWORLD/VEN/MEQ/LBN.

Ostrom, E. (1998) 'A behavioral approach to the rational choice theory of collective action', *American Political Science Review*, 92 (1): 1–22.

Ostrom, E. (2000) 'Collective action and the evolution of social norm', *The Journal of Economic Perspectives*, 3: 137–58, Summer.

Ostrom, E. (2005) *Understanding Institutional Diversity*. Princeton, NJ: Princeton University Press.

Ostrom, E. (2009) Analyzing Collective Action. Paper presented at the 2009 conference of the International Association of Agricultural Economists held in Beijing, China, August 16–22, 2009. https://ageconsearch.umn.edu/record/53215/files/W09-16%20Ostrom_IAAE%202009.pdf.

Otele, O (2023) 'More than money: the logic of slavery reparations', *The Guardian*, 31 March. Available at: www.theguardian.com/news/ng-interactive/2023/mar/31/more-than-money-the-logic-of-slavery-reparations

Ouma, M. and Adésínà, J. (2019) 'Solutions, exclusion and influence: exploring power relations in the adoption of social protection policies in Kenya', *Critical Social Policy*, 39 (3): 376–95.

Owens, P. (2010) 'Torture, "Sex and Military Orientalism', *Third World Quarterly,* 31 (7), 1042.

Owolabi, O.P. (2023) 'Historical institutionalism, critical junctures, and the divergent legacies of forced settlement and colonial occupation', in O.P. Owolabi, *Ruling Emancipated Slaves and Indigenous Subjects: The Divergent Legacies of Forced Settlement and Colonial Occupation in the Global South.* New York: Oxford University Press.

Oxfam (2007) 'Spread of free trade agreements threatens poor countries'. Available at: www.oxfamamerica.org/press/spread-of-free-trade-agreements-threatens-poor-countries/

Oxfam (2022) 'Ten richest men double their fortunes in pandemic, while incomes of 99 per cent of humanity fall'. Available at: www.oxfam.org.uk/media/press-releases/ten-richest-men-double-their-fortunes-in-pandemic-while-incomes-of-99-per-cent-of-humanity-fall/#:~:text=The%2010%20richest%20men%20were,Steve%20Ballmer%20and%20Warren%20Buffet

Pailey, R.N. (2020), De-centring the 'White Gaze' of Development. *Development and Change,* 51: 729–745.

Parsons, C. (2016) 'Ideas and power: four intersections and how to show them', *Journal of European Public Policy,* 23 (3): 446–63.

Patnaik U. (2019) The revenue impact on the Indian masses of exchange rate changes in the context of the drain of wealth: 1871 to 1901. *Social Scientist,* 47 (11–12).

Pateman, C., (1988) *The Sexual Contract,* New York: Polity Press.

Paternotte, D. (2015) 'Global times, global debates? Same-sex marriage worldwide', *Social Politics: International Studies in Gender, State & Society,* 22 (4): 653–74. Winter.

Pavcnik, N. (2017) 'The impact of trade on inequality in developing countries', Working Paper Series 23878. Available at: www.nber.org/papers/w23878

Peiffer, C. and Alvarez, L. (2016) 'Who will be the principled-principals? Perceptions of corruption and willingness to engage in anticorruption activism', *Governance,* 29 (3): 351–69.

Peiffer, C. and Rose, R. (2018) 'Why are the poor more vulnerable to bribery in Africa? The institutional effects of services', *The Journal of Development Studies,* 54 (1): 18–29.

Peluso, N.L. (1992) *Rich Forests, Poor People: Resource Control, and Resistance in Java.* Berkeley, CA: University of California Press.

Pepinsky, T., Pierskalla, J.H. and Sacks, A. (2017) 'Bureaucracy and service delivery', *Annual Review of Political Science,* 20 (1): 249–68. Available at: https://doi.org/10.1146/annurev-polisci-051215-022705

Pereira, A. (2015) *What was Life Like During the Dictatorship for Ordinary Brazilians?* Providence: Brown University. Available at: www.choices.edu/video/what-was-life-like-during-the-dictatorship-for-ordinary-brazilians/ (accessed 5 April 2023).

Perrigo, B. (2022) 'Why a blank sheet of paper became a protest symbol in China', Time. Available at: https://time.com/6238050/china-protests-censorship-urumqi-a4/ (accessed 5 April 2023).

Persson, A. Rothstein, B. and Teorell, J. (2013) 'Why anticorruption reforms fail—systemic corruption as a collective action problem', *Governance,* 26 (3): 449–71.

Pew (2021) Available at: www.pewresearch.org/religion/2021/06/29/attitudes-about-caste/#large-shares-of-indians-say-men-women-should-be-stopped-from-marrying-outside-of-their-caste

Pham, J.P. (2010) 'Putting Somali piracy in context', *Journal of Contemporary African Studies*, 28 (3): 325–41.

Phillips, S. (2020) *When there was no aid: War and peace in Somaliland*. Ithaca, New York: Cornell University Press.

Pierce, S. (2007) 'Identity, Performance, and Secrecy: Gendered Life and the "Modem" in Northern Nigeria', *Feminist Studies*, 33 (3), 539–565.

Pierson, P. (2004) *Politics in Time: History, Institutions, and Social Analysis*. Princeton: Princeton University Press.

Piliavsky, A. (2014) Introduction. In, Antonia Poliavsky (ed.), *Patronage as Politics in South Asia*. Cambridge: Cambridge University Press.

Piquard, B. and Delft, L. (2018) 'Valuing local humanitarian knowledge: learning from the Central African Republic', *Forced Migration Review*. Available at: www.fmreview.org/GuidingPrinciples20/piquard-delft

Potter, R.T., Binns, J., Elliott, E.N. and Smith, D.W. (2018) *Geographies of Development: An Introduction to Development Studies* (4th edn). London: Routledge.

Prasad, R. and Pardhasaradhi, Y. (2020) 'Twenty-five years of the constitution Seventy-fourth Amendment Act: promise and performance', *Indian Journal of Public Administration*, 66 (2): 159–78.

Premium Times (2022/updated 2023) 'APC fixes presidential forms for N100 million, adopts indirect primaries'. Available at: www.premiumtimesng.com/news/headlines/524823-updated-2023-apc-fixes-presidential-forms-for-n100-million-adopts-indirect-primaries.html?tztc=1 (accessed 28 March 2023).

Presbitero, A.F. and Zazzaro, A. (2012) 'IMF lending in times of crisis: political influences and crisis prevention', *World Development*, 40 (10): 1944–69. Available at: https://doi.org/10.1016/j.worlddev.2012.04.009.

Pruce, K. (2022) 'The politics of who gets what and why: learning from the targeting of social cash transfers in Zambia', *The European Journal of Development Research*, 35, 820–839.

Pruce, K., Hudson, D., Mcloughlin, C., Do Céu, M. Gusmão, J.O., Brancher, L., Carvoeiras Do Nascimento Pires, C., Noronha, R., Noano Ximenes, D. and Da Ressureição Das Neves Baptista, L. (2023) "This is our right": Social Protection and Fairness in Timor-Leste. DLP Research Brief, Birmingham: Developmental Leadership Program.

Pruce, K. and Hickey, S. (2019) 'The Politics of Promoting Social Cash Transfers in Zambia' in Hickey, S., Lavers, T., Niño-Zarazúa, M. and Seekings, J. (eds.) *The Politics of Social Protection in Eastern and Southern Africa*. Open access at: Oxford University Press.

Prunier, G. (1997) *The Rwanda Crisis: History of a Genocide*. New York: Columbia University Press.

Przeworski, A., Alvarez, M.E., Cheibub, J.A. and Limongi, F. (2000) *Democracy and Development: Political Institutions and Well-being in the World, 1950–1990*. Cambridge: Cambridge University Press.

Puar, J.K. (2007) *Terrorist assemblages: Homonationalism in queer times*. New York: Duke University Press.

Pun, N. (1999) 'Becoming dagongmei (working girls): the politics of identity and difference in reform China', *The China Journal*, 42: 1–18.

Pun, N., Shen, Y., Guo, Y., Lu, H., Chan, J. and Selden, M. (2016) 'Apple, Foxconn, and Chinese workers' struggles from a global labor perspective', *Inter-Asia Cultural Studies*, 17 (2): 166–85.

Qayyum, U., Sohail, and Sabir, S. (2020) 'Religion and economic development: New insights', *Empirica*, 47: 793–834.

Quijano, A. (2000) 'Coloniality of power, eurocentrism, and Latin America' (English translation). *Nepantla: Views from South*, 1 (3): 533–80.

Radil, S., Walther, O., Dorward, N., Pflaum, M., and Trémolières, M. (2022) 'Conflicts are becoming increasingly rural in North and West Africa', *OECD Development Matters*, 26 July. Available at: https://oecd-development-matters.org/2022/07/26/conflicts-are-becoming-increasingly-rural-in-north-and-west-africa/ (accessed 1 May 2023)

Rai, S. (2021) 'How big tech is importing India's caste legacy to Silicon Valley', Bloomberg, 11 March.

Rai, R.K., Bhattarai, D. and Neupane, S. (2019) 'Designing solid waste collection strategy in small municipalities of developing countries using choice experiment', *Journal of Urban Management*, 8 (3): 386–95.

Ramalingam, B., Gray, B. and Cerruti, G. (2013) 'Missed opportunities: the case for strengthening national and local partnership-based humanitarian responses'. Available at: https://actionaid.org/publications/2013/missed-opportunities-case-strengthening-national-and-local-partnership-based

Randazzo, E. (2016) 'The paradoxes of the everyday: scrutinising the local turn in peacebuilding', *Third World Quarterly*, 37 (8): 1351–70.

Rao, K.D., Makimoto, S., Peters, M. et al. (2019) 'Vulnerable populations and universal health coverage' in H. Kharas, J.W. McArthur and I. Ohno (eds) *Leave No One Behind: Time for Specifics on the Sustainable Development Goals*. Washington, DC: Brookings Institution Press.

Rapoport, H. and Docquier, F. (2006) 'The economics of migrants' remittances', *in Handbook of the Economics of Giving, Altruism and Reciprocity,* Vol. 2: 1135–98.

Ravenhill, J. (ed.) (2017) *Global Political Economy*. Oxford: Oxford University Press.

Raworth, K. (2012) 'A safe and just space for humanity'. Oxfam Discussion Paper. Oxford: Oxfam.

Raworth, K. (2017) *Doughnut Economics: 7 Ways to Think Like a 21st Century Economist*. London: Random House.

Resnick, D. (2018) 'Foreign aid and democratization in developing countries', in *The Oxford Handbook of the Politics of Development*, Ch. 20, 409–428.

Reuters (2021) 'World has entered a stage of vaccine apartheid – WHO head'. *Reuters*.

Reutlinger, A. (2020) 'What is epistemically wrong with research affected by sponsorship bias? The evidential account'. *European Journal for Philosophy of Science*, 10: 1–26.

Richmond, O.P. (2007) *The Transformation of Peace*. Basingstoke: Palgrave Macmillan.

Riehl, V. (2001) *Who is Ruling in South Sudan? The Role of NGOs in Rebuilding Socio-Political Order*. Uppsala: Nordiska Afrikainstitutet.

Riggan, J. (2016) *The Struggling State: Nationalism, Mass Militarization, and the Education of Eritrea*. Philadelphia. PA: Temple University Press.

Robbins, P. (2004) *Political Ecology: A Critical Introduction*. Oxford: Blackwell.

Robertson, P. (2016) 'North Korea's caste system: the trouble with Songbun'. Available at: www.hrw.org/news/2016/07/05/north-koreas-caste-system (accessed 7 April 2023).

Robeyns, I. (2005) 'The capability approach: a theoretical survey', *Journal of Human Development*, 6 (1): 93–117.

Robins, S., Gready, P., Aloui, A., Andrieu, K., Hamza, H.B. and Ferchichi, W. (2022) 'Transitional justice from the margins: collective reparations and Tunisia's truth and dignity commission'. *Political Geography*, 94: 102565. Available at: https://doi.org/10.1016/j.polgeo.2021.102565

Roche, C., and Denney, L. (2021) 'COVID-19: an opportunity to localise and reimagine development in the Pacific?' Paper 3 in G. Varughese et al. *Reimagining Development: Interdisciplinary Perspectives on Doing Development in an Era of Uncertainty.* UNSW Institute of Global Development, Sydney.

Rockström, J. et al. (2023) 'Safe and just Earth system boundaries', *Nature*, 619: 102–11.

Rockström, J., Steffen, W., Noone, K., Persson, Å., Chapin III, F.S., Lambin, F.S., Lenton, T.M.. Scheffer, M., Folke, C., Schellnhuber, H., Nykvist, B., De Wit, C.A., Hughes, T., van der Leeuw, S., Rodhe, H., Sörlin, S., Snyder, P.K., Costanza, R., Svedin, U., Falkenmark, M., Karlberg, L., Corell, R.W., Fabry, V.J, Hansen, J., Walker, B., Liverman, D., Richardson, K., Crutzen, P. and Foley, J. (2009) 'Planetary boundaries: exploring the safe operating space for humanity', *Ecology and Society*, 14 (2): 32. Available at: www. Ecologyandsociety.org/vol14/iss2/art32/

Rodney, W. (1972) *How Europe Underdeveloped Africa*. London: Verso Books.

Rodrik, D. (2000) Institutions for High-quality Growth: What they are and how to Acquire them. *Studies in Comparative International Development*, 35 (3): 3–31.

Rodrik, D. (2018) 'Populism and the economics of globalization', *Journal of International Business Policy*, 1: 12–33.

Rodrik, D. (2018) 'What do trade agreements really do? *Journal of Economic Perspectives*, 32 (2): 73–90.

Rodrik, D., Subramanian, A. and Trebbi, F. (2004) 'Institutions rule: the primacy of institutions over geography and integration in economic development', *Journal of Economic Growth*, 9: 131–65.

Roepstorff, K. (2020) 'A call for critical reflection on the localisation agenda in humanitarian action', *Third World Quarterly*, 41 (2): 284–301. Available at: https://doi.org/10.1080/01436597.2019.1644160

Roht-Arriaza, N. and Orlovsky, K. (2009) 'A complementary relationship: reparations and development', in P. de Greiff and R. Duthie (eds), *Transitional Justice and Development: Making Connections*. New York: Social Science Research Council. pp. 170–213.

Rose-Ackerman, S. (1978). *Corruption: A Study in Political Economy*. Academic Press. https://doi.org/10.1016/C2009-0-22067-8

Max Roser (2019) *"Child mortality: achieving the global goal for 2030 would be a huge achievement – but we are currently far away"* Published online at OurWorldInData.org. Retrieved from: 'https://ourworldindata.org/child-mortality-global-goal' [Online Resource]

Rosser, A., Wilson, I. and Sulistiyanto, P. (2011) 'Leaders, elites and coalitions: the politics of free public services in decentralised Indonesia', Developmental Research Program Policy Paper 16. Development Leadership Program.

Rostow, W.W. (1960) *The Stages of Growth: A Non-communist Manifesto*. Cambridge: Cambridge University Press.

Rostow, W. and Baker, R.J. (2016) *The Economics of Take-off into Sustained Growth*. Springer.

Rothstein, B. (2011). *The Quality of Government: Corruption, Social Trust, and Inequality in International Perspective*. University of Chicago Press.

Rothstein, B. (2021) *Controlling Corruption: The Social Contract Approach*. Oxford University Press.

Routley, L. (2014) 'Developmental states in Africa: a review of ongoing debates and buzzwords', *Development Policy Review*, 32 (2): 159–77.

Roy, P., Khan, M. and Slota, A. (2022) 'A new approach to anti-corruption: when rule-breakers rule: anti-corruption evidence (ACE). Available at: https://ace.soas.ac.uk/publication/a-new-approach-to-anti-corruption-when-rule-breakers-rule/

Ruan, J. and Wangm, P. (2023) 'Elite capture and corruption: the influence of elite collusion on village elections and rural land development in China', *The China Quarterly*, 253: 107–22.

Rubenstein, J.C. (2015) *Between Samaritans and States: The Political Ethics of Humanitarian INGOs* (1st edn). Oxford: Oxford University Press.

Ryan, Y. (2011) 'The tragic life of a street vendor', *Al Jazeera*, 20 January. Available at: www.aljazeera.com/features/2011/1/20/the-tragic-life-of-a-street-vendor (accessed 5 April 2023).

Said, E., (1978). *Orientalism*. New York: Pantheon Books.

Said, E. (2003) Introduction to orientalism. In *Imperialism* (pp. 30–52). Routledge.

Sabaratnam, M. (2017) *Decolonising Intervention: International Statebuilding in Mozambique*. London: Rowman & Littlefield.

Salem, Sarah Mamdouh Ibrahim and Jibrin, Rekia (2015) 'Revisiting intersectionality: reflections on theory and praxis', *Trans-Scripts*, 5.

Samman, E., Roche, J.M., Sarwar, M.B. and Evans, M. (2021) '"Leave no one behind:": five years into Agenda 2030: guidelines for turning the concept into action'. London: Overseas Development Institute.

Sampaio, P.R.P. and Daychoum, M.T. (2017) 'Two decades of rail regulatory reform in Brazil (1996–2016)', *Utilities Policy*, 49: 93–103.

Sandvik, K.B. and Dijkzeul, D. (2019) 'Humanitarian governance and localization: what kind of world is being imagined and produced?' *PRIO Blogs, Humanitarianism* (blog). Available at: https://blogs.prio.org/2019/11/humanitarian-governance-and-localization-what-kind-of-world-is-being-imagined-and-produced/

Sanga, K., Reynolds. M., Paulsen, I. Spratt, R., and Maneipuri, J. (2018) 'A tok stori about tok stori: Melanesian relationality in action as research, leadership and scholarship', *Global Comparative Education*: Journal of the WCCES.

Schady, N.R. (2000) 'The political economy of expenditures by the Peruvian Social Fund (FONCODES), 1991–5. *The American Political Science Review*, 94 (2): 289–304.

Schaffer, F.C. (2007) *Elections for Sale: The Causes and Consequences of Vote Buying*. Boulder, CO: Lynne Rienner Publishers.

Schmelzle, C. and Stollenwerk, E. (2018) 'Virtuous or vicious circle? Governance effectiveness and legitimacy in areas of limited statehood', *Journal of Intervention and Statebuilding*, 12 (4): 449–67.

Schmidt, V.A. (2008) 'Discursive institutionalism: the explanatory power of ideas and discourse', *Annual Review of Political Science*, 11 (1): 303–26.

Schmidt, V.A. (2010) 'Taking ideas and discourse seriously: explaining change through discursive institutionalism as the new "fourth" institutionalism', *European Political Science Review*, 2 (1): 1–25.

Schneider, B. (1999) 'The desarrollista state in Brazil and México', in M. Woo-Cumings (ed.) *The Developmental State*. Ithaca, New York: Cornell University Press: 235–51.

Schulz, P. (2018) 'Displacement from gendered personhood: sexual violence and masculinities in Northern Uganda', *International Affairs*, 94 (5): 5.

Schulz, P. and Touquet, H. (2020) 'Queering explanatory frameworks for wartime sexual violence against men', *International Affairs*, 96 (5): 1169–87.

Schumpeter, J.A. (2013) *Capitalism, Socialism, and Democracy*. Basingstoke: Routledge.

Schuster, R., Germain, R.R, Bennett, J.R., Reo, N.J. and Arcese, P. (2019) 'Vertebrate biodiversity on indigenous-managed lands in Australia, Brazil, and Canada equals that in protected areas', *Environmental Science & Policy*, 101: 1–6. Available at: https://doi.org/10.1016/j.envsci.2019.07.002

Scott, E. (2022) 'The political economy of local aid: a new research agenda', in D.A. Deese (ed.), A *Research Agenda for International Political Economy*, 183–98. Cheltenham: Edward Elgar Publishing.

Scott, J.C. (1998) *Seeing Like a State: How Certain Schemes to Improve the Human Condition Have Failed*. New Haven, CT: Yale University Press.

Sejan, S.S. (2022) 'Strategic denial of Rohingya identity and their right to internal self-determination', *International Studies*, 59 (3): 234–51.

Sen, A.K. (1977) Rational Fools: A Critique of the Behavioral Foundations of Economic Theory. *Philosophy & Public Affairs*, 6 (4), 317–344. http://www.jstor.org/stable/2264946

Sen, A. (1982) 'Poverty and famines: an essay on entitlement and deprivation'. Oxford: Oxford University Press.

Sen, A. (1985) "Well-Being, Agency and Freedom: The Dewey Lectures 1984." *The Journal of Philosophy* 82(4): 169–221.

Sen, A. (1993) The Economics of Life and Death. *Scientific American*, May 1993.

Sen, A. (1999) *Development as Freedom*. Oxford: Oxford University Press.

Sen, A. (2000) 'Social exclusion: concept, application, and scrutiny', Social Development Papers No. 1. Manila: Asian Development Bank.

Sengupta, M. (2009) 'Making the state change its mind – the IMF, the World Bank and the politics of India's market reforms', *New Political Economy*, 14 (2): 181–210.

Shandra, J.M., Rademacher, H. and Coburn, C. (2016) 'The World Bank and organized hypocrisy? A cross-national analysis of structural adjustment and forest loss', *Environmental Sociology*, 2 (2): 192–207. Available at: https://doi.org/10.1080/23251042.2016.1160471.

Shaw, M. (2005) *The New Western Way of War: Risk-Transfer and its Crisis in Iraq*. Cambridge: Polity.

Shaw, R.M., Howe, J., Beazer, J., & Carr, T. (2020) 'Ethics and positionality in qualitative research with vulnerable and marginal groups', *Qualitative Research*, 20 (3), 277–293.

Shoesmith, D., Franklin, N. and Hidayat, R. (2020) 'Decentralised governance in Indonesia's disadvantaged regions: a critique of the underperforming model of local governance in Eastern Indonesia', *Journal of Current Southeast Asian Affairs*, 39 (3): 359–80.

Shuayb, M. (2022) 'Stop referring to people like me as "local"', *The New Humanitarian*, 8 February. Available at: www.thenewhumanitarian.org/opinion/2022/2/8/Localisation-lip-service-fixing-aid-colonial-legacy

Sikkink, K. (1991) *Ideas and Institutions: Developmentalism in Brazil and Argentina*. Ithaca, New York: Cornell University Press.

Silver, H. (2007) Social Exclusion: Comparative Analysis of Europe and Middle East Youth, Middle East Youth Initiative Working Paper No. 1, Available at SSRN: https://ssrn.com/abstract=1087432 or http://dx.doi.org/10.2139/ssrn.1087432

Simandan, D. (2019) "Beyond Haraway? Addressing constructive criticisms to the 'four epistemic gaps' interpretation of positionality and situated knowledges", *Dialogues in Human Geography*, 9 (2), 166–170.

Singh, P. (1996) *How Solidarity Works for Welfare: Subnationalism and Social Development in India*. Cambridge: Cambridge University Press.

Sivakumaran, S. (2007) 'Sexual violence against men in armed conflict', *European Journal of International Law*, 18 (2): 253–76.

Sirnate, V. (2014), 'Positionality, personal insecurity, and female empathy in security studies research', *PS: Political Science & Politics*, 47 (2), 398–401.

Slim, H. (2021) 'Localization is self-determination', *Frontiers in Political Science*, 3: 80.

Smith, A. ([1776] 2003) *The Wealth of Nations*. London: Penguin Classics.

Snow, D.A., & Benford, R.D. (1988) Ideology, frame resonance, and participant mobilization. *International Social Movement Research*, 1 (1), 197–217.

Solomon, H. (2014) 'Somalia's Al Shabaab: clans vs Islamist nationalism', *South African Journal of International Affairs*, 21 (3): 351–66.

Soss, J. and Weaver, V. (2017) 'Police are our government: politics, political science, and the policing of race-class subjugated communities', *Annual Review of Political Science*, 20: 565–91.

Spectator, The (2022) Full text: 'Putin's declaration of war on Ukraine', 24 February. Available at: www.spectator.co.uk/article/full-text-putin-s-declaration-of-war-on-ukraine/ (accessed 1 May 2023).

Spivak, G.C. (1993), *Outside in the teaching machine*. London: Routledge.

Spivak, G.C. (1994) 'Can the subaltern speak', in P.J. Cain and M. Harrison (eds), *Imperialism*. Basingstoke: Routledge. pp. 49–72.

Spivak, G.C. (2005). Scattered speculations on the subaltern and the popular. *Postcolonial studies*, 8 (4): 475–486.

Steffen, W., Richardson, K., Rockström, J., Cornell, S.E., Fetzer, I., Bennett, E.M., Biggs, R., Carpenter, S.R., de Vries, W., de Wit, C.A., Folke, C., Gerten, D., Heinke, J., Mace, G.M., Persson, L.M., Ramanathan, V., Reyers, B. and Sörlin, S. (2015) 'Planetary boundaries: guiding human development on a changing planet', *Science*, 347 (6223): 1–11.

Steinberger, P.J. (2004) *The Idea of the State*. Cambridge: Cambridge University Press.

Stewart, F. (2000) 'Crisis prevention: tackling horizontal inequalities', *Oxford Development Studies*, 28 (3): 245–62.

Stewart, F. (2002) 'Horizontal inequalities: a neglected dimension of development', *Oxford Development Studies*, 30 (2): 121–38.

Stewart, F. (2008) 'Horizontal inequalities and conflict: an introduction and some hypotheses', in F. Stewart (eds) *Horizontal Inequalities and Conflict: Conflict, Inequality and Ethnicity*. London: Palgrave Macmillan.

Stewart, F. (ed.) (2016) *Horizontal Inequalities and Conflict: Understanding Group Violence in Multiethnic Societies*. Basingstoke: Palgrave Macmillan.

Stiglitz, J.E. (2017) *Globalization and its Discontents Revisited: Anti-globalization in the Era of Trump*. New York: W.W. Norton & Company.

Stirk, C. (2015) 'An act of faith: humanitarian financing and zakat. Development initiatives'. Available at: https://devinit.org/resources/humanitarian-financing-and-zakat/

Stokes, S., Dunning, T, Nazareno, M., and Bravo, V. (2013) *Brokers, Voters, and Clientelism: The Puzzle of Distributive Politics*. New York: Cambridge University Press.

Storer, E., Leonardi, D.C. and Fisher, J. (2021) 'Geographies of unease: witchcraft and boundary construction in an African Borderland, *Political Geography*, 90.

Stubbs, Thomas H., Kentikelenis, A.E. and King, L.P. (2016) 'Catalyzing aid? The IMF and donor behavior in aid cillocation', *World Development*, 78: 511–28.

Stuckler, D., Basu, S. and McKee, M. (2011) 'International Monetary Fund and aid displacement', *International Journal of Health Services*, 41 (1): 67–76.

Subramanian, A. and Wei, S.-J. (2007) 'The WTO promotes trade, strongly but unevenly', *Journal of International Economics*, 72 (1): 151–75.

Surucu, C. (2002) 'Modernity, nationalism, resistance: identity politics in post-Soviet Kazakhstan', *Central Asian Survey*, 21 (4): 385–402.

Szeftel M. (1998) Misunderstanding African politics: corruption & the governance agenda. *Review of African Political Economy*, 25 (76): 221–240.

Tadros, M. (2011) 'Working Politically Behind Red Lines: Structure and agency in a comparative study of women's coalitions in Egypt and Jordan'. DLP Research Paper 12. Birmingham: Developmental Leadership Programme.

Tangri, R. and Mwenda, A. (2010) 'President Museveni and the politics of presidential tenure in Uganda', *Journal of Contemporary African Studies*, 28 (1): 31–49.

Tankard, M. and Paluck, E. (2016) 'Norm perception as a vehicle for social change', *Social Issues and Policy Review*, 10 (1): 181–211.

Tankebe, J. (2009) 'Public cooperation with the police in Ghana: does procedural fairness matter?, *Criminology*, 47 (4): 1265–1293.

Tanner, L. and Moro, L. (2016) 'Missed out: the role of local actors in the humanitarian response in the South Sudan conflict'. Available at: www.oxfam.org/en/research/missed-out

Tapscott, R. (2021) *Arbitrary States: Social Control and Modern Authoritarianism in Museveni's Uganda*. Oxford: Oxford University Press.

Tarrow, S. (2022) *Power in Movement: Social Movements and Contentious Politics*. Cambridge: Cambridge University Press.

Taylor, C. (1994) *Multiculturalism: Examining the Recognition*. Princeton, NJ: Princeton University Press.

Taylor, V., & Whittier, N. E. (1992) 'Collective identity in social movement communities: Lesbian feminist mobilization', in Freeman, J., and Johnson, V. (eds), *Waves of protest: Social movements since the sixties*. London: Rowman & Littlefield. pp. 169–194.

Teichman, J. (2016) *The Politics of Inclusive Development: Policy, State Capacity, and Coalition Building*. New York: Palgrave Macmillan.

Terpstra, N. (2020) 'Rebel governance, rebel legitimacy, and external intervention: assessing three phases of Taliban rule in Afghanistan', *Small Wars & Insurgencies*, 31 (6): 1143–73.

Tharoor, S. (2018) *Inglorious Empire: What the British Did to India*. London: Penguin.

Thelen, K. (2004) 'How Institutions Evolve: Insights from Comparative Historical Analysis' in (eds) Rueschemeyer, D., and Mahoney, J. *Comparative Historical Analysis in the Social Sciences*. Cambridge: Cambridge University Press.

Thelen, K. (1999) 'Historical institutionalism in comparative politics', *Annual Review of Political Science*, 2 (1): 369–404.

Thompson, M.S. (2021) 'Cultivating "new" gendered food producers: intersections of power and identity in the postcolonial nation of Trinidad', review of *International Political Economy*, 28 (1): 177–203. Available at: https://doi.org/10.1080/09692290.2019.1663748.

Thompson, M.S. (2019) 'Still searching for (food) sovereignty: why are radical discourses only partially mobilised in the independent Anglo-Caribbean? *Geoforum*, 101.

Thompson, M.S. (2020) 'Milk and the motherland? Colonial legacies of taste and the law in the Anglophone Caribbean', *Journal of Food Law & Policy*, 16 (1): 135–57.

Thorat, S. and Sabharwal, N.S. (2015) 'Caste and social exclusion: concept, indicators, and measuremen', *India's Children: Essays on Social Policy*. New Delhi: Oxford University Press. pp. 392–774.

Tierney, M.J., Nielson, D.L., Hawkins, D.G., Roberts, J.T., Findley, M.G., Powers, R.M., Parks, B., Wilson, S.E. and Hicks, R.L. (2011) 'More dollars than sense: refining our knowledge of development finance using AidData', *World Development*, 39 (11): 1891–906. Available at: https://doi.org/10.1016/j.worlddev.2011.07.029

Tilly, C. (1993) *Coercion, Capital, and European States AD 990–1990*. London: Wiley-Blackwell.

Tilly, C. (1999a) *Durable Inequality*. Berkeley, CA: University of California Press.

Tilly, C. (1999b) 'From interactions to outcomes in social movements', in M. Giugni, D. McAdam and C. Tilly (eds), *How Social Movements Matter*. Minneapolis, MN: University of Minnesota Press.

Tilly C., (2007) 'Poverty and the Politics of Exclusion', in Narayan, D. and Petesch, P. (ed.), *Moving out of Poverty: Cross-Disciplinary Perspectives on Mobility*, World Bank, Washington DC, pp 45–75.

Tilly, C. and Tarrow, S. (2007) *Contentious Politics*. Boulder: Paradigm Publishers

Toye, J. (2016) *Assessing the G77: 50 years after UNCTAD and 40 years after the nieo in Emerging Powers and the UN*. Basingstoke: Routledge.

Transparency International (2021) 'Corruption free climate finance: protecting forests & people'. Available at: www.transparency.org/en/publications/corruption-free-climate-finance-protecting-forests-and-people

Treen, K.M., Williams, H.T. and O'Neill, S.J. (2020) 'Online misinformation about climate change', *Wiley Interdisciplinary Reviews: Climate Change*, 11 (5): e665.

True, J. (2020) 'Continuums of violence and peace: a feminist perspective', *Ethics & International Affairs*, 34 (1): 85–95.

Tsai, L. (2015) 'Constructive noncompliance in rural China'. *Comparative Politics*, 47 (3): 253–79.

Tuastad, D. (2003) 'Neo-Orientalism and the new barbarism thesis: aspects of symbolic violence in the Middle East conflict(s)', *Third World Quarterly*, 24 (4): 591–99.

Tudor, M. (2013). *The Promise of Power: The Origins of Democracy in India and Autocracy in Pakistan*. Cambridge: Cambridge University Press.

Turner, C., Khrais, R., Lloyd, T. et al. (2016) '*Why American's schools have a money problem*', NPR. Available at: www.npr.org/2016/04/18/474256366/why-americas-schools-have-a-money-problem (accessed 8 August 2023).

Tyler, T. (2011) *Why People Cooperate: The Role of Social Motivations*. Princeton, NJ: Princeton University Press.

Tyler, T. and Huo, Y. (2002) *Trust in the Law: Encouraging Public Cooperation with the Police and Courts*. New York: Russell Sage Foundation.

ul Haq, M., (1995) *Reflections on Human Development*. Oxford: Oxford University Press.

Uesugi, Y. (ed.) (2020) *Hybrid Peacebuilding in Asia*. New York: Palgrave Macmillan.

UK Government (2019) *The UK Government's Approach to Stabilization: A Guide for Policymakers and Practitioners*. London: Stabilization Unit.

UN (2016) 'International community has obligation to prevent ethnic cleansing in South Sudan – UN rights experts'. New York: UN. Available at: https://news.un.org/en/story/2016/12/546722 (accessed 5 April 2023).

UN (1962) *The UN Statistical Office. International Trade Statistics 1900–1960*. UNDP, 2023. Human Development Index (HDI). Available at: https://hdr.undp.org/data-center/human-development-index#/indicies/HDI

UN (2022) '*COP27 reaches breakthrough agreement on new loss and damage fund for vulnerable countries*'. Available at: https://unfccc.int/news/cop27-reaches-breakthrough-agreement-on-new-loss-and-damage-fund-for-vulnerable-countries (accessed: 30 March 2023).

UN (2023) '*Global issues peace and security*'. Available at: www.un.org/en/global-issues/peace-and-security#:~:text=Within%20the%20United%20Nations%2C%20peacebuilding,foundations%20for%20sustainable%20peace%20and (accessed 1 May 2023).

United Nations High Commission for Refugees (UNHCR) (2023) 'Sudan and South Sudan: refugees, asylum-seekers, and IDPs'. Geneva: UNHCR. Available at: https://data.unhcr.org/en/documents/details/99798 (accessed 5 April 2023).

United Nations Office for the Coordination of Humanitarian Affairs (2008) *OCHA Glossary of Humanitarian Terms 200* (accessed 15 August 2023).

United Nations Office of the High Commissioner for Human Rights (UN OHCHR) (2022) 'UN report details summary executions of civilians by Russian troops in northern Ukraine'. Geneva: UN OHCHR. Available at www.ohchr.org/en/press-releases/2022/12/un-report-details-summary-executions-civilians-russian-troops-northern (accessed 5 April 2023).

UN Security Council (2022) 'Ninety percent of war-time casualties are civilians'. New York: UN Security Council. Available at: https://press.un.org/en/2022/sc14904.doc.htm#:~:text=Despite%20countless%20Council%20resolutions%2C%20civilians,homes%20by%20conflict%20and%20disaster (accessed 5 April 2023).

UNOCHA (2023) 'UN and partners appeal for US$5.6 billion to help millions affected by Ukraine war'. Available at: www.unocha.org/story/un-and-partners-appeal-us56-billion-help-millions-affected-ukraine-war

Uppsala Conflict Data Program (UCDP) (2022) 'Frequently asked questions'. Available at www.pcr.uu.se/research/ucdp/faq/ (accessed 5 April 2023).

USAID (2022) 'Integrating local knowledge in development programming'. USAID. Available at: https://usaidlearninglab.org/sites/default/files/2022-07/integrating_local_knowledge_07112022-400pm.pdf

Utomi, P., Duncan, A., and Williams, G. (2007). Nigeria: The Political Economy of Reform. Strengthening the incentives for economic growth. The Policy Practice. https://ngfrepository.org.ng:8443/jspui/handle/123456789/1737

Uwazuruike, A.R. (2020) '#EndSARS: The movement against police brutality in Nigeria', *Harvard Human Rights Journal*.

Van der Veen, A.M. (2011) *Ideas, Interests and Foreign Aid*. Vol. 120. Cambridge: Cambridge University Press.

Van Dijk, T.A. (1985) *Discourse and Society*. London: Sage Publications.

Vanguard (2020) '#EndSARS: Youth inclusion in governance will check restiveness — Ikpeazu'. Available at: www.vanguardngr.com/2020/11/endsars-youth-inclusion-in-governance-will-check-restiveness-%E2%80%95-ikpeazu/ (accessed 28 March 2023).

van Heerde, J., & Hudson, D. (2010). 'The Righteous Considereth the Cause of the Poor'? Public Attitudes Towards Poverty in Developing Countries. *Political Studies*, *58*(3), 389–409. https://doi.org/10.1111/j.1467-9248.2009.00800.x

VDEM (2023) *Country Data*, VDEM website. Available: https://v-dem.net/data_analysis/CountryGraph/

Veenendaal, W. and Corbett, J. (2020) Clientelism in small states: how smallness influences patron–client networks in the Caribbean and the Pacific, *Democratization*, 27:1, 61–80,

Véron, R. (2001) 'The 'new' Kerala model: lessons for sustainable development', *World Development*, 29 (4): 601–17.

Waage, J., Yap, C., Bell, S., Levy, C., Mace, G., Pegram, T., Unterhalter, E., Dasandi, N., Hudson, D., Kock, R. and Mayhew, S. (2015) 'Governing the UN sustainable development goals: interactions, infrastructures, and institutions', *The Lancet Global Health,* 13 (5): e251–2.

Walker, G. (2012) *Environmental Justice: Concepts, Evidence and Politics*. London: Routledge.

Wampler, B. (2008) 'When does participatory democracy deepen the quality of democracy? Lessons from Brazil', *Comparative Politics*, *41*(1): 61–81.

Wang, Y., Mechkova, V. and Andersson, F. (2019) 'Does democracy enhance health? New empirical evidence 1900–2012', *Political Research Quarterly*, 72 (3): 554–69.

Watkins, K. and Quattri, M. (2014) '*Lost in intermediation: how excessive charges undermine the benefits of remittances for Africa*'. London: Overseas Development Institute. Available at: https://gsdrc.org/document-library/lost-in-intermediation-how-excessive-charges-undermine-the-benefits-of-remittances-for-africa/

Weale, A. (2004) *Politics as Collective Choice. What is Politics? The Activity and It's Study*. A. Leftwich. Cambridge, England, The Polity Press.

Weaver, C. (2008) *Hypocrisy Trap: The World Bank and the Poverty of Reform*. Princeton, NJ: Princeton University Press.

Weber, H. (2017) Politics of 'Leaving No One Behind': Contesting the 2030 Sustainable Development Goals Agenda, *Globalizations*, 14 (3): 399–414.

Weber, M. (1919) 'Politics as vocation'. Lecture.

Weber M (1921 [1978]) *Economy and Society: An Outline of Interpretive Sociology*. Berkeley, CA: University of California Press

Weber, M. ([1919] 2015) *Weber's Rationalism and Modern Society*, T. Waters and D. Waters (trans. and ed.). New York: Palgrave Macmillan.

Webster, C. (2002) *The National Health Service: A Political History*. London: Oxford University Press.

Weiss, L. (1998) *The Myth of the Powerless State*. Ithaca, New York: Cornell University Press.

Weston, K. (2010) 'Me, myself, and I', in Taylor, Y., Hines, S. and Casey, M.E. (eds), *Theorizing Intersectionality and Sexuality*. Springer. pp. 15–36.

White, A. and J. S. Migdal (2013) *The Everyday Life of the State : A State-in-Society Approach*. Seattle: University of Washington Press.

White, A.R., Nathan, N.L. and Faller, J.K. (2015) 'What do I need to vote? Bureaucratic discretion and discrimination by local election officials', *American Political Science Review*, 109 (1): 129–42.

Whitfield, L. and Buur, L. (2014) 'The politics of industrial policy: ruling elites and their alliances', *Third World Quarterly*, 35 (1): 126–44.

WHO and UNICEF (2021) 'Progress on household drinking water, sanitation and hygiene 2000–2020: five years into the SDGs'. Geneva: World Health Organization and the United Nations Children's Fund.

Williams, M. (2008) *The Roots of Participatory Democracy: Democratic Communists in South Africa and Kerala, India*. Basingstoke: Palgrave Macmillan.

Williams, P.D. (2018) *Fighting for Peace in Somalia: A History and Analysis of the African Union Mission (AMISOM), 2007–2017*. Oxford: Oxford University Press.

Williamson, J. (1990) 'The progress of policy reform in Latin America'. Washington, DC: Peterson Institute for International Economics.

Williamson, J. (1994) 'The political economy of policy reform', Washington, DC: Peterson Institute for International Economics.

Willis, R. (2020) *Too Hot to Handle?: The Democratic Challenge of Climate Change*. University of Bristol: Policy Press.

Willitts-King, B., Bryant, J. and Spencer, A. (2019) 'Valuing local resources in humanitarian crises', London: Overseas Development Institute. www.odi.org/publications/11480-valuing-local-resources-humanitarian-crises

Wilson Center (2021) '#EndSARS youth protests in Nigeria: lessons and opportunities for regional stability the southern voices newtork for peacebuilding, Washington, DC: The Wilson Center Africa Program'. Available at: www.wilsoncenter.org/sites/default/files/media/uploads/documents/SVNP-2021-Joint-Paper-Frimpong-Commodore-EndSARS_0.pdf (accessed 28 March 2023).

Wilson, M. (2013) 'From colonial dependency to finger-lickin' values: food, commodization, and identity in Trinidad', in H. Garth (ed.) *Food and Identity in the Caribbean*. London: Bloomsbury Academic. pp. 107–20.

Woods, N. (2008) 'Whose aid? Whose influence? China, emerging donors and the silent revolution in development assistance', *International Affairs*, 84 (6): 1205–21. Available at: https://doi.org/10.1111/j.1468-2346.2008.00765.x

Wood, T. (2016) "Is Culture the Cause? Choices, Expectations, and Electoral Politics in Solomon Islands and Papua New Guinea." *Pacific Affairs* 89 (1): 31–52.

World Bank (1999) *World Development Report 1999/2000*. Oxford: Oxford University Press.

World Bank (2000/2001) *World Development Report 2000/2001: Attacking Poverty*. Oxford: Oxford University Press.

World Bank. (2013). *What do we mean by social exclusion?* Washington, D. C: The World Bank.

World Bank. (2014). *Discriminated against for speaking their own language*. Washington, D. C: The World Bank. Available at: https://www.worldbank.org/en/news/feature/2014/04/16/discriminados-por-hablar-su-idioma-natal-peru-quechua

World Bank (2015) *The World Bank Group A to Z 2016*. Washington, D. C: The World Bank. Available at: https://doi.org/10.1596/978-1-4648-0484-7

World Bank (2020) *World development indicators*. Washington, D.C.: The World Bank.

World Bank (2020) *'Fragility and conflict: on the front lines of the fight against poverty'*. Washington, D. C: World Bank. Available at: www.worldbank.org/en/topic/poverty/publication/fragility-conflict-on-the-front-lines-fight-against-poverty (accessed 5 April 2023).

World Bank (2021) 'Personal remittances, received (% of GDP)'. Washington, D. C: The World Bank Available at: https://data.worldbank.org/indicator/BX.TRF.PWKR.DT.GD.ZS?most_recent_value_desc=true

World Bank (2021) 'A changing landscape: trends in official financial flows and aid architectures'. Washington, D. C: The World Bank Available at: https://thedocs.worldbank.org/en/doc/9eb18daf0e574a0f106a6c74d7a1439e-0060012021/a-changing-landscape-trends-in-official-financial-flows-and-the-aid-architecture

World Bank (2022) 'Remittances grow 5% in 2022, despite global headwinds'. Washington, D. C: The World Bank Available at: www.worldbank.org/en/news/press-release/2022/11/30/remittances-grow-5-percent-2022#:~:text=Growth%20in%20remittance%20flows%20is,%24100%20billion%20in%20yearly%20remittances

World Bank (2022) *'Fragility, conflict, and violence'*. Washington, DC: The World Bank. Available at: www.worldbank.org/en/topic/fragilityconflictviolence/overview#3 (accessed 5 April 2023).

World Bank (2023) 'What we do: financing'. Washington, D. C: The World Bank Available at: www.worldbank.org/en/what-we-do/products-and-services/financing-instruments

World Bank (2023) *Indigenous Latin America in the Twenty-First Century The First Decade Washington*, D. C: The World Bank.

World Bank (2023) *World Bank Open Data*. Washington, D. C: The World Bank. Available at: https://data.worldbank.org/

World Bank (2023) *'The World Bank in South Sudan'*. Washington, DC: The World Bank. Available at: www.worldbank.org/en/country/southsudan/overview#:~:text=South%20Sudan%20remains%20in%20a,to%20be%20the%20most%20affected (accessed 5 April 2023).

World Commission on Environment and Development (WCED) (1987) *Our Common Future*. Oxford: Oxford University Press.

WTO (2004) 'Special and differential treatment in the WTO: why, when, and how?' Available at: www.wto.org/english/res_e/reser_e/ersd200403_e.htm

WTO (2011) *'World Trade Organization international trade statistics'*. Available at: www.wto.org/english/res_e/statis_e/its2011_e/its11_world_trade_dev_e.pdf

WTO (2023a) *'Principles of the trading system'*. Available at: www.wto.org/english/thewto_e/whatis_e/tif_e/fact2_e.htm

WTO (2023b) *'Total merchandise export 2021'*. Available at: https://stats.wto.org/dashboard/merchandise_en.html

WTO (2023c) 'Understanding the WTO – the case for open trade'. Available at: www.wto.org/english/thewto_e/whatis_e/tif_e/fact3_e.htm

WTO (2023d) 'Members and observers of the WTO'. Available at: www.wto.org/english/thewto_e/countries_e/org6_map_e.htm

WWF (2022) 'Living Planet Report 2022 – Building a nature-positive society'. Gland, Switzerland: WWF.

Wyns, A. (2023) 'COP27 Establishes Loss and Damage Fund to Respond to Human Cost of Climate Change', *The Lancet Planetary Health*, 7 (1): e21–22. Available at: https://doi.org/10.1016/S2542-5196(22)00331-X

Xie, K. (2021a) *Embodying Middle Class Gender Aspirations: Perspectives from China's Privileged Young Women*. Singapore: Palgrave Macmillan.

Xie, K. (2021b) 'The affective life of the Nanjing massacre: reactivating historical trauma in governing contemporary China', *HAU: Journal of Ethnographic Theory*, 11 (3): 1000–1015.

Xu, M. (2016) 'Millions of unregistered individuals await legal status after China scraps one-child policy', *Global Times*. Available at: www.globaltimes.cn/content/965972.shtml

Yakubu, A. (1993) 'Coercing old guard emirs in Northern Nigeria: the abdication of Yakubu III of Bauchi, 1954', *African Affairs*, 92 (369): 593–604.

Yang, D. (2011) 'Migrant remittances', *Journal of Economic Perspectives*, 25 (3): 129–52.

Yeh, E.T. (2013) *Taming Tibet: Landscape Transformation and the Gift of Chinese Development*. Ithaca, New York: Cornell University Press.

Yergin, D. and Stanislaw, J. (2002) *The Commanding Heights: The Battle for the World Economy*. New York: Simon & Schuster.

Yeros, P. (ed.) (2016) *Ethnicity and Nationalism in Africa: Constructivist Reflections and Contemporary Politics*. Springer.

York, G. (2022) 'Tigray war has seen up to half a million dead from violence and starvation, say researchers', *Globe and Mail*, 15 March. Available at: www.theglobeandmail.com/world/article-tigray-war-has-seen-up-to-half-a-million-dead-from-violence-and/ (accessed 1 May 2023).

Young, I.M. (2001) 'Activist challenges to deliberative democracy', *Political Theory*, 29 (5): 670–90.

Yuichi Kono, D. and Montinola, G.R. (2009) 'Does foreign aid support autocrats, democrats, or both?' *The Journal of Politics*, 1 (2): 704–18.

Zagzebski, L. (2017) 'What is knowledge?, in J. Greco and E. Sosa (eds), *The Blackwell Guide to Epistemology*. Oxford: Blackwell. pp. 92–116.

Ziai, A. (2017) 'Post-development 25 years after *The Development Dictionary*', *Third World Quarterly*, 38 (12): 2547–2558.

Index

Page numbers in **bold** indicate tables and in *italic* indicate figures.